I0889823

East of East

Latinidad

Transnational Cultures in the United States

This series publishes books that deepen and expand our understanding of Latina/o populations, especially in the context of their transnational relationships within the Americas. Focusing on borders and boundary crossings, broadly conceived, the series is committed to publishing scholarship in history, film and media, literary and cultural studies, public policy, economics, sociology, and anthropology. Inspired by interdisciplinary approaches, methods, and theories developed out of the study of transborder lives, cultures, and experiences, titles enrich our understanding of transnational dynamics.

Matt Garcia, Series Editor, Professor of Latin American, Latino and Caribbean Studies, and History, Dartmouth College

For a list of titles in the series, see the last page of the book.

East of East

The Making of Greater El Monte

EDITED BY ROMEO GUZMÁN, CARRIBEAN FRAGOZA,
ALEX SAYF CUMMINGS, AND RYAN REFT

Rutgers University Press
New Brunswick, Camden, and Newark, New Jersey, and London

Library of Congress Cataloging-in-Publication Data

Names: Guzmán, Romeo, editor. | Fragoza, Carribean, editor. | Cummings, Alex Sayf, editor. | Reft, Ryan, editor.
Title: East of east: the making of greater El Monte / edited by Romeo Guzmán, Carribean Fragoza, Alex Sayf Cummings, and Ryan Reft.
Description: New Brunswick, New Jersey: Rutgers University Press, [2020] | Series: Latinidad: transnational cultures in the United States | Includes bibliographical references and index.
Identifiers: LCCN 2019017115 | ISBN 9781978805491 (cloth) | ISBN 9781978805484 (pbk.)
Subjects: LCSH: El Monte (Calif.)—History. | El Monte (Calif.)—Social life and customs. | Popular culture—California—El Monte—History. | El Monte (Calif.)—Biography.
Classification: LCC F869.E4 E27 2020 | DDC 979.4/93—dc23
LC record available at https://lccn.loc.gov/2019017115

A British Cataloging-in-Publication record for this book is available from the British Library.

This collection copyright © 2020 by Rutgers, The State University of New Jersey
Individual chapters copyright © 2020 in the names of their authors
All rights reserved

No part of this book may be reproduced or utilized in any form or by any means, electronic or mechanical, or by any information storage and retrieval system, without written permission from the publisher. Please contact Rutgers University Press, 106 Somerset Street, New Brunswick, NJ 08901. The only exception to this prohibition is "fair use" as defined by U.S. copyright law.

∞ The paper used in this publication meets the requirements of the American National Standard for Information Sciences—Permanence of Paper for Printed Library Materials, ANSI Z39.48-1992.

www.rutgersuniversitypress.org

Manufactured in the United States of America

For Aura, Camila, and the Guzmán and Fragoza clans
Romeo Guzmán

To those who imagine radical futures for Greater El Monte
Carribean Fragoza

For Betsy and Barbara
Alex Sayf Cummings

For Soo
Ryan Reft

Contents

East of East

Introduction

Finding Silenced Histories, Lost Intersections, and Radical Possibilities in Greater El Monte

ROMEO GUZMÁN, CARRIBEAN FRAGOZA, ALEX SAYF CUMMINGS, AND RYAN REFT

For three days in May 1935, El Monte's white residents worked tirelessly to cement their place in history by performing the past on the community's streets and in its auditorium. To set the scene, men, women, and children wore their grandparents' and great-grandparents' old clothes: overalls for the men, dresses and sunbonnets for the women. Working from T. H. Cooney's scholarship on western expansion, El Monte High School staged an ambitious performance of "The End of the Santa Fe Trail" with a cast of five hundred. In the ensuing years, the celebration stretched into a five-mile street parade of canvas-covered wagons and horse-drawn buggies and included a rifle and pistol tournament, rodeo, quilt and antiquity showcase, and barbeque. Collectively, the various activities and performances of the first annual El Monte Pioneer Homecoming sought not only to articulate a history for the community's residents, but also to situate El Monte within the larger history of Southern California and the U.S. western expansion following the Mexican-American War of 1846–1848.

Like Spaniards before them, white settlers were attracted to the region's fertile soil, abundant water supply, and green and lush landscape. Beginning in 1851, Americans from Texas and other Southern states settled in this region and formed two villages, Lexington and Willow Grove, with the former eventually emerging as the larger one. The majority of settlers pursued farming, and by the 1860s there were at least thirty-six farms with an average of ninety-three acres.[1] The arrival of 500,000 white Americans in California was accompanied by a shift in power relations, which included a new racial hierarchy—albeit one that continued to view the indigenous population as inferior—and a distinctly different social, economic, and political order.[2] Though many whites (along with much smaller numbers of Asian and Latin American prospectors) hoped to cash in on the Gold Rush in Northern California, many would eventually move south to places like Los Angeles and El Monte. By 1866, notes the historian William F. King, "El Monte was well established as an important farm center."[3]

Economic change paralleled demographic change in the San Gabriel Valley (SGV). New arrivals from the American South settled and brought with them the political and racial beliefs dominant in their place of origin. The frontier environment only exacerbated their dependency on such ideologies and encouraged vigilantism. In El Monte, vigilantism might have represented popular conceptions of so-called frontier justice, but this form of enforcement was hardly free of the racial and class biases inherent in the nation's formal legal system. As a well-armed mob on horseback, the El Monte Boys enforced their own brand of vigilante justice throughout Southern California, which frequently targeted Mexicans and Native Americans. "The 'El Monte Boys,'" in the words of Horace Bell, "were long celebrated for their proclivity to seek out trouble and add to it."[4] Residents of Alta California, many of whom were ethnically mixed due to the territory's long history of diversity, had embraced the identity of Californios. But the members of this group were soon dispossessed of land; voted out of political office; and in the end found themselves, like other so-called minorities in this new California: with few rights and forced to sell their labor.

Throughout California, one finds a similar trajectory of shifting economics, demographics, and political consolidation unfolding across the late nineteenth century. After settling in new territories, white Americans worked to solidify their political, economic, and social position. As the state entered the twentieth century, this process was followed by an effort to create a past that would serve the present. Particularly in the early decades of the twentieth century, white businessmen, politicians, boosters, and residents were eager to create a sense of place by pointing to California's past. But there was a problem: the contours of American racial hierarchy prevented any references to Native American history. Even Americans like Hubert Howe Bancroft, who

FIG. 1 Pioneer parade in El Monte during the 1930s. (Courtesy of El Monte Historical Museum.)

valued recording and documenting the past as carefully as possible, did not understand Native Americans' sophisticated relationship to the natural environment. In the words of the nineteenth-century historian, these people "went naked, or nearly so, ate grasshoppers and reptiles, among other things, and burrowed in caves or hid themselves away in brush huts or in thickets."[5] As California's newest arrivals, white Americans could not point to themselves, their ancestors, or even their own cultural achievements as a means of bolstering the state's cultural standing.

It was under these circumstances that white Americans looked to the old Spanish past and raised funds to restore the California missions, create a highway that would connect them throughout California, and structure its history in the service of the present.[6] This narrative, which scholars have dubbed the Spanish Fantasy Heritage, provided a romantic and idealistic vision of the past and most importantly portrayed both Spaniards and Mexicans as lazy and incapable of exploiting the state's rich resources. In short, the Spanish Fantasy Heritage firmly positioned white Americans as the only people equipped to lead California to its economic and political future.

In El Monte, white residents joined this statewide effort to imagine a past and present that would firmly place the future in the hands of white Americans. However, instead of looking to Spanish California, El Monte pointed to a much more recent past: the city's white pioneers. The city, residents claimed, not only marked the end of the Santa Fe Trail, thus linking the Midwest and East Coast to California, but also boasted "the first public school and the first Baptist church in the Los Angeles Basin"—both symbols of American civilization. In short, El Monte prided itself as the first American settlement in Southern California and thus the central hub connecting this new territory to the rest of nation.

Throughout the twentieth century, El Monte writers, residents, politicians, and educators promoted this pioneer narrative through publications, performances and celebrations, school curricula, and the erecting of monuments. In 1935, as mentioned above, El Monte launched its inaugural three-day pioneer homecoming. It grew in surprising ways. In the festival's second year, it attracted 60,000 Southern California residents. And just three years after the first homecoming, the El Monte Historical Society was founded and began to house material related to the community's pioneer history in the El Monte High School (at the time on Valley Boulevard).[7]

As the twentieth century pressed forward, El Monte experienced unprecedented growth and important demographic shifts. From 1930 to 1970, the population increased twentyfold, from 3,479 to 69,892. Such changes, though important, have often been ignored or underexplored, particularly with respect to how the city's diverse communities interacted and related. James Ellroy, a former El Monte resident and celebrated noir writer, described the mid-century SGV as "the rat's ass of Los Angeles County—a 30-mile stretch of contiguous hick towns due east of L.A. proper . . . white trash heaven." Housing covenants sequestered Latinos in "slum districts and tin roof shantytowns" across the valley. "Negroes were not allowed on the streets after dark," Ellroy wrote. El Monte was the "hub of the valley," where "you had Dust Bowl refugees and their teenage kids. You had pachucos with duck's-ass haircuts and Sir Guy shirts and slit bottomed khakis." Yet Ellroy collapsed the Mexican presence in El Monte to the "winos and hopheads" living in Medina Court and Hicks Camp.[8] A skilled storyteller, he nevertheless revealed the powerful sway that pioneer narratives still held over the ways people understood the region in his appraisal of mid-century El Monte and its residents.

Indeed, the pioneer narrative endured well past Ellroy's 1950s boyhood in El Monte. In 1973, Lilian Wiggins, the museum's director from 1961 to about 1990 and a descendant of El Monte's first American families, affirmed the museum's focus and perspective.[9] Its collection, she told the *Los Angeles Times*, "is strictly 'wagon train.'"[10] Well into the 1960s, El Monte High School students, regardless of their own ethnic background, were required to dress up as pioneers on "pioneer day." Finally, in preparation for the city's seventy-fifth anniversary in 1987 and after decades of proudly proclaiming this site as the end of the Santa Fe Trail, the city and a committee of residents succeeded in gaining recognition for it as a historic landmark.[11] The state Historical Resource Commission concluded that El Monte was the first place in Southern California to be settled by Americans rather than by Mexicans or Spaniards.

However, it also found that El Monte was not the end of the Santa Fe Trail. It marked the "end of some trail, but not the Santa Fe Trail," the *Los Angeles Times* wrote in reporting the commission's findings.[12] Following this new historical designation, the city council spent $226,000 to make improvements to the park and to add a marker and historical artifacts, including a covered wagon.[13]

The pioneer narrative's greatest achievement is its endurance and power. It is embedded in the city's official logo, proudly memorialized at Pioneer Park, and narrated in the city's museum. Its most egregious offense is placing white pioneers at the center of El Monte's history, excluding some of the region's most important ethnic groups and events. Most importantly, this narrative designates pioneers as the single most important actors in El Monte's past. In his classic 1995 text, *Silencing the Past: Power and the Production of History*, the anthropologist Michel-Rolph Trouillot offers a theory of the production of history that includes not just the writing of historical narratives but also the dissemination of history to the public—such as through museums, films, and folklore (the creation of *relevance*). The production of history, he argues, is deeply intertwined with power. We must expose the roots of power to unmask how it operates and show how the production of any history involves "silences" at four crucial moments: "the moment of fact creation (the making of *sources*); the moment of fact assembly (the making of *archives*); the moment of fact retrieval (the making of *narratives*); and the moment of retrospective significance (the making of *history* in the final instance)."[14]

Radicalizing the Archive

For the South El Monte Arts Posse (SEMAP)—an arts collective made up of writers, scholars, urban planners, and educators based in El Monte and South El Monte—these silences are personal, experienced, and felt. As children of migrants and grandchildren of Braceros, we found that the omission of Mexicans as well as our Asian classmates and neighbors stood in stark contrast to our experiences growing up in a multiethnic neighborhood, watching generations of people of color do the back-breaking labor of building these towns. It stood in contrast to the art, culture, and affirmation that emanated from places like East Los Angeles as well as from the stories we read in countless books that we devoured as high school students and eventually as undergraduates. Where, we wondered, were all the brown faces?

To evaluate historical narratives and explore the field's silences and conceptual framings, historians examine the history of historical writing, known within the profession as historiography.[15] From the late nineteenth to the mid-twentieth century, the children and grandchildren of white pioneers began writing the history of El Monte. These texts, like much scholarship from this era, celebrated American expansion and movement west, portrayed pioneers as rugged innovators, focused exclusively on white men, and adopted a national perspective and framework. In these narratives, Native Americans were either ignored or written in as figures in a larger narrative of American triumphalism. They emerge, the historian Ramón Gutiérrez writes, as "nameless, and usually faceless, victims of atrocities."[16]

The civil rights movement and the entry of people of color and women into the university since then have had a profound impact on historians and academics in general. New theories and methods provided the room and tools to include marginalized people and communities in larger historical narratives. New scholarship began to show that rugged pioneers did not succeed on their own but were aided by the government, often to the detriment of other ethnic groups. For example, while early works on El Monte describe white migrants as "pioneers" and "settlers," the term "squatter" more aptly describes their arrival and occupation of the land. Like many newcomers throughout California, they benefited from intermarriage with prominent Californio families and, perhaps more importantly, the application of American property law—notably the Land Act of 1851.[17] Land grants under both Spanish and Mexican rule often lacked geographic specificity, and in some instances documentation was judged to be inadequate by U.S. law—a point that American interlopers exploited. Mexican residents, now subjects of the United States, spent decades trying to defend their claims, and even when they succeeded, it was often at great personal cost.[18]

Since the 1990s, historians have increasingly adopted transnational and global perspectives, revealing the connections between California and people and places across the globe rather than viewing the process of American colonization from a purely regional or national perspective. Native Americans and multiethnic communities emerged as active agents rather than passive victims or props in a triumphal narrative. Historians and scholars started to think of space as they think about time: something that is always changing and relational. "Space is not a scientific object removed from ideology and politics; it has always been political and strategic," as the geographer Edward W. Soja has written. "If space has an air of neutrality and indifference with regard to its contents and thus seems to be 'purely' formal, the epitome of rational abstraction, it is precisely because it has been occupied and used, and has already been the focus of past processes whose traces are not always evident on the landscape."[19] Last, and perhaps most important, students of the West started to study different ethnic groups in relationship to each other to explore how one's ethnic makeup (or citizenship status) affected one's place in society.

Amid the celebration of greater El Monte's multiculturalism, an absence exists: the dearth of blackness. Though encountering discrimination as well, Asian and Mexican Americans have been able to suburbanize at much higher rates when compared with their black counterparts. Reasons for this inequality include federal, state, and municipal housing policies such as redlining that over time penalized all nonwhites and immigrants, but at differing levels and with a particularly heavy impact on African Americans.[20]

Other factors also contributed to the relatively limited presence of African Americans in El Monte. Since the early twentieth century, Mexican and Asian Americans often resided in small colonies within a short distance of their work; though segregated and often lacking services, they established footholds in the region. El Monte Hicks Camp and Medina Court serve as two examples.[21] Most notably, Asian Americans also benefited from the anxieties of the Cold War, when elected officials promoted the integration of Asian Americans into California suburbs as a way to combat Communism and promote the goals of U.S. foreign policy.[22] Urban renewal, highway construction, and other economic development schemes in Los Angeles victimized each group, but Asian Americans and Mexican Americans were able to integrate the working and middle-class suburbs of the SGV. Historians such as Eric Avila, Emily E. Straus, and Andrew Wiese have shown that African Americans did pursue the suburban dream but suburbanized at lower rates in more segregated communities.[23]

Still, in the face of this imbalance, one must at least ask: to what extent have today's SGV residents contributed to this reality? George Lipsitz and other scholars have explored the consuming power of whiteness and how people of color sometimes embraced its implicit ideology as a means to access greater resources, property, and wealth.[24] "Whatever the ethnicity or nationality of the immigrant, his nemesis is understood to be African Americans," Toni Morrison wrote in 1993.[25] And whatever the answer to this larger question, its exploration extends beyond the scope of this work; even with the multicultural successes of the SGV, let it serve as a reminder that troubling inequities remain across racial lines, even in a landscape as diverse and multifaceted as that of greater El Monte.

Indeed, despite El Monte's multiethnic past and present, decades of new scholarship on the West, and new theories and methods about the historical process, the pioneer narrative remains intact in the official history of El Monte under the care of the city's museum and its director and board. To continue to imagine a white past in the face of a multiethnic nation is akin to calls to "Make America Great Again": perpetual erasure. We prefer the (admittedly sardonic) call of Langston Hughes, to "Let America be America again . . . America never was America to me."[26]

The city's centennial in 2012 encouraged new ways of thinking about its history and new methods of conveying its present and past to its residents and the broader public. SEMAP used this historical date as an opportunity to launch the public history and place-making project called "East of East: Mapping Community Narratives in El Monte and South El Monte." The project aspired to build a new, multiethnic, transnational, and radical history of South

El Monte and El Monte, one that began before the arrival of white pioneers and continued into the present. To build this new history, we needed to build a new archive. The process of building this new archive and history is central to the entire endeavor.

SEMAP launched the "East of East" project in collaboration with La Casa de El Hijo del Ahuizote, a cultural space in Mexico City that houses the papers of the Mexican and transnational anarchist Flores Magón brothers.[27] La Casa and SEMAP are linked by Carribean Fragoza and Romeo Guzmán's friendship with Diego Flores Magón, as well as by a shared epistemology and overlapping disciplines. As an arts collective, SEMAP uses the arts to transform how we think about and experience place and to foster a grassroots and collective sense of ownership of space, both public and private. The friendship between SEMAP and La Casa was further cemented by a historic connection: in 1917 Ricardo Flores Magón delivered an important speech in El Monte. It was from here that he wrote letters to his brother, Enrique, who at the time was hiding out in the SGV—most likely in La Puente.

Since 2012, we have worked with archivists, educators, historians, artists, and community members to host discussions, lectures, bike tours, and creative writing workshops with Spanish-speaking migrant women and youth; conducted more than a hundred oral histories; digitized more than 1,500 city and personal archives; created original art about El Monte and its sister city, South El Monte; partnered with Tropics of Meta and KCET to share this content; and built a new digital archive of South El Monte and El Monte. Throughout this process, we have invited scholars to write essays about El Monte and South El Monte's past and novelists and community members to produce first-person creative nonfiction stories connected to place.

Beyond the Santa Fe Trail: Greater El Monte in the Long View

East of East writes against the pioneer narrative and the myth of the end of the Santa Fe Trail in an effort to view Greater El Monte—El Monte and the city of South El Monte—as a site of contestation. Rather than simply adding a new set of actors, themes, or perspectives, *East of East* understands history and culture as both an act of governance and resistance. As Edward Said pointed out in his influential 1993 work, *Culture and Imperialism*, governance and empire remain primarily about land, but it is through culture and the appropriation of history that such contestations are decided.[28]

Like Southern California in general, El Monte and South El Monte have always existed at the intersection of larger forces—be they Spanish colonialism, distant Mexican rule, or a contemporary federal government at odds with Californian notions about immigration and civil liberties. Together the communities provide a setting in which to examine the history of Spanish

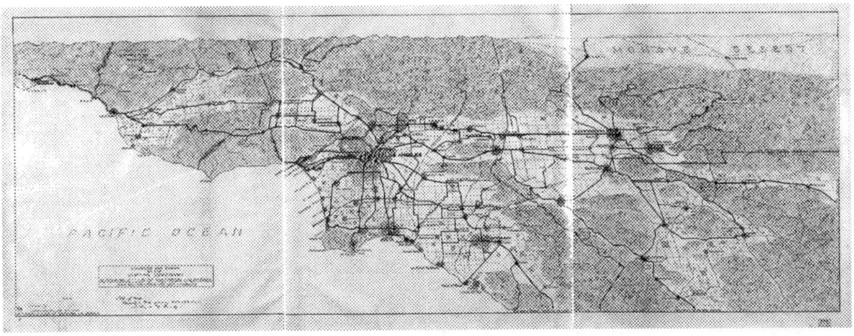

FIG. 2 "Map of Los Angeles and the San Gabriel Mountains." Automobile Club of Southern California, 1915. (Courtesy of the Library of Congress, Geography and Map Division.)

California; the rise of the urban West; and the social, cultural, and political transformation of twentieth-century suburbs in a way that studies centered strictly on Los Angeles or its inner suburbs cannot. These communities are part of a much bigger story of colonization and conquest, labor and culture, race and suburbanization at the fringe that has not yet been told.

Fluidity defines the interplay between city center and suburb. The political, cultural, and economic flows between the two cannot be separated or cordoned off into compartmentalized entities. As liminal spaces between both cities and suburbs, points of departure and transition amid the flow of labor, migrants, music, politics, and cultures (in this case, in the vast metropolitan sweep of Greater Los Angeles), El Monte and South El Monte have been points of contact between farmworkers, punks, white supremacists, suburbanites, Zumba dancers, and civil rights activists. This part of the urban fringe—a fringe beyond the fringe, truly "east of east"—offers a fresh perspective on the cross-cutting currents that nonetheless still flow into the diverse, multiethnic suburbia of the twenty-first century United States.

East of East springs from the intersection of major developments in the field of urban history. First, scholars such as Mike Davis, Michael Dear, Edward Soja, and other members of the Los Angeles school began to frame Los Angeles not as an outlier of U.S. suburbanization but as the model for the nation's metropolitan areas.[29]

Second, it draws on the "new suburban history," which has ventured beyond central cities to see what was happening in "the little boxes on the hillside," and to examine the tension between city and suburbs.[30] The growth of the SGV—particularly the demographic change at the heart of this expansion, largely driven by Asians and Latinos—has caught the attention of scholars and students of suburbs and cities. Los Angeles's sprawl, increasing cost of living, and connection to foreign capital have driven countless individuals and families to the SGV, producing a novel form of suburbanization that promises to be increasingly replicated in California and elsewhere. Charlotte Brooks, Wendy Cheng, Matt Garcia, Becky Nicolaides, James Zarsadiaz, Rudolfo D. Torres, and Victor M. Valle all have provided new insights into the growth of multiethnic suburbs by showing how these new and old migrants are transforming cities and by articulating new ideas about belonging and racial hierarchies. As working-class communities east of East Los Angeles and in the heart of the SGV, El Monte and South El Monte are defined by their majority-minority status and their ambivalent relationship to Greater Los Angeles.[31]

Third, collectively, the cities and suburbs that make up this fringe in the SGV and parts of Southeast Los Angeles—or what Torres, and Valle labeled the "Greater Eastside . . . an interdependent network of newer and maturing near-in cities and suburbs"—cast a significant economic shadow, one that the authors argue transformed the region into "one of the nation's most dynamic industrial landscapes." El Monte and South El Monte lie within its central orbit and exist as part of the Greater Eastside.[32] El Monte and South El Monte capture this transformation, and in these ways, *East of East* answers Torres and Valle's plea for a view of the Los Angeles metropolitan region that better accounts for its Latino and Asian residents—economically, politically, and culturally—and looks past black-white binary racial debates.

East of East carries these developments further by providing a consistent setting for untangling the identities, conflicts, and solidarities over three centuries of American life. Rather than seeing a multiethnic suburb as a novelty, *East of East* understands it as part of a long and rich trajectory from Spanish to American colonization and from white supremacy to the assertion of power by people of color throughout the twentieth century and today. Racial hierarchies were articulated, enacted, and contested again and again, in public and private space, in ways that became significant not only to Greater El Monte but also to California. Indeed, El Monte's built environment, political and economic history, and diverse population emerge out of its interaction with Los Angeles—but they also shape the larger metropolis.

This book offers a longer and more enduring view of this urban trajectory than most traditional scholarship has offered. The stories of El Monte and South El Monte's diverse communities must be told, or they will be lost. Their lives might be erased just as the history of indigenous and Mexican residents was whitewashed by the mythic narrative of the End of the Santa Fe Trail celebrations in 1935 or, even more prosaically, by economic development and sprawl amid metropolitan Los Angeles's expansion and foreign investment. Such a loss would be especially painful in a century when the United States finds itself again reckoning with a long love affair with whiteness, its exclusionary notions of citizenship and belonging, and the reluctance to include diverse communities as part of the nation's historical narrative.

Like America itself, El Monte was always already diverse, and the city shows how America's multiethnic multiplicity is now unfolding in new and different ways. *East of East* proposes to incorporate these stories in a way that is unconventional, heterogeneous, and disciplinarily promiscuous. It employs a broad American Studies methodology, engaging in issues of memory and myth, oral history and creative nonfiction, and place making and archive building. It is organized both chronologically and thematically, and through our digital archive readers have the opportunity to dig deeper and contribute to an evolving project of community history. It is both a time capsule and a statement of intent—that the activists, artists, farmworkers, musicians, and writers portrayed here not only mattered historically, but that they and their descendants actually represent the vanguard of metropolitan America.

The future will not happen in the cities or the suburbs, but in the middle, and El Monte and South El Monte have always been in the middle. Indeed, this project aims to decenter and recenter our histories of labor, migration, music, race, and urban development in the metropolitan West. What El Monte and South El Monte can teach us is that a borderland, fringe, edge city, and place of transit and departure might be a middle, but that the middle is often also the center of the action—in a real sense that too often goes unrecognized.

Notes

1 William F. King, "El Monte, An American Town in Southern California, 1851–1866," *Southern California Quarterly* 53, no. 4 (December 1971): 317–332.
2 Kevin Starr, *California: A History* (New York: Modern Library, 2007), 103.
3 King, "El Monte," 317. See also Starr, *California*, 81.
4 Horace Bell, *On the Old West Coast: Being the Further Reminiscences of a Ranger-Major Horace Bell* (New York: Grosset and Dunlap, 1930), 310.
5 Hubert Howe Bancroft, *Literary Industries: A Memoir* (San Francisco: History Company, 1891), 651.
6 Phoebe S. K. Young, *California Vieja: Culture and Memory in a Modern American Place* (Berkeley: University of California Press, 2006).
7 The museum moved from the high school to its current location, the former city library, in 1968. This building, coincidentally, was built through President Franklin Delano Roosevelt's Works Progress Administration program. See Mayerene Barker, "El Monte Preserves Past in City Museum," *Los Angeles Times*, September 30, 1973.
8 James Ellroy, *My Dark Places: An L.A. Crime Memoir* (New York: Alfred A. Knopf, 1996), 18–21.
9 After Wiggins's death, the museum appointed Helen Huffing and Mary Schaffer as directors—both of whom died shortly after becoming director. From 1992 to about the mid-2010s, the museum was run by Donna Crippen, the wife of Jack Crippen, a prominent politician. See Donna Crippen, oral history interview, January 15, 2014, South El Monte Arts Posse (SEMAP), East of East: Mapping Community Narratives in El Monte and South El Monte, http://www.semapeastofeast.com.

10 Barker, "El Monte Preserves Past in City Museum."

11 In 1930 the California State Society of the American Revolution erected a plaque in El Monte that read, "This tablet commemorates the site of the oldest Protestant Evangelical Church in Southern California, the erection of the first school house and the end of the Santa Fe Trail." See Denise-Maria Santiago, "Wagons Ho: El Monte Insists Trail Didn't End in Santa Fe," *Los Angeles Times*, June 21, 1987.

12 Elizabeth Caras, "Trail's End? Maybe Not, but El Monte Is Historic," *Los Angeles Times*, August 16, 1987. For more on the Old Spanish Trail and El Monte, see "El Monte," in *Los Angeles A to Z: An Encyclopedia of the City and County*, ed. Leonard Pitt and Dale Pitt (Berkeley: University of California Press, 2000), 136–137.

13 "Los Angeles," California State Parks Office of Historic Preservation, accessed February 17, 2018, http://ohp.parks.ca.gov/?page_id=21427.

14 Michel-Rolph Trouillot, *Silencing the Past: Power and the Production of History* (Boston: Beacon Press, 1995).

15 Ramón Gutiérrez, "Contested Eden: An Introduction," *California History* 76, no. 2/3 (1997). For more on the recent developments in the field, see Stephen Aron, "Convergence, California, and the Newest Western History," *California History* 86 (2009): 4–13 and 79–81.

16 R. Gutiérrez, "Contested Eden," 6.

17 Even King, who provides a rather neutral, if not laudatory, portrayal of white settlers, argues that "most of the farmers were 'squatters' on the land" ("El Monte," 323).

18 Starr, *California*, 103–105; Carlos Manuel Salomon, *Pio Pico: The Last Governor of Mexican California* (Norman: University of Oklahoma Press, 2010), 118; Paul Gates, "The California Land Act of 1851," *Southern California Historical Quarterly* 50, no. 4 (December 1971): 395–430. In his interpretation of the act, Gates argues that it did not affect Californios as unfairly or as extensively as others have since suggested.

19 Edward W. Soja, *Postmodern Geographies: The Reassertion of Space in Critical Social Theory* (London: Verso, 1989), 80.

20 Richard Rothstein, *The Color of Law: A Forgotten History of How Our Government Segregated America* (New York: Liveright, 2017); Andrea Gibbons, *City of Segregation: One Hundred Years of Struggle for Housing in Los Angeles* (Brooklyn, NY: Verso, 2018); Josh Sides, *L.A. City Limits: African American Los Angeles from the Great Depression to the Present* (Los Angeles: University of California Press, 2003).

21 Matt Garcia, *A World of Its Own: Race, Labor and Citrus in the Making of Greater Los Angeles, 1900–1970* (Chapel Hill: University of North Carolina Press, 2001).

22 Charlotte Brooks, *Alien Neighbors, Foreign Friends: Asian Americans, Housing and the Transformation of Urban California* (Chicago: University of Chicago Press, 2009).

23 Eric Avila, *Popular Culture in the Age of White Flight: Fear and Fantasy in Suburban Los Angeles* (Los Angeles: University of California Press, 2004), and *The Folklore of the Freeway: Race and Revolt in the Modernist City* (Minneapolis: University of Minnesota Press, 2014); Emily E. Straus, *Death of a Suburban Dream: Race and Schools in Compton* (Philadelphia: University of Pennsylvania Press, 2014); Andrew Wiese, *Places of Their Own: African American Suburbanization in the Twentieth Century* (Chicago: University of Chicago Press, 2004).

24 George Lipsitz, "The Racialization of Space and the Spacialization of Race: Theorizing the Hidden Architecture of Landscape," *Landscape Journal* 26, no. 1 (2007): 10–23.

25 Toni Morrison, "On the Backs of Blacks," Time, December 2, 1993, 57. See also Wendy Cheng, *The Changs Next Door to the Diazes: Remapping Race in Suburban California* (Minneapolis: University of Minnesota Press, 2013), 41.

26 Langston Hughes, *Let America Be America Again: And Other Poems* (New York: Vintage, 2004), 3.

27 For a history of La Casa see Romeo Guzmán, "Rebel Archive: A History of La Casa de El Hijo Del Ahuizote," in *Regeneración: Three Generations of Revolutionary Ideology*, ed. Pilar Tompkins Rivas (Mexico City: Vincent Price Art Museum and La Case de El Hijo del Ahuizote, 2018).

28 Edward Said, *Culture and Imperialism* (New York: Vintage, 1994), 78.

29 Joel Garreau, *Edge City: Life on the New Frontier* (New York: Anchor Books, 1991), 3.

30 Indeed, as the historian Michelle Nickerson has argued, the "new suburban history" is hardly new anymore; see "Beyond Smog, Sprawl, and Asphalt: Developments in the Not-So-New Suburban History," *Journal of Urban History* 41 (2015): 171–180.

31 Brooks, *Alien Neighbors, Foreign Friends*; Cheng, *The Changs Next Door to the Diazes*; Garcia, *A World of Its Own*; Becky M. Nicolaides and James Zarsadiaz, "Design Assimilation in Suburbia: Asian Americans, Built Landscapes, and Suburban Advantage in Los Angeles's San Gabriel Valley since 1970," *Journal of Urban History* 43 (2017): 332–371; Rudolfo D. Torres and Victor M. Valle, *Latino Metropolis* (Minneapolis: University of Minnesota Press, 2000).

32 Torres and Valle, *Latino Metropolis*, 21, 24, and 42.

Part I

Origins and Departures

FIG. 3 Phung Huynh, "In the Meadow." El Monte Station. (Courtesy of the Los Angeles County Metropolitan Transportation Authority.)

Historians make choices, and choices are neither neutral nor apolitical. When a study begins and ends, for example, can produce profound exclusions. For too long historians worked in the service of the nation-state by writing histories that celebrated the rise of the nation and privileged a temporal frame that was aligned with nation building.[1] El Monte's early historians (much like its official historical museum) began their narratives of El Monte with the conclusion of the Mexican-American War of 1846–1848. Their romantic and uncritical perspectives of the so-called pioneers erased conflict, conquest, and the region's previous inhabitants. The region was not only home to the Tongva but was also part of the Spanish empire and Mexican state and experienced profound social, cultural, and political changes. Far from the sprawling, multiethnic landscape of today, the colonial era witnessed a tumultuous clash between the native Tongva people and the Spanish, who faced fierce resistance from iconic rebels such as Toypurina. Throughout the nineteenth century, indigenous, Mexican, and American interlopers jostled for power. White vigilantes, who supported the Confederate cause during the Civil War, brought rough Southern justice to impose order on a new Anglo-dominated California, which was increasingly connected to the broader United States by markets and railroads. Through force and the law, Californios lost political power, land, and even their social standing in society. Through historical actors like Toypurina and the El Monte Boys, El Monte and Los Angeles residents remember the past and in the process reveal competing historical interpretations.

Note

1 Prasenjit Duara, *Rescuing History from the Nation: Questioning Narratives of Modern China* (Chicago: University of Chicago Press, 1995).

1

The Tongva People

AURELIE ROY

In recent years, the enduring legacies of the original people of the Los Angeles (LA) Basin, referred to as the Tongva or Gabrielinos,[1] have become increasingly apparent in the landscape of the region. Right behind LA's world-famous Hollywood sign lies Cahuenga (or Kawenga) Peak, the Tongva's "place in the mountains." People can hike the Gabrielino Trail in Angeles National Forest, just north of El Monte, and up Tongva Peak[2] in the Verdugo Mountains, north of LA; go to the public Tongva Park in Santa Monica;[3] go to the Tongva Memorial Garden at Loyola Marymount University;[4] and see the San Gabriel Mountains on a daily basis. These markers of indigenous heritage are important reminders of the region's roots as well as of indigenous life today. Our exploration of El Monte invites readers to think of the LA Basin as an indigenous space as well as to imagine how its heritage has interacted with other waves of migration, politics, and modes of cultural and artistic expressions over the course of its history.

Indigenous Life from Pre-European Contact to American Colonization

The Tongva or Gabrielinos migrated from the Mojave Desert to the current-day LA Basin around 7,000 years ago, displacing some of the Chumash who had been living in the area since at least 8,000 B.C.[5] By 1500, present-day LA County had around twenty-five Tongva villages, each of which had a population of 300–500 hunter-gatherers who spoke one of the Shoshonean Uto-Aztecan languages and relied on nuts (particularly acorns and pine nuts), berries, game, and fish for subsistence. They settled on territories ranging from present-day Santa Monica to the northeast, the San Gabriel Mountains to the north, and Riverside to the east, stretching all the way southeast to Corona and southwest to Newport Beach and including the islands of Santa Catalina, Santa Barbara, San Nicolas, and San Clemente.

The Spanish started exploring the shores of Southern California in the early sixteenth century. They began with an expedition to Santa Catalina Island in 1520, followed by a series of failed expeditions sent by Hernán Cortés in the 1530s.[6] The Spanish explorer Juan Rodriguez Cabrillo traveled to the coast of California in 1542 and landed on Catalina Island, and Sebastian Vizcaíno was received peacefully by indigenous people of the LA Basin in 1602. But it was not until the travels by land in 1769 of Gaspar de Portolà, governor of the province of Las Californias in the Viceroyalty of New Spain, that Spanish settlement started. At the time, approximately 5,000 Tongva people were living in the LA Basin.

Between 1769 and 1823, Spanish Franciscan friars of the Catholic Church led by Junípero Serra replaced the Jesuit order's control of Alta California and established twenty-one missions financed by the king of Spain. Spread along the Californian Camino Real, also known as California's Historic Mission Trail and superseded nowadays by the long highways of the Californian coast, the missions stretched all the way from San Diego to Sonoma, just north of San Francisco. Misión San Gabriel Arcángel, the fourth of California's missions, was established in 1771 some nine miles east of the indigenous village of Yangna, which in 1781 would become the site of the administrative pueblo of Los Angeles (in present-day downtown LA).[7]

The negative impact of the Franciscan missions on the indigenous population of the LA Basin loomed large, and indigenous groups immediately resisted the establishment of the missions, as exemplified by the crushed 1785 rebellion led by Toypurina, an indigenous female spiritual leader. Despite their acts of resistance and rebellion, however, the indigenous peoples were soon submerged by the wave of Christianization that swept the region. Of the estimated 310,000 Native Americans living in current-day California in 1769, only about one-sixth remained after a hundred years of colonization—a history that many missions still fall short of acknowledging.[8]

The missions relied on the original inhabitants of the LA Basin to gain power in the region, starting a movement of Christianization, exploitation, and decimation of the indigenous peoples and renaming the Tongva as Gabrielinos in the process. The Tongva served to build the missions and were often separated from their families and communities; many were Christianized and forbidden to speak their native tongue, while others ran away into the nearby mountains.

Those who were captured had their feet or heads cut off and put on sticks for the public to see as examples of punishment inflicted by the Spanish on those who sought to escape. Many died from the diseases brought by the Spanish, while others were raped. The denial of Tongva identity remains evident today, as the bodies in mass graves remain nameless at the Missions of San Diego and San Francisco de Asís, among others.[9] In 1859, Mission San Gabriel was returned to the Catholic Church by President James Buchanan, and it still operates as a Catholic parish.[10]

After Mexico won its independence from Spain, the Mexican government retained the system put in place by its predecessor. Alta California remained for the most part privately owned through land grants provided to rancheros, with indigenous workers serving to sustain the ranchos until the mid-nineteenth century. Thus, even with the secularization of the missions by the Mexican government in 1834, political, economic, and social freedom remained elusive for the LA Basin's indigenous people.[11] Alta California fell under the protection of the Presidio of Sonoma, which replaced the older Spanish military forts of San Diego (1769; which had controlled and protected the San Gabriel Mission), Monterey (1770), and Santa Bárbara (1782).[12] And Los Angeles became an important hub of power as the new capital city of (Alta) California (1835–1854).

In 1848, under the Treaty of Guadalupe Hidalgo, Mexico ceded Alta California (present-day Southern California) to the United States. By the time the first American settlers arrived in the LA Basin, the indigenous population of California had declined by half.[13] After gold was discovered in Placerita Canyon (on the western edge of present-day Angeles National Forest) in 1842, the Gold Rush brought a massive wave of immigrants to the LA Basin in 1849 and 1850. In 1850, California became an American state; in the next three years eighteen treaties were negotiated with the federal government in order to establish reservations, but they were never ratified.[14] Today, the Tongva are still not recognized by the federal government, although the State of California recognized them formally as the original people of the LA Basin in 1994.[15]

Significance of Tongva to El Monte, South El Monte, and the LA Basin

Located about fifteen miles east of Los Angeles, in the San Gabriel Valley, the communities of El Monte and South El Monte are located in the heart of Tongva or Gabrielino lands, at a richly layered historical and geographical crossroads. According to some sources, the area was formerly known as Houtngna or Hautngna, meaning "the place of the willow"; and according to other sources it was called Sheevanga or Sheevangna, meaning "the wooden or willow area."[16] It was named *la misión vieja* (the old mission) by the Spanish when they colonized the area.[17] But over the past few years, the area has witnessed a budding revival of Tongva identity.

The Tongva, like most other Indian nations in the United States, are still here despite numerous efforts to remove indigenous peoples and practices from the American landscape.[18] This is not simply a story of indigenous enslavement by the missions, or of displacement of indigenous populations and land grabs by individual settlers. In the 1930s and 1940s, the descendants of the Tongva in El Monte and South El Monte moved farther away to work in the sugar beet fields. Fortunately, at least some of the native people living in the area managed to find refuge among Mexican families.

Cross-cultural collaborations continue to shape the region, and intermarriage added to this ethnic diversity. Descendants of the Tongva were also able to use the names of Mexican families for protection well into the twentieth century, at a time when it was still safer to be Mexican than Indian. And when several citizens of Japanese lineage were interned during World War II, Tongva neighbors preserved their businesses until their return.[19]

More recently, attempts to superimpose development projects onto the original landscape continue. A "$30 million project, which includes the building of a 14,000 square foot building, a 116-car parking lot, and other structures"[20] in South El Monte threatened to remold the Whittier Narrows Nature Center into yet another part of American consumer society, which tends to dissociate people from the natural world.

This was not a new fight; plans for a dam at Whittier Narrows started in the 1920s and continued through the New Deal, threatening the communities and natural areas, including a local bird sanctuary. At the time, the El Monte Citizens Flood Control Committee organized to fight the plan.[21] In recent years, the Friends of the Whittier Narrows Natural Area fought local politicians who are not attuned to the area's environmental importance and historical meaning to people.[22]

Many other Indian tribes of California also lack a tribal land base recognized by the state or federal governments, and some of those tribes are still seeking such recognition to this day. Without that recognition, tribal lands cannot exist legally.[23] This makes it even more difficult for the Tongva to protect their ancestral connections to the land and stall development projects.

For the Tongva, attempts by outsiders at disappearing first the people and then their cultural practices when the people survived took many forms: from religious conversion to cultural assimilation through schooling in the Spanish missions. That, too, is part of a larger history of assimilation that has continued into the American era in various forms. Less than an hour east, in Riverside County, in 1892 the American government established the Perris Indian School, supervised by a man with the appropriate name of M. S. Savage.[24] The school was "the flagship among 25 federal off-reservation American Indian boarding schools,"[25] following the national model of vocational training and cultural assimilation for Native American students set up by the Carlisle Indian School—the first of such schools, built in Pennsylvania in 1879.[26] Ten years later, the Perris Indian School was relocated to Riverside and renamed the Sherman Institute. It "is still operating today as Sherman Indian High School, a modern off-reservation boarding high school for Native American Indian students."[27]

As a result of the discriminatory policies and practices described above, simply identifying oneself as Tongva was unthinkable for many people just a few decades ago. According to Gloria Arellanes, who identifies herself as Tongva and lives in El Monte, her identity was nipped in the bud at home because her family had told her about the threat of discrimination and violence should she be identified by others as Tongva. As a result, she was taught to blend in and speak Spanish or English, not Tongva. Similarly, Mark Acuña, a Tongva tribal council member,

> had been raised by his father and grandparents as white. They wanted him to be able to get an education and assimilate into the American culture. He did. He studied ethnobotany and became a college professor. It wasn't until he was around 50 years old that he went to hear a Tongva woman speak about medicinal plants that the tribe had used. He was ready to argue with her that the tribe was extinct. Then he recognized the plants she was talking about as the same plants his grandfather grew. He remembered someone saying his grandfather had been a Tongva medicine man. Then his father told him how the family decided to keep his ancestry from him so he could pass as white.[28]

Acuña's story exemplifies how a culture's various elements are carried by people in their day-to-day experiences and yet easily made invisible in more or less subtle ways. Acuña's Tongva identity survived through his grandfather's relationship to plants. But the fact that those practices had remained unnamed to him, as if practiced in a cultural vacuum, disconnected him from both his own identity and his conception of Tongva history. The fact that people are no longer afraid to identify themselves as Tongva today therefore illustrates the desire to restore their own visibility and identity and the possibility of doing so.[29] At the University of California, Los Angeles, for instance, the linguist Pamela Munro set up a Facebook page to help revive the Tongva language with the help of Tongva speakers.[30] But obstacles persist. On the one hand, the legal barriers to Tongva self-determination are numerous. A few years ago, the Gabrielino-Tongva Tribe submitted a proposal to the city of Garden Grove, requesting permission to build a casino near Disneyland. The project could not move forward due to lack of federal recognition of the tribe, which prevents the Tongva from establishing a casino since there is no "Indian land" to provide the proper jurisdiction to administer it.[31]

On the other hand, the Tongva's cultural presence in the LA Basin keeps growing. If local names and places remain subjects of debate today, they have allowed a revival of Tongva culture in the LA Basin. These names provide points of entry into the region's many layers of history and constitute a shift in the indigenous history of the Americas: giving the Tongva themselves a renewed sense of confidence in their heritage, and giving the larger society a (relatively) reduced discriminatory attitude toward indigenous peoples. Puvungna, or "the gathering place," on the campus of California State University, Long Beach constitutes to this day the main gathering point for Tongva people for cultural events and was chosen by at least some Tongva descendants for its historical significance as the place where the creation deity Chinichinich—spellings of the name vary—appeared to the Tongva long before colonization.[32] And a cultural center and museum opened in 1992 in Kuruvungna Springs, on the campus of University High School in west Los Angeles, to celebrate the Tongva's cultural heritage. One of their signature events is the Life before Columbus Festival, held every year in October.[33]

As noted by some Tongva people, what has allowed them to survive until this day has been, in part, their ability to pass as people of different ethnicities, based on whichever was most protective at different points in time. Examples abound. During the Gold Rush, some Tongva, who lived under the informal protection of neighborly Mexican families, took on a Mexican identity. And in the twentieth century, it became common to try to pass as white to blend into mainstream society as fully as possible.[34] It is time to make living together while respecting our cultural differences a priority.

Notes

1 There is disagreement about what name should be given to the indigenous people of the LA Basin. Some advocate for Tongva and others for Gabrielino or a hyphenated version of the two, while still others advocate for Kizh. This chapter seeks not to settle this dispute, but rather to trace and celebrate indigenous presence in the region as one of its many layers of settlement. For an illustration of the controversy over the correct name for the indigenous people, see Ashley Archibald, "Turf War Rages On over Name of Tongva Park," *Santa Monica Daily Press*, March 3, 2013, http://smdp.com/turf-war-rages-on-over-name-of-tongva-park/119202.

2 The peak was renamed in 2002. See Liana Aghajanian, "Intersections: Descendants of the Tongva Look to Their Past," *Glendale News-Press*, October 15, 2012, http://articles.glendalenewspress.com/2012-10-15/opinion/tn-gnp-1015-intersections-descendants-of-the-tongva-look-to-their-past_1_tongva-language-tongva-indians-tongva-tribe.

3 For information about the Santa Monica Tongva Park, which got its name in 2013, see Tongva Park, "Overview of Tongva Park and Ken Genser Square," accessed June 22, 2019, http://tongvapark.squarespace.com/about/.
4 For more information, see Loyola Marymount University, "Tongva," accessed July 18, 2019, https://mission.lmu.edu/cis/peacefulplaces/tongvamemorial/.An archival collection on the original people of the LA Basin can be consulted at Loyola Marymount University. To access the catalog entry, go to http://www.oac.cdlib.org/findaid/ark:/13030/c89g5p09.
5 Los Angeles Almanac, "History Timeline: Los Angeles County, Pre-History to 1799 A.D.," accessed June 22, 2019, http://www.laalmanac.com/history/hi01a.htm.
6 Four Directions Institute, "Gabrielino," 2007, http://www.fourdir.com/gabrielino.htm.
7 Aghajanian, "Intersections."
8 Carol Pogash, "To Some in California, Founder of Church Missions Is Far from Saint," *New York Times*, January 21, 2015, http://www.nytimes.com/2015/01/22/us/to-some-indians-in-california-father-serra-is-far-from-a-saint.html?_r=0.
9 Gloria Arellanes (a Tongva from El Monte), phone interview by author, September 20, 2014; California Missions Resource Center, "California Missions Facts," accessed July 18, 2019, https://www.missionscalifornia.com/mission-facts.
10 Four Directions Institute, "Gabrielino."
11 Jesse La Tour, "A History of the Kizh (Orange County's Native Inhabitants)," accessed June 22, 2019, http://jesselatour.blogspot.com/2012/07/a-history-of-tongva-tribe-orange.html.
12 California Missions, "The Four (+ One) California Presidios," accessed June 22, 2019, http://www.californiamissionguide.com/presidios/california_presidios.html.
13 La Tour, "A History of the Kizh."
14 For more detail, see http://www.gabrielinotribe.org/TribalHistory/tribal_history.cfm.
15 For more on this, see Alice Mirlesse, "Identity on Trial: The Gabrielino-Tongva Quest for Federal Recognition," (2013), Pomona Senior Theses, Paper 90, http://scholarship.claremont.edu/pomona_theses/90/.
16 Members of the Kizh-Gabrieleño Band of Mission Indians, oral history interview, January 10, 2015, South El Monte Arts Posse, East of East (SEMAP): Mapping Community Narratives in El Monte and South El Monte, http://www.semapeastofeast.com.
17 Ibid.
18 See, for instance, "Tribal History—Lost Treaty Rights and Current Status," Gabrielino-Tongva Tribe, accessed July 18, 2019, http://www.gabrielinotribe.org/historical-sites-1/. For information about the Tongva language revitalization, see "Tongva Language," accessed June 22, 2019, https://www.facebook.com/TongvaLanguage/.
19 Members of the Kizh-Gabrieleño Band of Mission Indians, oral history interview, SEMAP.
20 Laura Vena, "Shaping the Landscape at Whittier Narrows Nature Center," KCET, January 26, 2015, https://www.kcet.org/shows/departures/shaping-the-landscape-at-whittier-narrows-nature-center.
21 See David Reid, "Whittier Narrows Park," chapter 18 in this volume.

22 See Friends of the Whittier Narrows Natural Area, home page, November 15, 2015, http://www.naturalareafriends.net/home.

23 Seventy-eight tribes are currently seeking recognition. See California Courts, "California Tribal Communities," accessed June 22, 2019, http://www.courts.ca.gov/3066.htm.

24 The History of the Perris Indian School," Perris Valley Museum Historical Archives, accessed July 19, 2019, http://www.shermanindianmuseum.org/perris.htm.

25 Bettye Miller, "New Book Recounts History of Sherman Institute," *UCR Today*, November 29, 2012, https://ucrtoday.ucr.edu/10497.

26 For more information about the Sherman Institute and the national Indian boarding school policy, see Charla Bear, "American Indian Boarding Schools Haunt Many," *National Public Radio*, May 12, 2008, http://www.npr.org/templates/story/story.php?storyId=16516865.

27 California Indian Education, "Indian Boarding Schools," 2008, http://www.californiaindianeducation.org/indian_boarding_schools/. For the current school's website, see Sherman Indian High School, "About Us," accessed June 22, 2019, http://www.shermanindian.org/home/.

28 Accessed January 10, 2016, http://www.pbs.org/indiancountry/challenges/tongva.html (documentary link discontinued).

29 Arellanes, phone interview by author.

30 Letisia Marquez, "UCLA Linguist, Gabrielino-Tongva Indians Use Social Media to Revive Extinct Language," *UCLA Newsroom*, June 27, 2014, http://newsroom.ucla.edu/stories/ucla-linguist-gabrieleno-tongva-indians-use-social-media-to-revive-extinct-language.

31 Gabrielino-Tongva Tribe, "Garden Grove Casino Resort Proposal," accessed January 10 2016, http://www.gabrielinotribe.org/garden_grove/index.cfm (article link discontinued).

32 Gloria Arellanes, Facebook messenger interviews by author, September 21 and 23, 2014. For more information about Puvungna, see California State University, Long Beach, "About Puvungna," modified October 24, 1996, http://www.csulb.edu/~eruyle/puvudoc_0000_about.html.

33 Gabrielino Tongva Springs Foundation, "Home," accessed June 22, 2019, http://gabrielinosprings.com/wpsite/.

34 Members of the Kizh-Gabrieleño Band of Mission Indians, oral history interview, SEMAP.

2

Toypurina

A Legend Etched in the Landscape

MARIA JOHN

Nestled within communities throughout Southern California, three vibrant works of public art commemorate the life and the legend of Toypurina. In East Los Angeles (LA), a mural sixty feet by twenty feet in the neighborhood of Boyle Heights adorns the main wall of Ramona Gardens, a large and well-known public housing complex historically tenanted by Latino families. At the center of the mural, the striking face of a youthful indigenous woman commands the viewer's attention. Around her, in technicolor, all the vitality of the Ramona Gardens community is depicted—from its children enjoying the recently established library to the lively sporting activities of the community's many young residents. According to Raul Gonzalez, one of the mural's creators, Toypurina, the woman holding our attention, is representative of "the ultimate strength, the woman fighter, the mother who protects her children from harm at Ramona Gardens."[1]

A little east of El Monte, at the busy Baldwin Park Metrolink Station, a sprawling monument pays tribute to this spirited Gabrielino woman. Consisting of an arch twenty feet high and a plaza a hundred feet long, the LA artist Judy Baca's "Danza Indigenas" (1993) centers on an artistic recreation of an archway from the nearby San Gabriel Mission. Beneath the arch, the mission's floor plan is etched into the colored concrete of an open plaza that leads commuters to shelters along the train platform. On the platform itself commuters continue to engage with the monument as they stand atop the floor plans of several other nearby missions. Superimposed on all these floor plans, interweaving shapes representing two lines of indigenous dancers are the key feature giving this monument its name (in English, "Indigenous Dances"). According to Baca, her artwork seeks to actively "put memory back into a piece of the land."[2] In particular, the memory of indigenous resistance within the missions is symbolized by a stone mound located on the San Gabriel Mission floor plan near what would have been the church altar. It is a replica of one the Gabrielinos would have used as a place of prayer, and is meant, Baca explains, as "a tribute to Toypurina."[3]

Finally, in central LA, animating the streets of Koreatown, another Toypurina mural can be found as part of the Gabba Alley Project—an initiative of a local art gallery to revitalize alleyways across LA with colorful and socially engaged artwork. To date, over 110 murals by more than eighty-five local and international artists have been created.[4] In February 2018, a mural by LMNOPI, an activist, painter, and printmaker based in New York City, became one of the most politically engaged pieces to join the project.[5] The artist's six-by-ten-foot mural of Toypurina is centered on the young woman's face. She gazes resolutely at the viewer. At eye level, the word "decolonize" sits brightly atop topographical map lines that are layered across Toypurina's image. According to the artist, the map lines "could be seen as a prison and a representation of colonization of a people and a land."[6] However, by weaving the lines "in and out of the contours of Toypurina's face," the intention is to "convey a rebellion against that subjugation, a way of owning and transforming it into adornment."[7]

The placement of these artworks in such prominent, accessible, and populated public spaces, their larger-than-life scale, and the veneration of Toypurina that is their shared goal mark the presence of an active and shared community memory. These artworks also attest to the fact that even though Toypurina's home was originally in the area closest to the San Gabriel Mission, her life and legend have extended their relevance far beyond the geographical confines that mapped her mortal life. Through art, history, and memory, Toypurina's story has been woven into the very fabric of the landscape surrounding the specific places where historical events unfolded to make her legendary. This chapter touches upon the history of Toypurina's life in connection to the foiled uprising at Mission San Gabriel in 1785, the emergence of new historical theories about Toypurina's role in the rebellion, and what the longevity of her story might suggest about the communities that claim her.

FIG. 4 Daniel González, "Toypurina." (Courtesy of Daniel González.)

Toypurina and the San Gabriel Mission, 1785

Few details survive about the life of the Gabrielino medicine woman Toypurina, but she is undoubtedly best remembered for her involvement in a planned revolt against Spanish colonial rule in 1785. Born into the Kumivit tribe of Southern California in the area around Mission San Gabriel, Toypurina's tribe became known as the Gabrielino (today, their descendants also refer to themselves as the Tongva people) after Spanish contact in the late eighteenth century.[8] Franciscan missionaries had founded more than twenty missions from San Diego to Sonoma between 1769 and 1823.[9] These missions encroached on the lands of numerous tribal nations in the area, exploited the labor of the tribes' people, and proselytized for their conversion to the Roman Catholic faith. From the perspective of the colonists, these missions were intended to act as a chain of defense around the Spanish empire in the north.[10]

It was in this context that Mission San Gabriel was established in September 1771, near the banks of the Río Hondo on the southern edge of the San Gabriel Valley. The mission remained at its original site until May 1775, when it was moved several miles north to its present site—on Gabrielino land. Historians estimate that in 1770, the Gabrielinos were one group among more than fifty-competing indigenous communities in the LA basin. The Gabrielino population was high, numbering about five thousand, and their territory encompassed about 1,500 square miles.[11] By the time Toypurina became involved in the rebellion against the mission in 1785, it is estimated that "well over 1,200 Indians" from the area had been baptized by the missionaries at San Gabriel, including approximately 843 Gabrielinos.[12]

In an effort to protect the self-sufficiency of their communities, retain their tribal cultures, and uphold their religious practices and beliefs, many native people at this time had long been actively resisting the imposed Spanish rule and attempts at acculturation. Toypurina emerged as one such individual. In October 1785, she joined a group of Gabrielino neophytes from Mission San Gabriel in their plot against the mission. Most prominent among the instigators of this rebellion was the discontented neophyte Nicolás José, who not only initiated talk of the plan among other Gabrielinos inside the mission but also rallied key individuals, including Toypurina, from as many as eight Indian villages in the surrounding area.[13]

Historians have concluded that their plan was provoked in the final instance when Spanish officials forbade the practice of traditional dances.[14] Up until this point, the padres had shown some degree of leniency, permitting a number of Indians to maintain their roles in traditional ceremonies. José in particular is said to have been accustomed to living in ways that allowed him to balance his commitments to both of his cultural worlds.[15] The authoritarian decision to suddenly ban all traditional dances among the mission Indians was thus the latest in a long string of ongoing affronts and atrocities (violence, rapes, forced religious conversions, and slave labor) committed against the Gabrielinos since the beginning of the Spanish invasion. José and his allies therefore set out to destroy the San Gabriel Mission.

Toypurina's support of this effort is believed to have been crucial, due to her powers as a medicine woman. It was intended that she would use her divine influence to restrain the Catholic priests during the revolt, while her male counterparts would eliminate the Spanish soldiers.[16] On the night of October 25, 1785, Toypurina and the other insurgents attacked the mission as planned, but unbeknown to them, a corporal of the guard had been informed of the revolt ahead of time—which allowed the Spanish to mount an ambush. When Toypurina arrived, she and several others were arrested. Spanish officials held a trial, sentencing five people to twenty-five lashes each, and another twelve to receive fifteen or twenty lashes each.[17] Rather than torture or kill the offenders behind closed doors, these floggings were carried out in public, so the entire mission population would see the consequences of the rebels' actions.

In addition, the Spanish officials found Toypurina, José, and two other men (Temejasaquichí and Alijivit) guilty of leading the attack.[18] As punishment, Toypurina was exiled from Mission San Gabriel after being held there as a prisoner for the duration of her trial, during which time she was also baptized into the Catholic faith. She was sent to live out her life further north, first at Mission San Carlos Borromeo, located near Monterey in present-day Carmel. There she married a Spanish soldier named Manuel Montera[19] Between 1789 (the year of their marriage) and 1794, Toypurina and Montera had three children: Cesario, Juana de Dios Montero, and Maria Clementina. In 1799, Toypurina passed away at Mission San Juan Bautista and was buried there.[20]

New Historical Understandings

The precise nature of Toypurina's role within the uprising is a matter of some historical debate. It is unclear to what extent she should be understood as its principal leader, and her motivations for getting involved in the first place have been reconsidered by scholars in recent years in light of new historical evidence. At the time of the rebellion, the Spanish reportedly depicted her as a seductress and sorceress—a witch who used her powers of persuasion to orchestrate the events. While the Spanish may have acknowledged that the idea for the uprising originated with José and others among the mission Indians, at the trial, they reportedly attributed most responsibility to Toypurina because of her kinship connections and her renown in the area as a powerful medicine woman, which served to intimidate people into joining the cause. Toypurina and her brother were said to have contacted and convinced several people in surrounding villages to participate in the rebellion, giving the plan the necessary momentum and the numbers it needed to get off the ground.

Since the 1960s, historians have continued to view Toypurina as a central player in the rebellion, but they cast her actions as that of a freedom fighter, resisting colonialism in the name of her people. This interpretation has dominated academic circles since 1958, when the historian and genealogist Thomas Workman Temple II became the first scholar to examine the transcripts from Toypurina's trial. He subsequently published an influential article about the rebellion based on his reading of the proceedings.[21] Temple's interpretation of the interrogation transcripts identified Toypurina as the star witness, and he dramatized various key events that have now become staple features in multiple retellings of her story.

According to Temple's account, as Toypurina's interrogation began she kicked over a stool provided by her captors, preferring instead to stand while delivering her testimony. Temple also reported that she was the last of the witnesses to testify and was quick to take credit for organizing and leading the attack, stating her motives plainly: "I hate the padres and all of you, for living here on my native soil, for trespassing upon the land of my forefathers and despoiling our tribal domains. . . . I came [to the mission] to inspire the dirty cowards to fight, and not to quail at the sight of Spanish sticks that spit fire and death, nor [to] retch at the evil smell of gunsmoke—and be done with you white invaders!"[22] According to Temple, these were Toypurina's "exact words," and moreover he claimed that they were corroborated by the testimonies of the other Indian defendants at the trial, who not only spoke of Toypurina's "bewitching powers" but also identified her as the prime instigator and leader of the rebellion.[23]

For the most part, this is also the version of events that has become popularized outside of academic settings and that still reverberates most widely in the community memories of places and people connected to this history. In this prevailing understanding of events, Toypurina has become the symbol of Gabrielino resistance to the missions and an icon of California Indian women's resistance to colonial oppression. Toypurina's dramatic story has been publicly and permanently memorialized in this way through the three public artworks discussed at the opening of this chapter, as well as in a short film.[24] The Mission San Gabriel Playhouse also hosted a production about her life titled *Toypurina: A Story of Love, Determination and Loss*, which opened in July 2014 and toured California in 2016.[25] The publicity for this play promotes Toypurina's heroism and her leadership as the focal point of the story: "Written by two members of the Gabrieleno/Tongva San Gabriel Band of Mission Indians, and based on real-life events of their ancestors, *Toypurina* charts the life and times of the play's namesake, a young Native American woman who led a rebellion against injustice and oppression. In 1785, at the young age of 25 and pregnant with her first child, Toypurina used her vision, charisma and determination to challenge the authority of the Spanish settlers. It was an action that would impact the rest of her life."[26]

In addition to providing creative inspiration for a new generation of local native and Latino artists, this popularized understanding of Toypurina's legacy even captured the attention of the internationally renowned Chilean author Isabel Allende, who paid tribute to Toypurina's courage in her 2005 novel *Zorro*, basing a key character on the historical figure.[27]

By contrast, the historian Steven Hackel has reinterpreted Toypurina's involvement in the rebellion.[28] While not calling into question her bravery or her important role in the uprising, Hackel's new historical narrative casts Toypurina's actions in a more nuanced light and furnishes us with new possibilities for understanding the diverse and complex motivations of the various participants. In contrast to the widely held belief—both at the time and in current popular understandings of history—that Toypurina was the rebellion's main orchestrator, Hackel suggests that more attention should be paid to the roles of José and another organizer, Temejasaquichí.[29] Hackel writes that, "All four of the suspects questioned, including Toypurina, identified Nicolás José, a thirty-seven year-old mission Indian—not Toypurina—as the rebellion's prime instigator."[30] Moreover, according to Hackel, it was Temejasaquichí—not Toypurina—who visited the mission to convince the neophytes "not to believe in the Padres but rather only in her."[31] Whether or not these new insights change our perspective on Toypurina's role in the rebellion, at the very least, they might encourage us to reconsider the extent to which any one person can be held responsible for the execution of the plan.

In revisiting the transcripts from the trial, Hackel also reports that the records provide no indication that Toypurina implicated herself through insolent conduct during her interrogation—she did not kick over a stool, speak of white invaders, fire-spitting sticks, dirty cowards, or the despoiling of her forefathers' land.[32] Rather, the soldier who recorded her testimony reported only that "she was angry with the Padres and with all of those of this Mission because we are living here in her land."[33] Whereas Temple and later scholars have embellished Toypurina's testimony to emphasize the ways in which her actions and words were an indictment of the "white invaders," Hackel reads the evidence in a slightly different way. Toypurina's statement clearly indicates that her anger was directed toward "all of those of this Mission," not only the padres and soldiers. This is significant, Hackel reasons, because it suggests that Toypurina's grievances may have been directed equally toward "all of those" Indians who lived at Mission San Gabriel. In other words, Hackel tries to move us beyond a straightforward story of Indian solidarity against the Spanish. Instead, he emphasizes the likelihood of multiple and overlapping motivations among the many participants.

To substantiate this suggestion, Hackel takes the local political, social, and economic context into account. For instance, he points out that between 1780 and 1785, the number of Indians, as well as the livestock population, at the mission had increased dramatically. In almost five years, the mission population had nearly doubled, while the numbers of livestock had increased threefold.[34] These dramatic changes were not due to a natural increase of livestock and people already in the area, but rather to the relocation of more than 560 Indians into the San Gabriel Valley from numerous distant villages.[35] Many of these newly transplanted neophytes had come to San Gabriel from communities that were historically antagonistic to villages near the mission.

Thus, if we bear in mind that these changes in the five years prior to the rebellion were placing inordinate pressure on preexisting Indian subsistence patterns in the area and bringing numerous conflicting groups into the San Gabriel Valley, we can start to understand the actions of Toypurina, the other unbaptized insurgents, and the Indians from within the mission as being motivated by a far more complex, and potentially quite varied, set of considerations. The attack, according to Hackel's reinterpretation—while obviously part of a general and long-standing effort to resist colonialism and expel the Spanish—was thus also a specific and targeted response led by the Gabrielinos to reassert their dominance over other newly arrived Indians in the area. In understanding what motivated Toypurina and other participants in the revolt, Hackel therefore underscores the significance of recognizing that multiple goals were at stake. Moreover, Toypurina's actions as a freedom fighter were not simply and only a response to the Spanish presence; they were also influenced by a long history of intertribal conflict and competition that predated colonialism.

Toypurina's Importance for the History of El Monte and South El Monte

Tribal historians have compared Toypurina to Joan of Arc because "both were religious leaders of their people, both organized revolts against invading foreign powers, both led rebel forces in the field, both were betrayed, both were subjected to sham trials, and both suffered tragic ends."[36] Toypurina's story has therefore been taken up today by communities whose members either trace their lineage to the Gabrielinos or might in some way relate to a narrative of oppression and resistance. The three works of art first discussed in this chapter attest to the ways in which quite distinct communities in LA have embraced Toypurina's story as representative of their own. For the artists commissioned to create the mural in Ramona Gardens, it was Toypurina's exemplary strength and her role as a protector of her peoples that made her an obvious choice for their piece, titled "Conoce Tus Raices" (Know Your Roots). The artists drew on Toypurina's image and legend as a means of conveying the important role played by mothers within the Ramona Gardens community in protecting the culture and safety of their children.[37]

For the Gabrielino traditionalist and Chicana artist Judy Baca, who was commissioned by the LA County Metropolitan Transportation Authority (MTA) and the City of Baldwin Park to create a mission-themed monument in this largely Latino community, it felt "appropriate" to use her artwork "to put [Toypurina] back into her own territory."[38] In an interview with the *Los Angeles Times*, Baca explained that her artwork as a whole aims to portray an "authentic" and "truthful" vision of the area's history.[39] Returning Toypurina to her homeland was one means of expressing this vision. Baca also achieved it by etching carefully chosen words and quotes into different parts of the monument. Under the central arch, for example, is the word *Sunigna,* the Gabrielino name for the area, and a quote from the queer Chicana scholar and writer Gloria Anzaldúa: "This land was Mexican once, was Indian always and is, and will be again."[40] At the most distant shelter from the plaza are engravings of the words "memory" and "willpower," which, according to Baca, are "what any culture—the ones living then and those living now—has to have to preserve itself."[41] The memory of Toypurina and the willpower she demonstrated to protect the survival of her people and culture are thus integral features of this work of public art and memory.

Similarly, for LMNOPI, who identifies herself primarily as an activist whose art is "a vehicle for messaging around indigenous sovereignty, climate justice and human rights," the decision to draw on Toypurina's story as the focus of her mural for the Alley Project was made to represent the intersection of these themes. In the first instance, the mural was a way to "pay homage to the Tongva people as some of the original inhabitants of the Los Angeles basin."[42] LMNOPI especially chose Toypurina out of a respect and reverence for "her effort to organize a rebellion against the Spanish colonizers to remove them from her homeland."[43] And as seen most vividly through the distinctive use of map lines in the mural, drawing on Toypurina's story was also seen by this artist as a way of bringing attention to historical and ongoing processes that simultaneously subjugate land and people, thus reinforcing the message that humans must be understood as a part of the landscape.[44] Moreover, the significance of the word "decolonize" within the mural is to suggest "the possibilities that exist when we recognize our intrinsic connection to place beyond ownership, beyond structures imposed by mankind. It is also a nod to the ancestors to let them know we are still fighting."[45] Again, the ability of Toypurina's story to represent an unbreakable connection between people and place and, most significantly, to symbolize a continued struggle against the subjugation of people and land stands as a reminder not only of what has survived and what has been overcome, but also of all that remains to be done to honor that past.

Throughout her life, Toypurina stood as an exemplar of the challenging circumstances and choices that California Indians faced in the wake of Spanish contact, violence, and settlement. She openly resisted the mission and participated in an attempt to destroy this symbol of Spanish colonialism in her homeland. After the revolt failed, Toypurina made several adjustments in her life to Spanish colonialism, including her baptism and marriage to a Spanish soldier. As historians have recently pointed out, though, these changes in her later life did not necessarily entail a full acceptance on Toypurina's part of either Catholicism or the Spanish order. Instead, what they show is that she and other native Californians adapted to their circumstances and attempted to shape events to their advantage. It is questionable, for example, whether Toypurina or any other native people genuinely accepted baptism or knew the full extent of its meaning.[46] In Toypurina's case, this is especially complicated given that the evidence suggests that she was coerced into baptism, since she was still imprisoned at the time.

Her adoption of Catholicism may therefore have been evidence of a survival strategy rather than any abandonment of her traditional culture. A similar interpretation might be made of her marriage to Montera. Rather than signaling her acceptance of Spanish religion and ways of life, Toypurina may have just been seeking ways to protect herself and survive. Marrying a soldier may have been the most expedient way of safeguarding her future. Though the revolt at Mission San Gabriel was ultimately thwarted, it therefore stands as a symbol of, and testament to, the spirited survival of the Gabrielinos and wider indigenous resistance to oppression.

The ongoing significance of Toypurina's story in particular clearly does not end with the foiled rebellion, or even with her banishment from her traditional homeland. Rather, her life's story in its entirety reflects a narrative of resilience, survival, and a persistent will to adapt to changing—and often very difficult—circumstances. Toypurina emerges from the historical record as a woman who not only confronted Spanish colonialism in Southern California but who also lit a path for the survival and endurance of future generations of her people. Herein lies the continuing significance of her memory and her legend for the present-day communities whose members claim her, in and around El Monte and South El Monte.

Notes

1 Quoted in Lisbeth Espinosa, "The Changing Aesthetics of Murals in Los Angeles" (MA thesis, California State University, Los Angeles, 2011), 81.

2 Quoted in Zan Dubin, "Muralist Honors California Indians Art," *Los Angeles Times*, August 10, 1993.

3 Quoted in ibid.

4 Gabba Gallery, "Gabba Alley Project," accessed June 22, 2019, https://www.gabbagallery.com/alley-project/.
5 LMNOPI, "About LMNOPI," accessed June 22, 2019, https://lmnopi.com.
6 LMNOPI, correspondence with author, September 5, 2018.
7 Ibid.
8 In 1994, the state of California recognized the Gabrielino-Tongva Tribe in Assembly Joint Resolution 96 (Resolution chapter 146, Statutes of 1994). Extending out from LA and into the Southern California region, there are nineteen federally recognized tribes and hundreds that are not yet recognized. While the Gabrielino or Tongva people do not have federal recognition (they filed for it in 1990, and the application remains pending), the passage of the 1994 resolution has caused some tension. As the tribe states on its website: "State recognition also goes to 'who' the Tongva are, for only one Tribe is recognized. Any attempt to separate the Tongva into 'bands' might be helpful for those interested in multiple casino locations. But recognizing several 'bands' instead of one 'Nation' would be contrary to California's public policy" (Gabrielino-Tongva Tribe, "Tribal History," accessed June 22, 2019, http://www.gabrielinotribe.org/historical-sites-1/). This speaks to the fact that some Gabrielino or Tongva people do not accept only one organization or government as representing them. For more about the Gabrielino or Tongva people and other tribes in the LA area, see University of California Los Angeles, "Mapping Indigenous LA," accessed June 22, 2019, https://mila.ss.ucla.edu/. For information on the history of the Los Angeles Indian population, its demographic characteristics, and the making of the Indian Community of Los Angeles, see Joan Weibel-Orlando, *Indian Country L.A.* (Urbana: University of Illinois Press, 1991).
9 Steven Hackel, "Sources of Rebellion: Indian Testimony and the Mission San Gabriel Uprising of 1785," *Ethnohistory* 50, no. 4 (Fall 2003): 648.
10 Ibid.
11 Ibid.
12 Ibid.
13 Ibid.
14 Ibid., 651.
15 Ibid.
16 Ibid.
17 Ibid., 655.
18 Ibid.
19 Ibid., 658. Montera was Toypurina's second husband. Historians don't know a great deal about her first husband—a native man who remains unnamed in historical records. According to some scholars he was staunchly opposed to the Spanish religion and so his marriage to Toypurina was annulled within the church so that she could later enter a "Christian" marriage. See Ernest P. Salas Teutimes, Christina Swindall Martinez, Andrew Salas, and Gary Stickel. *Toypurina: The Joan of Arc of California* (San Gabriel, CA: Kizh Tribal Press, 2011).
20 Hackel, "Sources of Rebellion," 658.
21 Thomas Workman Temple II, "Toypurina the Witch and the Indian Uprising at San Gabriel," *Masterkey* 32, no. 5 (1958): 136–152.
22 Quoted in ibid., 148–149.
23 Ibid., 144.

24 For a trailer, see Ralph Nabor, "Toypurina: A True Story," accessed June 22, 2019, http://www.youtube.com/watch?v=I25x9aJJbZs.

25 San Gabriel Mission Playhouse, *Toypurina: A Story of Love, Determination and Loss*, accessed June 22, 2019, http://www.toypurina.org/.

26 San Gabriel Mission Playhouse, "Toypurina," accessed June 22, 2019, http://www.missionplayhouse.org/wp-content/uploads/Toypurina-Sponsor-Page.pdf.

27 Isabel Allende, *Zorro* (London: Harper Collins, 2005).

28 In addition to his 2003 "Sources of Rebellion," see Steven Hackel, *Children of Coyote, Missionaries of Saint Francis: Indian-Spanish Relations in Colonial California, 1769–1850* (Chapel Hill: University of North Carolina Press, 2005). For other historical discussions of Toypurina's life, see Rose Marie Beebe and Robert M. Senkewicz, eds., *Lands of Promise and Despair: Chronicles of Early California 1535–1846*, (Norman: University of Oklahoma Press, 2015); James A. Sandos, "Between Crucifix and Lance: Indian-White Relations in California, 1769–1848," *California History* 76, nos. 2–3 (1997): 196–229.

29 Hackel, "Sources of Rebellion," 654–657.

30 Ibid., 651.

31 Ibid., 654.

32 Ibid.

33 According to Hackel's reading of the testimony, these were Toypurina's exact words: "Estaba enojada con los Padres y con todos los de esta mision porque estamos viviendo aqui en su tierra" (quoted in ibid., 655, n.75).

34 Ibid., 656.

35 Ibid.

36 Teutimes et al., *Toypurina.*

37 Espinosa, "The Changing Aesthetics of Murals in Los Angeles," 81.

38 Quoted in Dubin, "Muralist Honors California Indians Art." While Baca provided the artistic vision behind "Danza Indigenas," it should be noted that the monument was a collaboration involving Baca and LA architects Kate Diamond of Siegel Diamond Architects and Gustavo Leclerc of Adobe LA. Baca also interviewed Gabrielinos and other residents of Baldwin Park in order to include community voices in the project.

39 Quoted in ibid.

40 Quoted in ibid.

41 Quoted in ibid.

42 LMNOPI, correspondence with author.

43 Ibid.

44 Ibid.

45 Ibid.

46 It should be noted that these historical interpretations are not unique to the Californian context. Indeed, historians writing about missions, missionaries, and the history of colonialism in various contexts have made similar arguments about indigenous negotiations of new cultural and social realities. For a recent example, see Vicente M. Diaz, *Repositioning the Missionary: Rewriting the Histories of Colonialism, Native Catholicism, and Indigeneity in Guam* (Honolulu: University of Hawai'i Press, 2010).

3

From Alta California to American Statehood

Race, Change, and the Californio Pico Family

RYAN REFT

In 2014, the last great-grandchild of Pío Pico, Josephine "Josie" Pico Marquez, died in El Monte. The daughter of Celestino and Ramona Pico, Marquez had been born in Whittier in 1913 and moved to El Monte in 1948. The Whittier–El Monte connection was furthered by the fact that Celestino, Pío Pico's grandson, had been born in Whittier as well, in 1883, and Ramona had been born in El Monte in 1880. "It's the end of that generation," Marquez's nephew, John Albitre, told the *San Gabriel Valley Tribune*.[1]

Even with Marquez's passing, Pío Pico's presence in the San Gabriel Valley persists—though more metaphysically than corporeally. Pío Pico State Park, the location of the former California governor's mansion, sits just a few dozen feet away from Whittier Boulevard and stands as testament to the Californio businessman who lived through three epochs in California history: Spanish colonial rule, Mexican independence, and American statehood. The Pico name, as the historian William Estrada has noted, flourishes across Southern California in Pico Boulevard, Pico Rivera, Pío Pico Koreatown Library, and Pico Canyon, for example. "And yet, despite the veneration in the popular mind, much of what we know about Pío Pico remains clouded in myth," writes Estrada.[2]

Even attempts at capturing his history and those of other notable Californios, at least in terms of public awareness, have been only marginally successful. "California's Mexican past is often distorted, shrouded in museums, relegated to street names and old Spanish missions," writes the historian Carlos Manuel Salomon.[3]

Accounts of Alta California, the period stretching from 1769 to 1846, often envision Spanish settlers populating a bucolic landscape dotted with Catholic missions overseen by priests and friars, with Native Americans happily laboring away. Arguing that such idealized notions amount to a "Spanish fantasy" that ultimately denudes California of its Mexican and indigenous past, replacing it with an anodyne European nostalgia, historians such as William Deverell, Phoebe S. Kropp, Kevin Starr, Eric Avila, and Mike Davis have deconstructed this history. This sort of popular memory "repressed from view . . . the actual plight of Alta California's descendants," notes Davis, but equally importantly, it also obscures the state's long history of racial and ethnic diversity.[4]

The reality as represented by the San Gabriel Valley native and last Mexican governor of California proves much more complicated. Under Spanish and later Mexican rule, the future American state was a land of diversity, opportunity, and exploitation. Californios such as Pico were both exploiters and the exploited. Few families epitomize the racial and ethnic mélange, inequality, and complexity of El Monte and the San Gabriel Valley that stretched from Spanish colonization to American statehood better than the Pico family, and perhaps no one inhabited this milieu like the last governor of Mexican California, Pío Pico.

The Pico Family

Santiago de la Cruz Pico, Pío Pico's grandfather and the founder of the Pico family in California, arrived in the territory as an escort to the Juan Bautista de Anza expedition in 1775, initially settling in San Francisco before moving to Southern California when he transferred to San Diego. He later retired to Los Angeles, then just a pueblo. All of his sons would serve in the military as well, and the Pico brood would become one of few select families of enlisted personnel to receive land grants during the Spanish colonial period.[5]

Pío Pico's father, José María Pico, served as a sergeant for the Spanish crown. He worked at several Spanish missions and died at the San Gabriel Mission in 1819.[6] Jose's racial background—like those of many of his fellow settlers—reflected the larger diversity of Alta California. Granted, the region was demographically far smaller at the time. Even on the eve of the Gold Rush in 1848, only about 18,000 people resided within Alta California, but the territory drew a "wide variety of people mostly poor pobladores or townspeople . . . a racially diverse group who . . . saw California as an economic opportunity," writes Salomon.[7] For example, of the forty-two founders of Los Angeles in 1781, twenty-six claimed Afro-Mexican ancestry, while many of the others were descended from Native Americans, Spaniards, mestizos, and other mixed castes.[8]

Undoubtedly, the Spanish colonial system placed great emphasis on racial difference, enforcing a none-too-subtle caste system on its population: Africans and Native Americans on the bottom rungs, mestizos and mulattos in the middle, and *peninsulares* (Spanish-born transplants to the Americas) and creoles (American-born people of Spanish ancestry) at the top. Though hardly on equal terms, Spaniards, Native Americans, mestizos, and mulattos interacted to create a sort of hybrid culture unique to California, but not uncommon in what were then Spain's and later Mexico's northern territories.

Like many borderlands far removed from bureaucratic centers, Alta California shook off arbitrary distinctions and embraced a more fluid conception of race. Mestizos and mulattos could win land grants and even occupy significant political positions.[9] "Access to land meant access to honor and dignity," the Yale University historian Stephen Pitti observed in 2013.[10] Californios, as residents of Alta California called themselves, "thought of themselves as a proud people, an emerging people." Far from Mexico City, they developed a sense of independence and self-government. Tejanos in Texas and Nueva Mexicanos in New Mexico exhibited a similar identity, though each remained unique to its local circumstances.

Multiracial heritage, however, did not necessarily ensure solidarity with other traditionally marginalized groups. The Pico family, like many other residents of Alta California, could not claim a pure Spanish heritage but had rather emerged from the unique culture of New Spain, tracing its ancestry back to a mix of Spanish, Indian, and African roots. Despite his own racially mixed status as a mulatto, Santiago de la Cruz Pico had been a soldier—helping spread Spanish imperialism across Mexico, often at the expense of indigenous populations.

As evidenced by the Pico family, many settlers of mixed ancestry wanted to identify as Spanish or European, and the Californio identity did not fully erase racial and class distinctions. For example, perhaps due to his lengthy service for the crown, José María Pico was listed as a Spaniard in the 1790 census, although his father and brothers were recorded as mulattos. Moreover, like his father, Santiago, José María would suppress Native American resistance, for example in 1785. José María, who spoke the local Tongva language, overheard a plot by the local Indians involving the female Native American leader Toypurina. He informed the San Gabriel Mission of the impending uprising, and the conspirators were arrested.[11]

Spaniards and Californios viewed indigenous people as inferior and undoubtedly exploited the labor and bodies of the local populations. "It is difficult . . . to see the mission system as resulting in anything other than wholesale anthropological devastation," notes Starr, "whatever the sincerely felt evangelical intent of the missionaries and the civilizing goals of the [Spaniards]."[12] Even as the mission system declined after Mexican independence in 1821 and with secularization after 1833, many Native Americans (some historians estimate as many as 10,000) served the wealthier Californio families as servants. While prosperous Californios might have looked upon this time as the height of Mexican California, "rancho society" had cruel and barbaric aspects to it, as Native Americans continued to endure harsh treatment.[13] Observers such as Charles Dwight Willard drew comparisons to the own racial hierarchy of the United States. Renowned California writer Carey McWilliams paraphrased Willard's observations: "The Indians were the slaves, the *gente de razon* were the plantation owners or 'whites' and the Mexicans were the 'poor whites.'" The gente de razon, peninsulares, and Californios "looked down upon the Mexicans and Indians as a different breed of people—darker, illiterate, churlish, incapable of progress or understanding." Novels such as Helen Hunt Jackson's *Ramona* cast the Franciscans (and after them, the Californios) as benevolent employers despite the fact that, as McWilliams argued, such "fine old Spanish families . . . were among the most flagrant exploiters of the Indian in Southern California.[14]

Once it gained independence from Spain, Mexican California's diversity increased. Economic ties with Latin America, New England, and the Far East grew. More and more non-Mexicans settled in the region and married into Californio families, enlarging conceptions of citizenship in Alta California. Secular culture gained a stronger foothold as the newcomers brought with them prosperity, along with different lifestyles and values.[15]

Pío Pico Rises and Falls

Born to José María and Maria Eustaquia on May 5, 1801, at the Mission of San Gabriel, growing up around San Diego, and dying in Los Angeles on September 11, 1894, Pío Pico serves as a useful figure with which to explore the history of El Monte and San Gabriel Valley. Pico was born in relative poverty and one of ten children—three boys and seven girls—and his rise and fall stretches from California's period as a New Spain colony to its American statehood. Though he would become one the most resilient and successful Californio businessmen in post-1846 California, building a mansion in Whittier on his land grant of nearly 9,000 acres, he would be buried in a "pauper's grave" in Los Angeles, ending his life in poverty.[16]

Family mattered emotionally and professionally to Pico, like many wealthy Californios. By the 1830s, a small number of military families, including the Picos, had managed through marriage and "godfathering" to control territorial politics. Pío Pico's relationship with his younger brother, Andres, would prove durable, lasting, and profitable; to a lesser extent the same was true of the relationship between Pío and his other brother, José Antonio. In addition, Pío would deftly create familial alliances with several of his brothers-in-law. Californio familial ties would prove critical to his political and economic success throughout his career up and into the 1860s and 1870s, when US statehood and demographic change would conspire to undue such bonds.

With an almost innate ability to insert himself into political debates, Pío Pico had emerged as a prominent businessman and politician by the time of Mexican independence in 1821. At age twenty-six, he was elected to the San Diego town council, and in 1828 he found himself seated in the California *diputacion* (legislature). Three years later, Pico had assumed the position of *primer vocal*, the senior member of the legislature. From this position he would lead a revolt against the Mexican government in 1831, an expression of Californios' sense of independent identity. He briefly found himself governor of the territory, until Mexico reestablished authority in early 1833 and appointed Brigadier General José Figueroa to the position. Still, Pico and his fellow Californios had forced Mexico's hand and established California as an "independent force within the Mexican republic."[17]

Independence from Spain had sparked a questioning of the role of the Catholic Church in Mexican life, and particularly the role of the missions. By the early 1830s, secularization had come to seem inevitable. In theory, the process was meant to liberate Native Americans from the Catholic Church and provide them with lands for cultivation and other uses, while distributing some of the properties to Californios. In reality, Native Americans received little from secularization, but Californios profited immensely.

Pico stood at the forefront of the secularization process and took advantage of its various aspects to increase his land holdings and enrich his cattle business. By 1835, Pico had been appointed the administrator of one of California's most profitable missions, San Luis Rey, just east of San Diego. To say that he treated Native Americans connected to the mission cruelly would be an overstatement, but he undoubtedly exploited their labor and to some extent cynically applied Mexican law to limit their protests and increase production.

Like many Californios, Pico was more interested in profitability than empathy for Native Americans. As result, Native American uprisings became increasingly common, and Pico's Rancho Jamal property fell victim to one in 1838. Pico relinquished his position at San Luis Rey in 1840 soon after he received a land grant of 131,000 acres at Rancho Santa Margarita. His brother

FIG. 5 "The Old Spanish and Mexican Ranchos of Los Angeles County." Title Insurance and Trust Company, Los Angeles, circa 1937. (Courtesy of the Library of Congress, Geography and Map Division.)

Andres also received a large rancho in San Fernando Valley. In 1849, Pío made arrangements to purchase Rancho Paso De Bartolo, which he called El Ranchito, in San Gabriel Valley—in what is today Whittier, Montebello, and Pico Rivera.[18]

Geographic conflict plagued political relations in California: influential Northern Californio families often feuded with those of the South. In 1844, Pío Pico led another rebellion against the Spanish governor, eventually being installed as governor on an interim basis in the same year and permanently in 1845. He moved the capital to Los Angeles and attempted to relocate the very profitable customs house from Monterrey as well. Unsurprisingly, Pico seemed to be stuck in a near-constant struggle with Northern California power brokers. During his second term as governor, he spent as much time battling Northern political interests and mending fences between the two regions as he did preparing for the American invasion.[19] Though Los Angeles and San Diego put up a strong fight in resistance to the Americans, Monterrey folded without a single gunshot.

Pico in America's California

Statehood brought great change. The English language soon became dominant, and especially after 1849 Anglos rushed in. By the late 1850s, 300,000 Anglos far outnumbered their 13,000 Mexican counterparts. Californios owned large swaths of land in the state—perhaps as much as 13,000,000 acres of coastal property—but the newcomers found ways to make that ownership moot.[20]

In the Treaty of Guadalupe that ended the Mexican-American War, Mexicans were given the choice to leave or become US citizens. The U.S. government promised to honor Mexican and Spanish land grants. Many Californios chose to become citizens, hoping that the new arrivals would resemble those who had settled in California during the 1830s and afterward. Walter Colton, the author of *Three Years in California*, remarked that in the wake of prospectors and others, "American avarice has hardened the heart and made a god of gold." In his view, the new arrivals represented the worst of America: "speculator[s], piker[s], and cardsharp[s]."[21]

Though change came rapidly to Northern California, the state's southern half remained somewhat buffered from radical change. As late as the 1870s, beginning in Santa Barbara and extending south, Californios maintained large landholdings and demographic dominance and held political power.[22] Still, the arrival of so many Anglos—bringing with them beliefs related to Manifest Destiny—soon took a toll, as they physically and ideologically trickled south from the north. Many Californios witnessed the dissolution of their political power and economic wealth as the American legal system, combined with extralegal measures of Anglo settlers, undermined the traditional families of the region. Mexican land grants lacked the kind of specificity found in American property law; there was no Northwest Ordinance grid system that rigidly defined ownership, so Anglos found ways to challenge land claims in court.

The Land Act of 1851 required Mexican landholders to prove the legitimacy of their holdings to a three-person Board of Land Commissioners in San Francisco. While 604 out of 813 cases were upheld in favor of Mexican—now Mexican American landholders—the process of defending these claims took years and often depleted the coffers of Californio families. Americans squatting on land disrupted family economies so that property would have to be sold off to pay debts or continue funding legal actions. Lawyers' fees, even in victory, would often be paid in land, and thus Californio properties were transferred to Anglos legally but no less painfully.[23] Having written numerous land grants in the waning days of Mexican California, Pico provided endless testimony defending the property transfers before the board in the period 1851–1856.[24]

American statehood also brought much more rigid conceptions of race. The new state constitution barred African Americans from testifying in court against whites, serving on juries, attending public schools, and voting and generally discouraged black migration to the state. Pico endured disparaging remarks from whites that demonstrate the new racial logic: Isaac Hartmann, a San Francisco land claim attorney, described Pico as a "corrupt, non-English-speaking negroid, dwarfist."[25]

Admittedly, many Californios sought to ally themselves with Anglo elites, thereby distinguishing themselves socioeconomically from their less well-off Mexican counterparts. Predictably, this largely failed. If average Mexicans suffered stereotypes that depicted them as untrustworthy "dangerous, swarthy figures," notes Pitti, Californios were depicted as men and women outside of time, "feudal lords" from another era and culture.[26]

Racial violence exploded as well. Even before the discovery of gold, El Monte residents witnessed several lynchings in the 1850s. Taking a longer view, from 1850 to 1890, local records abound with references to Mexican lynchings. Over 300 Mexicans were lynched during the Gold Rush era. "The practice of lynching Mexicans soon became an outdoor sport in Southern California," writes McWilliams.[27]

Beyond lynchings, violence more generally defined the region. In 1854, Los Angeles recorded a murder a day, with the vast majority of victims being of Mexican or Indian descent. In the previous year, California had witnessed more murders than the rest of the nation, and Angelenos had seen more than any other Californians. Los Angeles became the most violent city in the state, as lynch mobs accosted average Mexicans and Californios alike.

What we would call racial profiling today occurred as well. All Mexicans, including Californios, found themselves more subject to arrest and violence than their white peers. Systematic legal discrimination also meant that Californios and other Mexicans were more likely to be hanged for crimes than Anglos guilty of the same infraction.[28] The prevalence of assaults, murders, and lynchings and the presence of a legal system biased against nonwhites signified that the Mexican-American War concluded in 1848 had in essence resumed.[29]

Mexican banditry arose in response to Anglo hostility, but this split the Californio community. Some supported the bandits as a form of resistance to oppression, while others advocated cracking down on them to impose law and order. Pico's nephew Salomon Pico may have been one such bandit, organizing

Californios in the 1850s to avenge injustices visited upon them by violently hostile Anglos.[30] Hortense Rendon Aguirre, the daughter of one of Pico's nephews, remembers "the hideout of the famous Mexican bandits," obscured by the thick brush that grew along the Old Mission Road toward Whittier Road near El Ranchito. In her own way, Aguirre acknowledges what historians such as Eric Hobsbawm have labeled "social banditry" or banditry as unorganized political protest or resistance when she writes that the bandits "never harmed anyone of their own nationality, only the gringos. It was something more of revenge."[31]

Amazingly, Pico managed to thrive despite this climate of hostility. During the 1850s, he and other Southern Californios realized that the booming region of Northern California required endless amounts of cattle and consumer goods. The prevalence of squatting and prospecting in Northern California made cattle ranching in the region difficult. Due in part to its climate and the lack of gold discoveries, Southern California attracted fewer Anglo setters. Pico and other Californios in the south made enormous profits from cattle ranching.

El Ranchito's a twenty-room adobe mansion provided Pico with a home away from the violence and crowds of the city, while also sustaining him economically. The property's proximity to Los Angeles, temperate climate, and location near the San Gabriel River made it a perfect location for farming and the cultivation of orchards. Tenants farmed the excess land, including a scattering of Gabrielino Indians living in *jacales* (thatched-roof huts). Renters such as the Indians provided Pico with a great deal of wealth into the 1880s.[32]

The results of his success were clearly visible at Pico's San Gabriel Valley residence, where he came to spend a great deal of time. "We came by way of the Ranchito, on the east side of the San Gabriel River," Joseph Pleasants wrote in 1849 as he and others made their way down to what is today Orange County for a hunting expedition. Pico "lived at that time in all the state of a feudal lord. The picturesque old ranch house at the Ranchito stood in the midst of a beautiful garden, fragrant with the flowers of 'ye olden time.'"[33] Harriet Strong, a Pico ally, remarked on the uniqueness of its drawing room, its lush Brussels carpeting, and the "unmatched" wallpaper, paintings, and ancient weapons that adorned its walls while "china cuspidors, white with pink moss-rose decorations were plentifully distributed in all the rooms."[34]

During this period, Pico also discovered a litigious side, frequently challenging business and land decisions in court. Though he lost many cases, he also won plenty.[35] He maintained alliances with Californio families, his brother Andres, Mexicanized Anglos, and even some of the new American elite. None of this proved easy, as Americans expressed distrust of Pico due to his role as the last governor of Mexican California and his racial ancestry, but he maintained significant wealth for decades.

Pío even dabbled in proto-urban renewal when he began buying up land around LA Plaza, which had slipped in value due to decline. He first built Pico House—at the time the most luxurious hotel in all of California—there and later began buying up other parcels for development. Eventually, the area did rebound, but Pico failed to fully capitalize on the rising property values. Over-time, his success would be undone not only by demographic change and racism, but also by poor business decisions.[36]

Pico's struggles came into full view during the 1880s, when his dependence on the legal system as a means to arbitrate disputes boomeranged on him. At the age of ninety in 1891, Pico lost all of El Ranchito. Through various legal contests and court rulings, the ranch was reduced to less than half of the original nearly 9,000 acres. The case of *Pico v. Cohn* would take care of the rest, though many observers found the ruling dubious at best. "Anyone who has examined the Court's opinion is convinced that the elderly ex governor was the victim of outrageous fraud," wrote the attorney Leo Friis.[37]

If El Ranchito manifested Pico's successes in flush times, it reflected his descent into pauperism as well. "No wallpaper, tapestries or rugs" adorned the home in Pico's twilight years; a few coyote and goat skins covered some of El Ranchito's now otherwise bare wood floors; and cooking was done not on a "fancy Yankee range" but rather "the same masonry type stove prevailing for centuries in Spanish culture," remembered Aguirre.[38]

The completion of the Transcontinental Railroad resulted in many more Anglos' coming to California, especially Los Angeles. If climate and lack of gold had initially stunted migration to the city, the addition of the iron horse quickly made up for that. With the growth of Whittier, Santa Ana, Anaheim, and Fullerton, more horse and buggy traffic passed by El Ranchito. Pico "contented himself more and more with sitting on the *casa* porch, watching a new world passing his doorstep," writes Martin Cole, longtime curator of the Pío Pico State Park. The rising number of white families weakened familial alliances between Californios, as did their declining economic and political power. And Cole notes that the newcomers "would jostle Pío Pico out of vast wealth and leave him destitute."[39]

Southern California retained its diversity, but it did so in spite of widespread discrimination. With its history of exploitation and racial cruelties, Alta California had never been a purely egalitarian, color-blind culture, but the imposition of American statehood amid sectionalism and attempts to expand slavery to the West in the mid-nineteenth century clearly introduced even more rigid conceptions of race. Even the abolition of slavery after the Civil War failed to significantly improve circumstances.

Just over a decade after Pico's death, Whittier purchased El Ranchito to gain access to the wells located on the property. Harriet Russell Strong, by then a prominent businesswoman, led preservation efforts that resulted in El Ranchito being deeded to the state. In 1927, it became one of the California's first state parks.

In the ensuing decades, San Gabriel Valley would undergo massive transformation from a largely agricultural region dominated by white homeowners and farmers to an urbanized suburban metropolis consisting largely of Latino and Asian American homeowners. As Mike Davis wrote, "the Anglo conquest of California in the 1840s has proven to be a very transient fact indeed."[40] Pico experienced firsthand the erasure of Mexican California, yet one wonders if his spirit doesn't still sit out on the porch of El Ranchito on clear San Gabriel Valley nights, gazing across modern-day Los Angeles County to his birthplace in El Monte and his grave in Los Angeles, and marveling at the people and places that have come to define Southern California. Perhaps he and Josephine reminisce about Celestino and Ramona, El Ranchito, and how the Pico legacy contributed to the modern day San Gabriel Valley.

Notes

1 Quoted in Sandra T. Molina, "Last Great-Grandaughter of Pío Pico, Last Mexican Governor of California, Dies at 100," *San Gabriel Valley Tribune*, July 10, 2014, https://www.sgvtribune.com/2014/07/10/last-great-grandaughter-of-po-pico-last-mexican-governor-of-california-dies-at-100/.

2 William D. Estrada, "The Life and Times of Pío Pico, Last Governor of Mexican California," KCET, October 10, 2017, https://www.kcet.org/shows/lost-la/the-life-and-times-of-Pío-pico-last-governor-of-mexican-california.

3 Carlos Manuel Salomon, *Pío Pico: The Last Governor of Mexican California* (Norman: University of Oklahoma Press, 2010), 5.

4 Mike Davis, *City of Quartz: Excavating the Future in Los Angeles* (New York: Verso, 1990), 27. See also Eric Avila, *Popular Culture in the Age of White Flight: Fear and Fantasy in Suburban Los Angeles* (Los Angeles: University of California Press, 2004), 201; Kevin Starr, *Americans and the California Dream, 1850–1915* (New York: Oxford University Press, 1973), 16; William Deverell, *Whitewash Adobe: The Rise of Los Angeles and the Remaking of Its Mexican Past* (Los Angeles: University of California Press, 2004).

5 Salomon, *Pío Pico*, 16–17.

6 Henry D. Barrows, "Pío Pico: A Biographical and Character Sketch of the Last Mexican Governor of Alta California," *Annual Publication of the Historical Society of Southern California, Los Angeles* 3, no. 2 (1894): 55.

7 Salomon, *Pío Pico*, 12. See also Starr, *Americans and the California Dream*, 46.

8 Salomon, *Pío Pico*, 12.

9 Ibid., 15.

10 *Latino Americans*, episode 1, "Foreigners in Their Own Land," directed by David Belton and Sonia Fritz, aired 2013, on PBS, https://www.pbs.org/video/latino-americans-episode-1-foreigners-their-own-land/.

11 Salomon, *Pío Pico*, 18.

12 Kevin Starr, *California: A History* (New York: Modern Library, 2007), 41.

13 Ibid., 50.

14 Carey McWilliams, *Southern California: An Island on the Land* (Salt Lake City, UT: Gibbs Smith Publishers, 1973), 52; see also 76.
15 Starr, *California*, 54.
16 Salomon, *Pío Pico*, 126. See also Davis, *City of Quartz*, 27.
17 Salomon, *Pío Pico*, 43.
18 Ibid., 63–67 and 130.
19 Ibid., 76 and 95.
20 Starr, *California*, 103.
21 Quoted in Starr, *Americans and the California Dream*, 31.
22 McWilliams, *Southern California*, 64.
23 Starr, *California*, 103–105; Salomon, *Pío Pico*, 118.
24 Salomon, *Pío Pico*, 112.
25 Quoted in ibid., 115.
26 *Latino Americans*, episode 1.
27 McWilliams, *Southern California*, 60.
28 Rosaura Sanchez and Beatrice Pita, "The Literature of the Californios," in *The Cambridge Companion to the Literature of Los Angeles*, ed. Kevin R. McNamara (Cambridge, MA: Cambridge University Press, 2010), 18; Salomon, *Pío Pico*, 121; McWilliams, *Southern California*, 60.
29 McWilliams, *Southern California*, 60.
30 R. Sanchez and Pita, "The Literature of the Californios," 17; Salomon, *Pío Pico*, 121.
31 Quoted in Martin Cole, "Pío Pico Mansion: Fact, Fiction, and Supposition," in *Pío Pico Miscellany*, ed. Martin Cole (Whittier, CA: Governor Pico Mansion Society, 1978), 30. See also Eric Hobsbawm, *Primitive Rebels: Studies in Archaic Forms of Social Movements in the 19th and 20th Centuries* (New York: Norton, 1959).
32 Salomon, *Pío Pico*, 132–133.
33 Quoted in Cole, "Pío Pico Mansion," 21.
34 Ibid., 24.
35 Salomon, *Pío Pico*, 133–136.
36 Ibid., 157.
37 Quoted in Cole, "Pío Pico Mansion," 35. See also Salomon, *Pío Pico*, 212.
38 Quoted in Cole, "Pío Pico Mansion," 32.
39 Ibid, 34.
40 Mike Davis, *Magical Urbanism: Latinos Reinvent the U.S. City* (New York: Verso, 2000), 49.

4

Here Come the El Monte Boys

Vigilante Justice and Lynch Mobs in Nineteenth-Century El Monte

KAREN S. WILSON AND
DANIEL LYNCH

"Law and Order Monte Boys Style" is the title of a chapter in one of the more recent histories of El Monte.[1] Those six words capture the popular stories associated with the men of the nineteenth-century township. Any written history of Los Angeles County has to at least mention the Monte boys. Their involvement with the repression of crime is characterized variously as the work of righteous citizens, frontier-savvy former Texas Rangers, or all-too-eager vigilantes. From the 1850s through the 1870s and perhaps beyond, if there were bandits to be caught, murderers to be punished, or horse thieves to be hanged in the county, the men from El Monte always seemed to be on the scene. Their contemporaries, at times admiringly and at other moments critically, referred to them generically as the Monte boys (with a little *b*). Popular histories have capitalized the *b*, suggesting that the group was an organized institution that was important to the quality of life in old Los Angeles.

But who were these men? In the various accounts of their escapades individual names were mentioned only rarely. Other than that they resided in El Monte, owned fast horses, and wielded deadly weapons, what do we know about them? Much of what is known comes from contemporary newspaper accounts and memoirs by neighboring witnesses. Why have they remained a centerpiece of local history? Their long-lasting fame suggests significance beyond their role in past events. Most importantly, how do the facts and legends about the Monte boys connect with El Monte and Los Angeles today?

El Monte took shape during the 1850s as a community of settlements along the banks of the San Gabriel River about twelve miles east of the central plaza of Los Angeles. Located at the end of a trail, it functioned as a way station between Southern California and the interior Southwest. In the aftermath of the Mexican-American War, many migrants from the United States came through the El Monte area on their way to Los Angeles and other parts of California. Some chose to stay in the region, while others returned to it after trying their luck in the crowded gold-mining counties up north. The stretch of willows along the river (El Monte means "the wooded place" in archaic Spanish) attracted farmers looking for fertile, well-watered land in a semiarid landscape. Although the land was claimed under grants made to William Workman (an English immigrant and Mexican citizen) and a few others prior to American sovereignty, uncertainty as to the authenticity of some claims and little enforcement provided an opening for squatters to establish small farms and ranches in the area. Most of the Anglo-Americans settlers were Southern-born, and many had briefly settled in the westernmost slave state, Texas, before heading further west. El Monte, and in particular a clump of homes and businesses called Lexington, became known as an American town with a Southern flair.

The American town acquired a number of nicknames that suggest it was held in low regard by both residents and outsiders. Lexkill, Lickskillet, Porkerville, and Hell's Half-Acre were some of the more colorful names. Those names no doubt referred to the living and social conditions of the town. The Southern roots of its Anglo settlers showed through, particularly in its residents' politics and approach to law enforcement. As fiercely partisan Democrats, their anti-Republicanism and proslavery sentiments prevailed right through to the end of the Civil War. Accustomed to the brutalities of slavery and imposing their own sensibilities of law and order on those they viewed as inferior, they stood out and fit in with the clash of cultures that marked Gold Rush California.[2]

At a time when the American system of justice was thinly and loosely present in the West, citizens' committees of vigilance or militias were popular and acceptable approaches for dealing with criminal activity. While leading merchants, doctors, lawyers, and ranchers often formed these seemingly respectable committees, they often served as cover for mob justice that on numerous occasions resorted to lynching. The state of California tried to exercise some control over groups of armed men formed to aid a marshal or sheriff in protecting a town or village against bandits or to fight Native Americans. Local militias could be chartered and receive free guns and ammunition through an application to the state. A group named the Monte Rangers petitioned for weaponry in 1854, apparently the second militia formed in the county after the Los Angeles Rangers. Organized to take advantage of the state's offer, the Monte Rangers were short-lived. But this group may have helped start the legend of the Monte boys.

In 1856, the panicked white population of Los Angeles feared being overrun by a Spanish-speaking mob after a Hispanic man was killed by an Anglo Los Angeles City marshal. The *Los Angeles Star* reported that shortly after receiving a call for help, "a party of citizens from the Monte, mounted and armed, numbering thirty-six muskets, arrived in town, and were received with loud cheers." The firearms were likely the remains of forty rifles given to the Monte Rangers by the state. The Monte Rangers had each also received a cavalry saber and a Colt revolver. Some of the Monte men hailed from Texas where they may have used Colts to fight Mexicans and Native Americans. Colts proved a highly effective weapon for Texas Rangers, who learned to fire revolvers from horseback while in pursuit or in close combat.[3]

From 1856 onward, men from El Monte became known for their actions on horseback outside of their own community. They rode to other settlements in Southern California to enforce their own brand of vigilante justice, and Mexican men frequently bore the brunt of their violence. Never identified at the time as the Monte Rangers or any organized militia or law enforcement organization, they were essentially a well-armed mob on horseback. As summed up by one memoirist, "the 'El Monte Boys' were long celebrated for their proclivity to seek out trouble and add to it."[4]

In 1857 the press reported that "men from the Monte" were cooperating with a "company of Californians [native-born, Spanish-surnamed Californios]" and other bands of armed men as they hunted the gang of Juan Flores and Pancho Daniel. The Flores-Daniel gang had ambushed and assassinated Los Angeles County Sheriff James Barton, triggering one of largest manhunts in the county's history. Through a combination of local intelligence gathering and superior horsemanship, the Californio company tracked down the bandit leaders and then transferred them to the custody of the El Monte men. Later that evening, the prisoners untied each other's hands under a shared blanket and escaped into the night. Although the El Monte men recovered Flores, Daniel remained at large despite their efforts to find him. "Monte is not popular just now," the Los Angeles correspondent for the *Daily Alta California* commented on the episode. As the correspondent explained, "the Monte men—those frontier savages, who spent their whole lives fighting Indians," had gone soft. "Just at the moment when they were desired to be ferocious, they took a freak to being kind-hearted."[5]

In all probability, though, the failure of the El Monte men to retain Flores and Daniel had more to do with incompetence than kindness. *El Clamor Publico*, a Spanish-language newspaper, claimed that at least twelve Spanish-surnamed men were "murdered" in the wake of Barton's assassination and that "of these, three were murdered unjustifiably." The *Clamor* implicated the El Monte men in one particularly appalling incident. A man suspected of possessing Barton's shotgun was cornered by Anglos in a field near San Gabriel when "citizens from the Monte" appeared and set fire to the grass. The *Clamor* reported that the suspect was shot dead as he ran from the blaze and that "immediately the head was cut off and taken to El Monte."[6] The decapitation may have been inspired by that of the legendary bandit Joaquin Murrieta, the scourge of Anglo and Chinese gold miners whose severed head toured the state in 1853. But this brand of violence was new to Los Angeles County, where Spanish-surnamed people remained in the majority and elite ranching families maintained a great deal of influence. Hispanic men had been lynched since the Mexican-American War, but always in ways moderated by local custom and a spirit of cross-cultural cooperation. Trying to make sense of the orgy of Anglo violence that followed Barton's death, the *Clamor*'s editor wondered, "What civilized man cuts the head off a cadaver?"[7]

In addition to local newspaper editors, other Angelenos held poor opinions of El Monte and its eager vigilantes. With their tendency to dash about the countryside, supposedly in support of law and order, the men from El Monte developed a notable reputation not for bravery, but rather for reactionary ineptitude. The organizer of the Los Angeles Rangers, Horace Bell, scathingly called them out for the escape of Flores and Daniel on their watch. In his 1881 memoir he wrote that the "Monte gringos" had been "in some mysterious way outwitted" by their prisoners, who had fled in the night from the "gringo camp." As Bell explained earlier in his book, "in its literal signification," gringo "means ignoramus." Bell (born in Indiana, raised in the South, and fluent in Spanish) was a man of adventure and many contradictions who had known the "disgrace" of being a gringo. He dismissed the Monte boys as ignorant and stupid, worthless for law enforcement, and outside the customs of Californio culture. Tolerated, even celebrated, by their fellow residents of El Monte, these men failed to impress members of neighboring communities.[8]

Harris Newmark, a Jewish immigrant from Prussia and another early arrival in American Los Angeles, also wrote disparagingly of the Monte boys, using irony to draw attention to their flawed characters. Calling them "recognized disciplinarians," Newmark noted that "the peculiar public spirit animating these early settlers" was such "that no one could live and prosper at the Monte who was not extremely virile and ready for any dare-devil emergency." The "peculiar public spirit" made the Monte boys regular participants in "neck-tie" parties—lynchings of untried suspects by mobs of self-righteous citizens. A few days after the capture of the Flores-Daniel gang, the *Daily Alta California* correspondent reported that "the people have come in from the Monte, expecting there will be a hanging." Soon a "triangle" was struck, "calling the people together" for a public meeting at which a judge argued for "a little delay" to allow some of the twenty prisoners being held to prove their innocence. The crowd concurred with the judge, though "considerable opposition was made by the Monte men." Nineteenth-century El Monte became known for its walnut groves, pig farms, and galloping horsemen who could be counted on to show up whenever frontier justice reared its head.[9]

During the Civil War, in which California remained part of the Union despite its sizable population of Southerners, the outlier reputations of El Monte and its boys reached new heights. On May 7, 1861, scarcely a month after the guns firing at Fort Sumter signaled the beginning of the war, U.S. Army Quartermaster of Los Angeles Winfield Scott Hancock reported to his superior in San Francisco that "the 'bear flag' was paraded through the streets of El Monte" and "was escorted by a number of horsemen." As with the vigilante episodes of the 1850s, the horsemen parading the bear flag were not described by Hancock as the Monte Rangers or as a formal militia of any kind. They came together in a collective display of their Southern sympathies under a familiar California symbol. The image had its origins in the 1846 Bear Flag Revolt, a movement by a small group of Anglo-American settlers to declare California independent from Mexico at the outset of the Mexican-American War. Now, at the outset of the Civil War, secessionists used the bear flag in support of California independence from the Union.[10]

The Confederate sympathies and anti-Republicanism of the majority of El Monte's residents were clearly displayed and well known by their neighbors before and during the war. Those who held the strongest attachments to those positions left Southern California to defend them on battlefields thousands of miles away. But those who stayed behind demonstrated a telling willingness to defend the small town from the onslaught of a local pestilence—smallpox—that struck the Mexican and Native American population especially hard. An untreatable disease that has been eradicated worldwide because of effective vaccines, smallpox traveled to the Western Hemisphere with the Spanish conquistadors and spread across North America through the migrations of missionaries and settlers. The outbreak in Los Angeles County in 1862–1863 coincided with the great drought-driven die-off of vast herds of cattle, ending the reign of the ranchos as the economic engine of Southern California.

By January, 1863, 200 people had died from smallpox and at least 200 more were afflicted in the county.[11]

In contrast to community leaders in Los Angeles City, who took prudent measures to halt the spread of the highly communicable and often fatal disease and to aid the poorest sufferers, the men of El Monte organized a Committee on Health to keep its precincts free of those who might be carriers as well as the sick, dying, and dead. With six explicit charges from "a mass meeting of citizens," the twelve members of the committee were authorized and directed to prevent the "victims" (presumably those of the Catholic faith) from passing "through the streets and lanes of El Monte on their way to the San Gabriel Mission," to keep "strangers and other persons" suspected of being exposed to smallpox from stopping in the town, and "to use any measure in regard to straggling Indians that may become necessary" to keep them out of the area. These orders focused exclusively on preventing the ill and potentially ill from coming in proximity to the residents of El Monte.[12]

In the much larger and more affected city of Los Angeles, officials conducted house-to-house surveys to keep track of the spread of the epidemic, marking quarantined homes with yellow flags and designating a house four miles outside the city as a place where the Catholic Sisters of Charity could nurse the sickest. The Hebrew Benevolent Society (HBS), founded by Jewish Angelenos in 1854, donated $150 to feed the poor and sick and appointed five of its members to solicit and distribute additional funds in support of the indigent "during the prevailing sickness." On the day that El Monte's "precautionary measures" were published in the *Los Angeles Star*, the HBS announced its "Committee of Relief" in the same newspaper, drawing a commendation from the paper's editor for its "practical philanthropy" and "munificent donation." The leadership of Los Angeles's French-born mayor, the Sisters of Charity, and Jewish merchant members of HBS exemplified the necessary cross-cultural collaboration demanded by the epidemic that threatened the entire community. The concerned citizens of El Monte struck a posture of isolation and wariness that could only have sent chills down the spine of any Mexican or Native American who had the misfortune of living there or traveling through the town.[13]

On the eve of the national election of 1864, the men and boys of El Monte made another provocative demonstration that the *Los Angeles News* described as a "gorilla barbecue and procession" for the Democratic ticket. After much eating and drinking, the "Monteites marched and howled" through the streets of town, imitating "the African" while shouting the slogan, "America for white men." The *News* claimed that, ironically, "at least half of the procession could have no vote, being half-breeds and quarter-bloods." The Union-supporting *News* frequently mocked Spanish-speaking Democrats, and it is possible that the paper exaggerated the diversity of the crowd. Still, it is stunning that any mixed-race people participated in such a demonstration, considering that the intolerance and violence of El Monte had been and could so easily be turned against them.[14]

After the Civil War, a new era began that transformed El Monte. Most California land claim disputes were settled, and property values increased. The transcontinental railroad connected California to the rest of the nation. In 1873, the Southern Pacific Railroad built a depot at El Monte, expanding the markets for local agriculture. Having built up their wealth and status, a number of El Monte pioneer squatters left the area for better opportunities. The professionalization and expansion of police forces eliminated the need for vigilance committees. As the social upheaval of western expansion and civil war diminished, so did the tolerance for random acts of mob justice. The last lynching attributed to the Monte boys happened in 1887, with the capture and hanging of four Anglo horse thieves. Accounts of armed horsemen from El Monte spontaneously dashing about the county as self-appointed judge, jury, and executioner ceased to appear in newspapers and memoirs.

Despite twentieth-century histories that portrayed the early Anglo settlers of El Monte as resourceful pioneers, contemporaneous accounts tell a different story. Not unlike their peers in many communities established in nineteenth-century California, descendants of those pioneers and town leaders preferred to emphasize a positive tale. Among the facts that fell away as the history was recounted were the community's squatter origins. Among the facts altered were the escapades of some men of El Monte. The bully boys of the self-proclaimed "American town" became righteous men who tamed the Wild West ways of Los Angeles County. And thus the most famous export of El Monte came to be a heroic legend, despite evidence of mob justice and lynchings.

As social norms and sensibilities have changed, many of the events and attitudes of the past have become unacceptable, regrettable, and even shameful to those of us living in today's Los Angeles County. The ignoble assaults on Native Americans by European settlers, the squatting on lands once used communally or claimed by others, and the indiscriminate and discriminatory violence that made the West wild are just some examples of the dark side of how the United States and California came to be. The American town of El Monte has a particularly notorious place in the history of Los Angeles. For some contemporary residents, the notoriety of the El Monte boys serves best as a reminder of good prevailing over bad, civilized over uncivilized. For others, including the historians who have separated fact from legend, that interpretation underscores how history can be distorted to assuage the guilty and erase the victims. The truth about the Monte boys helps illuminate the too easily accepted tragedy of mob violence, an insight still unfortunately relevant today. Perhaps now it is time to say that the legend of the Monte boys has outlived its usefulness and to let the facts stand.[15]

Notes

1 Jorane King Barton, *El Monte: Images of America* (Charleston, SC: Arcadia, 2006), 53.
2 *A History of El Monte: The End of the Sante Fe Trail* (Los Angeles: El Monte Lodge No. 424—International Order of Odd Fellows [I.O.O.F.], 1923), 64; William F. King, "El Monte: An American Town in Southern California, 1851–1866," *Southern California Quarterly* 53, no. 4 (December 1971): 318.
3 "A Man Killed," *Los Angeles Star*, July 26, 1856. See also "Bond of Monte Rangers," March 25, 1854, California State Archives; "Interesting Letter from Los Angeles," *Daily Alta California*, February 15, 1857; Frederick Wilkins, *The Legend Begins: The Texas Rangers 1823–1845* (Austin, TX: State House Press, 1996), 184–185.
4 Horace Bell, *On the Old West Coast: Being the Further Reminiscences of a Ranger-Major Horace Bell* (New York: Grosset and Dunlap, 1930), 310.
5 "Interesting Letter from Los Angeles," *Daily Alta California*, February 15, 1857.
6 "Cronica Local," *El Clamor Publico*, February 21, 1857; "Muerte de Miguel Soto en San Gabriel," *El Clamor Publico*, February 7, 1857.
7 Untitled editorial, *El Clamor Publico*, April 11, 1857. See also Paul Gray, *A Clamor for Equality: Emergence and Exile of Californio Activist Francisco P. Ramirez* (Lubbock: Texas Tech University Press, 2012), 46–47.
8 Horace Bell, *Reminiscences of a Ranger: Early Times in Southern California* (1881; repr., Norman: University of Oklahoma Press, 1999), 49 and 406–407.
9 Harris Newmark, *Sixty Years in Southern California, 1853–1913, Containing the Reminiscences of Harris Newmark* (New York: Knickerbocker Press, 1916), 91 and 324; "Interesting Letter from Los Angeles," *Daily Alta California*, February 15, 1857.
10 Quoted in Winfield S. Hancock to W.W. Mackall, May 7, 1861, in *The War of the Rebellion: A Compilation of the Official Records of the Union and Confederate Armies: Series I, Volume L, Part 1* (Washington: Government Printing Office, 1897), 479–480.
11 Michael E. Engh, *Frontier Faiths: Church, Temple, and Synagogue in Los Angeles, 1846–1888* (Albuquerque: University of New Mexico Press, 1992), 81.
12 "Public Meeting at El Monte—Establishment of Board of Health," *Los Angeles Star*, February 14, 1863.
13 Ibid.
14 "The Gorilla Barbecue and Procession," *Los Angeles News*, November 8, 1864.
15 Additional works that have helped illuminate the history of California and the American West include Patricia Limerick, *The Legacy of Conquest: Unbroken Past of the American West* (New York: W. W. Norton, 1987); Howard R. Lamar, *Texas Crossings: The Lone Star State and the American Far West, 1836–1986* (Austin: University of Texas Press, 1991); Kevin Starr, *California: A History* (New York: Modern Library, 2007); and John Mack Faragher, *Eternity Street: Violence and Justice in Frontier Los Angeles* (New York: W. W. Norton, 2016).

Part II

Social and Political Movements

FIG. 6 Álvaro Márquez, "El Porvenir." (Courtesy of Álvaro Márquez.)

Though we often think of iconic political struggles unfolding in America's biggest cities, El Monte and South El Monte show how suburban communities on the metropolitan periphery often became critical spaces for radical politics, civil rights battles, labor disputes, identity struggles, and immigration debates across the twentieth century. The contradictions of a growing agricultural and industrial economy in Los Angeles became manifest in the radical, transnational struggles of early twentieth-century El Monte: the anarchism of Ricardo Flores Magón during World War I flows into the 1930s with the agency of El Monte's Mexican and Mexican American migrant workers, who in the face of the Depression struck for better wages and working conditions. As El Monte reaped the benefits of California's postwar boom, residents took up the mantle of desegregation in local schools and later pushed for the formation of South El Monte—an outgrowth of the expanding economy of its parent city and the larger San Gabriel Valley. During the late 1960s and early 1970s, Greater Los Angeles emerged as a key center of the Chicano movement, and El Monte's residents imbued with its spirit organized their own opposition, epitomized by outspoken Chicana feminists such as Gloria Arellanes, the artistic protests of muralists, and antideportation activism. Meanwhile, newcomers from Asia charted their own paths in the San Gabriel Valley—especially after the Immigration Act of 1965 eliminated racist national quotas for migration—and built their own businesses, communities, and movements. Each challenged racial and gender hierarchies and promoted ideas of community and belonging beyond national citizenship and traditional electoral politics. All serve as insightful previews of twenty-first century struggles over the same issues and capture the critical importance of places and spaces once viewed as liminal by historians but now seen as integral to local, regional, and national debates.

5

Rise, Fall, Repeat

El Monte's White Supremacy Movements

DAN CADY

The trail from East to West is littered with tales of heroic pioneers. In the preserved downtowns of California's peripheral municipalities, local history museums visually display a partial timeline of any given community's development. With the sensibilities of amateur archeologists, volunteer curators begin each city's nameless history with native artifacts. Under glass, these stone and woven treasures bear only tribal designations, and the individuals who crafted them remain anonymous, buried in the historical dustbin's unmarked graves. The intricate baskets abruptly end, and the tools and toys of named individuals pack the other display cases, walls, and ceilings. The visual crush tells a story: resilient, independent, and sturdy white pioneers left their homes, landed in this particular town, and imposed new order on the landscape. Despite its inherent violence, this imposition becomes legend. Plain-folks Americans—or, perhaps, the American *Volk*—tamed and then conquered the West. It is a tale that all white Americans carry with them in their DNA, and it remains ubiquitously reinforced in conservative political discourse, religious identity, country music, and truck advertisements.

Yet the history of intrepid whiteness rarely survives genuine scrutiny. We find instead a mixed tale of good deeds and genocide, valiant efforts and colossal failures, hubris and collapse. El Monte's self-conscious white past is no exception. As late as 2004, its historical society and museum claimed to have room for only a single group's perspective.[1] Uncritical and nationalistic, the historical society presents a shallow representation not only of the multiethnic city but also of its past whiteness. Ironically, this buried white history bears a significant resemblance to the officially recognized rendition. One could characterize both as the strange, episodic history of Anglo-American transplants attempting to establish a white moral order on the edges of an emerging metropolis through calls for a shared celebration of the pioneer myth. Both versions celebrate the American *Volk*.

In twentieth-century El Monte, migrants from the American South and Midwest led two notable campaigns on behalf of white supremacy, fueled by white racial mythology. In the 1920s, Ku Klux Klan members stationed themselves in the city and proclaimed the members of their hooded order to be caretakers of the region's morality. They viewed themselves as the keepers of a white American bloodline under assault by modernism, Catholicism, Jews, and blacks. Forty years later, neo-Nazis, again from the South and Midwest, disrupted the town through a violent comedy of errors during a time of dramatic demographic change. They too believed the white race that suffered the Santa Fe Trail (with its fabled end in El Monte) was destined by God to erase the histories of weaker, darker, and more corrupt races. In both cases, transient men employed the language of white Christian nationalism in crusades against nonwhites, so-called foreigners, and all things incompatible with the fabled pioneer archetype.

Location played a central role, as well. Klansmen and Nazis alike chose to set up shop in El Monte due to the city's proximity to metropolitan Los Angeles. The largest city in the West held a multitude of potential converts, and each group believed that its call for order would resonate in the chaos of the urban environment. But Los Angeles was not the only prize. The region's horizontal growth led the Klan and the Nazis to strategize ways to evangelize the periphery. Because of El Monte's place within a network of smaller municipalities that linked the San Gabriel Valley to Orange, San Bernardino, and Riverside Counties, the city served as a pragmatic point of origin for official operations.

Boys in the Hoods

Following World War I, the secret society of the Ku Klux Klan was hardly a secret at all. In cities and towns across the nation, white men in white robes paraded through the streets by the tens of thousands with little regard for anonymity. Nationwide, their numbers soared to nearly five million. Their prominence as one of the country's largest fraternal organizations suggests the line the order walked between overt racism and its much-advertised commitment to moral uplift, Christian fellowship, and "pure patriotism."[2] Klan publications of the era emphasize Christian nationalism and make few references to race. Through ambitious marketing, the Klan attracted scores of middle-class white men and women, most of whom lived in areas with little ethnic diversity. Brash Klansmen identified their loyalties on personal business cards, newspaper advertisements, and shop signs. On any given Saturday, one might spend the afternoon watching two Klan baseball teams competing in a league game: white hoods and apple pie.

Highly visible, the invisible empire resided openly in El Monte. At least once a month in the first years of the 1920s, local Klansmen met to perform rituals and organize campaigns. At least six of the hundreds of members needed to be present, and no ritual could be performed without a Klonkard (who oversees all rituals) and a Kludd (the resident Protestant minister and musical director). The Kludd was among the most visible of the Klansmen. Having mastered public speaking and jeremiads, Kludds spoke at larger Klan rallies and were often expected to proselytize in neighboring communities.

El Monte's Kludd was H. E. Wilhite. In the early twenties, Wilhite (a middle-aged native of Missouri) guided the First Christian Church of El Monte as its minister. He most likely introduced the Klan to his community in the typical way of the Kludd—that is, he invited the Klan to march into his church midway through a service, where they made a large cash donation. At that point, he feigned incredulity and lauded the hooded men for their generous gift.[3] This exact charade happened hundreds of times across the United States.

Wilhite was a traveling man. By the time he was twenty-five years old, he had visited almost every state in America as a journeyman evangelist and itinerant small-town preacher. Leaving the revival circuit in the early twentieth century, he laid his hat in California for good. From 1906 to 1925 he pastored churches in Oxnard, San Bernardino, Colton, Rialto, and El Monte. Not only was Wilhite a featured speaker at El Monte Klan rallies, but his rootless networking illustrates the interlinking of adjacent communities around the city. For example, Wilhite worked as a temporary pastor at Downey First Christian Church while also serving the El Monte Klan. The preacher to whom he passed the torch, Edward Seawall, was the Downey Klan's Exalted Cyclops, or chapter president. Wilhite also came to the aid of fellow Klansmen in Pasadena. In April 1924, he was among the dozen Klansmen (at least three of whom were Protestant ministers) who crashed Pasadena's City Hall to unsuccessfully demand the reinstatement of Klan-affiliated police officers.[4] With little protest, most white citizens saw members of the Klan as cross-burning Shriners.

Still, some city governments—like that of Pasadena—balked at the Klan's crusades and incidentally found themselves on the right side of history. The inability to force Pasadena to forgive its Klansman cops gives a little insight into the order's bumbling antics. Local Klansmen were caught hiding in closets in order to catch adulterers and, in one incident, attempted to tar and feather a woman, but the tar and feathers never arrived. Yes, they burned some crosses and unfurled flags, but they never affected the local culture the way that Klansmen in Orange County ruled city halls. Ultimately, the El Monte Klan's greatest battle was against the Klan itself. Five months after the Pasadena police debacle, three hundred El Monte Klansmen met in the Odd Fellow's Hall in an open rebellion against the national organization. Citing the dictatorial nature of the Klan's constitution, they formed the Independent Order of the Knight of the Ku Klux Klan as a democratic antidote to the original's top-down structure.[5] The national Klan banished them, and membership tanked. By the end of the year little remained of the El Monte Klan. As for Wilhite, he died in 1956, a registered Republican.

Beyond the antics of a few hundred disgruntled white men, there was a second layer of Klan activity that made a much larger impact. This layer harnessed the pioneer myth's endless reserve and fluently spoke the language of the American *Volk*. Loudly proclaiming his country roots and rural moral superiority, Virginia-born Reverend Robert "Fighting Bob" Shuler attacked Los Angeles's wickedness throughout the 1920s while lauding El Monte as a place of rural, spiritual regeneration. He also became the Klan's most prominent spokesperson in the West. From his perch at Trinity Methodist in downtown Los Angeles, Shuler spent most of the early 1920s advancing the Klan in word and deed. He hosted hundreds of hooded men, women, and children at his church and wrote effusively of the Klan's virtues. The Klan, he wrote in his monthly publication, *Bob Shuler's Magazine*, were "100 per cent (*sic*) American." To Shuler, that meant the organization stood for "the doctrine of white supremacy," loyalty to the Constitution, the Bible's placement in public schools, and the need of white Protestant men to "stand for the virtue of womanhood."[6] As an avowed Confederate, Shuler was an unrepentant adherent of white supremacy and segregation. His tirades against Jews, blacks, Catholics, and alcohol could fill books—and did. Throughout the 1920s he published his intolerance in *Bob Shuler's Magazine*, which had a readership of 20,000.

While Shuler received some condemnation for his backward-looking radicalism, his flock increased. Even detractors marveled at his work ethic. He wrote weekly sermons, preached, published magazines, and hosted a radio program. His secret? El Monte. According to Shuler, he found his energy to fight for Los Angeles's whiteness at his ten-acre suburban farm in the city's north end. The farm afforded him the opportunity to step into antebellum America daily. He milked cows and raised hogs, chickens, and rabbits. According to one observer, Shuler's pioneer playland "constitutes a daily storehouse of energy and vitality that keeps him going the rest of the day at typewriter, pulpit and microphone."[7] Like many other white transplants in Southern California, Shuler attempted to recreate a rural fantasy life as a buttress against modernity. He made his mark. One can still find a piece of this fetishized South in the Whittier Narrows in the form of Northern cardinals, whose ancestors from Virginia Shuler released into the wild in 1923.

Ironically, the Klan disappointed Shuler, but because of its moderation, not its excesses. He broke with the—in his estimation—tainted Klan but never disavowed its ideology. Thus, as the Klan faltered, Shuler remained steadfast. From his Los Angeles church, he continued to attack Jews, blacks, and Catholics, and thanks to the popularity he earned by doing so, he was able to get the candidate he favored elected mayor and nearly earned himself a seat in the U.S. Senate. Quite a feat for a simple farmer from El Monte.

The Dueling Nazis of El Monte

Cities like El Monte could stay white for only so long. Labor camps, housing covenants, and segregationist policies slowly gave way to multiethnic communities by the mid-1960s. During this time of demographic change, a series of bizarre episodes revolving around race and memory put El Monte in the national spotlight. Once again, a costumed paramilitary organization led by transient white outsiders stood in the center ring. In 1966, the Nazis came to El Monte, but it was not their first choice. A year earlier, George Lincoln Rockwell, the head of the Virginia-based American Nazi Party (ANP), had opened a West Coast office in Glendale in an effort to "resist communism, Zionism and race-mixing." According to Rockwell, he chose Glendale simply because "it's a white man's town." Rockwell handpicked his most ardent loyalist, the twenty-four-year-old Michigan-born Ralph Forbes, as the location's commander. Forbes saw the group's new site in more pragmatic terms. From Glendale, he said, the Nazis could service "Redondo Beach, Long Beach, the San Fernando Valley and other areas."[8] Unwavering in his convictions in the face of conflict, from his Glendale location he proclaimed that despite his landlord's efforts to evict the Nazis, they would "not be driven out." But in just over a year, and multiple court cases later, Forbes; his wife, Karen; and their two children were evicted.

The Forbes family moved to 4375 Peck Road, El Monte. Living upstairs in the two-story house, Forbes used the ground floor as a meeting place, propaganda center, and Christian Identity church. Seeing striking similarities between Jesus and Adolf Hitler, and moving from clerical collar to storm trooper uniform, Forbes hoped to draw on white Americans' religiosity and meld it with Nazi political and racial ideology to create a new form of holistic conservatism. He promised not to march in El Monte and use the location only as a home base from which to launch operations elsewhere. The flag pole in the front of the house, his wife said, would fly only the American flag.

FIG. 7 Michael Sedano, "El Monte, 1970." (Courtesy of Michael Sedano.)

To a degree, he kept his word. He spoke at college campuses, attacked antiwar marchers, and demonstrated in San Bernardino with local Klansmen, but he did little at home. Marches occurred outside the residence but had hardly any impact on Forbes's activities. Forbes was far more affected by the rebranding and intrafascist squabbling of the national party. Forbes's objective was to inform white Americans that plain folks and Nazis shared the same goals, and by 1967 the ANP had followed his lead. Wanting to enter the political mainstream, Rockwell traded swastikas for American flags and renamed his group the National Socialist White People's Party (NSWPP). This accommodation, however, caused multiple members to revolt or quit. Consequently, one alienated member demonstrated his frustration by shooting Rockwell dead. The reverberation's waves shook El Monte.

Forbes and Rockwell were, of course, not far off the mark. Well acquainted with *Mein Kampf*, both men understood Hitler's high regard of white American pioneers. Aryans on the American frontier, Hitler wrote, worked the land, displaced "aborigines," and developed settlements. Forbes and Rockwell also must have known of Hitler's love of the German author Karl May's books on American frontier wars with natives.[9] American Nazis tapped into the same pioneer mythology that launched Walt Disney's *Davy Crockett, King of the Wild Frontier* and a thousand westerns and constituted the bulk of white American historical identity. The Nazis also mirrored the Republican Party's quiet embrace of radicalized conservatism without its conspiratorial guise. Thus, Dixiecrats and John Birchers transformed themselves into New Right Republicans, evolving in parallel with the Nazis. Despite its efforts, however, the NSWPP failed to overcome the natural disdain toward Nazis felt by a generation of people who had fought them, escaped them, knew them, and despised them. American Nazis needed a new strategy.

Thus, Ralph Forbes's plan for kinder, gentler Nazis ultimately upended his command in El Monte and left him scrambling for a safe haven in Arkansas. In his absence came nineteen-year-old Joseph Tommasi. Born in Virginia but reared in El Monte, Tommasi was an odd bird for a Nazi. He smoked weed, listened to rock music, and let his girlfriend sleep over in Nazi houses. By the early 1970s he had effectively taken control of the El Monte Nazis (now called Storm Troop 5) through a campaign for greater visibility and direct confrontation. As a clarion call, Tommasi crafted a poster proclaiming in capital letters, "The future belongs to the few of us willing to get our hands dirty. Political terror." In this period, the El Monte Nazi house went from plain dilapidation to dilapidation featuring the Nazi flag and a swastika-stenciled exterior. The city attempted to fine Tommasi, and neighbors wanted the house vacated. So with the threat of eviction looming, Tommasi purchased the house, reportedly with money that came from President Richard Nixon's campaign funds, and continued radicalizing the local party.[10]

Demonstrations ensued, and Tommasi welcomed them. In January 1972, a hundred members of the militant Jewish Defense League and nine hundred other people demonstrated outside of the house on Peck Road. Protesters threw small explosives, rocks, bottles, and eggs and engaged in fistfights. Sixty uniformed Nazis, led by Tommasi, stood on the porch with rifles. After the melee, he told the *Los Angeles Times* that if the demonstrators had breached the property line, he would have ordered them shot.[11] The police arrested forty demonstrators, and the Nazis went about their day.

Emboldened by the fight's publicity, Tommasi further defied the NSWPP with more appeals for radical direct action. Rebuffed by the NSWPP, he then quit the group and formed the Nationalist Socialist Liberation Front (NSLF)—headquartered, of course, in El Monte. The national party, it seemed, had grown too liberal. Tommasi hoped his Aryan brothers from Peck Road's Storm Troop 5 would join in the revolt, but only a few answered the call. Instead, they exiled him from the property and denounced the NSLF as a rival (that is, hostile) party. Hence, the Nazis turned on each other and sealed their fate. In August 1975, Tommasi and a small contingent of the NSLF stormed the El Monte house with clubs in hand. Before Tommasi got to the house's threshold, Jerry Jones, an eighteen-year-old storm trooper, shot him through the right eye, killing him and effectually putting an end to the tenure of Nazis on Peck Road.[12] Tommasi died underneath a Nazi flag and feet away from Hitler's portrait and another Nazi barely old enough to drive a car. Within months, the Nazis vacated El Monte in 1976. They vowed to move to Pasadena to join white suburban parents in fighting the threat of school integration.[13] However, their assistance never materialized, and like members of the Klan, their identities receded into obscurity while their base ideology remained imbedded in the white American consciousness.

It is easy to look at El Monte's Ku Klux Klan and Nazis and marvel at their triumph of willful destruction. From one perspective, it suggests that overt racism and vigilantism occasionally find a voice in America, only to collapse in karmic absurdity. But this assessment reeks of convenience. Perhaps it is better to think of El Monte's past as a cautionary (and mildly speculative) tale of an unwritten future. The pioneer myth, which both groups fed on, fuels white identity—both radical and mundane, in politics, and at local museums. Periodically, that fuel combusts locally and nationally, at the hands of the radicals and to the delight of ordinary people. At the end of *The California Reich*, a 1975 documentary, the filmmakers inserted an appropriate quote from a 1923 *New York Times* editorial on Germany's nascent Nazi party. The party was a small force of "Boy Scouts having an outing, playing war," the paper said, describing them as "persons better fitted for a comic opera stage than a serious effort to overthrow the government."[14] As America has witnessed, these changes are not laughing matters, and they are manifest in elections, not costume parties.

Notes

1 Zeke Minaya, "In El Monte, Two Sides to the Past—Close Yet Far," *Los Angeles Times*, August 30, 2004, http://articles.latimes.com/2004/aug/30/local/me-museums30.

2 Klanman's manual (Knights of the Ku Klux Klan Incorporated, 1924), 8.

3 Joshua Rothman, "When Bigotry Paraded through the Streets," *Atlantic*, December 4, 2016, https://www.theatlantic.com/politics/archive/2016/12/second-klan/509468/.

4 Jane Beemer Schults, "The Ku Klux Klan in Downey in the 1920s" (master's thesis, California State University, Long Beach, 1991), 139 and 151; "Threat Issued by State Klan," *Los Angeles Times*, April 6, 1924.

5 "Klansmen Turn on Evans," *Los Angeles Times*, September 26, 1924.

6 Bob Shuler, "The K. of C. vs. The K. K. K.," *Bob Shuler Magazine*, September 1922, 98.

7 "Church and Ranch Keep Schuler Busy," *Los Angeles Record*, April 12, 1929.

8 "Glendale Unwilling Host to American Nazi Party," *The Spokesman-Review*, December 28, 1964.

9 Adolf Hitler, *Mein Kampf*, translated by James Murphy (Boston: Houghton Mifflin, 1939), 418–419. See also Michael Kimmelman, "Karl May and the Origins of a German Obsession," *New York Times*, September 12, 2007, https://www.nytimes.com/2007/09/12/travel/12iht-12karl.7479952.html.

10 Leroy F. Aarons, "Calif. Nazis Were Recruited," *Washington Post*, June 7, 1973.

11 Betty Liddick, "The Evolution of an American Nazi," *Los Angeles Times*, September 2, 1975.

12 Mayerene Barker, "Former Nazi Was a Rebel with a Cause," *Los Angeles Times*, August 21, 1975.

13 Greg Waskul, "US Nazi Party Ex-Official Slain," *Los Angeles Times*, August 6, 1975; Mayerene Barker, "Nazis Leaving El Monte, May Try Pasaden," *Los Angeles Times*, June 17, 1976.

14 Quoted in Keith Critchlow and Walter Parkes, dirs., *The California Reich* (Los Angeles: Intercontinental Releasing Corporation, 1975).

6

Ricardo Flores Magón and the Anarchist Movement in El Monte

YESENIA BARRAGAN AND
MARK BRAY

"Forward, comrades! Soon you will hear the first shots; soon the shout of rebellion will thunder from the throats of the oppressed . . . Land and Liberty!"[1] These were the prophetic words of the Mexican anarchist Ricardo Flores Magón that were printed in *Regeneración*, the bilingual anarchist newspaper published by the Magón brothers and their comrades, on November 19, 1910—just one day before the Mexican Revolution would radically transform world history. Decades later, the Zapatistas adopted the slogan "Land and Liberty!" as they occupied San Cristóbal de las Casas in early 1994 in defiance of the North American Free Trade Agreement and the neoliberal order. Nevertheless, Ricardo Flores Magón, one of the chief intellectual and political influences to the Mexican Revolution, made this declaration not in Mexico, but in the United States, where he had been living in exile since 1903 due to his radical activities. In 1905 in St. Louis, Missouri, Magón cofounded the Partido Liberal Mexicano (Mexican Liberal Party, or PLM)—which, despite its name, was a radical political organization rather than a party. From Missouri, he and his *compañeros* agitated against the Mexican dictator Porfirio Díaz and projected their anarchist vision of a world without bosses or borders.[2]

As an anarchist in exile, Magón had many stops during his stay in "El Norte," and one was none other than El Monte, California. There, in 1917, just a year before he and Enrique Flores Magón (his brother and fellow anarchist organizer) would be sent to Fort Leavenworth Prison near Kansas City, Ricardo delivered a moving speech, likely to a diverse crowd of working-class and poor Mexican Angelenos, Italian Americans, and others who formed a large part of the fabric of Greater Los Angeles at the time. As a 1917 *Los Angeles Times* article warned its readers, "If the people of Los Angeles knew what was happening on our border, they would not sleep at night. . . . German nationals hob-nob with Mexican bandits, Japanese agents, and renegades from this country. . . . Los Angeles is the headquarters for this vicious system, and it is there that the deals between German and Mexican representatives are frequently made."[3] Indeed, the anarchist Magón brothers were the "bandits" that authorities had in mind, for U.S. officials, at the behest of Díaz and other Mexican authorities, sought to suppress the PLM's activities on the northern side of the border.[4] Regardless of the continual arrests and repression, Ricardo continued to propagate his beliefs widely, as he did one day in El Monte.

The theme of Ricardo's speech in El Monte was indifference, perhaps in response to his dismay at the state of the revolution in Mexico in 1917. Although the revolutionary Mexican Constitution was drafted that year, it certainly did not present the liberatory vision that the anarchist brothers had fought hard for. Ricardo railed against the poor person who "looks after his own well-being and that of his family, and nothing more, without realizing that the well-being of the individual depends on the well-being of everyone else."[5] His voluntaristic focus on the latent potential of collective struggle rather than the ripeness of objective material conditions was indicative of the anarchist emphasis on action as opposed to the Marxist emphasis on social and economic conditions.

More importantly, however, Magón's argument that individual betterment required cooperation echoed the massive international influence of the Russian anarchist Pyotr Kropotkin's *Mutual Aid: A Factor of Evolution*, which was published serially in the 1890s and circulated widely throughout the English- and Spanish-speaking worlds. In response to the rising popularity of Social Darwinism and the racist and imperialist use of the concept of "the survival of the fittest" (a phrase coined by Herbert Spencer but often mistakenly attributed to Charles Darwin), Kropotkin's scientific research demonstrated that cooperation and mutual aid were as important to animal and human evolution as competition. Much to the dismay of many anarchists, Kropotkin (a signatory of the infamous 1916 Manifesto of the Sixteen) supported the Entente Powers in World War I. However, in his speech in 1917, the year that the United States entered the war, Magón asked his audience, "Aren't we ourselves, the disinherited, the oppressed, the poor, those who lend ourselves to receiving from the

FIG. 8 "Enrique and Ricardo Flores Magón." (Courtesy of La Casa de El Hijo del Ahuizote.)

hands of our oppressors the guns destined to exterminate our working class brothers . . . ?"[6] Like most anarchists, Magón dismissed the war effort as a capitalist scheme to divide the international working class. But as his words show, he considered anarchism to be an ideology not only for the standard (Marxist) industrial proletariat, but also the oppressed more broadly—thereby including peasants, who were utterly essential in the Mexican context.

In private letters from El Monte and La Puente during Ricardo and Enrique's stay there in 1917, we also get a different, perhaps more human, view of the two firebrands. Like many activists in exile, the Magón brothers became restless and occasionally sick (both literally and metaphorically) about their time away from home. In a letter from El Monte on June 28, 1917, for example, Ricardo wrote to a loved one that "the truth of the matter is that I can't stay here [in El Monte] for more than a week. The *compañeros* are wonderful, but it bothers me not being able to do anything, I feel like I'm missing something, because, although the reality is that I don't do much there [in Mexico], I entertain myself."[7]

Despite Ricardo's seeming boredom and inability to be active, it appears that El Monte was treating him well, for his health had improved. "I have not suffered not even an evening of insomnia," he wrote, and he mentioned taking relaxing baths in the nearby river that helped him sleep peacefully throughout the evening.[8] Enrique's time in what is known today as the San Gabriel Valley, however, was a bit more trying for his health. As he wrote from La Puente, California, his stomach was constantly bothering him—so much that one day in mid-February, he complained that his only meal was a cup of coffee before he set out to work his long ten-hour shift cutting and de-rooting trees at a nearby ranch, where he worked with some friends. It wasn't ideal, but it was something at least. Talking about his coworkers, he added that "we are all equal, [and work] without preferences and in perfect harmony."[9] As a working-class immigrant in exile, Enrique had to look for any available job opportunities, including this gig at a ranch. Of course, he faced challenges experienced by any laborer performing precarious, temporary work, as demonstrated by his complaint that "*el burgués*" (the boss) hadn't paid them yet. Again, this was not ideal, but he wrote that at least he didn't have to deal with "any *mayordomo*" who would scream at him.[10]

From the brothers' letters, we also get a special insight into the dynamic political world of El Monte in the early twentieth century. In one letter, Ricardo talked about a political meeting to be held at the house of a man named Aguirre. "In my opinion," Ricardo noted, "the people now express much interest in the struggle," likely referring to the ongoing situation of the Mexican Revolution.[11] But times were tough, and the stakes were getting higher. Ricardo lamented these conditions when he reported that few people had attended the last meeting at the Italian Hall in Los Angeles, where the Magón brothers were only able to raise $1.04 for the cause (in comparison, Enrique made $3 for one day's work at the ranch). One of the main problems, according to Ricardo, was that organizers weren't announcing the meetings well in advance. "For me," he wrote, "the meetings in the Italian [Hall] are very important for the movement in general, and I get restless if I'm not able to speak there every time."[12]

The stakes couldn't be made clearer than in a speech, later published in *Regeneración*, that Ricardo made in El Monte on September 23, 1917. Celebrating the sixth anniversary of the famous manifesto of September 23, 1911, issued by the organizing junta of the PLM, Ricardo stated that the anniversary was an "incredibly important date in the revolutionary history of the Mexican pueblo" because it clearly marked a "revolutionary tendency" that was antiauthoritarian, anticapitalist, and antireligious. Indeed, in 1917, toward the end of the revolution, Ricardo railed against the legacy of Díaz and the "*científicos*," referring to Díaz's technocratic advisers, and the many presidents who came in and out of office during the tumultuous years of the revolution. Maintaining his antiparliamentary, anarchist stance, Ricardo reiterated before the crowd in El Monte that "many today realize that the government itself is the problem, no matter if Pedro or Juan is in power."[13]

Enrique's letters also give us insights into El Monte's vibrant political networks, showing how Magonismo was being built on the ground in El Monte. After coming home late from work one evening, Enrique ran into some friends named Bakunin (Enrique was clearly using the name of the famed Russian anarchist as a pseudonym), Oscar, and Acracia (probably another pseudonym, since this term was synonymous with "anarchy" and commonly used in titles of anarchist periodicals at the time).[14] In a piece written by Enrique in *Regeneración*, he also reported on a benefit picnic near El Monte held on Sunday, August 26, 1917, to support the newspaper. Organized by the local anarchist groups Acracia of La Puente, Tierra y Fraternidad and Luz Libertaria of El Monte, and Regeneración of San Gabriel, the picnic was held just south of the Bassett Bridge between El Monte and La Puente.[15]

Was this the site of Ricardo's infamous El Monte speech? Perhaps. But what we know for sure is that the picnic was both a social and an economic success. The party lasted more than nine hours, with entertainment provided by a "great Mexican orchestra" as "comrades, men and women" danced the night away. Overall, the four groups chipped in about $85 to make the benefit happen, and nearly $74.61 was collected to support *Regeneración*. Enrique was so pleased with his El Monte comrades that he encouraged others to use the example of these groups when searching for ways to support *Regeneración*.[16] Moreover, in the issues of *Regeneración*, we can find some names of residents of El Monte who supported the newspaper directly. For example, a person named R. Andrade contributed $1 in 1912,[17] while a group of "active *compañeros*" met in the house of comrade Feliciano Macias in El Monte in September 1917 to "celebrate the anniversary of the promulgation of the Manifesto of September 23, 1911," the PLM's openly anarchist-communist manifesto that was proclaimed during the Mexican Revolution. At the celebration in El Monte, it was reported that anarchist hymns were sung, money was collected for the paper, and "everyone danced happily."[18] Without these vibrant political and cultural networks in El Monte and elsewhere, *Regeneración* would not have been able to continue to publish.

However, despite the warmth of his comrades in El Monte and La Puente, Enrique was also quite homesick. "How awful it is to be away from home," he wrote, "away from the people you hold dear, although the anarchists should not have any preferences!" A bit tongue-in-cheek, Enrique went on to describe his longing for Mexico: "But it's impossible for me, any other way. *Mi viejita, mi compañita de vida* [My mother, my life companion], my children, my close friends, everything is there [in Mexico]. My daily life, all the years, in other words a large part of me, me, and my affections, my love, it's all there."[19] But for the moment, El Monte was his loving, albeit temporary and imperfect, home away from home.

In the end, Ricardo Flores Magón died in Leavenworth Penitentiary in 1922, while serving a twenty-year sentence for violating the 1917 Espionage Act. The circumstances of his death remain in dispute, as some claim that prison guards murdered him. Nevertheless, his legacy remains stronger than ever. In 1997, for example, indigenous communities fighting for self-determination and autonomy in Oaxaca formed the Popular Indigenous Council of Oaxaca, "Ricardo Flores Magón" (CIPO-RFM) in his honor.

Notes

1 Quoted in Ricardo Flores Magón, "Land and Liberty," in *The Mexico Reader: History, Culture, Politics*, ed. Gilbert M. Joseph and Timothy J. Henderson (Durham, NC: Duke University Press, 2002), 338.
2 Ibid., 335–338.
3 Quoted in Mark Wild, *Street Meeting: Multiethnic Neighborhoods in Early Twentieth-Century Los Angeles* (Berkeley: University of California Press, 2005), 167.
4 Ibid., 160.
5 Ricardo Flores Magón, "Speech in El Monte, California, 1917," in Ricardo Flores Magón, *Dreams of Freedom: A Ricardo Flores Magón Reader*, ed. Charles Bufe and Mitchell Cowen Verter (Oakland, CA: AK Press, 2005), 280–281.
6 Ibid., 282.
7 Ricardo Flores Magón, letter to "Manito," June 28, 1917, La Casa de El Hijo del Ahuizote (hereafter La Casa), Mexico City, Mexico.
8 Ibid.
9 Enrique Flores Magón, letter to "Terita," February 4, 1918, La Casa, Mexico City, Mexico. See also Enriqué Flores Magón, letter to "Terita," February 14, 1918, La Casa, Mexico City, Mexico.
10 Ricardo Flores Magón, letter to "Tesorito," March 4, 1918, La Casa, Mexico City, Mexico.
11 Ricardo Flores Magón, letter to "Manito," June 28, 1917, La Casa, Mexico City, Mexico.
12 Ibid., 2.
13 Ricardo Flores Magón, "El manifiesto de 23 de septiembre," *Regeneración,* no. 260, October 6, 1917.
14 Enrique Flores Magón, letter to "Terita," February 4, 1918, La Casa, Mexico City, Mexico.
15 Enrique Flores Magón, "El Picnic," *Regeneración,* no. 259, September 1, 1917.
16 Ibid.
17 R. R. Palacios, "Para la defensa," *Regeneración,* no. 92, September 12, 1912.
18 Ricardo Flores Magón, "Ejemplo," *Regeneración*, no. 260, October 6, 1917.
19 Enrique Flores Magón, letter to "Terita," February 4, 1918, La Casa, Mexico City, Mexico.

7

Bitter Fruit

The El Monte Berry Strike of 1933

MELQUIADES FERNANDEZ

The El Monte Berry Strike of 1933 was one of the largest organized labor strikes to challenge the agriculture industry of Southern California during the Depression. Although it was not the first strike to arise in the season, it was the first to gain public recognition and attention. Just as the berry harvest was about to start, workers decided to put in place a work stoppage to address stagnating wages and declining working conditions during the economic crisis of the 1930s. It was a labor struggle that would involve the Cannery and Agricultural Workers' Industrial Union (CAWIU), the local (mostly, but not exclusively, Mexican) workers, Japanese growers, white elected officials with a vested economic interest in the berry industry, and Mexican consulate officials. However, despite the strike's visibility and intensity, workers and organizers won only marginal victories that kept many of the offending institutions and parties in place. Nonetheless, it provided fuel that would help ignite subsequent labor strikes throughout California.

The Berry Fields

In May 1933, Hicks Camp was nearing full capacity. More than 1,500 migrant workers were prepared to take part in the berry harvest, which would begin in May and last through August. Hicks Camp was, like the surrounding neighborhoods of Medina Court and Hayes Camp, a migrant labor camp set up to house the families who worked in the local fields. Hicks Camp was not envisioned as a permanent neighborhood, but it became one as people settled down to build homes and established a local culture. Men, women, and children would quickly assemble homes of cardboard and repurposed box carts on a nondescript tract of land that lacked paved roads or basic plumbing.

By the time of the strike, there were about 1,500 residents packed into the twenty-two-acre plot of land; the population would drop only as low as 1,000 residents during the off season. However, members of this large, mostly Mexican, labor force laid down their roots in El Monte in an especially precarious economic time, as workers in Hicks Camp faced a labor market that had 185 workers for every 100 available jobs.[1] Agricultural wages, historically meager and exploitative, were dropping throughout California as the market was gutted by arriving Dust Bowl migrants. A large population of displaced Arkansas and Oklahoma residents, fleeing severe drought and depressed economies back home, moved en masse to California seeking better opportunities.

Berry picking was backbreaking and tedious work. Workers would rise as early as 4:00 A.M. to prepare the day's food and arrive at the fields by 6:00. Work was fast paced, with the laborer having to expertly pick ripened berries while not damaging unripened ones and avoiding any bad berries. Work continued for ten to twelve hours a day. Since wages were based on the type of berry picked, it was difficult to accurately calculate a market wage earned by any individual worker. At its peak, pay for experienced workers picking raspberries averaged forty cents per crate, and those picking youngberries and blackberries got twenty cents per crate.[2] According to Charles Wollenberg, the Los Angeles Chamber of Commerce estimated average rates as high as twenty-five cents per hour, while Mexican workers placed the average at fifteen cents and argued that a low of nine cents was not unusual.[3] The variability of the wages hints at a constantly shifting and insecure work environment in which workers could not count on having a weekly or even daily guaranteed wage.

As a result, at the end of May 1933, a group of workers—Mexican, white, and Japanese—organized and presented demands to S. Fukami, secretary for the Japanese Growers Association, for higher, more consistent wages of thirty-five cents per hour that would allow them to have a secure and predictable income.[4] The workers, however, found little support among the Japanese farm operators, and in response a general meeting was scheduled for June 1 at Hicks Camp.

The Strike

During the general meeting, the organizers proposed a strike. Fifty workers—Mexican, Filipino, and Japanese—and two CAWIU organizers made up the strike committee. Over five hundred workers were present at the initial vote at Hicks to go on strike and took up the campaign by leafleting, posting bulletins, and organizing daily meetings to keep people up to date on the direction of the strike. CAWIU literature was disseminated in English, Spanish, and Japanese as organizers tried to recruit members for a farm workers' union. Augustine Ramos, one of the strikers, remembers: "In those days only the poor people worked for the farmers, the big shots. They were getting paid very low wages—people couldn't make a living any more. That prompted people; as small as they were, as unorganized as they were, they had something in common. They got together and went on strike."[5]

The conditions affecting the El Monte workers were not unique; instead, they reflected the operations of the larger agricultural industry in all of California that sought to exploit the poverty-ridden labor force. The work stoppage would grow and encompass other El Monte agricultural camps, including Chino and Medina Court. It expanded into areas of La Puente and spread as far as the celery fields of Santa Monica. According to the newspaper *La Opinion*, over two thousand workers were refusing to work by June 7. A week later the figure had risen to seven thousand.[6]

However, despite its early momentum, the Berry Strike soon faced internal and external challenges. In earlier decades Mexican workers had had support from and solidarity with Japanese farm laborers, who also faced historical discrimination and segregation by the dominant white Anglo culture. Though both communities were relegated to the same side of segregated theaters and the children of both groups attended Lexington Elementary School in El Monte, by the 1930s worker demographic characteristics had changed and the groups' relationship had shifted. By the time of the strike, their similarities were obscured by an overseer-worker relationship that was carried out on a daily basis in the fields. As one of the laborers, a Señora Torres, put it, "[The Japanese farmers] would work in the field, but you knew they were the *boss*."[7] The Japanese, perceived by the community as the "boss," became a logical target for striking Mexican workers, who saw the Japanese farmers as the visible agents who could address their concerns over wages and working conditions.

While Mexican laborers constituted most of the agricultural migrant labor force, the Japanese operated most of the land on which they worked. The San Gabriel Valley included about 700 acres of berries, and 80 percent of that land was operated by Japanese growers. Although the Japanese had established a presence in the industry, most of the land they operated was in fact owned by white landholders who leased it to Japanese foremen. This system was a result of the California Alien Land Act of 1913, which imposed severe restrictions on Japanese ownership of land and restricted leasing agreements to three years. However, these rules were circumvented by the practice of Issei (first-generation) parents passing land on to their Nisei children, second-generation immigrants who were exempt from the law because they were recognized American citizens.

During the strike, the Japanese community arranged for family members to work in the fields, and children were excused from school to salvage the berry harvest. On the weekend of June 30–31, people in the surrounding community were also invited to pick their own berries at discounted rates. The seeming benevolence of the Japanese land operators in allowing people to harvest their own berries both alienated the striking Mexican workers and built a level of public sympathy for the growers.

Radical versus Conservative Leadership

Internally, within a period of a few weeks, leadership disputes compromised the strikers' movement and eventually their gains. Although the CAWIU is often credited with instigating the strike, its role was short-lived—a result of both internal and external pressures. During the strike, the Comite Pro-Huelga was formed to support the region's striking Mexican workers. Its membership included nationalist leaders from local fraternal and *mutualista* self-help organizations, representatives of the Mexican consulate in Los Angeles, and strikers. The organization's leaders, Consul Alejandro Martinez and Vice-Consul Ricardo Hill, discouraged more militant direct worker action. At a community meeting held on June 9, Hill called for the expulsion of CAWIU's Lino Chacon and J. Ruiz from the Strike Committee for "frequently urging militant measures against scabs" and distributing Communist literature. While it should be noted that the CAWIU was indeed a Communist-aligned organization, the radical roots of many of El Monte's organizers were in a Mexican tradition strongly influenced by anarchist movements such as the one led by the prominent Ricardo Flores Magón—who had organized in El Monte and Greater Los Angeles in the 1910s.

As noted by Gilbert Gonzalez in *The 1933 Los Angeles County Farm Workers Strike*, the fervor with which Hill sought the termination of the radical leadership was in keeping with his upbringing as a member of the upper class in Mexico, which had viewed labor organizing as a controlled element of national politics. According to the *Los Angeles Times*, Hill urged the strikers "to run the agitators out and were told that when that was done an earnest effort will be made to obtain a settlement."[8] At the center of the disagreement between Hill and the CAWIU-style of organizing was a fundamental difference in tactics and vision. For Hill, labor was not concerned with bringing about any type of proletarian revolution. The growers understood that Hill's priority was to win a compromise, and to that end they moved to eliminate the radical union organizers as well. According to the local Japanese newspaper *Rafu Shimpo*, the growers believed that "if the radical element [were] weeded out of the union movement[,] the farmers [would] have a better chance to cooperate with labor."[9]

To this end, Hill relied heavily on external entities, mainly the Los Angeles Police Department's Red Squad, to undermine and eventually dismantle the radical leadership of the Berry Strike. On June 10, 1933, a large segment of the CAWIU was denounced by Hill as "reds" who did not stand for the interest of Mexican workers, and most of its leaders were arrested on June 13.[10] The Red Squad was notorious for infiltrating and dismantling all types of leftist organizations, especially militant labor unions. An officer in the squad observed, "I warned them to stay away, owing to their affiliation to the Communist Subsidiary organization . . . if their consul was advising and directing them, I was sure they would not get into trouble, but if they were communist led and directed, it might lead to trouble for them, such as deportations."[11] Beyond its use as a scare tactic, in the context of the 1930s—which saw the implementation of the Mexican repatriation program—deportation for all people of Mexican descent was a very real threat. People were systematically deported, irrespective of their actual citizenship, based on the perceived notion that they were Mexican.

Compromise and Legacy

Under these conditions, and without the radicalized influence of the CAWIU, Hill and the Comite Pro-Huelga were free to move forward with talks centered on compromise and agreement. As the Mexican strike organizers, the Japanese land operators, and white interests penned an agreement on July 6, the strike came to an end. Workers earned a substantial victory in acquiring a daily wage of one dollar and fifty cents, as well as agreements to hire back workers in an expeditious manner and prohibit reprisals. However, following the agreement, labor organizers found themselves with a quickly dissolving and Pyrrhic victory. Not only had many workers already lost a whole season of work, but on July 10 the Bureau of Industrial Relations announced that the July 6 agreement applied only to the vegetable farms on the coast and would not to be enforced in the berry farms of the valley. Although this decision was strongly protested by the Mexican unions, the bureau argued that there had been no lasting "binding agreement," and the Japanese growers were not held accountable for not honoring the July 6 agreement.[12] Furthermore, in an act of retribution in 1933, the Japanese Chamber of Commerce, with the support of the white community, proposed that "Mexican farm labor strikers . . . be deprived of further county relief aid if found participating in any labor agitation. . . . Deportation of foreigners implicated in such action is further recommended."[13] Such threats were made after a season of striking, in which many members of the laboring community had earned no income to support their families.

It is difficult to characterize the El Monte Berry Strike as a clear victory for the Mexican and working-class communities, yet its legacy would be manifested in the months and years that followed. While the victories secured by the union were easily and quickly pushed aside by the Japanese growers and white landowners, the strike was a clear indication of the mood of labor in the agriculture industry at the time, as thirty more major strikes affected California in the next twelve months. The legacy of the El Monte Berry Strike can be viewed as one of empowerment for a community that many contemporary observers viewed as foreign and un-American in its mind-set. The strike served to awaken the class consciousness of a generation of labor organizers whose members would continue to participate in strikes and agitate against the agribusiness industry. According to Wollenberg, one El Monte veteran was quoted as saying, "if there is no strike in the San Joaquin Valley now, there will be when we get there."[14] And he was right. The San Joaquin Cotton Strike of 1933 was the largest agricultural strike seen in California at that time, as 18,000 workers took to the picket lines demanding fairer wages and better working conditions. The El Monte Berry Strike instilled within workers a sense of their value and an understanding of collective struggle. As Augustine Ramos had observed at the beginning of the strike, people understood that they had a common struggle, and only through collective action would they be able to win it.

Notes

1 Charles Wollenberg, "Race and Class in Rural California: The El Monte Berry Strike of 1933," *California Historical Quarterly* 51, no. 2 (1972): 158.
2 Ronald Lopez, "The El Monte Berry Strike of 1933," *Aztlán: Chicano Journal of the Social Sciences and Arts* 1, no.1 (1970): 103.
3 Ibid., 157.
4 Lopez, "The El Monte Berry Strike of 1933," 103.
5 Diane Conover and Tony Estrada, "Interview with Augustine Ramos," in *Personal Stories from El Monte Communities*, ed. Susan Sellman Obler (Whittier, CA: Rio Hondo College, 1978), 90–91.
6 Wollenberg, "Race and Class in Rural California," 157.
7 Quoted in Vicki Ruiz, *From Out of the Shadows: Mexican Women in Twentieth-Century America* (New York: Oxford University Press, 1999), 76 (emphasis in original).

8 Gilbert Gonzalez, "Berry Strike Gets Violent," *Los Angeles Times*, June 10, 1933.
9 Quoted in John Modell, *The Economics and Politics of Racial Accommodation: The Japanese of Los Angeles 1900–1942* (Urbana: University of Illinois Press, 1977), 122.
10 Lopez, "The El Monte Berry Strike of 1933," 105.
11 Quoted in Gonzalez, "Berry Strike Gets Violent."
12 Wollenberg, "Race and Class in Rural California," 162.
13 Quoted in Modell, *The Economics and Politics of Racial Accommodation*, 124.
14 Wollenberg, "Race and Class in Rural California," 163.

8

Schools for All

The Desegregation Campaign in El Monte

RACHEL GRACE NEWMAN

> The professor started talking about segregation in the South, of blacks, of *Brown v. Board of Education* . . . so after class I went up to the professor, and I said, "Hey professor, were you aware of the segregation of the Mexican-American students all over the Southwest, including California?" . . . He said, "I know nothing about it."
> —Olga Gutiérrez, 2015

In Memory of Olga Gutiérrez, 1937–2016

Olga Gutiérrez, a Mexican American teacher and activist in El Monte, California, was working on a master's degree at California State University, Los Angeles. It was 1980, twenty-six years after the U.S. Supreme Court had ruled in *Brown v. Board of Education* that the policy of dividing children into different schools on the basis of race was illegal. Talking about segregation meant talking about the separation of white and black children in the South; but Gutiérrez knew that segregation was also part of the recent history of her own community.

Sharing this information with her professor, Gutiérrez realized that something had happened in El Monte that was historically important yet had been mostly forgotten. From the 1920s to the 1940s, Mexican American children had attended segregated schools, and a coalition of parents and Anglo allies had brought an end to this practice in 1945, well before the 1954 *Brown* decision. When Gutiérrez wrote a master's thesis to tell this story of desegregation in El Monte, she described it as a story of "things that ought not to be forgotten even though they are painful."[1] For her, this pain was personal. When she attended elementary school in the 1940s, she found that Spanish, the only language she spoke at the time, was prohibited. Her mouth was taped shut as punishment for speaking in her mother tongue at school.[2] In 1980, as an established Mexican American professional and graduate student, Gutiérrez set out to understand how segregation had begun and ended in El Monte.

In the Southwest, segregation was not technically based upon race, and it was not the result of state-level laws like those that existed in the South. In California, segregation was the product of decisions made at the local level by school district superintendents, school boards, and principals with the support of white communities. By law, Mexicans and Mexican Americans were considered white, even though they were actually treated as people of color and faced systematic violence and exclusion.[3]

School districts did not explicitly refer to race but used other criteria to keep Mexican American children in separate, inadequate schools. Because Mexican-origin families often lived apart from Anglo Americans, geography served as an apparently neutral rationale for school segregation. However, whites prevented people of color from buying homes in their neighborhoods, and thus geographic separation was not inevitable but the result of racism.[4] Educational officials also claimed that segregation actually benefited children with particular educational needs. As one Texas superintendent explained, his district separated Mexican and Anglo American children to provide Spanish speakers with English-language instruction and to accommodate the arrival of Mexican American migrant children in the district late in the school year.[5] In 1939 in Oxnard, California, local authorities claimed that a new school on the Mexican side of town was intended to keep children safe, so they would no longer need to cross railroad tracks to reach schools in the white part of Oxnard.[6] However, the poorly constructed, uncomfortable, and sometimes dangerous schools for Mexican-descended children were obviously worse than school facilities for Anglo American children.[7] Regardless of the reasoning they invoked, Anglo American community leaders deliberately created separate and inferior educational opportunities for Mexican American children throughout the Southwest.

FIG. 9 Lexington school's 4th grade class, 1944, El Monte. (Courtesy of La Historia Historical Society Museum.)

This process unfolded in El Monte as well, where segregation began in 1923. Until then, Mexican American children had attended school alongside Anglo American children. But in that year, as El Monte's Mexican-descended population was growing rapidly and school facilities were becoming overcrowded, the local school board decided that a new school (Columbia School) would be built to serve only the Anglo American population. Mexican American children would remain at the older facility, Lexington School, which was referred to in 1927 school board minutes as the "Mexican school."[8]

In fact, the students in the Lexington School were not entirely of Mexican descent, since Japanese American children also attended. Only in 1938 did the El Monte School District make its reasoning for segregation explicit: "children coming from non-english speaking (*sic*) families" were "required to attend the Lexington School regardless of the area in which they live."[9] In reality, arguments about language skills were only a weak justification for what was effectively racial segregation, as the historian Mario García notes: "Ironically, most children never left the Mexican schools even after they had learned English."[10]

At the segregated Lexington School, there were no Mexican American or Spanish-speaking teachers.[11] Former students interviewed by Gutiérrez remembered physical abuse from their teachers, low expectations for academic achievement, and inadequate facilities, as well as some well-meaning teachers.[12] In an oral history interview conducted in the late 1970s, Augustine Ramos spoke of his years at Lexington with Mexican and Japanese American classmates, noting that only in the fifth grade, when all the Lexington students were transferred to the Columbia School, did he see "little Anglo kids" for the first time. "You can imagine . . . how much we lagged behind," Ramos said.[13] From the 1920s to the 1940s, students at the Lexington School simply did not have the same resources, academic support, or opportunities as did their Anglo peers at other El Monte schools.

By World War II, as calls to end racial discrimination gained increasing public support throughout the country, many groups in El Monte sought to end segregation in their own community. Gutiérrez notes the contributions of Anglo allies. The key figures were the Reverend Dwight Ramage and his wife, Holly, who were affiliated with the Presbyterian Church, and Father John V. Coffield, who served Catholic parishioners in El Monte. Father Coffield is still remembered by many in El Monte as a staunch ally of Mexican Americans who stood alongside them in many civil rights struggles. When the Ramages arrived in El Monte in 1942, they were struck by the obvious segregation and inequality in the town's elementary schools, and along with Coffield, the Ramages wanted to change the situation. They collaborated with local Mexican American leaders like Don Ignacio Gutiérrez (Olga Gutiérrez's father-in-law) and a larger group of Mexican American parents.[14] Groups like the League of United Latin American Citizens and the Federation of Hispanic American Voters mobilized against segregation in El Monte as well.[15]

However, Olga Gutiérrez found that the catalyst for desegregation came from a Mexican American family's refusal to accept segregation in 1945. After this family moved to the area, they found that they could not enroll their young daughter in their local school, Cleminson, "because of her Spanish surname"; she would have to attend Lexington instead. The family hired a prominent lawyer, Manuel Ruiz, and along with the Mexican American community, they organized two large meetings to rally support for desegregation.[16] They planned to sue the school board, but Reverend Ramage and Father Coffield suggested "confronting the district at a school board meeting" first. Years later, Ramage remembered how "the Mexican-American community lent the spark" to desegregation efforts "by being so militant and angry" that they were willing to sue. In contrast, Ramage and Coffield were hoping "to end segregation with as little antagonism as possible."[17]

In the end, the lawsuit was not necessary. At the April 1945 school board meeting, El Monte's Mexican American parents and their allies successfully lobbied to end segregation in the district by the beginning of the following school year.[18] This decision seemed to spell the end of segregation in the school district after twenty-two years of separate schools for Mexican- and Anglo-American children.

El Monte parents were not the only ones to fight against segregation in their community during this era. Before and after their struggle, other communities brought cases against school districts to local courts, but judges often ruled in favor of school districts' right to separate students as they saw fit for so-called educational reasons. In two California cases in 1931 and 1946, parents' efforts did bring legal victories, although these rulings did not have the broader impact that parents might have hoped for.[19] While scholars have written about these court cases, the El Monte case has attracted less notice, perhaps because integration in that situation came from a school board decision. However, the fact that parents did not have to sue illustrates the strength of their community organizing. They were a force that school district officials could not ignore, and the board quickly assented to their demands.

But the story continued after the desegregation victory. Gutiérrez's research also showed that even a favorable decision from the school board could not eradicate racism in the broader community. Anti-Mexican prejudice had deep roots and would continue to affect Mexican American children in the community. Gutiérrez learned that in El Monte, "as soon as the Anglo community learned about desegregation" that would bring Anglo and Mexican American children together in the same school, Anglo parents asked for school-wide checks for head lice.[20] The district superintendent agreed to this request, which probably resulted from Anglo parents' racist stereotypes about the Mexican American community's supposed lack of hygiene.[21] Gutiérrez notes that "interestingly enough," the children who did have head lice were not Mexican American.[22]

With prejudice still strong in El Monte even after desegregation, it is not surprising that in Gutiérrez's interviews with former students of the Lexington School, she found that integration had also been a painful experience. Some even remembered segregated Lexington fondly. Never having seen the privileges they might have had at an integrated school, Mexican American children simply accepted as normal the school they had to attend.[23] Some Mexican and Japanese American students even enjoyed their time together. "Oh, we had a lot of fun. We didn't think anything of it," remembered Lupe Ruiz in a 1970s interview.[24] As one former student told Gutiérrez, after the move to the Columbia School, "the Anglo kids made fun of us—made fun of our food, our customs. In the segregated school, it was secure."[25] Another explained that it was only after being integrated that Mexican American students realized that they "were not prepared" compared to their Anglo peers.[26]

Clearly, the negative impacts of segregation in El Monte did not end with the school board's decision to integrate. Indeed, Gutiérrez points out that her interviewees were among the small number of Lexington graduates who had achieved professional success or middle-class stability.[27] As one interviewee pointed out, the experience of segregation at the Lexington School "set in motion a force that few were able to overcome."[28]

Furthermore, because Southwestern communities had used indirect de facto strategies to segregate children, there was no easy legal solution to achieve integration in places like El Monte. Segregation of Mexican American students persisted for several decades after the 1954 *Brown v. Board of Education* decision. Integration efforts were hampered by the fact that *Brown* could apply only in situations in which students were legally classified by their race and suffered as a result of this explicit racial discrimination, but segregation of Mexican Americans often operated in more subtle ways.[29] Only in 1970 did a Supreme Court case involving the Corpus Christi, Texas, school district firmly establish that Mexican Americans, regardless of their racial status, were a socially recognized ethnic minority, and that the provisions of *Brown* applied to them, too.[30]

Still, in 1971, the U.S. Commission on Civil Rights found that half of the Mexican American schoolchildren in the Southwest attended schools with a Mexican American majority, and a quarter of these students attended schools whose Mexican American population reached 85–100 percent.[31] As late as 1971, "nearly half of the 30 elementary schools" in the El Monte area were found to be ethnically "imbalanced," according to standards set by the state of California to ensure that the demographic characteristics of individual school populations matched those of the entire district population.[32]

In other words, even though El Monte parents formed a robust, politically active Mexican American community, their desegregation victory did not bring an end to the segregating tendencies and racist attitudes that continued to shape the school experiences of El Monte's Mexican American children. Nor could integration erase the harm done to the generations of students who attended the Lexington School. In 2015, Ernie Gutiérrez, Olga's husband and an El Monte community leader, said that school segregation had caused "severe damage" to the Mexican-descended population of his hometown.[33] Ernie Gutiérrez identified this damage as psychological harm to Mexican Americans' sense of self-worth: students coming from segregated schools suffered from "feelings of inferiority" when they "were forced to compete with Anglo students" who had received better academic preparation. In addition to this unfair competition, Anglo American students often mocked their Mexican American classmates for being culturally different.[34]

As the effects of segregation have lingered—and segregation in poorly disguised forms continues to exist—it is critical to document and share stories of segregation in places like El Monte. Olga Gutiérrez knew this in 1981 when she described her thesis as a "search for a truth that had to be told."[35] But there are only two available copies of her thesis, both shelved in university collections that are difficult for the public to access. Much like the history she recovered, Gutiérrez's research has not received the attention it deserves.

Notes

Epigraph: Olga Gutiérrez, oral history interview, January 8, 2015, South El Monte Arts Posse (SEMAP), East of East: Mapping Community Narratives in El Monte and South El Monte, http://www.semapeastofeast.com.

1 Olga Gutiérrez, "Analyzing Segregation in El Monte: The Lexington School," MA thesis, California State University, Los Angeles, 1981, iii.
2 Olga Gutiérrez, oral history interview, SEMAP.
3 Rubén Donato and Jarrod S. Hanson, "Legally White, Socially 'Mexican': The Politics of De Jure and De Facto School Segregation in the American Southwest," *Harvard Educational Review* 82, no. 2 (Summer 2012): 210.
4 On the connections between urban segregation and school segregation in the agricultural town of Oxnard in Southern California, see David G. García, *Strategies of Segregation: Race, Residence, and the Struggle for Educational Equality* (Oakland: University of California Press, 2018).
5 Donato and Hanson, "Legally White, Socially 'Mexican,'" 213–214.
6 D. García, *Strategies of Segregation*, 80–83.
7 Gilbert G. Gonzalez, *Chicano Education in an Era of Segregation* (Denton: University of North Texas Press, 2013), 183–185.
8 Quoted in O. Gutiérrez, "Analyzing Segregation in El Monte," Appendix B.
9 Quoted in O. Gutiérrez, "Analyzing Segregation in El Monte," Appendix D, 5.
10 Mario T. García, "Americans All: The Mexican American Generation and the Politics of Wartime Los Angeles, 1941–45," *Social Science Quarterly* 65, no. 2 (1984): 282.
11 O. Gutiérrez, "Analyzing Segregation in El Monte," 24.
12 Ibid., 23–24.
13 Diane Conover and Anthony Estrada, "Interview with Augustine Ramos," in *Personal Stories from the El Monte Communities*, ed. Susan Sellman Obler (Whittier, CA: Rio Hondo College, 1978), 85.
14 O. Gutiérrez, "Analyzing Segregation in El Monte," 16–17.
15 M. García, "Americans All," 283.
16 O. Gutiérrez, "Analyzing Segregation in El Monte," 18.
17 Ibid., 20.
18 Ibid., Appendix F, 3.
19 Donato and Hanson, "Legally White, Socially 'Mexican,'" 214–217. The 1946 case, while increasingly analyzed by scholars, still remains far more obscure to the general public than *Brown*. See Philippa Strum, *Mendez v. Westminster: School Desegregation and Mexican-American Rights* (Lawrence: University Press of Kansas, 2010).
20 O. Gutiérrez, "Analyzing Segregation in El Monte," 21–22.
21 For more about racism and public health in Los Angeles, see Natalia Molina, *Fit to Be Citizens? Public Health and Race in Los Angeles, 1879–1939*, (Berkeley: University of California Press, 2006).
22 O. Gutiérrez, "Analyzing Segregation in El Monte," 21.
23 For similar comments from Mexican American interviewees who experienced segregation (and integration) as children in Oxnard, California, see D. García, *Strategies of Segregation*, chapters 2 and 4.
24 Patti Barry and Andrea Lopez, "Interview with Lupe Ruiz," in *Personal Stories*

from the El Monte Communities, ed. Susan Sellman Obler (Whittier, CA: Rio Hondo College, 1978), 98.

25 Quoted in O. Gutiérrez, "Analyzing Segregation in El Monte," 25.

26 Ibid., 24.

27 Ibid., 22.

28 Ibid., 28.

29 Donato and Hanson, "Legally White, Socially 'Mexican,'" 218.

30 Ibid., 220.

31 United States Commission on Civil Rights, *Mexican American Education Study*, 6 vols. (Washington: Government Printing Office, 1971).

32 "13 Schools in El Monte Cited as Imbalanced," *Los Angeles Times*, November 28, 1971. In the El Monte City School District, this meant that each school should have a Mexican American population of 21.5–51.5 percent. Yet many school populations did not fall within this range, and the district had actually grown more "imbalanced" since the late 1960s, after an "influx of Spanish-surnamed families" to South El Monte (ibid.).

33 Ernie Gutiérrez, oral history interview, January 14, 2015, South El Monte Arts Posse (SEMAP), East of East: Mapping Community Narratives in El Monte and South El Monte, http://www.semapeastofeast.com.

34 O. Gutiérrez, "Analyzing Segregation in El Monte," 26–27.

35 Ibid., 3.

9

"City of Achievement"

The Making of the City of South El Monte, 1955–1976

NICK JURAVICH

The official seal of the City of South El Monte bears the phrase "City of Achievement" around its edge. Pictured inside are a gold trophy, a shield that reads "All America City," and the silhouettes of a factory and a 1950s-style ranch house, with the words "incorporated in 1958."

At first glance, this seal seems generic. Thousands of cities and towns in greater Los Angeles and across the United States were incorporated in the two decades after World War II. Nearly all of them were founded on a combination of industrial and residential development in suburban areas, development that was subsidized and segregated (racially and economically) by a combination of government programs and private actors. Nearly all of these new cities and towns promised "all-American" dreams of suburban prosperity to prospective business owners and residents, who they hoped would be primarily, if not exclusively, middle-class and white.[1]

The founding of South El Monte took place in the context of these regional and national transformations, and the city's founders hoped it would prosper like the suburbs around it. Early on, they did their best to lure businesses and middle-class white residents to South El Monte, but their efforts yielded little success. From its beginning, the city lacked the land, infrastructure, and racial exclusivity necessary to attract substantial suburban wealth in postwar America.[2]

However, the history of this "City of Achievement" is also a story of local organizing by Mexican and Mexican American residents, who repeatedly challenged the dominant racial order of suburban development and reimagined how their city could serve a diverse, working-class population.[3] Residents of the area fought to found South El Monte against the expectations of regional planners in the 1950s. Leaders of the new city built partnerships between voluntary organizations and city government to improve its landscape and infrastructure in the 1960s, creating a culture of civic involvement in the process. In the 1970s, inspired by the Chicano movement and led by a new generation of activists, the people of South El Monte expanded this local organizing tradition, working to improve schools, medical care, employment prospects, and recreational opportunities for themselves and their neighbors.

Their efforts did not go unnoticed, and South El Monte received several national awards for civic participation in its first twenty years, two of which now appear on the city's seal. There is something ironic about these victories: a city that was not particularly high achieving by the standards of suburban racial capitalism outshone its richer neighbors in measures of community engagement. Local organizing did not enrich South El Monte or its residents, but it did make people happier, healthier, and better able to meet the challenges of working-class life in the United States in the late twentieth century. What follows is a brief glimpse of some of the many ways that the people of South El Monte achieved this organizing tradition in their city.

For a multiracial group of property and business owners, the first struggle was creating a city where none existed. "They practically laughed us right out of that office," remembered Blanche Felix in 1977. She and a local factory owner had gone to meet with representatives of the city of El Monte in the early 1950s to discuss annexation. At the time, South El Monte was an unincorporated area of Los Angeles County. Thousands of residents, primarily farmworkers, lived in *colonias* in the area, but without an incorporated city government, they did not have access to adequate municipal services. For property owners and industrialists, the lack of infrastructure also limited their ability to develop their land and expand their businesses. Felix hoped that El Monte would annex the area, as it had many others, but she was told that "that area was only fit for chickens." The regional zoning board had designated South El Monte as "an agricultural area that actually nobody wanted," including the city to the north.[4]

Felix was not deterred. After "two years of fighting every inch of the way," she and several other local leaders won an industrial rezoning of the area in 1955. Residential developments began to grow as well. Beatriz Perez, whose father supervised the drainage of South El Monte for development and sewer construction, remembered that her family and others "weren't allowed to buy property in El Monte . . . the way the deeds read, no Mexican people could buy *no mas* . . . not even Japanese."[5] In response, her father bought ten acres on Loma Avenue and Fawcett Avenue in what became South El Monte. "He put up his own streets, his own lighting. He paid for everything," Perez recalled. He then sold the lots for houses "just to show them that we could have just as nice houses as anybody else."[6] Having been refused by El Monte, residents decided to incorporate on their own. In 1958, they voted to become a city by a two-to-one margin, achieving the official creation of the city of South El Monte.

Joseph Vargas owned a large swath of land called the Vargas Ranch in what became South El Monte. Like Felix and Perez, he recalled extensive segregation in the San Gabriel Valley as a motivating factor for incorporation. He had come to South El Monte in 1927, when "discrimination existing in this area was rampant," and caused a scene in El Monte just after World War II by threatening to sue a pool hall for posting a sign that read "No Mexicans Allowed." Years later, he marveled that "from this extreme set-up," he was elected to lead South El Monte in 1964, becoming the city's first mayor of Mexican descent.[7]

The stories told by Vargas, Felix, and Perez echo those collected by Wendy Cheng in the western San Gabriel Valley. Cheng found that the experiences of Latino/a/x and Asian residents who navigated the racial hierarchies of the housing and job markets in the 1950s "did not usually translate into a commitment to the exclusionary mandates" when these people became property owners. Instead, they "articulat[e] relationships to property based on distinctly antiracist, non-white identifications."[8] South El Monte's founders hoped the city would be a place to develop their land and businesses free from the discrimination they encountered elsewhere. They also sought a space where they could celebrate their Mexican heritage. Beginning in 1958, Vargas hosted annual fiestas to celebrate the city's birthday and Mexican Independence Day at his ranch. The events were well attended: across the four census tracts that cover South El Monte, 15–25 percent of residents had Spanish surnames in 1960.[9]

Most of these Spanish-surnamed residents, of course, did not own land or factories. Those who did, including Vargas, espoused formal commitments to antiracism, but they also aimed to shape South El Monte into an ideal suburb for investment in their property. In seeking to "unleash the value of land as real estate," these elites worked within a system of suburban property ownership and management structured by "a white supremacist politics" (as described by Nathan D. B. Connolly in his study of Miami).[10] The goal of building an antiracist city thus existed in tension with goal of making South El Monte attractive to investors. These tensions constrained elite antiracism by Vargas and others in the decade that followed.

The San Gabriel Valley, like much of suburban Los Angeles, grew rapidly in the 1960s. However, development continued to be an uneven process, reflecting the efforts of elite and middle-class white suburbanites "to monopolize and segregate the assets of postwar prosperity."[11] Cities like El Monte, which resident Frank Lara remembered as "kind of a racial town," catered to white residents in several ways.[12] For example, the cities annexed newly built subdivisions that were segregated by racist real estate and lending practices. These cities also offered financial incentives to lure businesses while allowing owners to segregate their establishments.

When suburbanites were required to address the needs of their nonwhite, working-class neighbors (as was the case in California's large unified school districts), the results were similarly unequal. Augustine Ramos, who moved to El Monte as a child in the 1930s, recalled that the school he attended was "strictly for Mexican and Japanese children."[13] Nearly thirty years later—after the construction of several new schools in the area, the Supreme Court decision in *Brown v. Board of Education*, and local and national protests demanding desegregation—the California Board of Education found that thirteen schools in the El Monte area still "fail[ed] to meet state regulations governing the racial composition of schools."[14]

The segregation of suburban spaces by race and class did not go unchallenged. South El Monte's Frank Lara remembered that "the Second World War did change a lot," as returning soldiers sought in their own communities the democracy they had fought for abroad.[15] Equally important in these years were the efforts of women. Mothers, including Felix and Perez, joined parent-teacher associations to demand quality education for their children.[16] Their teenage children created what the historian Matt Garcia calls "artistic expressions of alternative cultural formation" when they challenged geographies of exclusion by gathering at integrated rock-and-roll venues, including El Monte's American Legion Stadium.[17]

At the same time, participation in suburban real estate markets demanded repudiations of overt antiracist activism. In 1963, Vargas, then vice mayor of South El Monte, appeared at a seminar on "merit employment" and argued that Mexican Americans should not join an integration drive being led by black Angelenos. "I have a deep sympathy and understanding for the Negro situation," Vargas said, "but the fact is, the Mexican-American people do not have a common problem and cannot be helped—but only retarded—by linking their situation to the Negro."[18] Rather than challenge exclusion head-on, as he had in his youth, Vargas now sought to consolidate power and manage the needs of Mexican American residents of South El Monte through suburban investment and civic voluntarism. In the long run, the latter proved more successful than the former, leading later generations of South El Monte's leaders to embrace more robust activism.

Seeking to expand opportunities for growth in the early 1960s, South El Monte tried to annex some unincorporated areas, but this strategy was limited

FIG. 10 Men posing and working on the corner of Rush and Merced. (Courtesy of South El Monte Arts Posse and South El Monte City.)

by both natural geography and the presence of El Monte, a more aggressively expansionist neighbor, to the north. As a working-class community, South El Monte could not promise tax breaks or access to free-spending consumers to lure commerce in the same ways as wealthier cities. Instead, the city relied on the efforts of local businesses to grow its tax and employment base.[19] To improve and beautify the city, its leaders turned to voluntarism and local employment, opening up new spaces for residents to participate in government and articulate their own visions for the city.

As South El Monte developed this tradition of civic engagement, local leaders began to apply for, and win, awards for this work. These victories recognized campaigns that combined volunteer work with city-sponsored employment and educational programs, and they cemented the value of community organizing in the minds of many residents. In 1965, the city government organized a city beautification and cleanup project that involved one out of every eight residents. The impressive turnout earned them the grand prize in the National Cleanest Cities Achievement Award Contest. Lady Bird Johnson, the First Lady, presented the award to the mayor and city councillors in Washington, D.C., calling South El Monte "a small city with a big heart."[20] The award, a golden trophy, was added to the city's seal.

The city elites—business and property owners—who organized these campaigns espoused a wide range of political philosophies. Not all of them believed in using municipal power to address segregation and inequality. James Law, a white resident of South El Monte who owned a demolition business on Potrero Avenue, was a member of the John Birch Society who voted for Barry Goldwater in 1964; according to his son, he hated what he called "welfarism." At the local level, however, he supported Vargas, his neighbor, for mayor in 1964 and worked with the Rotary Club to sponsor volunteer beautification campaigns while also supporting business-friendly tax laws and opposing expanded social welfare programs.[21] Vargas's 1963 comments about civil rights activism may well have been influenced by the need to maintain good relations with conservative white residents and business owners such as Law. For many other residents, however, the public-private partnerships between volunteers and the city in the 1960s set the stage for more robust programs of municipal employment and education in the 1970s.

By the late 1960s, South El Monte had largely failed to attract businesses and middle-class residents through traditional suburban promises of cheap land, low taxes, and racial homogeneity. However, the city's commitment to community involvement did attract a new generation of professionally trained, civic-minded Mexican and Mexican American leaders. Pete Nuñez was born in Calexico and spent his youth migrating to Fresno and Merced in the summers with his farmworker parents. After returning to school to earn a degree in dentistry at the University of Southern California (USC) in 1973, he decided to practice in South El Monte, where "there was no dentist." As he explained in 1977, "my goal is eventually to set up the whole corner [where his office was located] as a dental center for this community." After choosing South El Monte, Nuñez "got involved in school activities," giving free dental exams to local children.[22]

Education also brought Fernando Ledesma, a Marine Corps veteran and USC track star, to El Monte and South El Monte. His college coach, who helped him land his first job, told him, "I'm going to send you where you can work with some Mexican-American people that need models" and got him an interview in the El Monte Unified School District. Ledesma's first job was coaching track and teaching Spanish at Arroyo High School, but as he remembered, "soon I found myself in the continuation school [Valle Lindo High School, on the site of what is now South El Monte High School] as a counselor and working the night school [for adults] as a counselor." Parents and administrators recognized Ledesma as a leader, and when gang activity became a problem at Mountain View High School in the early 1970s, they asked him to take over as principal.[23]

As Ledesma recalled, he planned to sidestep the challenge, but when he went home and told his wife about it, she rebuked him. "You went into [education] to help people in the community when they needed you" she told him, "And here you are, your people are wanting you over there." Ledesma took the job in 1974, pouring his passion for education into the challenges the students faced. "These are my people, my kids," he told an interviewer in 1977, "and I'll fight for them, and they know it, and I'll go to court for any one of these kids and I do." Gang violence did not disappear overnight, but conditions at the high school improved. Ledesma credited "unbelievable" support from the community, particularly in building a bilingual education program that "provided more jobs for people in the community, teachers as well as aides and kids."[24] Reymundo "Ray" Guzmán, who attended El Monte Unified schools in the 1970s, recalled that he "didn't speak a word of English" when his family moved to South El Monte from Mexicali.[25] He and his brothers encountered racism initially and, as they got older, gang violence. Still, Guzmán felt that the situation had improved by the time he graduated from high school in 1981, a testament to the efforts of many educators in these years.[26]

As these stories demonstrate, South El Monte faced new challenges in the late 1960s and early 1970s. The headlines of the annual economic development forecasts in the *Los Angeles Times* charted this change, as cheery prognostications of continued growth gave way to predictions like "Valley's Way of Life to Be Altered in 1969: Freeway Jobs Top List; Drug Use, Blight, Segregation, VD Are Targets for Eradication."[27] At the local level, suburban growth slowed as the San Gabriel Valley matured. Cities that had once expanded their tax bases through constant new construction and annexation now faced the prospect of either raising taxes or cutting services, while the workers who had built the freeways, factories, and houses faced layoffs and prolonged unemployment. Many became long-haul truckers, traveling far from home on the same freeways that had once promised to bring prosperity to the San Gabriel Valley.[28] These local challenges were compounded by the stagnation of the national economy during the 1970s, which led to cuts in federal funding for cities—particularly funding for social services.

South El Monte's working-class population was hit hard by rising unemployment. Still, local residents continued to organize. The people of El Monte, who now faced similar challenges, joined with them in greater numbers than ever before. South El Monte and El Monte share a school district, and many residents concentrated their efforts on improving local education. Many of these efforts connected explicitly with the emerging Chicano movement, in terms of both demands for self-determination and respect and everyday efforts to create new services and programs for underserved Mexican American communities.[29]

Valle Lindo High School, where Ledesma was a counselor, was one focal point of these efforts (the school was later renamed for Ledesma). A high school for students who "have become disciplinary problems in their regular classrooms or have to work part time to support their families," the school also served adults in the community with night classes, and people from all walks of life worked to support it. The Rotary Club of South El Monte created a "business buddy" system to generate jobs for students at the school.[30] In an acknowledgment of his community work, the principal of the school, Martin C. Montano, was hired as the consultant for Mexican affairs by the Pomona Unified School District after La Raza Unida de Pomona threatened a student strike on account of the district's lack of Mexican staff (La Raza described Montano as "the best pick").[31] After he left Valle Lindo, the school continued to innovate, offering pre- and postnatal care to young mothers in 1971 and adding a day-care center for students with children, staffed by community members, in 1976.[32]

At other schools, parents organized. In the Valle Lindo District, which served elementary schools in both South El Monte and El Monte, mothers calling themselves PICA (Parents Involved in Community Action) called meetings to demand that the superintendent keep them informed about the performance of their children and the district's plans for the use of federal monies, as required by law.[33] Maria Ávila, a local mother who went back to college at the age of forty-two, got her start organizing within the parent-teacher associations at her children's schools. In the 1970s, she founded the Mexican Youth Council and worked with the El Monte Boys Club, both of which worked with local gang members to reduce violence and provide job opportunities. She also took a position with a local health network, doing family education. Throughout her activism, she emphasized a direct message: "Vote. Educate. Participate at all levels."[34]

Of course, community action alone could not make up for the unequal distribution of resources, even as it provided jobs to local residents. Students who faced these kinds of inequalities responded by organizing. They chartered a chapter of Movimiento Estudiantil Chicano de Atzlan (MEChA) at Mountain View High School in 1973, the year before Ledesma arrived as principal. At the time, Mountain View served over half of South El Monte's high school students (South El Monte High School was not yet built), and 53 percent of students were of Mexican descent. David Flores, a student at the school, explained that organizing with MEChA "would help us in trying to get out and become something . . . the club would be basically helping ourselves in education."[35] PICA supported their efforts, even if many people in the older generation preferred to identify themselves as Mexican or Mexican American (as opposed to Chicano). Still, after the club encountered resistance from administrators and white students, these adults supported the rights of their students to organize. Ávila, a generation older, embraced the term, describing herself as "a Chicano militant in a different way."

Ávila's embrace of the new generation's activism was echoed, in a more muted way, by none other than Vargas. Interviewed in 1977, he said, "We are tremendously indebted to the Black minority, for what has developed in the civil rights field."[36] Vargas's change of heart is a reminder, in the words of the Southern Californian scholar Robin D. G. Kelley, that people do not take part in uniform activism across time and space but are "constantly inventing new ways to rebel, ways rooted in our own peculiar circumstances."[37] Now a local elder, Vargas witnessed the outpouring of activism that sustained the city in the 1970s and recognized the influence of the movement that he had once shunned in the name of moderation.

By the 1970s, then, elite-driven voluntarism had given way to more explicit programs of municipal employment, education, and empowerment in South El Monte. These programs did more than create entry-level municipal jobs, though the value of this income was significant for working-class residents. As earlier efforts had redefined an agricultural area as an urban community, these new programs defined working-class people as essential partners in achieving equality and prosperity in South El Monte. Programs of employment brought people into official spaces—schools, clinics, and community centers—as agents of both the city and the community, where they provided health care, improved education, and celebrated Chicano life and culture.[38]

The public, spatial quality of this work was most visible in the murals created by young *monteros* in South El Monte and El Monte as part of a federally funded Comprehensive Employment and Training Act program in 1974. On a wall of the Valle Lindo Continuation High School, where Ledesma worked for many years, they painted an interpretation of David Siqueiros's "America Tropical."[39] Their efforts brought the aesthetics and politics of what Andrew Sandoval-Strausz calls "Latino urbanism" into public view in an official, publicly owned space.[40]

One year later, in 1975, South El Monte received its sixth national civics award since its founding, the All-America City Award. In choosing South El Monte, the awards committee recognized a place that was, in many respects, representative of the future of American cities: proudly multiracial, with a program of public-sector jobs designed to mobilize the skills and values of residents and respond to increasing inequality and deindustrialization. As the *Los Angeles Times* reported, "Involvement of residents in efforts to cope with such problems as juvenile crime and a lack of health and childcare facilities has earned South El Monte an All-America City Award" from the National Municipal League. One of twelve cities selected across the nation, and the only one from California, South El Monte was honored for several programs, including Nuñez's free dental clinics, and particularly for "the involvement of residents and the volunteer leadership." The photo that accompanied the newspaper article pictured members of the local Flores gang painting over graffiti. South El Monte was not without many problems—as the article noted, it had the highest school dropout rate, the fewest doctors, and the highest crime rate in the area—but the city's response to these problems, rooted in community organizing, continued to win national awards.[41] Irony persisted, as well: a city that did not achieve wealth or elite status within the racial hierarchy of American suburbia was deemed all-American as a result of its thoroughly Mexican American organizing tradition.

The work of achieving a livable community was far from finished in 1975, but the residents of South El Monte remained committed to the task and to one another. The city's organizing tradition had evolved considerably from the elite-driven efforts of the 1950s, drawing inspiration from both local organizing and transnational movements for self-determination. The shield of the "All-America City" award was added to the South El Monte's seal, as a reminder of the city's robust community organizing and an inspiration to future generations. As Nuñez put it in 1977, "To the next generation, I would like to say don't underestimate yourself. The key to success is persistence."[42]

Notes

1 There is a vast scholarly literature on postwar suburbanization that illuminates the role of the state, in partnership with landowners and business owners, in building and segregating the metropolitan landscape. See, among many others, David Freund, *Colored Property: State Policy and White Racial Politics in Suburban America* (Chicago: University of Chicago Press, 2007); Andrew Highsmith, *Demolition Means Progress: Flint, Michigan and the Fate of the American Metropolis* (Chicago: University of Chicago Press, 2014); Kenneth T. Jackson, *Crabgrass Frontier: The Suburbanization of the United States* (New York: Oxford University Press, 1985); Kevin M. Kruse and Thomas J. Sugrue, eds., *The New Suburban History* (Chicago: University of Chicago Press, 2006); Lisa McGirr, *Suburban Warriors: The Origins of the New Right* (Princeton, NJ: Princeton University Press, 2001); Becky M. Nicolaides, *My Blue Heaven: Life and Politics in the Working-Class Suburbs of Los Angeles, 1920–1965* (Chicago: University of Chicago Press, 2002); Robert Self, *American Babylon: Race and the Struggle for Postwar Oakland* (Princeton, NJ: Princeton University Press, 2003).

2 The struggles of South El Monte to attract capital investments in land and businesses as a working-class, racially mixed city mirror the struggles of demographically similar suburbs elsewhere in California, including Compton in the Los Angeles area and Milpitas in the Bay Area. See Self, *American Babylon*; Emily E. Straus, *Death of a Suburban Dream: Race and Schools in Compton, California* (Philadelphia: University of Pennsylvania Press, 2015).

3 In making this point, this chapter argues that South El Monte is an early example of what Andrew K. Sandoval-Strausz has analyzed as Latino urbanism, fueled by sweat equity, small businesses, and community-building practices developed and sustained through transnational exchange ("Latino Landscapes: Postwar Cities and the Transnational Origins of a New Urban America," *Journal of American History* 101, no. 3 (December 2014). See also Mike Davis, *Magical Urbanism: Latinos Reinvent the U.S. Big City* (New York: Verso, 2000).

4 Jane Perry and David Rocha, "Interview with Blanche Felix," in *Personal Stories*

from the El Monte Communities, ed. Susan Sellman Obler (Whittier, CA: Rio Hondo College, 1978), 20–21.

5 Irma Hernandez and Javier Valencia, "Interview with Beatriz Perez." in *Personal Stories from the El Monte Communities*, ed. Susan Sellman Obler (Whittier, CA: Rio Hondo College, 1978), 64–65.

6 Ibid.

7 Ed Reyes and Bev Sahagian, "Interview with Joseph Vargas," in *Personal Stories from the El Monte Communities*, ed. Susan Sellman Obler (Whittier, CA: Rio Hondo College, 1978), 111.

8 Wendy Cheng, "The Changs Next Door to the Diazes: Suburban Racial Formation in Los Angeles's San Gabriel Valley," *Journal of Urban History* 39 (November 2012): 15–35. Cheng's analysis shares Sandoval-Strausz's conclusion that Latino/a/x property and business owners practiced and performed certain solidarities with their neighbors, tenants, and workers and thus did not exploit the privileges of class and property ownership to the extent possible within the system of suburban racial capitalism. In founding a suburb intentionally free of formal segregation, the efforts of South El Monte's founders echo the efforts of black suburbanites in the American South detailed by Andrew Wiese in *Places of Their Own: African American Suburbanization in the Twentieth Century* (Chicago: University of Chicago Press, 2004).

9 Social Explorer, Total Population: Puerto Rican or Spanish Surname (based on data from U.S. Census Bureau), 1960, accessed July 29, 2019, https://www.socialexplorer.com/58bf302bcf/view. By 1970, the majority of people living in these four census tracts had Spanish surnames: Total Population, Puerto Rican or Spanish Surname (based on data from U.S. Census Bureau), 1970, accessed July 29, 2019, https://www.socialexplorer.com/da858bccab/view.

10 N.D.B. Connolly, *A World More Concrete: Real Estate and the Remaking of Jim Crow South Florida* (Chicago: University of Chicago Press, 2014), 3 and 7. In contrast to the analysis of Cheng and Sandoval-Strausz, Connolly argues that property-owning black Miamians compromised with, and benefited from, the city's Jim Crow order. Their class interests thus substantially undermined their ability to seek true racial equality. On the inherent racism built into American real estate (and capitalism more broadly), see also Keeanga-Yamahtta Taylor "Housing Market Racism Persists Despite 'Fair Housing' Laws," *Guardian*, January 24, 2019, and *Race for Profit: How Banks and the Real Estate Industry Undermined Black Homeownership* (Chapel Hill, NC: University of North Carolina Press, 2019).

11 Self, *American Babylon*.

12 Sahagian and Reyes, "Interview with Frank Lara." On residential segregation, see Connolly, *A World More Concrete*; Freund, *Colored Property*; Jackson, *Crabgrass Frontier*; and Self, *American Babylon*.

13 Diane Conover and Anthony Estrada, "Interview with Augustine Ramos," in *Personal Stories from the El Monte Communities*, 85. On school segregation in El Monte, see Rachel Grace Newman, "Schools for All," chapter 8 in this volume.

14 Mike Castro, "Thirteen Schools in El Monte Cited as Imbalanced," *Los Angeles Times*, November 28, 1971.

15 Sahagian and Reyes, "Interview with Frank Lara," 45. On residential segregation, see Connolly, *A World More Concrete;* David Freund, *Colored Property: State Policy and White Racial Politics in Suburban America* (Chicago: University of Chicago Press, 2007); Jackson, *Crabgrass Frontier*; Self, *American Babylon*.

16 Perry and Rocha, "Interview with Blanche Felix," 26–27; Hernandez and Valencia, "Interview with Beatriz Perez," 70–71.

17 Matt Garcia, *A World of Its Own: Race, Labor, and Citrus in the Making of Greater Los Angeles, 1900–1970* (Chapel Hill: University of North Carolina Press, 2001), 7.

18 Quoted in "Mexican-Americans May Shun Integration Drive," *Los Angeles Times*, August 9, 1963.

19 In "Latino Landscapes," Sandoval-Strausz discusses the importance of small, community-oriented businesses for sustaining and reshaping urban spaces, a process visible in South El Monte.

20 Quoted in Lorraine Barnes, "Mrs. LBJ Makes Awards," *Washington Post*, February 16, 1966.

21 Dana Law, oral history interview, January 12, 2015, South El Monte Arts Posse, East of East: Mapping Community Narratives in El Monte and South El Monte (www.semapeastofeast.com). On Southern Californian conservatism, including the growth of the John Birch Society and the Barry Goldwater campaign for president, see McGirr, *Suburban Warriors*.

22 Greg Hoard, "Interview with Pete Nuñez" in *Personal Stories from the El Monte Communities*, ed. Susan Sellman Obler (Whittier, CA: Rio Hondo College, 1978), 53.

23 Tony Estrada and Greg Hoard, "Interview with Fernando Ledesma" in *Personal Stories from the El Monte Communities*, ed. Susan Sellman Obler (Whittier, CA: Rio Hondo College, 1978), 52–54.

24 Ibid., 55–58.

25 Reymundo Guzmán, oral history interview, January 9, 2015. South El Monte Arts Posse (SEMAP), East of East: Mapping Community Narratives in South El Monte and El Monte, http://www.semapeastofeast.com.

26 Ibid.

27 John Grover, "Valley's Way of Life to Be Altered in 1969," *Los Angeles Times*, December 29, 1968.

28 Robert Irwin, oral history interview, January 10, 2015. South El Monte Arts Posse (SEMAP), East of East: Mapping Community Narratives in South El Monte and El Monte, http://www.semapeastofeast.com; Guzmán, oral history interview, SEMAP.

29 On the Chicano movement in El Monte, see Juan Herrera, "¡La Lucha Continua!," chapter 10 in this volume. Gloria Arellanes explains, "We were trying to say we feel there should be better schools, our kids should be able to go to school, we should have health services and different issues that most communities had" (interview by Virginia Espino, "La Batalla Está Aquí: The Chicana/o Movement in Los Angeles," sessions 1–6, accessed September 11, 2014, UCLA Library Center for Oral History Research, University of California, Los Angeles, http://oralhistory.library.ucla.edu/viewItem.do?ark=21198/zz002cftg9&title=Arellanes,%20Gloria.

30 Peyton Canary, "Rotary Project to Help Continuation Graduates." *Los Angeles Times*, June 13, 1969.

31 Quoted in "Valle Lindo Principal Named Mexican-American Consultant." *Los Angeles Times*, June 25, 1970.

32 "Pregnant Girls Get Special Aid," *Los Angeles Times*, April 2, 1971; "School Nursery Helps Mothers—Fathers, Too," *Los Angeles Times*, February 12, 1976.

33 PICA is also short for *picar* (to poke).
34 Margie Saucedo and Helen Phillips, "Interview with Maria Ávila" in *Personal Stories from the El Monte Communities*, ed. Susan Sellman Obler (Whittier, CA: Rio Hondo College, 1978), 4.
35 Quoted in Mike Castro, "Student Polarization Feared," *Los Angeles Times*, June 1, 1973.
36 Reyes and Sahagian, "Interview with Joseph Vargas" 112.
37 Robin D. G. Kelley, *Race Rebels: Culture, Politics, and the Black Working Class* (New York, Free Press, 1994), 3.
38 The creative use of federal antipoverty and employment funds in South El Monte mirrors similar grassroots efforts to realize the promises of the War on Poverty across the country. For an overview, see Annelise Orleck and Lisa Hazirjian, *The War on Poverty: A New Grassroots History* (Athens: University of Georgia Press, 2011).
39 Ron Reeder, oral history interview, January 14, 2015. South El Monte Arts Posse (SEMAP), East of East: Mapping Community Narratives in El Monte and South El Monte, http://www.semapeastofeast.com. Images of the mural appear in a 16 mm film discovered by SEMAP. See chapter 11 in this volume.
40 Andrew K. Sandoval-Strausz, "Latino Landscapes: Postwar Cities and the Transnational Origins of a New Urban America," *Journal of American History* 101, no. 3 (December 2014).
41 Mayerene Barker, "South El Monte Wins Award as All-America City," *Los Angeles Times*, April 17, 1975.
42 Hoard, "Interview with Pete Nuñez," 63.

10

¡La Lucha Continua!

Gloria Arellanes and the Women of the Chicano Movement

JUAN HERRERA

"So we moved here to El Monte, and I remember all the neighbors were white," recalled Gloria Arellanes in a 2011 interview conducted by the University of California, Los Angeles, Library Center for Oral History Research.[1] This was extremely different from East Los Angeles, where she was born in 1941. Growing up in El Monte was not easy, she explained. Unlike East Los Angeles, where ethnic solidarity and family had sheltered her, in El Monte, discrimination and racism were omnipresent. It was not uncommon for her to hear disparaging comments about Mexicans: "that we were lazy. . . . We're dirty. [Y]ou couldn't show your culture, and we didn't have a culture. We didn't even know our own culture." A child of a Mexican American father and Native American Tongva mother, she wrestled with her racial and cultural identity. Arellanes attributes this to the intense Americanization she encountered at school: "I remember coming home one time telling my dad that I was an American, and he says, 'No, you're a Chicano.'" Arellanes laughingly recalls how this brought her to tears. "No way, no, no, no. I'm American," she bawled to her father.

It is difficult to imagine that Arellanes ever denied her Chicano and Tongva heritage. In the heyday of 1960s social movement activism, she became one of the most influential activists of the Chicano movement. She is best known for her participation in the Brown Berets, where she became the only woman to hold a major leadership position and the driver of the organization's establishment of a free health clinic. As a self-proclaimed advocate for the underdog, Arellanes has dedicated her life to a diversity of projects for community improvement. Yet little is known historically about this important figure or about the connections she helped forge between El Monte and national social movements. A humble and selfless person, she has happily remained outside the spotlight. There is no doubt that Arellanes's activism and that of other women in the movement has been overlooked by historical renderings of this period, which have centered on heroic male figures.[2]

Gloria Arellanes and the Context of Youth

"I was born in East Los Angeles at the Mayo Clinic over there on Soto Street, and we lived in the Maravilla projects probably the first five years of my life," remembered Arellanes. Like many Mexican Americans in Southern California, her family had deep roots in East Los Angeles. Her childhood was all about family. "My mother came from a family of sixteen. My father's family was fourteen," she recalled. Her father came from a middle-class family that had migrated from Chihuahua and settled in Los Angeles by way of Texas. Arellanes warmly remembers hearing heroic stories about her grandfather growing up. At the height of the Depression, her grandfather had helped run a food distribution program that brought fresh produce and other staples to barrios like East Los Angeles. Despite being labeled a communist for his efforts, he went on to run a successful family business. As Arellanes explained: "They were ironsmiths, and so my grandfather on my dad's side had this shop in East Los Angeles right there on Mednick and Dozier." Through this successful business venture, her grandparents reached some degree of economic mobility: "My grandmother's house . . . was this big, big huge property, a two-story home. . . . They had the first residential phone in Los Angeles, and I remember it was a big black heavy thing, and you had to dial."

Then one day her father relocated the family to a brand-new home in El Monte, using benefits from the GI Bill. Arellanes's family joined the waves of Mexican Americans who moved from Los Angeles to the San Gabriel Valley in search of new opportunities. Southern California's postwar Mexican American population boom transformed many cities like El Monte.[3] The city's predominantly white residents did not stand idle while it underwent historic racial transformations. Arellanes recalls how the city's Nazi Party spearheaded vigilante attacks that targeted Mexicans. As in many other neighborhood spaces, young people confronted racial tension in school. Instead of a place of learning, school became a site for the policing of Mexican American youth.

According to Arellanes, racial conflict escalated into full race riots in El Monte High School, in which Anglo and Chicano students harassed and picked fights with one another. "I'm very tall and I'm big boned, so people were very afraid of me, period, so nobody wanted to fight with me anyways," she proudly recalled. Additional policing by local authorities exacerbated tensions between white and Chicano youths, but it also created solidarity among Chicanos, who had to stick together for protection.

In high school Arellanes helped form the Mexican American Youth Council, which, under the guidance of an Anglo counselor, created an organizational space for young Chicanos to cultivate solidarity and craft their own agendas. This initial form of organizing convinced her of the need to develop a politics around race that not only valorized Chicano culture but also disproved the harsh stereotypes about the group. Most importantly, it motivated her to participate in community projects intent on defending and caring for the Chicano community.

The Brown Berets

"[Before the movement] I cruised Whittier Boulevard," Arellanes laughingly admitted. "Yes, that's what we did, and that's how I came in contact with the East LA community, cruising Whittier Boulevard for many, many years." She remembered how one day, she and her friends wound up in a new space called the La Piranya coffeehouse. Intrigued by youth activities there, they entered, thinking it was a party. Once inside they were greeted by other young people who immediately tried to recruit them into the Brown Berets, a new organization. As she recalled, "There was something there that attracted us, and so I wanted to know more." Arellanes and her friends were fascinated with the organization's leaders and their commitment to the community. "So we kept going back, and eventually I said, Okay, I'm going to join, and we joined," she casually recollected. This encounter with early Chicano movement organizing, by way of the Brown Berets, forever changed her life.

The Chicano movement was an epochal transformation in the long history of Mexican American mobilizations.[4] Unified by a strong valorization of Chicano culture, activists forged a new style of politics centered on mass protest and more radical mobilizations. This new generation of activists was inspired by Cesar Chavez and other Mexican American leaders and selectively borrowed from both the African American civil rights movement and Black Power mobilizations. Though this period is framed in academic literature as purely militant and radical, the bulk of the movement's goals were actually quite moderate. The Brown Berets, for example, are historically identified as a paramilitary organization that led the Chicano armed struggle. By privileging these masculinist and militant portrayals, most analyses of the Brown

FIG. 11 Gloria Arellanes in photo booth. (Courtesy of Special Collections and Archives, John F. Kennedy Memorial Library, California State University, Los Angeles, Gloria Arellanes Papers.)

Berets overlook the expansive grassroots organizing and community care focus that undergirded the organization's formation and subsequent mobilizations. Movement participants called for basic human rights such as fair and equitable education and employment, demanded resources for the Chicano community, and denounced abusive treatment from law enforcement.[5]

The East Los Angeles chapter of the Brown Berets was formed through the meeting of different youth activist organizations and leaders that convened at La Piranya. Created in 1967 with the help of local Catholic Church leaders, La Piranya drew prominent civil rights leaders and neighborhood youth from activist circles.[6] It was here that the Berets drafted an agenda for the improvement of the Chicano community that came to be known as the Ten Point Program.[7] Their mission was expansive, including demands for unity within the Chicano community, equitable wages and resources, and community control over policing.[8] Only one point stressed the right to bear and keep arms. As the historian Lorena Oropeza argues, the "Berets' militancy—and notoriety—derived primarily from their speech rather than their actions."[9]

The Berets were fundamentally concerned with improving living conditions for Chicanos in East LA. This included linking youth to broader Chicano mobilizations, such as the Moratorium to End the War in Vietnam and transforming street youth into active participants in the improvement of the Chicano community. The Berets endeavored to transform youth into productive citizens and, most importantly, fighters in the Chicano revolution. Toward this end, they recruited gang members to help with community projects. As Arellanes recalled, "I was always pleased to know that the Chicano Movement had something to do with the leveling-out of gang violence and activities."[10]

Politicizing Community Care

As members of a new generation of youth activists, the Brown Berets initially encountered resistance from neighborhood residents. The Berets realized that militancy and radicalism further distanced them from the community they sought to help. Recalling their early outreach to the community, Arellanes commented: "So we go in there in our Brown Berets, we didn't have our bush jackets yet, and we had some kind of a flyer for some event. I remember people getting [the flyer]—they would look at me, 'Chicano?' and they'd get the paper and wad it up and throw it down on the floor." Aside from distrusting the Berets' revolutionary aesthetic, older residents did not understand why youth chose to call themselves "Chicanos"—which older residents saw as a pejorative term.[11] Despite their use of a militia style, the Berets were primarily committed to protecting and caring for the East Los Angeles community. "We were trying to say we feel there should be better schools, our kids should be able to go to school, we should have health services and different issues that most communities had," Arellanes observed. "It took a long, long time to gain people's confidence in us."

The Berets improved their reputation in the community by establishing the Barrio Free Clinic. In so doing, they joined a movement throughout the United States in which communities of color created free health clinics and other social services for neighborhood residents. The clinic was open in the evenings and had full health services, including a pharmacy. It was staffed by numerous volunteers, including many white nurses and doctors, and was coordinated by Arellanes. Although she was initially reluctant to take on the responsibility because of her concerns about the white professionals who were involved, the clinic became her pride and joy. In July 1969 she became its official director. "The clinic became my passion because it really addressed a real need in the community," Arellanes proudly remembered.

The Barrio Free Clinic was among the first free clinics established in a low-income, Spanish-speaking community.[12] The Berets presented the clinic as a community-driven project that provided health services in the absence of state social welfare programs in urban barrios.[13] Here clients could avail themselves of a variety of programs designed for Spanish-speaking residents, including controversial sex education and reproductive health counseling for youth.[14] It was also a cultural center of sorts, and its walls were adorned with a multiplicity of movement posters and murals to cultivate cultural pride. The clinic, along with the Brown Berets' major efforts to transform Chicano youth, demonstrates a much more complex vision of the organization. In addition to serving as the armed vanguard of the Chicano revolution, the Berets deployed diverse strategies to improve community welfare.[15]

Another example of the movement's numerous lines of struggle included the Brown Berets' participation in the Poor People's Campaign in 1968. Organized by Martin Luther King Jr. and the Southern Christian Leadership Conference, the Poor People's Campaign fundamentally called for the federal government to change conditions for the nation's racialized poor. For Arellanes, participation in this campaign helped her understand that the fight for social justice was national and multiracial in scope. Brown Beret participation in the campaign connected El Monte and Los Angeles to other sites of struggle and allowed participants to see the commonalities among Chicano, African American, and Native American communities. As Arellanes remembered, "To me, that was the biggest experience I had in terms of meeting diversity and people from other parts of the country, because you're raised in an area, you don't leave it, you don't travel, you don't take vacations."

Her participation in the Poor People's Campaign also shows the complexities of the Brown Beret mode of mobilizing. The fact that the Berets participated in a campaign that pressured the federal government to play a more active role in alleviating poverty, particularly for racialized groups, meant that the

Berets were not just about militancy and armed revolution. They found various ways to enact change centered on a vision of community care. This included working with government officials and Anglo professionals.

Women and Politics in the Chicano Movement

Like other 1960s and 1970s political movements, Chicano mobilizations were not free of internal divisions and contradictions. Many of the most contentious points revolved around the militancy or insufficient radicalism of certain organizations. Another major point of contention was the movement's misogyny. As Chicana feminists have argued, women in the movement played a foundational role in building community institutions and rarely received recognition for their work. For example, Arellanes revealed the pivotal role that women played in maintaining the clinic: "While we were doing that clinic . . . the men were not involved in it. . . . They let the women do it." Many of the female clinic volunteers alleged that male Berets were disrespectful of the clinic. Arellanes clarified that the men "started wanting to party there when the clinic was closed and hang around when I had patients with children." As the clinic's director, Arellanes ordered men to stay out of the clinic if they were not there to help. "I was very protective of that clinic," she explained. "I was Mama Bear there. You don't mess with my clinic or my clients or my patients or my services."

Arellanes garnered attention because of her outspoken nature. Appointed minister of finance and correspondence for the Brown Berets in the spring of 1968, she transgressed many barriers that blocked many other women in the movement. The Berets used titles such as "minister" for leadership positions as a way to emphasize the militaristic and hierarchical nature of the group. She credited her entry into predominantly male spaces to her ability to command attention through her voice and body: "I was very large in stature, very large. I weighed close to 300 pounds, I'm five-foot-eight, I was very big, and I was very bigmouthed." She lamented that as the only female Brown Beret minister, she was continually shut out of decision-making processes. For Arellanes, the title of minister meant nothing because she was primarily given administrative tasks. As she saw it, she served primarily as the organizations' "glorified secretary."

Nonetheless, Arellanes continued to voice her opposition to discrimination against women. As she told the interviewer Virginia Espino, "I saw the abuse the women got, and I fought for them." According to Arellanes, men expected the women to do all the cooking and cleaning without ever giving them credit for their contributions. This created irreparable conflicts among the leaders, and eventually women from the East LA Brown Berets left the organization.[16]

Despite her gendered consciousness, Arellanes would not have described herself as a feminist at the time of her organizing. She recalled how the men disparagingly called feminists "women's libbers," implying that the women had betrayed the Chicano cause by embracing feminism. At that time the Chicano movement overwhelmingly considered feminism as a white woman's political project. Arellanes argued: "At that point in time, white women's liberation was take your bra off, burn your bra. They were still activists, but we couldn't relate to that. Culturally it was just not something we wanted to do or thought it was liberating to do that." Arellanes criticized the white women's liberation movement for its narrow focus on the individual rights of women. At that time, she and other Chicanas were focused on the liberation of the entire community. "It was liberating for us to see our community come up, be organized, go to school and get better housing and health, get jobs," she recalled. "Stop the police harassment, the brutality that went on, the racism that went on."

Arellanes's participation in the Brown Berets and the larger Chicano movement was not without struggle. She confronted gender discrimination and single-handedly raised two children as a single mother. Yet this work was not in vain, and she has many fond memories of the 1960s and 1970s. Despite all the struggles she encountered in the movement, she was forever positively touched by her activism: "I had fun with the Brown Berets. . . . We were all young. . . . We protested. We went to marches. We went to rallies. We were always trying to recruit new people, so you're always meeting people and talking . . . and traveling up and down the state to other areas that were interested in setting up Brown Beret groups, and that was always a lot of fun and interesting."

Arellanes's history of robust activism helps us see how movement practices interacted with geographies such as El Monte that do not automatically fall into the register of the Chicano movement. She also shows us the interrelationship in struggle between Chicanos and other racial groups such as African Americans and Native Americans. Inspired by the Chicano movement valorizations of indigenous culture, Arellanes also became involved in a movement to reclaim her Tongva heritage by collaborating with different Native American groups and recreating Tongva ceremonial practices. She is now a respected elder in the Native American community. She continues to be a proud resident of El Monte and throughout her life has engendered diverse projects of community care. She transferred her commitment to social justice to her work in Los Angeles County and later in the Los Angeles sheriff's department. Through her everyday struggles to defend and advocate for Chicanos and other minorities, Arellanes is a living legacy of the Chicano movement. Her story demonstrates that we need to interpret the movement not as a historical artifact but as a living movement and a continuing struggle. As 1960s and 1970s activists commonly asserted, "¡La lucha continua!"

Notes

1 Gloria Arellanes, interview by Virginia Espino, "La Batalla Está Aquí: The Chicana/o Movement in Los Angeles," sessions 1–6, 2011, UCLA Library Center for Oral History Research, University of California, Los Angeles, http://oralhistory.library.ucla.edu/viewItem.do?ark=21198/zz002cftg9&title=Arellanes,%20Gloria. All quotes from Arellanes in this chapter are from this interview.

2 For an extensive analysis of the central role that Chicanas played in the movement, see Dolores Delgado Bernal, "Chicana School Resistance and Grassroots Leadership: Providing an Alternative History of the 1968 East Los Angeles Blowouts" (PhD diss., University of California, Los Angeles, 1997); Maylei Blackwell, *¡Chicana Power! Contested Histories of Feminism in the Chicano Movement* (Austin: University of Texas Press, 2011); Lorena Oropeza, *¡Raza Si! ¡Guerra No! Chicano Protest and Patriotism during the Viet Nam War Era* (Berkeley: University of California Press, 2005); Dionne Espinoza, Maria Eugenia Cotera, and Maylei Blackwell, eds., *Chicana Movidas: New Narratives of Activism and Feminism in the Movement* (Austin: University of Texas Press, 2018); Rosie C. Vermúdez, "Alicia Escalante, the Chicana Welfare Rights Organization, and the Chicano Movement," in *The Chicano Movement: Perspectives from the Twenty-First Century*, ed. Mario T. Garcia (New York: Routledge Press, 2014), 95–116; Juan Herrera, "Spatializing Chicano Power: Cartographic Memory and Community Practices of Care," *Social Justice* 42, nos. 2–3 (2015): 46–66.

3 Many different factors led to this population surge after World War II. The historian Ernesto Chavez attributes this increase to the baby boom among Mexican Americans and other groups; see Ernesto Chavez, *"¡Mi Raza Primero!" (My People First!): Nationalism, Identity, and Insurgency in the Chicano Movement in Los Angeles, 1966–1978* (Berkeley: University of California Press, 2002). Another major factor was a sweeping change in immigration policy set forth by the Immigration Act of 1965. In stark contrast from previous restrictionist immigration policies, this reform established the principle of formal equality in immigration, which opened the door to greater numbers of non-European migrants. As a result of this reform, increasing numbers of people from Latin American and Asia migrated to the United States. For an extensive analysis of immigration reform and the making of the modern United States, see Mae Ngai, *Impossible Subjects: Illegal Aliens and the Making of Modern America* (Princeton, NJ: Princeton University Press, 2004).

4 Chavez makes an important argument about seeing the *longue durée* of the making of a Chicano movement that interacted with a long tradition of Mexican American organizing. For an extensive analysis of this history, see Chavez, *"¡Mi Raza Primero!"*

5 Oropeza, *¡Raza Si! ¡Guerra No!*, 49.

6 Chavez, *"¡Mi Raza Primero!,"* 44; Dionne Espinoza, "'Revolutionary Sisters': Women's Solidarity and Collective Identification among Chicana Brown Berets in East Los Angeles, 1967–1970, *Aztlán* 26, no. 1 (2001): 17–58.

7 Chavez, *"¡Mi Raza Primero!,"* 49. The Ten Point Program was specifically modeled after the Black Panther Party mobilizations. For an extensive analysis of the Black Panther Party and its projects of community care, see Alondra Nelson, *Body and Soul: The Black Panther Party and the Fight against Medical Discrimination* (Minneapolis: University of Minnesota Press, 2011).

8 Chavez, *"¡Mi Raza Primero!,"* 49.
9 Oropeza, *¡Raza Si! ¡Guerra No!*, 137.
10 The gang culture that Arellanes describes was significantly different from today's context of mega gangs. For more information on the development of gang culture in Los Angeles, see James Diego Vigil, *Barrio Gangs: Street Life and Identity in Southern California* (Austin: University of Texas Press, 1988); Edward Orozco Flores, *God's Gangs: Barrio Ministry, Masculinity, and Gang Recovery* (New York: New York University Press, 2013).
11 For a discussion of the term "Chicano" and 1960s youth redefinition of the identity category see Oropeza, *¡Raza Si! ¡Guerra No!*, 82–92.
12 Other Brown Beret chapters experimented with other social welfare programs, including free breakfast programs. The Black Panthers were the pioneers in these types of mobilizations, including similar community clinics. For an analysis of the Black Panthers' relationship to projects of community health care, see Nelson, *Body and Soul*. For an analogous example of Mexican American community institution building endeavors, see Juan Herrera, "Unsettling the Geography of Oakland's War on Poverty: Mexican American Political Organizations and the Decoupling of Poverty and Blackness," *Du Bois Review* 9, no. 2 (2012): 375–393, and "Spatializing Chicano Power."
13 Dionne Espinoza, "'Revolutionary Sisters,'" 36.
14 As Arellanes goes on to explain, this was a controversial point in the clinic. The clinic was initially funded through donations from the local Catholic church, which vehemently disapproved of the sex education programs. Therefore, Arellanes had to find alternative sources of revenue to help support these services.
15 In her interview with Gloria Arellanes, Espino refers to this movement practice as "straddling different lines" of struggle.
16 Jennifer G. Correa, "The Targeting of the East Los Angeles Brown Berets by a Racial Patriarchal Capitalist State: Merging Intersectionality and Social Movement Research," *Critical Sociology* 37, no. 1 (2010): 83–10; Espinoza, "'Revolutionary Sisters.'"

11

Toward a Radical Arts Practice

Theater and Muralism during the Chicano Movement

CARRIBEAN FRAGOZA

South El Monte and El Monte were culturally and politically engaged communities that participated in larger civil rights movements, including the Chicano movement. Through the arts, specifically theater and muralism—two of what many regard as pillars of the Chicano arts and cultural renaissance of the 1960s and 1970s—local artists and youth created spaces in which they could publicly and collectively address their experiences as marginalized members of a community marked by racism. However, little evidence of theater and muralism projects remains today, as both cities' lack of institutional support and deeply ingrained racist narratives effectively prevented these budding cultural movements from taking root. Nonetheless, by piecing together personal photographs, newspaper clippings, forgotten film reels, and the stories of artists and residents, we can begin to see the shape of a political and cultural movement as it emerged from these barrio suburbs.

In South El Monte, El Teatro Urbano, a homegrown theater troupe inspired by El Teatro Campesino, was founded in 1970 by Rosemary Rodriguez and Rene Rodriguez, two young South El Monte residents, in an effort to raise cultural and political awareness among locals and to respond to national and international issues. Though the Rodriguezes managed to build a significant network of *teatro* groups in Southern California and strengthened the overall *teatro* movement that was part of a Chicano cultural renaissance, they struggled to pick up traction locally as they faced overt and internalized racism from their own community. Nonetheless, Teatro Urbano continued to produce self-supported plays and even films over the next several decades.

In the early 1970s, South El Monte, together with community members, implemented numerous nationally lauded public social service programs that included a muralism project as part of a youth gang prevention program. This was followed by a short-lived arts program funded by the Comprehensive Employment and Training Act (CETA), a significant federal program that also funded artists to engage in public arts projects as a civic service.[1] In 1977, CETA funded a summer mural program for students at Valle Lindo High School, a continuation school for at-risk students that was then located in South El Monte. This brief mural project prompted CETA to fund a series of murals and projects in El Monte by thirteen artists—a project that, despite its sparkling promise, would bring muralism in the city to a crashing end. Both the *teatro* and mural projects grew from community members' need to express their unique and vibrant identities and creatively address the socioeconomic inequities and racial discrimination they experienced in their neighborhoods.

Teatro Urbano

Sometimes the most enduring art is as much an act of love as it is one of resistance against injustice. For Rosemary and Rene Rodriguez, *teatro* was a way to to assert their love for the community they had grown up in and to speak out against the discrimination they had witnessed and experienced. At least that was the initial impetus for their Teatro Urbano. Nearly fifty years later, it is their love for one another, the family of children and grandchildren they raised in the *teatro*, and the unending struggle for justice for all Chicanos that has kept their *teatro* alive.

The Chicano movement that gave birth to countless *teatros* in all corners of the Southwest in the 1960s and 1970s has come and gone, yet its legacy remains in the stories and practices that have been handed down over generations.[2] It is also alive in the stories that have been rescued from obscurity, despite the forces of erasure. An ephemeral art by nature, *teatro*'s presence was whitewashed almost as soon as it was performed in public parks and streets. In the spirit of political arts at the time, Rosemary and Rene held workshops and rehearsed and performed with the purposes of creating direct action and education and of generating mass participation and significant intervention in an array of issues such as the historically practiced discrimination against people of color and more current and urgent ones such as the Vietnam War draft.

Teatro Urbano was part of a theater movement in the 1970s that was spearheaded by Teatro Campesino. Teatro Urbano was given its name by Teatro Campesino's director, Luis Valdez.[3] By the time Rosemary and Rene met Valdez, Teatro Campesino and the farmworkers' movement had begun to build support and activism far beyond the rural fields of the Central Valley, reaching to cities where urban Chicanos were building a movement of their own. Located on the outskirts of East Los Angeles (LA) and LA, South El Monte and El Monte were suburbs that consisted of Latino and Chicano barrios yet demonstrated many characteristics of large urban centers then as they do today.

Like many other young Chicanos, Rosemary and Rene learned while attending college about their heritage and how systematic racism is used to discriminate and oppress people of color. Through organizations like Movimiento Estudiantil Chicano de Aztlan (MEChA), they began their process of political awakening and were initiated into activism. Before long, they decided to return to their hometown in the hope of sparking more local interest in activism and art. They recognized the need to educate Latinos in South El Monte and El Monte about current issues, using *teatro* as a pedagogical vehicle.

Rosemary and Rene remember that while people were curious about their often impromptu performances in public spaces such as Legg Lake in the Whittier Narrows Parks, some audience members disagreed with their pro-immigrant, pro-Chicano, and antiwar politics. "Aesthetically people seemed to like what we were doing. The problem for some of them was what we were saying. Sometimes they didn't like that," says Rene. Ever since he can remember, El Monte was always a very propolice city. Some white residents disapproved of their representations of police officers as pigs or their representations of white people in general. "Back then we used white-face make up and blonde wigs. I can see why they wouldn't like that. But that's how we did things back then," observes Rosemary, recalling the *teatro*'s use of archetypes—a signature characteristic of the influential Teatro Campesino. Their employment of archetypes was directly borrowed from a long history of agitprop theater and, most specifically, from commedia dell'arte, an improvised popular comedy based on stock characters in sixteenth-century Italian theaters.[4]

However, in addition to the disapproval of white residents, Teatro Urbano also met with some distaste from Mexican American locals. Rosemary and Rene recall that many Mexican Americans were too ashamed of their own heritage. "Our own people used words like wetbacks and TJs. We had to educate people that it wasn't right," says Rosemary. But internalized racism is difficult to uproot. Like many Mexican Americans at the time, Rosemary remembers feeling embarrassed by the Mexican music her mother would play at home. "It was amazing how at the time I was so in denial about who I was," she says.[5]

Teatro Urbano had difficulties finding a receptive audience in South El Monte and El Monte not only among older generations of Mexican Americans, but also among young people who understood so little about how systematic racism steered them into low-wage labor, jail, or war. Rene recalls that when he was a student at El Monte High School, teachers, counselors, and administrators were quick to advise male students, particularly ones with disciplinary issues, to enlist in the military lest they end up in jail instead. College education was rarely offered as an option. These failings, by design of the public education system, became the rallying issue in 1968 when thousands of students throughout LA walked out of their high schools in protest.[6]

El Monte High School students were not unaffected by the strong political currents that swept through the nation during the civil rights movement. Rosemary recollects walking out of the school to take part in what she recognized as an important and growing component of the Chicano movement. But something was amiss: "We didn't know what we were fighting for. We knew things weren't good but we didn't know why we weren't being educated. We didn't have direction."[7] Unlike East LA, El Monte and South El Monte had not developed an activist and cultural infrastructure driven by politicized and college-educated Chicanos returning to their communities. It should be noted that the Chicano movement in LA did not grow in a vacuum, as it was supported by the training and financial backing of groups such as the United Farm Workers and the more radical sectors of the Catholic church. Despite being historical strongholds for Mexicans and Chicanos, South El Monte and El Monte—two suburbs beyond the peripheries and scope of LA—fell out of the political reach that would have made significant organizing and change possible.[8]

Instead, El Monte's young activist movement dissipated before it had a chance to grow. Many student protesters wandered off into a nearby park, made their way to the Tastee Freez across the street from the high school, or simply went home.

"It was very difficult to organize in El Monte," says Rosemary, not only politically to address issues that directly affected Mexicans and Mexican Americans, but also to build a community-based *teatro*. "We offered workshops but lot of people didn't want to act," she recalls.[9] According to Rene and Rosemary, one of the reasons for this lack of interest in acting had to do with the fact that in high school students of color were often excluded from drama classes and clubs that were typically reserved for white students. Rosemary adds that in general, the arts had no presence in El Monte and South El Monte with the exception of popular music venues—most notably Legion Stadium, where the popular disc jockey Art Laboe hosted regular concerts featuring rock and roll and rhythm and blues.[10]

However, Teatro Urbano found support in a wide network of *teatros*. It joined an international network of *teatro* groups in the United States and throughout Latin America called Teatro Nacional de Aztlan (TENAZ), and in 1974, Rene and other *teatristas* traveled to Mexico City for a historic convening of *teatros*.[11] After two weeks of performances, workshops, and conversations, Rene returned to South El Monte with a renewed sense of commitment to *teatro* and an expanded awareness of the pan-Latino struggle, to which Chicanos in the United States contributed.

As *teatro* proliferated throughout California and the Southwest, Teatro Urbano also formed a regional network of *teatros* in Southern California, that included groups from Pico Rivera, Norwalk, and other neighborhoods well beyond the usual bastions of Chicano activism in East LA. This network became essential to Teatro Unido and other small *teatros*, as they supported and helped one another strategize and organize festivals and gatherings between the annual TENAZ festivals. According to Rosemary, this mutual support among *teatros* was especially important because *teatros* like Teatro Urbano often struggled to gain the support of the communities they were attempting to serve: "Not even our own people accepted us. That's why we had to connect with communities nearby."[12]

Nonetheless, it was in El Monte's and South El Monte's art desert that Teatro Urbano began to sow its seeds. And despite the inhospitable environment—including a lack of municipal support, if not opposition—they insisted on preparing new generations of Chicanos to become artists and activists. Indeed, it was among the youngest people that Teatro Urbano had most success, and its offshoot, a children's theater called El Teatro Pequeño, became an independent entity. By then, several children's theaters had been created, including one in Pasadena, just a few miles north of El Monte.

Teatro Urbano's insistence on remaining community-based in a city that continues to be immune to the arts has kept it alive for more than four decades. Despite the challenges and lack of support, Rene and Rosemary recognize the advantages of running a fiercely grassroots theater. "We were more independent, not tied to a school or city government. It made us more committed," says Rosemary. The couple notes that unlike college-based theaters, where members participate only while they are enrolled students, community *teatros* have deeper roots among members who continue to reside locally over the years. "It's more like a family," says Rosemary. In fact, Rosemary and Rene, happily married for about four decades, have made Teatro Urbano a family affair, having raised their children and grandchildren in the *teatro* tradition. Though Teatro Urbano is now based in Montclair, they recognize South El Monte as their home. They continue to operate as Teatro Urbano, staging plays and, more recently, shooting a film about the murder of the Chicano journalist Ruben Salazar. Though the couple acknowledges that while some advances have been made thanks to the labor of activists like Gloria Arellanes (also from El Monte) and professional Chicanos, there is much left to be done. They believe that *teatro* and the arts are as necessary as ever and have no plans to retire Teatro Urbano. "We keep going because we can't give up," says Rene.[13]

The Mural Movement That Never Was

Murals, like *teatro* and much of the art produced during the civil rights movement and other periods of deep sociopolitical upheaval, are produced out of need. From the traces of such murals in South El Monte, we can learn much about the conditions of their making as well as about the individuals who painted them.

In South El Monte and El Monte, where murals have been all but obliterated from public memory, their phantom traces give us glimpses into the lives of South El Monte residents through much of the 1970s. When these fragments—found in dusty film reels, personal photo collections, and newspaper clippings—are pieced together, an uneven yet enlightening narrative of a self-driven community begins to come into focus.[14]

Images of young men and women in South El Monte in the early 1970s come to life in a short film produced and eventually forgotten by the City of South El Monte.[15] This film celebrated the city's national recognition when it was given an All-America City Award for its creative, multipronged approach to addressing its many challenges, including unemployment and gang activity. Long-haired teenagers suppress laughter as they try to perform for the camera

FIG. 12 Youth in front of mural. (Courtesy of South El Monte Arts Posse and South El Monte City.)

a familiar yet already tired trope for Mexican Americans—gang members. Pretending to be derelicts plaguing the city, they smoke, fight, play hooky, and roam the streets in search of trouble. But they end up looking more like a group of boisterous, horseplaying friends than a band of young criminals. As the film progresses, they find productive ways to use their youthful energy, thanks to the award-winning services provided by the city: They are directed to organize field trips, concerts, and dances; participate in job training programs; and clean up graffiti and paint murals in their place.

Though the teenagers and their candid antics seem endearingly familiar, the murals depicted in the film appear almost out of place in a landscape currently so devoid of artistic expression. Even graffiti is hard to come by these days. Yet these glimpses of teenagers buffing walls clean of graffiti and carefully painting a detailed image of the Virgen de Guadalupe, as well as the neatly creased garb of figures made in their own image, show a unique period of conflict and grassroots unity in this community.

South El Monte had experienced a period of rapid growth and development since its founding in 1958 that lasted well into the 1960s—an experience similar to that of many American suburbs, especially in Southern California. South El Monte quickly grew its industrial and manufacturing base as an important source of revenue. However, in the 1970s, development and suburbanization slowed as the national economy entered a slump. By the early 1970s, South El Monte faced alarming new challenges as an influx of newly arrived immigrants was coupled with growing unemployment.[16] Members of a young and unemployed population, unprepared for a fluctuating, evolving labor market, increasingly turned to gangs.

With nothing to do and nowhere to go, young people often turned their frustrations into allegiances to local gangs, which proliferated throughout the 1970s and well into the 1990s. Small warring gangs aimed their discontent at each other and by claiming neighborhood territories fought for ownership over a city that had all but disowned them. Graffiti exploded into a huge problem that claimed too many walls for cleaning crews to keep up with. Residents, mainly white ones, outraged and panicked by what they saw, took to city hall to vent their grievances, and often resorted to anti-immigrant rhetoric.[17]

To be clear, gangs have existed for nearly as long as Chicanos have lived in U.S. barrios and have served as important, sometimes necessary, social networks. El Monte Flores, one of El Monte's oldest gangs, can be traced to one of the area's original barrios or camps, Las Flores—named after the flower farms that employed many local people. Here, workers' families settled and children grew up through the mid-twentieth century, among the beauty of flowers as well as the hard labor of agricultural life and the challenges of poverty that many people in the segregated barrios of El Monte and South El Monte experienced. It would be a mistake to consider gangs as the mere result of idleness.

As South El Monte found itself struggling with a growing gang problem, among other issues, residents and the local government sought creative solutions such as prevention, enrichment, and vocational training programs. As the production of socially responsive murals grew during the civil rights movement in the 1960s and into the 1970s, mural programs were increasingly used as antigraffiti and, more specifically, antigang methods. South El Monte's enrichment program, most likely influenced by the growing muralism of the Chicano movement, generated numerous murals in various private and public spaces throughout South El Monte. While it appears that none of these murals remain today, evidence of their existence is recorded in the film made by the city and a few newsletter photographs.

Though the spirit of the Chicano movement had begun to wane in the late 1970s, gang activity and mural making had not. In 1977, a short-lived arts program was established in El Monte as part of the Comprehensive Employment and Training Act (CETA), a significant federal program that also funded artists to engage in public arts projects as a civic service. Perhaps modeled after or building on South El Monte's youth program, specifically its mural component, CETA funded a summer muralism program for students at Valle Lindo High School, a continuation school for at-risk students. For one summer, the artist Ron Reeder was hired to teach these students to paint murals, though his most daunting task was to negotiate peace among warring gangs. These murals were also entirely lost over time as no conservation efforts were made, but they remain documented in Reeder's personal collection of photographs.[18]

Hired by a social services program at the Multi-Service Center in El Monte, Reeder went through a vetting process to determine whether he, a young white man from Norwalk, was fit to work in this Mexican American community. "They asked me questions like: what's the difference between a Mexicano and Chicano. I guess I answered well enough because they hired me," jokes Reeder in an interview.[19] But he also remembers that despite the program's good intentions, in some ways it was naïve of grant writers to think that art alone could solve the serious problems that fueled and were part of gang activity.

"It was tough at first, but I had a good group to work with," says Reeder, who experienced another unexpected level of vetting by the students.[20] In addition to harmless pranks, they also challenged his wits in more serious ways. Reeder found himself in the middle of knife fights between members of opposing gangs that social workers at the Multi-Service Center hoped would come to set aside their differences in the soul-inspiring labor of art. Reeder chuckles now at what was a series of averted crises at the time.

Early on, Reeder decided that his best approach was to share with the students works of art that had had an impact on him as a young artist. He dusted off a very old book on "Los Tres Grandes," the three great muralists of Mexico: José Clemente Orozco, Diego Rivera, and David Alfaro Siqueiros. Students were immediately drawn to Siqueiros's "America Tropical," a mural that had been whitewashed over after its completion in 1932 on Olvera Street in Los Angeles.[21] The image of the crucified Indian man depicted and its sharp critique of racist institutions resonated with the students, who understood what it was like to be a young person of color continuously subjected to discrimination, disenfranchisement, and punishment. Since Siqueiros's mural would lay under layers of white paint for decades longer, the students of South El Monte brought it back to life, even if briefly, to reflect back on the trajectories of their own young lives and the much longer chain of history they were inevitably part of.

By the end of the summer of 1977, social workers at the Multi-Service Center were convinced of the need to continue making art in these communities that resonated and was relevant to them. Dan Flaming, then assistant director of the center, applied for another CETA grant to produce a more extensive project with thirteen artists. "The idea was to make work that would mirror back to the community, including murals and other media," says Flaming.[22] The grant would also include a gallery at the Multi-Service Center where artists and local people could exhibit work.

During the following year, artists including Reeder, Harry Gamboa, Robert Gil de Montes, Gronk, Joe Janusz, Sarah Parker, Bill Fisher, Richard Hyland, Barry Scharf, David Scharf, Nancy Youdelman, and Mary Kemppanien explored and found inspiration in the city of El Monte. They produced and exhibited a series of photographs, experimental poems, paintings, and of course more murals. It would be the murals, painted in plain and public view, that would incite controversy and eventually expedite the dissolution of the CETA program in El Monte.

Whether or not city officials had any doubts or suspicions at the inception of this federally funded program, they certainly found cause for alarm when Gronk painted a mural of an *Adelita*, a revolutionary Mexican woman holding a rifle and red flowers, on the side of a Red Wing shoe store in the Valley Mall, El Monte's main outdoor commercial strip. Neighboring business owners were quick to complain to the city about the image that they found too aggressive and claimed was driving shoppers away. Flaming remembers the owner of the Red Wing store being pleased with the mural despite complaints.

However, it was a mural that was never painted that set city officials against all murals in the city of El Monte and made clear their lack of welcome for the artists.

Reeder had by then spent enough time in El Monte to have observed a pervasive hostility throughout the city, not only by whites toward people of color, but even among its various internal factions. "El Monte had the most divided group of people. The only way to get them to cooperate with each other was to unite them against an even larger threat," notes Reeder.[23]

FIG. 13 Ron Reeder and Joseph Janusz, "Godzilla Visiting El Monte." (Courtesy of South El Monte Arts Posse and Ron Reeder.)

So Reeder invited Godzilla to town. He made a detailed sketch for a mural scene in which Godzilla arrives in El Monte, crashing and stomping through buildings and terrorizing its residents. Most importantly, Reeder represented all members of the El Monte community, imagining how they might respond to such an emergency. "The redneck stands on his truck with a rifle, while the Chicano is standing in the shadows saying, 'I'll take you down, *ese*.' Everyone would be dealing in their own way but together," explains Reeder.[24] Simultaneously sardonic and genuine, it was supposed to be a proposition for community harmony.

City officials called a council meeting and, with no discussion or input from the artists or public, promptly slapped a moratorium on all murals in the city, effectively killing what could have easily grown into a vibrant muralism and art movement in El Monte.[25] "El Monte is a peculiar city. To be plainspoken, there was some element of racism there. When you have [a] social environment that is so skewed, it creates an environment that is ripe for critique. It sets itself up to be satirized and criticized," notes Flaming.[26]

By 1978, the program had drawn to an end, and the artists—perhaps invigorated with collective defiance and a renewed commitment to public art—went on to found Los Angeles Contemporary Exhibitions (LACE) in downtown LA. While LACE continues to operate in Hollywood and remains one of the most successful and long-standing artist-founded spaces of its generation, El Monte and South El Monte continue to struggle to build an adequate cultural infrastructure that is relevant to its predominantly Latino and Asian communities.

El Monte and South El Monte have historically been inhospitable environments for the arts. These cities have been insulated by their protective governments, which have insisted on adhering to sanitized yet inherently racist histories that have violated and disenfranchised their own communities of color. Even Latino council members in El Monte have shown only limited interest in the arts, while remaining inflexibly loyal to standard modes of law enforcement (also directly tied to racist histories) and prioritizing its police force over other social services. South El Monte, a significantly smaller city with less infrastructure, also persists in its insular governing practices that deliberately disregard political transparency and citizen participation.

El Monte currently prioritizes economic development by catering to investors and developers. South El Monte, when not embroiled in destabilizing scandals of political corruption, prioritizes economic growth by appeasing long-established industrial manufacturers and, more recently, by courting big-box retail. In both cases, support for the arts as a public service has largely fallen by the wayside. Generally, the arts have at best been supported when they suit political views and agendas and fit within narrowly defined notions of what art and culture are. At worst, the arts have been staunchly opposed, perceived as a threat, and banned.

As a result, El Monte and South El Monte continue to experience a severe creative and professional brain drain, in which young, educated, and creative residents are forced to look elsewhere for educational and professional opportunities in the arts. In spite of all of this, however, South El Monte and El Monte have inspired generations of artists, musicians, writers, filmmakers, and actors. The communities' densely layered and multicultural history has forged a unique Mexican American identity that is independent of East LA–centric Chicanidad.

It is no accident that El Monte and South El Monte incubated Teatro Urbano and the arts programs of CETA. Mexican American suburbs of Greater LA, the Inland Empire, and even Orange County have served as havens for multiple cultural underground scenes and movements. The existence of these suburbs outside of the LA's strictly policed territory provided young people of color with freedom to develop their own subcultures and self-sustaining networks. From the early days of rock and roll and rhythm and blues at El Monte's Legion Stadium to punk gigs in backyards and elaborate rave parties in discreet warehouses throughout the 1990s, Mexican American suburbia has long had an overlooked yet thriving cultural underground, one that it is hoped will continue to generate its own creative entities and nourish larger multicultural movements with its distinct character and vision.

Notes

1 Colleen Hooper, "Ballerinas on the Dole: Dance and the US Comprehensive Employment Training Act (CETA) 1974–1982" *Dance Research Journal* 49, no. 3 (2017): 70–90.

2 Alan Eladio Gómez, *The Revolutionary Imaginations of Greater Mexico: Chicana/o Radicalism, Solidarity Politics, and Latin American Social Movements* (Austin: University of Texas Press, 2016).
3 Rene Rodriguez and Rosemary Rodriguez, interview by author, August 17, 2018.
4 Rodriguez and Rosemary Rodriguez, interview by author.
5 Rodriguez and Rosemary Rodriguez, interview by author.
6 Mario T. García and Sal Castro, *Blowout! Sal Castro and the Chicano Struggle for Educational Justice* (Chapel Hill: University of North Carolina Press, 2011).
7 Rodriguez and Rosemary Rodriguez, interview by author.
8 Carribean Fragoza, "*La Raza*: The Community Newspaper That Became a Political Platform," KCET, April 4, 2018, https://www.kcet.org/shows/artbound/la-raza-the-community-newspaper-that-became-a-political-platform.
9 Rodriguez and Rosemary Rodriguez, interview by author.
10 For more on Laboe, see Jude Webre, "Memories of El Monte," chapter 22 in this volume.
11 Gómez, *The Revolutionary Imaginations of Greater Mexico.*
12 Rodriguez and Rosemary Rodriguez, interview by author.
13 Rodriguez and Rosemary Rodriguez, interview by author.
14 See Nick Juravich, "'City of Achievement,'" chapter 9 in this volume.
15 Hugh J. Triffet, writer and prod. dir., untitled video commemorating South El Monte's All-America City Award for 1974–1975 (South El Monte City: Unit T Production and South El Monte City, 1975), 16mm. Available for viewing courtesy of South El Monte Arts Posse at http://www.semapeastofeast.com.
16 See Adam Goodman, "American Dreams and Immigrant Realities in a South El Monte Shoe Factory," chapter 12 in this volume.
17 Mayerene Barker, "Angry Residents Demand Graffiti Be Stamped Out," *Los Angeles Times*, February 26, 1976.
18 Ron Reeder, oral history interview, January 14, 2015, South El Monte Arts Posse (SEMAP), East of East: Mapping Community Narratives in El Monte and South El Monte, http://www.semapeastofeast.com.
19 Reeder, oral history interview, SEMAP.
20 Reeder, oral history interview, SEMAP.
21 Erin Curtis, Jessica Hough, and Guisela Latorre, *¡Murales Rebeldes! L.A. Chicana/Chicano Murals under Siege* (Santa Monica, CA: Angel City Press, 2017).
22 Dan Flaming, interview by author, August 29, 2018.
23 Reeder, oral history interview, SEMAP.
24 Ibid.
25 Mayerene Barker, "El Monte Mural Stirs Ban Move," *Los Angeles Times*, March 10, 1977.
26 Flaming, interview.

12

American Dreams and Immigrant Realities in a South El Monte Shoe Factory

ADAM GOODMAN

Arthur Sbicca and Guadalupe González did not have much in common. Nor did they know each other particularly well. But their lives intersected in the late 1970s in South El Monte. Today, the Thuan Phat Asian Supermarket occupies the place where they met on Rosemead Boulevard, just south of Garvey Avenue and immediately to the north of the swap meet at the old Starlite Drive-In. From the late 1950s to the early 1990s, long before the grocery store had opened its doors, Sbicca and his family owned and operated a shoe factory on the property that employed people like González to make the latest styles in women's footwear.

What brought Sbicca and González together? Their stories and distinct paths to South El Monte can best be understood as part of the broader history of mass migration to the United States during the past 150 years. Since the late nineteenth century, tens of millions of people from all over the world have crossed the Atlantic and Pacific Oceans and the land borders with Canada and Mexico for a variety of reasons. Some have fled religious and political persecution, poverty, violence, and natural disasters; others have sought to reunite with loved ones; and many have come in hope of securing a better future for themselves and their families.[1] Immigration has shaped the United States in profound ways, but the histories of conquest, slavery, race- and gender-based discrimination, and the economic exploitation and exclusion from citizenship of entire groups of people have also played a central role in constructing the nation's identity. As a result, rather than finding a meritocratic society in which hard work led to social mobility regardless of one's background, many newcomers discovered that a variety of factors restricted their access to the so-called American dream.[2]

Examining Sbicca and González's experiences together and exploring how and why they converged and diverged sheds light not only on their personal histories, but also on the histories of El Monte and South El Monte and the making of modern America over the course of the twentieth century. And it uncovers an uncomfortable truth: some immigrants' American dreams have been built on the backs of other immigrants.[3]

European Immigration and American Dreams before 1965

Ernesta Rossi was just twelve years old in 1907 when she, her mother, and her seven siblings left their town in the Umbria region of central Italy and set out to reunite with her father in Philadelphia. After traveling more than 200 miles south to Naples, the family boarded a U.S.-bound ship on November 6. When the nine Rossis arrived in New York two and a half weeks later, authorities detained them. At the time, to be admitted into the country, immigrants had to prove that they would not be dependent on the state. Those deemed likely to become "public charges" faced exclusion and deportation. So officials held Ernesta and her family until her father, who had arrived a few months earlier, could send money to demonstrate that they would be self-sufficient. Six years later, another Italian emigrant left Italy for the United States. Twenty-one-year-old Francesco Sbicca, a shoemaker by trade, traversed the Atlantic aboard a passenger vessel called the *America* and arrived at Ellis Island on September 27, 1913. He also settled in Philadelphia, and at some point soon thereafter he started seeing Ernesta. The couple married in May 1916 and used their modest savings to buy furniture for their home. Less than ten months later Ernesta gave birth to Arthur, the first of their six children.[4]

Arthur's parents were just two of more than twenty-five million Europeans who immigrated to the United States in the period 1880–1920. Unlike previous eras, during which most people came from England and Ireland, the vast majority of these new migrants arrived from Italy, Russia, and other parts of Southern and Eastern Europe. Poverty and pogroms in migrants' countries of origin, combined with urbanization, industrialization, and heightened labor demand in the United States, could explain part of this unprecedented transoceanic migration. Innovations in transportation technology also made mass movement possible. Whereas it once took six weeks to cross the Atlantic by sail from Western Europe to the Americas, the widespread use of steamships had cut the length of the voyage to just two weeks by the end of the 1860s, turning the Atlantic into what one historian has described as a "two-way street."[5] Though 30–40 percent of the migrants returned to Europe, most of them stayed, fueling demographic and economic growth in the United States. Immigrants toiled in factories, fields, and mines and on railroad tracks crisscrossing the continent. Some, like the Sbiccas, became entrepreneurs. In September 1920, they started selling shoes out of their house. Francesco made them, and Ernesta kept the books, managed the business, and translated for her husband, who still did not speak English at the time. They later incorporated the company, creating job opportunities for other Italians and recent arrivals.[6]

Fears of foreign subversion during and after World War I and the influx of millions of Southern and Eastern Europeans considered racially inferior, culturally distinct, and—perhaps most important—unassimilable led Congress to pass a series of restrictive immigration laws in the 1910s and 1920s. These measures extended the preexisting bar on the entry of Chinese laborers and expanded it to include people from all of Asia. They also implemented a literacy test and established quotas based on people's country of origin that cut immigration from Southern and Eastern Europe to a small sliver of what it had been.[7]

Through a stroke of serendipity, Ernesta and Francesco had arrived in the United States just before the nation's gates closed. By the time the 1924 National Origins Act had passed, they were naturalized U.S. citizens with three children who were also citizens since they had all been born in Philadelphia. Their legal status and Francesco's skill as a shoemaker helped their company thrive in the years ahead. Two other factors also facilitated their success. First, although Europeans faced discrimination upon arriving, their white ethnic identity eventually allowed them to integrate into the mainstream. Second, contrary to the myth of the self-made man that is central to the American dream, the support of the federal government set many first-generation European immigrants and their second-generation children on a path of upward mobility. President Franklin Delano Roosevelt's New Deal of the 1930s and 1940s provided home loans, educational benefits, and welfare assistance to white Americans while frequently excluding African Americans from such programs. Decades later, Sbicca received a federal loan equivalent to $3.1 million today.[8]

The Sbicca family business flourished in the middle of the twentieth century. In July 1943, with Arthur serving in the U.S. Navy during World War II, Francesco (who by then went by Frank) and Ernesta moved the family to Los Angeles, where they opened a second factory that employed seventy-five people and produced 500 pairs of shoes a day. Frank told the *Los Angeles Times* that the company had decided to relocate "because easterners [were] turning more and more to California-made merchandise and consumers [were] particularly avid for Los Angeles products which [were] manufactured with an eye to Hollywood styling."[9] In the years ahead, the booming postwar economy led many other Americans to follow the Sbiccas west, resulting in the dramatic growth of California and the Sunbelt.

When Frank died a decade later in 1953, at the age of sixty-one, Ernesta and her children inherited an estate valued at more than $220,000 (some $2 million today). Arthur and his two brothers took over the company, and it flourished under their leadership. In the mid-1950s, the construction of I-10 freeway pushed the Sbiccas' business out of downtown Los Angeles. The brothers purchased a six-acre plot on Rosemead Boulevard (in what was then El Monte but would soon become South El Monte), where they built a 50,000-square-foot factory that employed more than 400 people. As the company's public profile grew along with its production and profits, the Sbicca family gained prominence within the local community, participating in Italian American social clubs and patriotic and charitable organizations. Arthur received a special commendation from the Italian government and sat on the advisory council to the president of La Verne College. He, his wife Virginia, and their three children lived in San Marino, a well-to-do suburb less than ten miles from South El Monte but worlds away.[10]

While the Sbiccas' continued success could be attributed in part to their business acumen, racial identity, and economic privilege, it also had much to do with their employees' labor. Unlike in Philadelphia, where the company had hired white workers from various ethnic groups, Mexicans comprised the majority of its workforce in California. By the late 1970s, the 750 documented and undocumented workers in Sbicca's South El Monte factory were making more than a million pairs of women's casual and dress shoes each year. One of the employees was Guadalupe González.[11]

Mexican Immigration and American Realities since 1965

The Mexicali Valley sits in the northeast corner of Baja California, wedged between a desert lake to the southwest and the border with the United States to the north. Long home to a multiracial Mexican and Asian community, it is one of the hottest and driest places in all of Mexico. But in the middle of the twentieth century, binational irrigation efforts using runoff from the Colorado River created rich agricultural lands and opportunities for people willing to move to the valley. This is where Guadalupe González's parents worked the fields and raised their eight children. Born in November 1957, Guadalupe grew up on a rancho and attended the local elementary school. When she was five her father died, and after that her mother raised the children by herself. The family was not well off but always had food. Over the next decade and a half, four of Guadalupe's siblings migrated to the United States and settled in El Monte. In 1977, after Guadalupe got pregnant at the age of nineteen, her mother kicked her out of the house and sent her north. She also went to El Monte, where she moved in with an older sister.[12]

Millions of other Mexicans joined the Gonzálezes in migrating to the United States during this period. Mexicans had been crossing the border in large numbers since the early twentieth century, when labor recruiters brought tens of thousands of people to the United States as temporary workers during World War I. People continued migrating throughout the 1920s, after powerful southwestern agricultural interests that profited from a steady supply of exploitable labor convinced legislators that the National Origins Act, which set restrictive quotas for migrants from various countries, should not apply to the Western Hemisphere. A new era of accelerated migration began in 1942, when U.S. and Mexican officials created the Bracero Program. Although the two governments first envisioned the agreement just as a wartime measure, they repeatedly extended it, issuing a total of 4.6 million short-term contracts (mostly in agriculture) to around 400,000 Mexican men. When the Bracero Program finally ended on December 31, 1964, U.S. employers depended on Mexican labor as much as Mexicans depended on employment in the United States—but now there was no legal way for people to enter the country or return to the same jobs they had held for years, if not decades.[13]

The Immigration Act of 1965 compounded this problem. Though it ended the discriminatory quota system that had been in place for over forty years and led to dramatic increases in migration from Latin America, Asia, and Africa, the act also put the first restriction on immigration from the Western Hemisphere. In 1976, Congress further limited Mexican immigration by instituting a country cap of 20,000 people per year. While Mexican men, women, and children had long migrated without documents, these changes in law, combined with ongoing labor demand in the United States and population pressures and lack of economic opportunities in Mexico, resulted in a spike in the number of people considered undocumented. From 1965 to 1986, Mexicans made some twenty-eight million unauthorized border crossings, more than twenty times the number of legal entries during the same period. Yet most Mexicans migrating to the United States at the time (70 percent of whom went to California) had little choice but to go without authorization. While employers and consumers continued to depend on their labor, politicians and the media stigmatized Mexicans as so-called illegal aliens. Most people eventually returned to Mexico or went back and forth between the two countries, but Guadalupe González and an estimated 5.7 million others stayed north of the border.[14]

Mexican immigrants transformed communities across California and the country in the postwar period. In the thirty years after 1960, El Monte's population increased by 815 percent and South El Monte's population quadrupled.

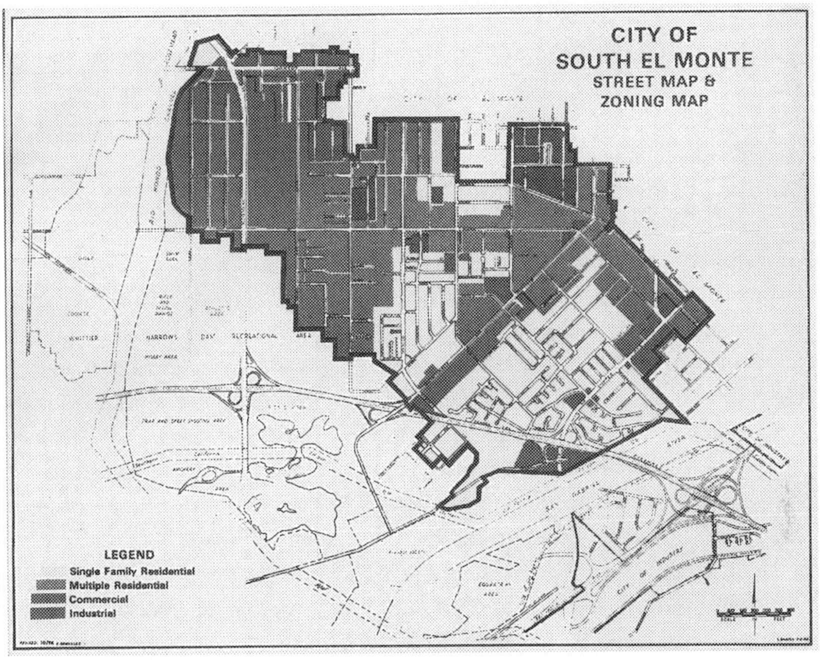

FIG. 14 For most residents, it is common to live in close proximity to factories. (Courtesy of South El Monte Arts Posse and South El Monte City.)

By 1990, Latinos (the vast majority of them Mexican) accounted for 72 percent of El Monte's 106,000 residents and 84 percent of South El Monte's 20,000-plus residents; and people born outside the United States (many of whom had arrived during the previous decade and spoke Spanish at home) made up half the population of the two working-class cities.[15] Unlike previous generations, these immigrants came from Mexico instead of Europe, and they arrived at a time of economic crisis rather than expansion. Moreover, a series of factors—from global economic forces such as the 1973 oil embargo and the proliferation of free trade to harsher immigration enforcement policies and practices—meant that the reality Guadalupe González faced and the opportunities available to her looked much different than the ones Francesco and Ernesta Sbicca had encountered sixty years earlier.

After giving birth to her son in the summer of 1977, Guadalupe found herself as a young, undocumented, single mother more than 200 miles from home and in need of a job. She soon found an opportunity at Sbicca's South El Monte factory through her sister-in-law, who also worked there. That September Guadalupe took a position in the cement department, laboring alongside some fifty other Mexican and Central American women. They talked, sang, and ate sweets to pass the time. She worked five days a week and sometimes also half a day on Saturday, earning $3.50 per hour (around

$14.30 today) to attach leather shoe straps to polyurethane soles. The work was repetitive, and the most difficult part of the job, according to González, was "enduring the smell of the cement." The company, then run by Arthur Sbicca (whom the workers referred to as Arturo) and his two sons, did not provide its employees with face masks or safety equipment, let alone medical benefits. "But we had to do it," González said. "We were all there for one reason: out of necessity, not because we wanted to be."

While toiling in factories under precarious conditions had a high physical cost for immigrant workers across the Los Angeles metropolitan region, being undocumented exacted a psychological toll on González and hundreds of thousands of others. In the 1970s, as the Immigration and Naturalization Service (INS) cracked down on interior enforcement and regularly conducted workplace and neighborhood raids, undocumented people—especially undocumented Mexicans—found themselves living under the constant threat of deportation. Racial profiling resulted in authorities targeting other Latinos, as well, including some U.S. citizens and permanent residents.[16]

Widespread fear existed throughout South El Monte's and El Monte's Mexican communities by the time González arrived. "If someone went to the store, it was like, 'Well, let's see if I come back,'" she recalled. "'If someone went to the movies: 'Let's see if they let us watch the film.' If someone left their house: 'Maybe I won't return. Maybe I'll wake up in Tijuana.'" The INS raided the Sbicca factory alone nearly twenty times in the period 1967–1978, apprehending more than a thousand workers in all. Investigators picked up González during a raid just weeks after she started working. Later that same day they put her on a crowded bus headed to the border. Knowing that her four-month-old son had remained behind in El Monte, she began to cry. But because the border was still relatively porous, she was able to return to El Monte the following day and was back at her old job the day after that. Though that was the only time authorities deported her, the possibility of being expelled again shaped the way that she went about her daily life. Instead of getting off the bus right in front of the Sbicca factory each morning, she got off a stop or two before, so that she could look north on Rosemead and make sure no immigration officials were waiting for her up ahead. She preferred walking the extra seven or eight minutes to reliving the trauma of being apprehended, deported, and separated from her son.[17]

González and other undocumented workers at Sbicca also took additional steps to improve their physical, psychological, and material well-being. In late 1977 and early 1978, a group of employees attempted to form a union at the factory. González supported the initiative at the risk of having her hours cut or losing her job altogether. When the unionization effort failed by just nine votes, workers decided to contest the result with the National Labor Relations Board based on more than 200 challenged ballots and widespread intimidation by management. Less than a week later, with the election still uncertified, more than three dozen INS investigators carried out a morning raid on the factory, apprehending 119 workers—including González's brother-in-law and many people involved in the unionization campaign. However, in contrast to other raids at the time, this one did not end in mass deportations. Sbicca workers' prior mobilization helped activate a rapid response network of labor organizers, immigration lawyers, and community activists who fought on their behalf. In the end, some sixty-five workers decided to contest their cases, and the majority of them eventually had their deportation orders canceled. Yet despite this significant victory, immigration raids persisted, and undocumented workers continued to live under the threat of expulsion in the following decades.[18]

Unlike Arthur Sbicca, a second-generation Italian American, Guadalupe González and other Mexicans who arrived after 1965 did not have a burgeoning postwar economy to help them get ahead. Nor did they have the benefit of intergenerational wealth or a white ethnic identity. These factors mattered in determining economic opportunities and outcomes. But the Sbicca family's rags-to-riches tale also depended on something else: the physically taxing, low-wage labor of people like González, and the fact that she no longer had access to the American dream. Her immigrant reality consisted of spending more than three decades inhaling dust and glue fumes, first at Sbicca and then at another shoe company, where she spent the majority of her career. Today, as a result, she suffers from regular nosebleeds and headaches and occasional vision problems.

Notwithstanding the hardships she endured, González fashioned a life for herself in the United States, and like so many other immigrants before and after her, she did so with dignity. She regularized her legal status under the Immigration Reform and Control Act of 1986 and made considerable sacrifices to provide for her family.[19]

Now, more than forty years after arriving in El Monte, González cannot imagine leaving. She likes going to Diana's on Durfee Avenue for tortillas and enjoys walking around the city's old downtown. El Monte is where she raised her four children, two of whom still live with her, along with a grandchild. Four of her siblings and their families are nearby as well. "We're going to live here forever," she says. El Monte is home.

Notes

1 Douglas S. Massey, Jorge Durand, and Nolan J. Malone, *Beyond Smoke and Mirrors: Mexican Immigration in an Era of Economic Integration* (New York: Russell Sage Foundation, 2002), 7–23.

2 The historian James Truslow Adams coined the term "American dream" in 1931, describing it as the "dream of a land in which life should be better and richer and

fuller for every man, with opportunity for each according to his ability of achievement" (*The Epic of America* [Boston: Little, Brown, 1931]) 405.

3 Unlike studies that compare the social mobility of European immigrants a century ago and Mexican immigrants during the past fifty years as if they are entirely unrelated, this chapter reveals the integral connection between them. For an example of the former type of study, see Joel Perlmann, *Italians Then, Mexicans Now: Immigrant Origins and Second-Generation Progress, 1890 to 2000* (New York: Russell Sage Foundation, 2005). On the importance of recognizing connections both between immigrant groups and across time, see Nancy Foner, "Then and Now or Then to Now: Immigration to New York in Contemporary and Historical Perspective," *Journal of American Ethnic History* 25, nos. 2–3 (Winter–Spring 2006): 33–47.

4 "List or Manifest of Alien Passengers for the United States" and "Record of Detained Aliens," November 23, 1907, Microfilm Serial T715, 1897–1957, Roll 1046, Line 4, pp. 185 and 236, *New York, Passenger Lists, 1820–1957* (accessed through Ancestry.com, July 27, 2018); "List or Manifest of Alien Passengers for the United States," August 12, 1907, Microfilm Serial T715, 1897–1957, Roll 0973, Line 12; p. 218, *New York, Passenger Lists, 1820–1957* (accessed through Ancestry.com, July 27, 2018); U.S. Department of Labor, "Certificate of Arrival—For Naturalization Purposes, Francesco Sbicca" November 11, 1919, and "Petition for Naturalization, Francesco Sbicca" January 22, 1920, *Pennsylvania, Federal Naturalization Records, 1795–1931*, District Court, Roll 180, Petition Numbers 38041-38390 (accessed through Ancestry.com, December 9, 2017); "Estate of Frank Sbicca, Deceased, Ernesta Sbicca and Arthur Sbicca, Executors, Petitioner, v. Commissioner of Internal Revenue, Respondent," *Reports of the Tax Court of the United States*, October 1, 1960 to March 31, 1961, vol. 35 (Washington: U.S. Government Printing Office, 1961): 96–107. On the exclusion and deportation of people deemed likely to become public charges, see Torrie Hester, *Deportation: The Origins of U.S. Policy* (Philadelphia: University of Pennsylvania Press, 2017), 142–146.

5 Walter Nugent, *Crossings: The Great Transatlantic Migrations, 1870–1914* (Bloomington: Indiana University Press, 1992), 34.

6 It should be noted that return migration rates varied widely. For example, while around half of all Italians went back to Europe, just 5 percent of people who had fled violence or famine in places like Russia and Ireland returned. Despite considerable return migration, immigration and high birthrates resulted in the U.S. population doubling from 50 million in 1880 to 106 million in 1920. See Nugent, *Crossings*, 14–18, 30–37, and 150; Raymond L. Cohn, *Mass Migration under Sail: European Immigration to the Antebellum United States* (New York: Cambridge University Press, 2009), 1–2, 8–13, 152–154, and 223–224; Kevin H. O'Rourke and Jeffrey G. Williamson. *Globalization and History: The Evolution of a Nineteenth-Century Atlantic Economy* (Cambridge, MA: MIT Press, 1999), 119–121; David A. Gerber, *American Immigration: A Very Short Introduction* (New York: Oxford University Press, 2011), 35 and 83; "Estate of Frank Sbicca," 96–107.

7 On the restrictive immigration laws of the 1910s and 1920s, see Daniel J. Tichenor, *Dividing Lines: The Politics of Immigration Control in America* (Princeton, NJ: Princeton University Press, 2002), 114–149.

8 Department of Commerce—Bureau of the Census, "Sixteenth Census of the United States: 1940," Population Schedule, Philadelphia, Pennsylvania, Ward 26,

Block 82, Sheet 15A (accessed through Ancestry.com, July 27, 2018); Ira Katznelson, *When Affirmative Action Was White: An Untold History of Racial Inequality in Twentieth-Century America* (New York: W. W. Norton, 2005); Juanita M. Kreps, *1976 Annual Report, Economic Development Administration* (Washington, D.C.: Department of Commerce, 1977), 59.

9 "City Gets First National Shoe Factory Branch," *Los Angeles Times* (hereafter, *LAT*), July 24, 1943.

10 "Estate of Frank Sbicca," 96–107; "Shoe Plant Work Started," *LAT*, October 21, 1956; Sheldon L. Pollack, "Application for Building Permit—Division of Building and Safety, Department of County Engineer, County of Los Angeles," July 21, 1957; Nick Juravich, "City of Achievement," chapter 9 in this volume; Ruth Billheimer, "California Fashion Pasadenans' Business," *Independent Star-News*, November 9, 1958; "Six Men Here Honored by Italian Government," *LAT*, November 5, 1957; "Two Appointed to Advisory Council," *LAT*, January 8, 1967; Julie Byrne, "Shoemakers Get Designs off the Ground," *LAT*, March 20, 1967; "Virginia Sbicca," *LAT*, August 28, 2013.

11 In the late 1970s, Sbicca's shoes sold for the equivalent of $105–$148 today. Arthur Sbicca, Sr., "Open Meeting on: The Immigration and Naturalization Service's Policies and Practices in the State of California, and the Civil Rights Effects of the Carter Administration's Proposed Immigration Legislation" (Los Angeles: California Advisory Committee to the United States Commission on Civil Rights, June 16, 1978), 400–402.

12 Guadalupe González, oral history interview, April 30, 2016, South El Monte Arts Posse, East of East; Mapping Community Narratives in El Monte and South El Monte, www.semapeastofeast.com. Interview conducted in Spanish and translated by author. All of the information about González and quotes from her that follow in this chapter are from this interview. On the history of the Mexicali Valley, see Verónica Castillo-Muñoz, *The Other California: Land, Identity, and Politics on the Mexican Borderlands* (Berkeley: University of California Press, 2016).

13 On the history of the Bracero Program and its impact on men, women, and children on both sides of the border, see Deborah Cohen, *Braceros: Migrant Citizens and Transnational Subjects in the Postwar United States and Mexico* (Chapel Hill: University of North Carolina Press, 2011); Ana Elizabeth Rosas, *Abrazando el Espíritu: Bracero Families Confront the US-Mexico Border* (Berkeley: University of California Press, 2014); Mireya Loza, *Defiant Braceros: How Migrant Workers Fought for Racial, Sexual, and Political Freedom* (Chapel Hill: University of North Carolina Press, 2016).

14 On the 1965 Immigration Act and the politics of immigration in the 1970s, see Tichenor, *Dividing Lines*, 176–241. On the history of Mexican migration from 1965 to 1985, see Massey, Durand, and Malone, *Beyond Smoke and Mirrors*, 41–47 and 52–72; Ana Raquel Minian, *Undocumented Lives: The Untold Story of Mexican Migration* (Cambridge, MA: Harvard University Press, 2018).

15 U.S. Bureau of the Census, *U.S. Census of Population: 1960*, Vol. 1—Characteristics of the Population, Part A—Number of Inhabitants (Washington, DC: U.S. Government Printing Office, 1961), 6–28 and 6–30; U.S. Bureau of the Census, *1990 Census of Population*, Social and Economic Characteristics—California (Washington, D.C.: U.S. Government Printing Office, 1993), 4, 9, 58, 98, 848, and 870.

16 Adam Goodman, *The Deportation Machine: America's Long History of Expelling Immigrants* (Princeton, NJ: Princeton University Press, forthcoming 2020).
17 "List of INS raids on Sbicca Shoes of California, 1967–1978, *Vallejo v. INS*, Deposition & Discovery," Records of the Center for Human Rights & Constitutional Law (Los Angeles, California).
18 Goodman, *The Deportation Machine.*
19 Some three million people (three-quarters of them Mexican) regularized their immigration status under the Immigration Reform and Control Act of 1986. See Massey, Durand, and Malone, *Beyond Smoke and Mirrors*, 89–91.

13

Dreams of Escape and Belonging

The Making of Asian El Monte since 1965

ALEX SAYF CUMMINGS

> The only thing we had in common was, what? McDonald's? I remember somebody calling me "Chinese sushi," and I had no idea what sushi was.
> —Christine Tran, 2018

On a dark early morning in 1992, 4:00 A.M., Win Chuai Ngan made the choice. It was the decision that would carry him far from the way station where he had languished on the long journey from poverty to freedom: a stop called slavery. Once everyone else was asleep, Chuai Ngan scaled the wall around the apartment complex on Santa Anita Avenue and ran madly into the night, with the phone number of a Thai temple crumpled in his pocket. He had scavenged it from a newspaper in the garbage when his masters let him take out the trash one evening.[1]

Chuai Ngan was one of dozens of Thai laborers who were forced to work from early in the morning until late in the night, sewing garments in an unassuming apartment complex in El Monte. Labor contractors had lured the victims from Thailand, promising them a voyage to the United States and a job in sewing, with reasonable hours and an opportunity to romp through the joys of American freedom in Los Angeles.

What they found instead was chilling. "Maliwan Clinton recalls her first taste of America with a shudder," the journalist Teresa Watanabe wrote in 2008. "In this fabled land of the free, she was enslaved behind razor wire and around-the-clock guards in an El Monte sweatshop, where she and more than 70 other Thai laborers were forced to work 18-hour days for what amounted to less than a dollar an hour."[2]

It was a classic grift, with a brutal authoritarian streak. The ringleaders told the captives that they would have to work—for less than minimum wage—to pay off the cost of their travel to the United States, making them indentured servants at best. They had to buy their food and other basic necessities from a commissary run out of a garage by their masters, a kind of company store. They were told that their families would be punished if they rebelled, and American police would shave their heads and brand their scalps if they managed to escape.[3]

There were no armed guards at the complex when Chuai Ngan made his daring escape, but afterward, the bosses were more careful. Three years later, in 1995, a group of government officials and community activists gathered late in the night at a nearby Yum Yum Donuts to work out their plan.[4] They had been working for years to build enough evidence to raid the El Monte compound, and now a team of representatives from the California Department of Industrial Relations, the Thai Community Development Center, and other groups was set to storm the complex.

When they arrived, the officials made sure to block the exit to the compound, forced their way in through the gates, and broke down doors to apartments that were locked from the outside, in some cases using a hammer. Unit by unit, they freed terrified and alarmed workers and eventually found and arrested the seven ringleaders who were holed up in the last apartment.[5] The whole operation was reminiscent of Allied armies rolling into Germany or Poland during World War II. "They had it so highly organized—systemized," Chancee Martorell of the Thai Community Development Center said. "It was like a Nazi concentration camp. I couldn't believe this could be happening in our country, in our own backyard."[6]

The workers were eventually freed to enjoy the vagaries of American life—though they had to endure an arduous stint in the hands of the former Immigration and Naturalization Service (INS), treated like criminals in orange jumpsuits, before being released.[7] Chuai Ngan became a successful restauranteur, most notably of the Win's Thai Cuisine spot in Van Nuys—which he owned with Sokanya Sutthiprapha, another detainee of the El Monte sweatshop.[8]

This bizarre and horrific episode tells many stories. Most notably, it was perhaps the single most widely known instance of systematic forced labor in the United States since the Civil War. It pierced, albeit briefly, the consciousness of an America that believed something like that could not possibly happen here (despite the fact that, of course, "it" had happened in America for several hundred years). It speaks of the enormous hardships and vulnerability that Asian migrants to the United States have faced, even after the Immigration Act of 1965 lifted racist quotas and liberalized immigration.[9] That ticket to America and that tourist visa were worth gambling everything for many people coming from Vietnam, Thailand, China, and other places in Asia and the Pacific.

Those fleeing war, poverty, and persecution in their home countries might have arrived somewhere else at first—in New York, Florida, Louisiana, or Georgia—but many ended up in El Monte.

Of course, not everyone was a slave in a sweatshop. But low-wage work in manufacturing was one of many factors that brought migrants to El Monte, in addition to the political upheaval that drove so many Vietnamese, Cambodians, and Chinese to Southern California. Christine Tran, an educator and sociologist from South El Monte, remembers her mother's journey through the wearisome and capricious world of piecework. "My mom worked in sweatshops, and I was around sweatshops my whole childhood," Tran recalled in 2018. "A lot of people want to live and be near the factory work." She continued: "Very strange market things influenced garment factories. At a time, it was a very popular thing for women, the one-button cardigan. It took a toll on a lot of the button workers. Imagine putting in eight buttons, and getting paid for eight buttons, right? Then all of a sudden the one button cardigan is in—all of a sudden your salary has decreased."[10] In El Monte, the fortunes of whole families could depend on the number of buttons on a sweater.

Roadblocks and Exit Ramps: The Uneven History of Asian Migration to Southern California

What brought so many Asians and Pacific Islanders to El Monte? The San Gabriel Valley (SGV) alone boasts more Asian Americans than any one of forty-two other states in the United States, with a population of over half a million in 2010. "The San Gabriel Valley is home to more Asian-Americans than Los Angeles, San Francisco, and Chicago," the journalist Christopher Yee reported in 2018.[11] If the SGV were a city, it would likely be the most Asian major city in the country, outside of Honolulu. Though other communities in the SGV had majority-Asian populations by this time, El Monte had 26 percent of its population hailing from Asia or the Pacific Islands—a fraction that rivaled the dominant Latino population in the city, and a number that has grown steadily over time.[12]

Conflict and loss has defined the experience of Asians and Asian Americans in El Monte from the beginning. Chinese immigrants had, of course, come to North America—known colloquially as Gum San, or Gold Mountain—during the age of the Gold Rush and railroad construction in the mid-nineteenth century. The profound hostility of native-born workers, especially whites, led to prodigious racial demagoguery by enterprising politicians, resulting most significantly in the Chinese Exclusion Act of 1882—which choked off almost all immigration from China until the measure was lifted in 1943.[13]

Meanwhile, Japanese immigrants and Japanese Americans faced much the same marginalization. Those who managed farms owned by whites faced turmoil when agricultural workers went on strike in the 1930s, setting up a sort of hopeless racial struggle between white, Latino, and Asian players. In the 1940s, when the shade of Japanese internment fell over California, many Japanese residents lost their homes and businesses—"a community erased," as the historian Andre Deckrow puts it.[14] In a land that once belonged to indigenous people, was taken over by Spain and Mexico before the conquest by American Anglos, and then was made more diverse by Asian and Latino migration, the events of the 1940s represented a stunning reversal—the wiping away of the Japanese trace on El Monte's landscape.

The story of Asian El Monte began anew in the 1960s, as immigration reform and new flows of immigrants and refugees changed the face of the city, the SGV, and California as a whole. The Immigration Act passed in the administration of President Lyndon Johnson was a watershed for ethnic diversity in the United States, opening up migration on a more evenhanded basis to people from Africa, Asia, and the Middle East. The aftermath of the Vietnam War and the genocide in Cambodia brought many newcomers to the region in the 1970s and early 1980s, and like immigrants past, they tapped into existing networks of kin and friends to locate themselves, build communities, and in some cases raise capital to build businesses.[15]

Consider the circuitous path that Van Vo took to America. Following the Communist victory in Vietnam, his family experienced brutal hardship because of his father's connections with the former South Vietnamese regime. At dawn one day when Vo was eighteen, he boarded a shaky raft that was barely able to accommodate him and thirteen other people who were willing to risk everything to escape. He eventually made it to Indianapolis, but before long he joined the Government of Free Vietnam, a group that aimed to overthrow the Communist regime. An ill-fated trip with the organization to Thailand resulted in a ten-year prison sentence in that Southeast Asian kingdom. Finally, in 2011, he returned to the United States to live in El Monte and pursue a career in the law.[16]

Like so many refugees from the conflicts of Southeast Asia, Vo eventually made his way into the middle class in Southern California. However, in many cases it took longer for refugees to achieve their dream than they might have imagined.

Indeed, the experience of Asian migration to Southern California communities such as El Monte says a great deal about the hopes and perils of the American Dream. It could mean freedom and prosperity, shackles and abuse, or myriad things in between—including a low-paying service job in a nail salon or massage parlor and praying to scratch out enough to send your kids to college.[17]

For many, the dream remained real, even if the results sometimes came up short. In fact, some detainees of the El Monte sweatshop evinced no regrets about their choice to come the United States. "[Maliwan] Clinton and the Chuai Ngans said that whatever travails they endured here, their American journeys have been well worth taking," Watanabe reported. "'American people have such big hearts,' Clinton said, 'and now I'm proud to say I'm one of them'" upon earning her citizenship.[18]

In the twenty-first century, in fact, Asians have outpaced and arguably displaced some Latinos who had long been part of the community.[19] Though El Monte was still remote enough to be relatively immune to the gentrification and skyrocketing cost of living that afflicted most of Los Angeles and its environs, prices have gone up in the early years of this century. Ernie Gutierrez, a resident of El Monte since 1937, was a firsthand witness to its long and gradual transition from segregation to diversity, and he eventually became the city's mayor. "Hispanic people that have immigrated here and haven't been long enough to save up money are probably finding rent here too expensive," Gutierrez remarked in 2008. "They might be moving near relatives in other parts of the state or country where jobs are plentiful and housing is cheaper."[20]

At the same time, though, Asian Americans experience the same cost-of-living pressure as all other residents of El Monte and the SGV. "Nearly 69,000 Asian Americans in the San Gabriel Valley are housing-cost burdened," Asian Americans Advancing Justice reported in 2018, "spending 30% or more of their household income on housing costs."[21] All people—Indian, Thai, Hmong, or Chinese—find themselves in the same boat, even if resources and privileges fall unevenly across racial categories and within the broad Asian American and Pacific Islander category.

In one way, this story is like any other of gentrification unfolding across a vast, metropolitan landscape—the way the churning of wealth and privilege and the lack of it reshapes neighborhoods and cities. But another part is the evolution of a truly multiethnic suburbia in America, whether that is in the SGV or the formerly lily-white subdivisions and shopping malls of Atlanta or Houston. Writing of Latino enclaves, the historian Mike Davis termed this phenomenon "magical urbanism" in 2000. Far away in the American South, the anthropologist Stanley Thangaraj tracked the transformation of suburban

FIG. 15 South El Monte native Christine Tran celebrating Buddha's birthday at a Vietnamese temple in 1987. (Courtesy of Christine Tran.)

Atlanta through the development of basketball leagues among Asian and Arab Americans in the former stomping grounds of the conservative icon Newt Gingrich. Back in the SGV, the historian Wendy Cheng spoke of "the Changs next door to the Diazes" in her own work on the changing face of Southern California neighborhoods and suburbs. Since 1965 and especially since 1975, El Monte's story has been more and more that of the Lings next to the Gutierrezes next to the Nguyens.[22]

Indeed, conventional narratives of white flight, chocolate cities, and vanilla suburbs no longer work in the age of the suburbanization of poverty and the back-to-the-city movement of affluent young people.[23] Instead of a binary story told about binary people in binary places, one finds a much richer and more complicated braid of stories in places like El Monte.

El Monte and South El Monte may not have been the epicenter of Asian American life in greater Los Angeles, but the Asian presence there has grown more deeply rooted since the 1970s. "Vietnamese people still congregate in Little Saigon in Orange County, and Cambodians still go to the Long Beach area for their community, mainly for celebrations and whatnot, but home is El Monte and South El Monte," Christine Tran recalled. "Some of that could be attributed to the sweatshops that existed, because it was a low-skill job that a lot of Vietnamese and Cambodian people could get."[24]

Living in the 626: "Sometimes I Want to Reconcile with a Past That's Not Really Mine"[25]

After their families came to Southern California, young people of first- or second-generation immigrant status sought to find their way in the region's high schools, community colleges, and universities. Frances Huynh experienced both a sense of difference and one of belonging as part of a Chinese Vietnamese, or Chiuchow, family in El Monte. Born in 1992, she recognized the changing demographic characteristics of her community but still remained nestled within her ethnic or racial group, even if there was no group that exactly mapped onto her own Chinese Vietnamese identity. Huynh's parents were of Chinese descent but grew up in Vietnam: "El Monte is predominantly Latina, but over the years it has becoming (*sic*) more API [Asian Pacific Islander] and more diverse. I feel like that really affected my own identity because even though I surrounded myself with all the Asian kids and my group and this diverse environment, at the same time I didn't know much about other people and other backgrounds, outside of my own. I just stuck into my bubble. And anyone in the 626 [area code], you can ask them—there's this 'Asian bubble' living here."[26] Huynh grew into her identity in college and increasingly identified as API—a racial designation that was more capacious than her ethnic heritage as Chinese Vietnamese. She remains committed to her community in El Monte and sees Vietnam as a second home through the stories her parents have told. She hopes someday to visit, though her brothers appear to be less interested: they see themselves as American through and through and prefer not to dwell on the past.

Asians may have attained greater visibility in the SGV since the 1970s, but at least 15 percent of them in El Monte remain under the poverty line, and the majority there have limited English proficiency.[27] The store signs along Garvey Avenue in El Monte were once all in Spanish, but now many cater to Asian consumers.

Yet El Monte is also a place where an "Asian bubble" can easily exist, and even a former slave like Chuai Ngan could become a prosperous entrepreneur, selling Thai food to Anglo and Asian alike. But different ethnic worlds converged more and more as the twentieth century gave way to the twenty first. By the 2010s, Asians still did not make up the majority of the population of El Monte as they did in SGV towns such as Rosemead or Monterey Park, and Vietnamese residents were a relatively tiny part of that group compared to Chinese Americans—though their presence was growing steadily.

The life of Bang Tran traces this arc: an escape from Vietnam, an uneasy landing in America, and eventual inclusion in a rapidly diversifying El Monte. Piling onto a tiny scooter, Tran, his parents, and four siblings somehow managed to flee their home country in 1975. A brief detention by Communist forces and passage on a ship that broke down in the Pacific followed, but the family made it to Guam, then Hawaii, and then Monterey Park. Tran's parents started selling food out of the back of a Ford Pinto before upgrading to a so-called roach coach—or a "food truck before they got hip," as he puts it. A spot in Los Angeles followed, and then, in 2004, a pho restaurant in El Monte, where Tran grew up eating *albondigas* and speaking Spanish.[28]

Even over a brief period, Tran and his siblings witnessed rapid demographic change at Arroyo High School. "When I grew up here, it was all Hispanic people," he said in 2008. "I only knew about three or four Asian people."[29] Their family was among the few Vietnamese in the community at first, but soon more and more Asian students appeared. "Back then, there were seven Asian students, and three of them were my brothers and sisters," Tran joked.[30]

Today, Garvey Avenue in El Monte and South El Monte is celebrated for its Vietnamese cuisine: Thien Tam vegetarian and the Trans' Viet Huong jostle side by side with King Taco, Krazy Boba bubble tea, and Little Caesars.[31] As the late food critic Jonathan Gold marveled in 2014, "the best pho parlors this side of Little Saigon" could be found on "an unlovely stretch of Garvey Avenue in South El Monte, a town best-known for its unusual concentration of auto-body shops."[32] Garvey Avenue had become yet another raffish corner in the expanding world of Asian life in twenty-first century Southern California.

Like Chuai Ngan—contemplating whether to flee his captivity at possibly the greatest human cost—many people from Thailand, Vietnam, and other neighboring countries had to decide whether to take the chance and leave where they were. Most did not end up in as dire circumstances as Chuai Ngan's, doing forced labor in a sweatshop behind barbed wire. But none knew what really awaited them. Many were trying to escape violence amid the wars and revolutions of the turbulent 1960s and 1970s in Southeast Asia, hoping to leave refugee camps for the sunny shores of Boca Raton or San Diego. As Viet Thanh Nguyen put it in his award-winning 2015 novel *The Sympathizer*, about Vietnamese desperately floating away from the collapsing regime in the South: "Now that we are to be counted among these boat people, their name disturbs us. It smacks of anthropological condescension, evoking some forgotten branch of the human family, some lost tribe of amphibians emerging from ocean mist, crowned with seaweed. But we are not primitives, and we are not to be pitied."[33] But Nguyen also offered up a stirring call: "We confess to being certain of one and only one thing—we swear to keep, on penalty of death, this one promise: We will live!"[34] And live they did, despite being thrown to the wind by the geopolitics that shattered their homes and by the poverty and the hope that drove untold numbers to leap into unknown futures. In the late twentieth and early twenty-first centuries, the Asian Americans of El Monte and the SGV have clung to this conviction, in the face of struggles mundane, terrifying, and everything in between.

Notes

Epigraph: Christine Tran, phone interview by author, August 23, 2018.

1 George White, "Workers Held in Near-Slavery, Officials Say," *Los Angeles Times*, August 3, 1995; Karen Robinson-Jacob, "From Virtual Slavery to Being Boss," *Los Angeles Times*, October 25, 2001.
2 Teresa Watanabe, "Home of the Freed," *Los Angeles Times*, August 14, 2008.
3 Ibid.
4 Hector Gonzalez, "Once-Enslaved Garment Workers Continue Fight," *Pasadena Star News*, August 2, 2010.
5 Ibid.; White, "Workers Held in Near-Slavery."
6 Quoted in Gonzalez, "Once-Enslaved Garment Workers Continue Fight."
7 Asian Americans Advancing Justice, "El Monte Garment Workers Case Sets Precedents Beneficial for All Low-Wage Workers," accessed June 28, 2019, https://www.advancingjustice-la.org/blog/el-monte-garment-workers-case-sets-precedents-beneficial-all-low-wage-workers#.W2yghuhKg2J.
8 Robinson-Jacob, "From Virtual Slavery to Being Boss."
9 For impressions of the act's impact, see Charles B. Keely, "Effects of the Immigration Act of 1965 on Selected Population Characteristics of Immigrants to the United States," *Demography* 8 (May 1971): 157–169; Raymond A. Mohl, "Asian Immigration to Florida," *Florida Historical Quarterly* 74 (Winter 1996): 280; Maria Möller and Kathryn E. Wilson, "Images of Latino Philadelphia: An Essay in Photographs," *Pennsylvania Magazine of History and Biography* 128 (October 2004): 385–398.
10 Tran, phone interview.
11 Christopher Yee, "More Asian-Americans Live in San Gabriel Valley than in 42 States, Report Says," *Pasadena Star News*, February 22, 2018.

12 Asian Americans Advancing Justice, "A Community of Contrasts: Asian Americans, Native Hawaiians and Pacific Islanders in the San Gabriel Valley," 2018, https://www.advancingjustice-la.org/sites/default/files/A_Community_of_Contrasts_SGV_2018.pdf, 6.

13 Monica Mong Trieu, "Ethnic Chameleons and the Contexts of Identity: A Comparative Look at the Dynamics of Intra-National Ethnic Identity Construction for 1.5 and Second Generation Chinese-Vietnamese and Vietnamese Americans," (PhD diss., University of California, Irvine, 2008), 99–100. For the historical context of anti-Asian xenophobia in the late nineteenth and early twentieth centuries, see Gary Gerstle, *American Crucible: Race and Nation in the Twentieth Century* (Princeton, NJ: Princeton University Press, 2001).

14 Andre Kobayashi Deckrow, "A Community Erased," chapter 17 in this volume.

15 Robinson-Jacob, "From Virtual Slavery to Being Boss"; Wendy Cheng, *The Changs Next Door to the Diazes: Remapping Race in Suburban California* (Minneapolis: University of Minnesota Press, 2013), 73. For kin networks and entrepreneurship in Asian American communities more broadly, see Huping Ling, *Voices of the Heart: Asian American Women on Immigration, Work, and Family* (Kirksville, MO: Truman State University Press, 2007), xxxv.

16 Courtney Tompkins, "El Monte Man, Long Beach Woman Tell How Many Vietnamese Refugees Escaped," *Pasadena Star News*, May 1, 2015.

17 Brenda Gazzar, "Diversity in Southern California's Asian Immigrant Community," *Los Angeles Daily News*, October 3, 2015.

18 Watanabe, "Home of the Freed."

19 Yen-Fen Tseng, "Chinese Ethnic Economy: San Gabriel Valley, Los Angeles County," *Journal of Urban Affairs* 16, no. 2 (June 1994): 169–189.

20 Quoted in Yvonne Villarreal, "Census Snapshot: Asians Find Homes in Historically Latino El Monte," *Los Angeles Times*, December 8, 2008.

21 Asian Americans Advancing Justice, "A Community of Contrasts," 3.

22 Mike Davis, *Magical Urbanism: Latinos Reinvent the U.S. City* (New York: Verso, 2000); Stanley Thangaraj, *Desi Hoop Dreams: Pickup Basketball and the Making of Asian American Masculinity* (New York: New York University Press, 2015); Cheng, *The Changs Next Door to the Diazes*; Joel Garreau, *Edge City: Life on the New Frontier* (New York: Anchor Books, 1991).

23 Emily Badger, "The Suburbanization of Poverty," *CityLab*, May 20, 2013, https://www.citylab.com/life/2013/05/suburbanization-poverty/5633/; Derek Hyra, "The Back-to-the-City Movement: Neighbourhood Redevelopment and Processes of Political and Cultural Displacement," *Urban Studies* 52 (2015): 1753–1773.

24 Tran, phone interview.

25 Francesca Huynh, "Frances Huynh," Narrating the Chinese Vietnamese Identity, accessed June 28, 2019, http://chinesevietnamese.com/frances-huynh.

26 Ibid.

27 Asian Americans Advancing Justice, "San Gabriel Valley," accessed June 28, 2019, https://advancingjustice-la.org/who-we-are/about-us/san-gabriel-valley; Gazzar, "Diversity in Southern California's Asian Immigrant Community."

28 Quoted in Alejandro Bryan Rosas, "Viet Huong: Bringing Vietnamese Flavors to El Monte," KCET, March 31, 2015, https://www.kcet.org/shows/departures/viet-huong-bringing-vietnamese-flavors-to-el-monte.

29 Quoted in Villarreal, "Census Snapshot."

30 Quoted in Alejandro Rosas, "Viet Huong."

31 Mike Sonksen, "Garvey Avenue from Alhambra to El Monte," KCET, January 8, 2015, https://www.kcet.org/history-society/garvey-avenue-from-alhambra-to-el-monte.

32 Jonathan Gold, "What's Better than One Pho Filet? Pho Filet 2 Debuts," *Los Angeles Times*, January 14, 2014, http://www.latimes.com/food/dailydish/la-dd-jonathan-gold-pho-filet-2-in-rosemead-20140113-story.html.

33 Viet Thanh Nguyen, *The Sympathizer* (New York: Grove Press, 2015), 382.

34 Ibid.

Part III

Nature and the Built Environment

FIG. 16 Jennifer Renteria, "Trees on Chico Avenue." (Courtesy of South El Monte Arts Posse and Jennifer Renteria.)

When this place was known to all its inhabitants as Houtngna (or Hautngna), it was encircled by rivers, existing almost as a kind of island. When the Spanish named this place El Monte, water continued to surround it. But slowly this became a different island, one surrounded not by water but by freeways. This section shifts slightly from the social history of the San Gabriel Valley to consider how the physical landscape shapes its residents and how they in turn shape the environment. Readers learn about the natural contours of the region, such as the San Gabriel River and Rio Hondo that border South El Monte and El Monte on the east and west, as well as the variegated social environments that its human inhabitants have created—from the recreational space of Legg Lake Park, part of the larger Whittier Narrows Recreational Area explored by David Reid in his essay, to the fluid commercial zone of the Starlite Swap Meet documented by Jennifer Renteria. Daniel Morales tells the story of Hicks Camp, an improvised community, whose homes were built from scraps discarded from the Santa Fe and Southern Pacific railroads, and yet which served as the headquarters for the Berry Strike of 1933 (see chapter 7). Hicks Camp became the largest and one of the oldest Mexican barrios in Southern California; one of numerous unofficial spaces that have become enduring markers of the remembered landscape, but events within and around it included not only Mexican laborers and white landowners but also Japanese and Japanese American tenant farmers. Andre Deckrow chronicles their history long obscured by World War II internment and post-1945 suburbanization. Another location lost to memory was Marrano Beach, discussed by Daniel Medina—a riverside retreat not only for locals but also for nearby Mexican urbanites. El Monte was also home to subsistence homesteads, part of a federal program described by Ryan Reft that provided a hundred Depression-era white families with a home and enough land to try their luck at "rurban" living. Together, these essays show the ways in which race, class, and space intersected to shape the people and the land.

14

Hicks Camp

A Mexican Barrio

DANIEL MORALES

> I remember the queen was beautiful, and the parade came down from Hicks Camp to Medina Court. The streets were decorated like in Mexico and it was real pretty. Cinco de Mayo they made the fiesta and we had to dance in the street.
> —Lucy Flores

From the 1910s until its demolition in 1972, Hicks Camp was one of the most vibrant barrios of El Monte. Named after the family who owned the land, Hicks Camp (renamed Hicksville in the 1950s) had a population that had grown from several dozen people in 1915 to over a thousand by 1930.[1] Never recognized as an official part of El Monte, the twenty-two-acre barrio was bounded by the Rio Hondo, Valley Boulevard, Lower Azusa Road, and Arden Drive. Half a mile away was Hayes Camp (later named Medina Court), another unplanned migrant camp that grew into a large settlement.[2] For six decades Hicks Camp and Hayes Camp were home to hundreds of families, as generations of Mexican migrants arrived and made their lives there.

Settlers first came to the San Gabriel Valley from what is present-day Mexico in the late eighteenth century, when soldiers, priests, and others from

New Spain colonized the area as the San Gabriel Mission. In the nineteenth century, many more ranchers and small landowners came, as the Mexican government encouraged migration to its northern frontier. In 1848, following the Mexican-American War, the area—along with the rest of what is today the western United States—became part of that country. However, it was not until the establishment of railroads across Mexico and the United States that large numbers of migrants started to arrive in Southern California. Mexicans came in the tens of thousands per year in this era, aided by the railroads and lured by job opportunities.

The Mexican population of Los Angeles County had tripled in size by 1920, reaching nearly a quarter of a million. The county developed a polynuclear landscape, an integrated regional economy where a mixture of agricultural and industrial operations in the same areas gave rise to multiple urban centers.[3] Industries such as oil and automobile and textile manufacturing arose across Southern California. As the Santa Fe and Union Pacific Railroads delivered food to markets, new towns sprouted up at railroad junctions, where food processing plants were centered. Based on this model, dozens of towns were founded in Los Angeles and Orange Counties, including El Monte, Azusa, Upland, La Verne, Riverside, and Santa Ana.[4]

Hicks Camp was only part of a larger world of *colonias* (segregated communities) that sprouted across the landscape to serve the mixed agricultural and industrial economy.[5] People came to work in a new form of large-scale industrial agriculture that relied on irrigation systems; close connections to associated manufacturing; refrigerated railroads to transport produce to faraway markets; and, most of all, large numbers of seasonal wage laborers. This is what the founders of El Monte meant when they described the area as a bountiful winter garden in promotional literature throughout California. Indeed, by the mid-twentieth century the valley was covered by large farms that produced oranges, lemons, walnuts, apricots, strawberries, and tomatoes, as well as dairy farms, horse ranches, and one lion ranch. Migrant communities—some planned, others not—arose alongside these new towns and provided the critical labor for economic development. El Monte, located fifteen miles east of downtown Los Angeles, where the San Gabriel River split in two, was ringed by a series of *colonias* where Mexicans and Asians lived: Hicks Camp, Medina Court, La Misión, Las Flores, Chino Camp, Wiggins Camp, La Granda, La Sección, and Canta Ranas.[6]

For the migrants who came to Hicks Camp, the place was a stop on a long journey. Most came from the central Mexican states of Guanajuato, Michoacán, and Jalisco, while a smaller number came from the northern states of Chihuahua and Sonora, and had worked and lived elsewhere in the United States before coming to El Monte.[7] Most workers labored in agriculture, and for many this meant a migratory existence up and down California. "We would migrate back and forth to Fresno, Merced, and so forth in the summers," Pete Nuñez recalled of his childhood in the 1950s. "And then we'd come back sometime between September and November, and go back to school."[8] Lucy Flores, who grew up outside the camp, told Pat Aroz, a college student: "Every summer, by August, you'd go into Hicks Camp, and there wouldn't be fifty people in it. Everybody would take off, and go up north, and pick cotton, or pick grapes, and come back. So if you went there in August or September, or whenever the seasons were, it was a ghost town. By October everybody would be back."[9]

Robert Hicks, a labor contractor, used fliers to recruit Mexicans in the 1910s and originally seemed to envision the camp as a source of contract labor for the farms of the area. By the 1920s, however, most Mexican migrants came to Hicks Camp on their own and paid rent to Hicks rather than take his contracts. Rent paid for the leveling of dirt streets and the annual spreading of gravel, but not much else. Even more prosperous Mexicans had to live in the camps, as they and other nonwhites were prevented by El Monte's racial housing covenants from purchasing a home in the city proper. Homes were built by the families living in them, mostly from repurposed boxcars that were torn up for their wood and frames. "There were holes in the streets, dirt roads, outhouses," Maria Ávila remembered. Yet, as in many barrios throughout Southern California, migrants found creative ways to adorn their rented spaces. "You found the prettiest plants in all kinds of coffee cans, lard cans, all kinds of things. Really, but it was poor."[10]

The City of El Monte refused to provide basic police and fire service for Hicks Camp for several decades, and the camp instead relied on Los Angeles County services from Temple City, which increased response times. This delay proved particularly disastrous in times of crisis, especially as Hicks Camp lay next to the Rio Hondo. "There was a flood here and [it] wiped out half of Hicks Camp and then, God, you could see pigs floating down the street and cows," recalled Beatriz Pérez.[11]

However, not all natural disasters produced negative memories. Pérez fondly remembers her family's introduction to earthquakes. She was jumping rope with her friend when an earthquake started, and "you could see the sidewalk open up like little waves. My mother had just gotten out of hospital and she kept yelling at us and said, 'Stop jumping, you're going to break the house down.' She thought we were making all this noise and it was the earthquake."[12]

In addition to frequent flooding and poor housing conditions, residents of Hicks Camp had to survive hard economic times. The Depression began in 1929 and continued until the United States entered World War II, in 1941. Throughout this time the residents of Hicks Camp struggled to make ends meet, stay in the country, and organize for better conditions. Most families relied on a mixture of seasonal jobs, local mutual aid societies, and their own backyard gardens and chicken coops to avoid the worst effects of the Depression. However, the economic downturn increased competition for jobs and the hostility between residents of Hicks Camp and the newly arrived white Okies.

In the early 1930s, 400,000 Mexicans and Mexican Americans left the United States for Mexico as repatriation campaigns ravaged communities across the country, particularly in Southern California. Repatriation was not a single policy, but rather a word used for a range of policies that were pursued in the United States to push Mexicans back into Mexico. Los Angeles County was the center of the campaign, and more than a third of ethnic Mexicans there were repatriated to Mexico in these years. In El Monte, Robert Hicks began demolishing the homes of those who had left, in an effort to prevent new residents from moving into the camp.[13] Hicks's actions may have been spurred by the momentum that union organizers had gained in the camp during the 1930s, especially after the participation of many residents in the El Monte Berry Strike of 1933.

In the 1940s the struggle for better conditions shifted to desegregation of El Monte's public accommodations. Officials in El Monte were suspicious of educating people of color and often steered them toward dropping out or following technical vocations. In 1947 a coalition of Mexican civil rights groups won a victory against school segregation in the U.S. Federal Appeals Court for the Ninth Circuit ruling in *Mendez v. Westminster*, but the El Monte School District remained segregated for years afterward. When Pérez began to show promise as a student and went to high school, the superintendent—none other than Robert Hicks—told her father, "Well, I think it's no use, Joe, because she's not going to learn anything in school."[14]

Led by Father John V. Coffield of San Juan Bosco Church, residents in Hicks Camp successfully organized to improve the neighborhood and end housing and educational segregation. Despite the 1948 U.S. Supreme Court decision in *Shelley v. Kraemer* that struck down racial housing covenants, the Los Angeles County housing market remained segregated. Housing agent associations followed strict guidelines not to sell to Mexicans.[15] A lot of residents who bought their own property in Hicks Camp and other unincorporated areas did so because they were not allowed to buy property in El Monte or other Southern California cities. Pérez's father could not buy property in the city proper "because the way the deeds read, no Mexican people could buy *no mas*. Just what they called the white race. I guess they didn't consider us white. So we couldn't buy any property. Not even Japanese."[16] Felix Ramos (like other residents who grew up in that era) remembered Coffield for a different reason: "He used to stop by and pick us up, every Sunday go by the streets honking and we would go with him and he would take us to mass. . . . I used to go with Fr. Coffield and had a great time. But at 10 o'clock another church with Holy

Rollers [evangelicals], and they would have a feast on Sundays so I got to go have the feast. . . . And at 7 o'clock they had another church with a lot of parties so I would go."[17]

Coffield exposed the kids to scouting, the outdoors, pools, and other places Mexicans normally would not be allowed to go because of city ordinances that segregated local parks and pools. Ramos credits Coffield with helping fight segregation and keeping students in school, which allowed many of them to finish high school and attend college. Several teachers, a principal, and even someone who earned a PhD in education came out of the neighborhood. As Ramos put it, "even though we were poor and we were a minority a lot of them progressed because of Fr. Coffield." Coffield was eventually sent to New York, and many people suspect that was because of his sympathies for the Brown Berets and the Chicano movement.[18]

During World War II many young men from Hicks Camp served in the armed forces and earned many distinctions, but these accomplishments did not save them from discrimination on the home front. In 1943, when the Zoot Suit Riots exploded in neighboring Los Angeles, residents of El Monte's barrios braced for the arrival of violence. When a lockdown took effect in the city, the violence spread to the *colonias* of Los Angeles County. Lupe Ruiz said that rumors were prevalent in those chaotic first days. "One night they came to Hicks Camp, a whole bunch of cars, full of sailors, all Anglos," Ruiz remembered. "They [*sic*] was, oh, maybe fifteen, twenty cars challenging the fellows from Hicks Camp to come out and fight with them. Well, they weren't going to come out you know, they didn't know whether they had guns or what."[19] On June 7 groups of drunken sailors arrived in Hicks Camp and Medina Court. Coffield tried to get the El Monte police to intervene, yet the sailors swarmed through the neighborhood—beating people and destroying the windows of the stores.[20] After the war many returning men and women found that their service had not qualified them for full citizenship in the eyes of whites. In one case, a young man was taking women to a dance in El Monte when "he was turned away and told Mexicans were not admitted. The veteran produced his citizenship papers and then was told he wasn't an American just because he had citizenship papers, he was still Mexican."[21]

Throughout the postwar years, Hicks Camp and its residents became more integrated into the area, attending events in nearby Medina Court and Legion Stadium and taking short drives to the racetrack at Irwindale or the big city of Los Angeles. Most people interviewed by historians for the South El Monte Arts Posse's oral histories remember Hicks Camp during those years as a poor but vibrant community. Growing up in Hicks Camp after World War II, Felix Ramos was raised by his godparents, who owned a small store there. His godmother had a *metate* (stone mortar) and used it to sell *masa* (corn dough) and tortillas—an enterprise that grew into a grocery store. "I was raised in that

FIG. 17 Lily and Vincent Rojas Jr. in Hicks Camp, 1952. (Courtesy of South El Monte Arts Posse and Vincent Rojas Jr.)

store," Felix recalled. "I would take care of it on the weekends, taking care of whatever had to be done." In the neighborhood, "the streets were all dirt, we didn't have no pavement. Our houses were all wooden, and everyone built their own home according to how they wanted to build their home. We owned the home but not the land."[22]

By 1950 Hicksville (as it had been renamed) had become smaller but more established, with about 200 families, four churches, and a thriving social and civic life. Zagarazo Hall, a former walnut factory, served as everything from a theater to a church. In 1954 the barrio was chosen as the backdrop for the film *Carmen Jones* thanks to its similarity to poor Southern towns.[23] Ramos remembers the era as more prosperous than the 1940s. His godparents' store thrived on serving the braceros who came every year from Mexico to pick in the fields, and Ramos also often worked in the grape, corn, cotton, and prune orchards. Ramos left Hicksville to join the army and spent several years in Europe. When he returned, he used the GI Bill to buy a house in South El Monte and the skills he learned in the army to get a series of decent jobs, a progression that allowed many Mexican Americans to enter the middle class.[24] The generation that had grown up during the Depression and then served in the armed forces came back with different expectations. They pressed for change in the 1950s, and a generation later many of their children joined the Chicano movement.

Hicksville's days, however, were numbered. Across Southern California, large redevelopment projects funded by the federal government took aim at Mexican *colonias*. Depicted as places of poverty, disease, and crime, *colonias* were seen as incompatible with a modern suburban metropolis. Many were torn down to make way for freeways, private tract housing, and public works projects that encased rivers in concrete.[25] While the original Hicks Camp encompassed a large area, sales to large-scale redevelopers and private home owners had made the camp much smaller by the 1960s. One area became a factory, while Rio Vista School replaced another section. After the land's value increased, the City of El Monte sought to redevelop and incorporate it into the city, and eventually, the Hicks family was able to sell the last plots to the city. Slowly at first, and then with increasing speed, the neighborhood was torn down, and in 1973 the last fifty-seven households in Hicks Camp were forced to move out. Most families received compensation for their houses and the option to buy into the new residential redevelopments that replaced them, but most never returned. Most of the last area was redeveloped into modern suburban houses, sold to families that were part of the first generation of the Mexican American middle class. Many families who left, however, stayed in the area—if not in El Monte or South El Monte, then in the San Gabriel Valley.

While Hicks Camp no longer exists, its influence is still felt in El Monte and beyond. For hundreds of the people who grew up in and around in the city, Hicks Camp in the 1950s and 1960s defined their youth: a world of crops, Mexican music and culture, and a struggle against adversity. The area that was Hicks Camp has been redeveloped into housing and industrial zones, but in the center of the nondescript neighborhood lies Rio Vista Park. Redeveloped in 2008 to commemorate the history of the area, the park features historical pictures with plaques that tell the story of Hicks Camp. Inscribed on the sidewalk are the names of former residents.[26]

On Tyler Avenue stands La Historia Society, a museum and archive to help people remember the time when Mexicans lived literally on the wrong side of the river. In addition to preserving countless photographs, the museum sells photo calendars and a small collection of books written by former barrio residents. And of course remnants of the barrio can be found not just in the stories of former residents, but also in their photo albums, homes, and even garages. While it has been more than fifty years since Ramos's family ran their grocery store, he still carefully stores many of the items the store sold for decades to Mexican families. There is the old *metate*, countless postcards of actors from Mexico's golden age of cinema, and bottles of old soda pop. The presence of Hicks Camp remains alive in the built environment and the collective memory.

Notes

Epigraph: Pat Aroz, "Interview with Lucy Flores" in *Personal Stories from the El Monte Communities*, ed. Susan Sellman Obler (Whittier, CA: Rio Hondo College, 1978), 33–36.

1 Cecilia Rasmussen, "The Heyday and Decline of a Lively Barrio," *Los Angeles Times*, November 27, 1995.
2 Ibid.
3 Stephanie Lewthwaite, *Race, Place, and Reform in Mexican Los Angeles: A Transnational Perspective, 1890–1940* (Tucson: University of Arizona Press, 2009).
4 For a longer discussion of these places, see Matt Garcia, *A World of Its Own: Race, Labor, and Citrus in the Making of Greater Los Angeles, 1900–1970* (Chapel Hill: University of North Carolina Press, 2001); José Alamillo, *Making Lemonade out of Lemons: Mexican American Labor and Leisure in a California Town, 1880–1960* (Urbana: University of Illinois Press, 2006); Gilbert G. González, *Labor and Community: Mexican Citrus Worker Villages in a Southern California County, 1900–1950* (Urbana: University of Illinois Press, 1994); Jerry González, *In Search of the Mexican Beverly Hills: Latino Suburbanization in Postwar Los Angeles* (New Brunswick, NJ: Rutgers University Press, 2017).
5 J. González, *In Search of the Mexican Beverly Hills*, 1–46.
6 Ibid., 25.
7 "Hicks Camp Study: Outline of Camp Study," 1949, Box 12, Papers of Ralph Leon Beals, National Anthropological Archives, Smithsonian Institution, Washington.
8 Greg Hoard, "Interview with Pete Nuñez," in *Personal Stories from the El Monte Communities*, ed. Susan Sellman Obler (Whittier, CA: Rio Hondo College, 1978), 59–64.
9 Pat Aroz, "Interview with Lucy Flores," 33–36.
10 Margie Saucedo and Helen Phillips, "Interview with Maria Ávila," in *Personal Stories from the El Monte Communities*, ed. Susan Sellman Obler (Whittier, CA: Rio Hondo College, 1978), 1–9.
11 Irma Hernandez and Javier Valencia, "Interview with Beatrice Perez," in *Personal Stories from the El Monte Communities*, ed. Susan Sellman Obler (Whittier, CA: Rio Hondo College, 1978), 59–64.
12 Ibid., 69.
13 Beherm Report, 1939–1940, interview summaries in "American You," Ralph Leon Beals Papers, E 154-SSRC Article, Box 12, p. 27.
14 Quoted in Hernandez and Valencia, "Interview with Beatrice Perez," 69.
15 J. González, *In Search of the Mexican Beverly Hills*, 46–75.
16 Quoted in Hernandez and Valencia, "Interview with Beatrice Perez," 61.
17 Felix Ramos, oral history interview, South El Monte Arts Posse (SEMAP), East of East: Mapping Community Narratives in El Monte and South El Monte, http://www.semapeastofeast.com.
18 Ibid.
19 Patti Barry and Andrea Lopez, "Interview with Lupe Ruiz" in *Personal Stories from the El Monte Communities*, ed. Susan Sellman Obler (Whittier, CA: Rio Hondo College, 1978), 101.
20 J. González, *In Search of the Mexican Beverly Hills*, 35.

21 Beherm Report, 1939–1940, interview summaries in "American You," Ralph Leon Beals Papers, E 154-SSRC Article, Box 12, p. 25.
22 Ibid.
23 Rasmussen, "The Heyday and Decline of a Lively Barrio."
24 Ramos, oral history interview, SEMAP.
25 J. González, *In Search of the Mexican Beverly Hills*, 103–131.
26 Ryan Reft, "Archiving Memories of El Monte in a Transnational Space," KCET, July 25, 2013, https://www.kcet.org/history-society/archiving-memories-of-el-monte-in-a-transnational-space.

15

Life at Marrano Beach

The Lost Barrio Beach of Los Angeles

DANIEL MEDINA

Marrano Beach never appeared on maps of Los Angeles County's seventy-five-mile coastline. It acquired no international acclaim, like the behemoths of Santa Monica, Manhattan, or Redondo. It had no brackish tide pools or cool Pacific breezes. There was not a chance of a surf advisory, because waves didn't even lap its shores. Marrano was a beach without an ocean.

It was an anomaly that raised the question: "Where in the hell is Marrano Beach?"

Marrano Beach was actually deep in the San Gabriel Valley, unfolded on a swath of marshland wedged in the Whittier Narrows along the Rio Hondo. It was miles from the sea, but its history as an inclusive recreational destination popular with local Mexican American communities throughout the twentieth century, endowed it with a tenacious cultural heritage unlike any other beach in Los Angeles.

The origin of Marrano Beach can be traced to the early barrios that arose around the original San Gabriel Mission in the late 1700s. Adobe homes of a Mexican village known as La Mision Vieja arose on mission land in the lush floodplain between the San Gabriel River and Rio Hondo. The barrio was one of several communities established in the Narrows, housing laborers tending to the region's robust plain of crops that was regularly enriched by river sediment.

Within a few decades, neighborhoods near La Mision Vieja came to include La Mision, Canta Ranas and El Rancho de Don Daniel. Marrano Beach was born on the riverfront property of El Rancho de Don Daniel, a Mexican land grant from the nineteenth century that had belonged to the Repetto-Alvarado family, whose members were prominent California landowners.[1] El Rancho de Don Daniel encompassed riparian wetlands and ponds surrounding the Rio Hondo, which flowed year-round, and the seasonal Mission Creek. With few opportunities for respite after toiling in the fields, residents of the barrios cultivated recreational lifestyles around this section of the river and embraced it as a bucolic resource for community and family activities.

In the twentieth century, the profile of El Rancho de Don Daniel was transformed from a pastoral space of leisure to a symbol of active cultural identity in an era of segregation. By serving as an alternative space of recreation for Mexican Americans affected by policies of racial discrimination applied at recreational zones in Los Angeles, the beach became a place to enforce their cultural claims to the land. Locals created what Victor M. Valle and Rodolfo D. Torres call "an oppositional model of cultural space."[2]

In the early 1900s, Mexican Americans and members of other minority groups in California were forbidden from entering "whites only" spaces such as parks, beaches, and swimming pools. Public park options were limited to East Los Angeles, due to the hostility encountered in green spaces in other parts of the city. By 1923, all public pools were racially segregated. Mexican, Asian, and African Americans could often use the pools only when the whites vacated the swimming areas once a week—the day before the city cleaned the pools.

The historian Lawrence Culver notes in *A Companion to Los Angeles* that neither backyard pools nor air-conditioning were common in the homes of middle-class residents until the 1950s, leaving working-class residents few options for relief from the oppressive heat of summer.[3] Relief was also difficult to find on the beaches of Los Angeles's coastline. In the 1920s, the city and county of Los Angeles purchased beaches within its borders to ensure the white ownership of seaside properties, protecting one of the city's most prized recreational and tourist assets from the perceived menace of racial intermingling.

In response, Mexican Americans in the far inland reaches of the San Gabriel Valley devised their own "beach." It was during this era in the 1930s that El Rancho de Don Daniel came to be known as Marrano Beach. In the book, *Blowout! Sal Castro and the Chicano Struggle for Educational Justice*, the Mexican American educator and activist Sal Castro recalled his experience growing up in East Los Angeles in the 1940s: "To compensate for this discrimination and exclusion in swimming pools and parks, Mexicans, including my family, went

FIG. 18 Youth hanging out at Rio Hondo River. (Courtesy of La Historia Historical Society Museum.)

to what was called Marrano Beach."[4] The possible origins of the name Marrano (meaning a pig or hog) are numerous, including that the murky stretch in the river resembled a pig trough, that a pig farm once existed upstream, or a that a flood swept through a local ranch and deposited pigs on the river's shore.

The name linked the space to the agricultural heritage of barrio life in the Narrows. It was a self-deprecating reference to the socioeconomic realities of local residents, a name choice that Valle and Torres posit "stressed their class orientation, especially their lack of public recreational and transportational resources, but also their resourcefulness in the face of poverty." Unable to attend or afford swimming lessons in city pools, children like Castro learned to swim in the beach's shallow waters. Couples could socialize on the shore with a pot of menudo, and children enjoyed refreshing *raspadas* (snow cones) sold from small stands. Singers and mariachis would work the sandy shores, serenading sunbathers and accompanying dances into the night. "If they could not afford to live in homes with swimming pools or transportation to a real beach," Valle and Torres add, "they could at least enjoy their imagined beach during the hottest months of summer."[5]

When freeways struck through the San Gabriel Valley in the middle of the twentieth century, the pastoral allure of the beach began to rust. On the heels of freeways that brought easier access to the Pacific coast, oil wells and factories followed and soon spoiled the area's peaceful vitality. Pollutants seeped into the Rio Hondo, leaving an acrid smell in the water. In his memoir *Always Running: La Vida Loca: Gang Days in L.A.*, Luis Rodríguez recalled the scene, depicting the pride that nonetheless survived the more abrasive elements:

> In the summer time, Marrano Beach got jam-packed with people and song. *Vatos Locos* [crazy guys] pulled their pant legs up and waded in the water. Children howled with laughter as they jumped in to play, surrounded by bamboo trees and swamp growth. There were concrete bridges, covered with scrawl, beneath which teenagers drank, got loaded, fought and often times made love. At night, people in various states of undress could be seen splashing around in the dark. And sometimes, a body would be found wedged in stones near the swamps or floating face down. The place stunk, which was why we called it what we did. But it belonged to the Chicanos and Mexicanos. It was the barrio beach. Ours.[6]

It remained for Rodríguez and others a preferred destination, given the animosity that still lingered on the beaches of the *gabachos* (white people). On his weekly "The Sancho Show" on KPCC-FM in the 1990s, Dr. Daniel Castro (aka Sancho) would jokingly refer to his past visits to the Marrano Beach Club. The fictitious club was a local lampooning of the exclusive institutions of leisure in Los Angeles's Westside, a symbol serving to deflate the stigma of discrimination. "If one knows Marrano Beach, one knows something of the Mexican, Chicano, East Los Angeles experience," Rita Lesdesma writes in *Culturally Diverse Populations: Reflections from Pioneers in Education and Research.*[7]

Despite the beach's heritage and its strong connection with local residents, the increasingly polluted area was eventually strangled by unchecked riparian growth. The prolific bamboo and invasive swamp plants of Rodríguez's Marrano

Beach cut off access to the river's shores, shuttering a blazing era of recreation in this small patch of the Narrows.

The beach was lost, but this buried portion of the Rio Hondo still flowed unrestrained, spared the concrete lining that eventually dressed the rest of the river. The value of this free-flowing waterway and the potential for reclaiming its riverfront shores was eyed by advocates of revitalization efforts in the 1990s and championed by County Supervisor Gloria Molina, a La Puente native with fond memories of Marrano Beach.[8] Nonnative plants were removed, picnic tables were installed, and the area was renamed Bosque Del Rio Hondo Park (the name means forest of the deep river). Los Angeles's Emerald Necklace network of parks and trails, spearheaded by Amigos de los Rios, links the five-acre Bosque to other parks located along a seventeen-mile loop of trails and greenways adjacent to the river.

Visitors to Marrano Beach today are warned by signs to stay out of the river. It's now a beach without access to its water, which may strike some as odd. But Marrano Beach, nearly thirty miles from the Pacific Ocean, was never a common shore. It was born of those spurned by discrimination, who were led to conceive their own spot in the sand.

Notes

A version of this chapter was previously published on KCET Departures as "Life at Marrano Beach: The Lost Barrio Beach of the San Gabriel Valley," April 17, 2014, https://www.kcet.org/shows/departures/life-at-marrano-beach-the-lost-barrio-beach-of-the-san-gabriel-valley.

1 Metea Gold, "Riverbank's Transformation into Park Triggers Flood of Memories," *Los Angeles Times*, August 29, 1997.
2 Victor M. Valle and Rodolfo D. Torres, *Latino Metropolis* (Minneapolis: University of Minnesota Press, 2000), 159.
3 Lawrence Culver, "America's Playground: Recreation and Race," in *A Companion to Los Angeles*, ed. William Deverell and Greg Hise, (Hoboken, NJ: Blackwell Publishing, 2010), 428.
4 Mario T. García and Sal Castro, *Blowout! Sal Castro and the Chicano Struggle for Educational Justice* (Chapel Hill: University of North Carolina Press, 2011).
5 Valle and Torres, *Latino Metropolis*, 159.
6 Luis J. Rodríguez, *Always Running: La Vida Loca: Gang Days in L.A.* (New York: Touchstone, 1993).
7 Rita Ledesma, "Lessons from Marrano Beach: Attachment and Culture," in *Culturally Diverse Populations: Reflections from Pioneers in Education and Research* (Abingdon, Oxfordshire: Routledge, 2009), 70.
8 Gold, "Riverbank's Transformation into Park Triggers Flood of Memories."

16

From Small Farming to Urban Agriculture

El Monte and Subsistence Homesteading

RYAN REFT

"People want to get outdoors . . . and the small farms home gives them that opportunity," Ross H. Gast told an audience of San Diegans in 1933. "It is a good home in good and bad times and a place to save earnings with an incidental production of food supply." The writer—an editor at the *Los Angeles Times*'s *Farm and Garden Magazine* and an El Monte resident—had long advocated for the "small farm lifestyle," a return-to-the-land movement that stretched back to the turn of the century. "The way I see it, the small farm home is not just a piece of property but a mode of living, one that is being adopted generally in Southern California," he noted.[1]

Through Gast and others, the *Los Angeles Times* had spent much of the 1920s promoting what had become known as the small farm movement. For many working- and middle-class Angelenos, the home held value productively rather than speculatively. Wage laborers, clerks, and even underpaid professionals by day, residents augmented their income with small acreage food cultivation. In suburbs like South Gate, working- and middle-class homeowners built their own bungalows and planted their own gardens as much out of economic necessity as any pretense to lifestyle or any hope of improving their financial portfolios.[2] As one federal official would tell the public in 1934, the hope was for the small farm movement to "develop a better standard of living and increase the security of families by eliminating their complete dependence on a paycheck."[3]

The San Gabriel and San Fernando Valleys had also experienced a boom in the numbers of white settlers looking to live a small farms existence. As an El Monte resident, Gast had witnessed the fruits of his promotional work close at hand. Estimates suggested that 5,000 newcomers had settled on small plots across metropolitan Los Angeles, with 2,500–3,000 in El Monte alone.[4] At least six hundred El Monte families already cultivated their own fruits and vegetables on small farm plots. Advertisements "extolling the virtues" of small farm living appeared regularly in local newspapers.[5]

Therefore, when New Dealers created the Department of Subsistence Homesteads (DSH), led by M. L. Wilson and organized within the Department of the Interior, leaders of the new organization looked to Southern California for model sites. With $25 million dedicated to the experimental, federally supervised small farms program known as Subsistence Homesteads, Gast would oversee both the forty-unit San Fernando Valley and hundred-unit El Monte homesteads: planning them, building them, and selecting 140 families from a pool of thousands of hopefuls to live on them. The historian Dona Brown argues that El Monte's project proved to be one of the most successful of the subsistence homestead communities.[6]

Yet while the two projects would offer struggling Depression-era families a chance to combine rural and urban lifestyles in what Gast called "rurban" living, the projects would remain exclusively white and in many ways demonstrate the racial impulses that had long fueled the small farms movement. In addition, subsistence homesteads served as symbols of the limitations of New Deal and progressive thought, as well as the racialized land and housing policies that would undermine the homeownership dreams of minority laborers in California and the nation for decades afterward.[7]

Los Angeles County as the Spot

The combination of its film, agricultural, and manufacturing industries made Los Angeles County a prime location for the small farms movement. During the 1920s, manufacturing boomed as hundreds of local and national firms established plants in the county, including Ford, Goodrich, Firestone, and U.S. Steel.

The Depression gave the idea of rurban living an added impetus. From 1929 to 1934, workers' average weekly earnings declined precipitously by nearly 26 percent. In a climate of lowered incomes and joblessness, the idea of producing one's own food took on greater significance. Paradoxically, at the same time as wages dropped, some employers expanded their operations in Southern California. In 1929 Bethlehem Steel bought the California Iron and Steel Company, and in 1936 General Motors built its famous plant in South Gate. Despite the economic downturn of the 1930s, by the middle of the decade, Los Angeles County ranked as fifth in industrial productivity nationally and was considered by many as the most significant industrial region west of Chicago.[8]

El Monte and the San Fernando Valley sat within commuting distance of such employment. Only fourteen miles from downtown Los Angeles and within seven miles of the city's industrial sector, the fertile land of El Monte offered working- and middle-class residents a promising small farm existence. From the San Fernando Valley, a thirty-seven-mile drive to the center of the city and the local Pacific Electric Red Car routes expanded such opportunities.

Then again for all the promise of employment, the number of people on the federal dole boomed. In 1932, the county recorded 37,500 residents on the relief rolls; by 1933 that number had ballooned to 120,000. Employment might have been available, but it depended on service employers and low-income workers. A rapid population increase meant that a greater number of Los Angeles citizenry depended on such employment. In addition to the population's dependence on low wage employment, the county's high percentage of elderly citizens left Los Angeles particularly vulnerable as most elderly had no work to speak of which left them in precarious economic straits. The city's swift growth, from 936,455 in 1920 to 2,208,492 in 1930, added further pressure. Even people with jobs had to make do with less, as their yearly incomes declined; the best paid workers in the region earned at most $1,000 annually.[9]

Moreover, except for Republican Mayor Frank Shaw, elected in 1933, most of California's and Los Angeles's politicians were either resistant to New Deal policies (like Republican Governor James Rolf), uninterested (like William Elmore Evans, the Republican who represented the Ninth Congressional District in the U.S. House), or mired in political scandal (like James Henry Hoeppel, the Democrat who represented the Eleventh Congressional District). Though Senator Hiram Johnson supported many New Deal policies, he washed his hands of the subsistence homesteads. "I have made a distinction . . . between those projects which are designed to help some and profit some," he wrote Secretary of Interior Harold Ickes. "I have been extremely wary of the latter class, and if any time I am compelled to communicate with you respecting them, [I] will frankly advise you of that fact." Considering all these factors, it should come as no surprise that in terms of relief, the journalist Lorena Hickok described Los Angeles as "the blackest spot in the United States"—hardly the famous "white spot" that inhabited the dreams of out-of-work Midwesterners, Easterners, and Southerners.[10]

Planning El Monte's Rurban Homes

Despite local political ambivalence toward the homestead program, the enthusiasm and political support provided by Shaw, combined with Gast's stewardship and expertise, helped guide the El Monte and San Fernando projects into existence—and, for the most part, success. As a writer and editor for the *Los Angeles Times*'s *Farm and Garden Magazine* and an official with the Los Angeles Chamber of Commerce, Gast knew how to pitch an idea, which he did to Washington bureaucrats in early 1934. "The story's around too," Harold Finley, an editor at *Farm and Garden Magazine*, wrote, "that Gast confronted the division with a trunkful of clippings, photographs, charts, plans, diagrams and reports relating to small farm homes and that they hastened then and there to break the news of his appointment [to the DSH] lest he attempt to exhibit them all."[11]

Gast moved quickly, buying up forty acres in San Fernando Valley and a hundred in El Monte. He purchased the former from Irvin Pertz and his wife for $335 an acre and the latter from Jonas Killiam and Minnie Joughlin at $500 per acre. He tapped Joseph Weston, an architect and El Monte resident, to design all 140 homes.

Much as with his other decisions, Gast carefully vetted the El Monte architect before hiring him. Weston had won a 1928 contest sponsored by the *Los Angeles Times* and Los Angeles Chamber of Commerce devoted to small farming. Gast had overseen the competition and drew upon this experience when appointed to his position with the DSH. Weston also had the necessary credentials: a graduate of the University of Pennsylvania's School of Architecture, he had practiced architecture in California, Europe, and Mexico, designing respected homes in Bel Air, on Arizona's Hope Ranch, and at Hollywood's American Legion Club. Moreover, he had helped Gast with the original proposal to the DSH, which included Weston's home designs—based largely on the New England style popular at the time.[12]

Weston's designs proved economical, pragmatic, and aesthetically pleasing. The *Los Angeles Times* celebrated the El Monte architect's dedication to form and function, noting that he had figured out how to "shorten a room a few inches and save enough to get a better kitchen sink, and where to put his doors so Mr. and Mrs. and the kids can save steps to and from various corners of the outdoors." The federal government applauded his efforts as well: "probably in no other instance has greater care been taken in the matter, type, design, and placement of houses than at Rurban Homes." Rex Tugwell, head of the Resettlement Administration (RA), declared the two projects, San Fernando Valley and El Monte, as the most successful in the United States and "by far the most beautiful." Visitors from twenty-two states and four countries descended upon the projects to see their visionary progress. Gast estimated that nearly

FIG. 19 Dorothea Lange, "El Monte Federal Subsistence Homestead, 1936." (Courtesy of Library of Congress, Farm Security Administration, Office of War Information Photograph Collection.)

100,000 people visited.[13] Completed several weeks early, the two projects were ready by September of 1935, Rurban Homes cost just over $402,000 (collectively, El Monte's units cost $299,400, and the San Fernando Valley's units cost $102,735)—several thousand under the $410,000 dedicated to the project. Throughout the country, most other DSH projects ran over budget.

Organized under and administrated by Rurban Homes Inc, a federally controlled nonprofit corporation, the homesteads would not be relief projects. Placing the project under the auspices of the Department of Interior rather than the Federal Emergency Relief Administration signaled President Franklin Roosevelt's intent that the program be aimed at social reform rather than charity—Dust Bowl refugees arriving in the state would find no opportunities to acquire subsistence homesteads. Though only 1.3 percent of those selected were native Californians, most had lived in the state for over a decade. According to the California State Planning Department, the most common occupations among the new homesteaders were mechanics or work in the building trades. Employment in transportation was third and commerce fourth, and five applicants identified themselves as miners. The average income of the El Monte small farmers was $971 a year, while the San Fernando Valley's selected residents averaged $1,156.[14]

Still, the combined confusion and excitement surrounding the plan required Gast and the DSH to clearly outline just what they meant by subsistence homesteads. "To clear up any misconception which may arise from the title, the circular makes it plain that the [DSH] does not offer free lands nor lands for homesteading," a *Los Angeles Times* article pointed out, "but through local corporations will establish model communities of small farm homes and sell those homes to approved applicants on a loan amortization basis which will not allow transfer of title for five years."[15] As the *Los Angeles Times* columnist Lee Shippey wrote in 1935, families "had to make good for five years, no matter how rapidly [they paid] out."[16] Estimated total costs to homesteaders ranged from $2,600 to $3,000, depending on the location and size of the home. When the first families moved in during November 1935, they assumed a forty-year monthly payment of $23.34, a bargain compared to what private lenders offered at the time.[17]

Race, Class, and Ethnicity in the Building Subsistence Homesteads

Thousands of prospective homesteaders applied for one of the 140 homes, though exactly how many did so seems to be in dispute. At some moments, Gast claimed that 30,000 had applied, but at other times he said that 1,850 had. Tugwell told the U.S. Senate that 37,000 hopeful people sent in applications. The RA later said that 2,027 had applied for homes in El Monte alone. Regardless, we do know that Gast selected 1,500 applicants for personal interviews and whittled that pool down to 140.[18]

Who were the members of the two communities? They were all native born and white. While the DSH had planned communities for Native Americans, African Americans, and Jews, all were to be racially or ethnically distinct, a reflection of the racial biases afflicting New Deal policies. Creating a mixed-race homestead would threaten its viability. Gast wanted the project to demonstrate the benefits of part-time farming and low-income employment, and any challenge to that was unwelcome. He would make clear he had little interest in reforming society. "We simply tried to create an intensely practical environment for 100 fine families," he later told observers.[19] In addition to government policies that privileged white males, the back-to-the-land small farm movement had promoted a white ideal for decades. Admittedly, in its early stages, the movement was seen as radical in nature. The Progressive Era reformer and a leading proponent of gentlemen farming, Bolton Hall saw small farms as a way to achieve a more egalitarian society with a greater distribution of wealth.[20]

However, many of the movement's leading lights based their beliefs on racist understandings of nonwhites. William Smythe, a small farms pioneer, used restrictive covenants to exclude Asians, Latinos, and African Americans from his colonies in San Ysidro and Tujunga, thereby reserving them for whites. In 1908, he wrote that "the Chinaman can no more compete with the 'little lander' than he can compete with the white laundry which has reduced his business in that line to the most insignificant proportions."[21] Following suit were other less notable small farm proponents such as Charles Weeks, who excluded "Orientals" and "Negroes" from his San Fernando "little lands." And Elwood Mead, a vocal supporter of the subsistence homesteads and a former professor at the University of Southern California, described Japanese farmers as "alien renters" who "put 'rural life on the downhill grade'" and thereby threatened to ruin American agriculture.[22]

During the 1920s, Los Angeles boosters and real estate interests called whites who returned to the land "gentleman farmers," seeing in them an ideal of masculine, rugged individualism on one hand, and a means of increasing suburbanization and land speculation on the other hand. The *Los Angeles Times*, particularly through Gast, provided a promotional outlet for these developments. In essence, the "little landers," merged with the rural or urban ideal of the Southern California lifestyle and carried with them all the racial implications embedded within it.[23]

San Fernando Valley serves as a prime example. As Laura Barraclough has demonstrated, this image of the Jeffersonian independent farmer (or gentleman farmer) rested heavily on the labor of Japanese and Mexican workers: "Gentlemen farming . . . cultivated a collective sense of entitlement among whites to live a rural lifestyle with the urban state's subsidy and protection, with few strings attached, that remains meaningful to this day." In San Fernando and Pacoima, Mexican and Japanese workers clustered in multiracial communities in close proximity to "gentleman farmers" and larger agricultural interests.[24]

El Monte's Hicks Camp experienced a similar process to that which unfolded in San Gabriel Valley. Though never recognized officially as part of the city, the twenty-two-acre barrio (or *colonia*, as historians such as Matt Garcia have described it), served as a migrant camp and home for Mexican and Mexican American field laborers working in the local agricultural industry. El Monte officials refused to provide police or fire service to the community, forcing it instead to rely on Los Angeles County—a situation that had dire effects in several instances. In 1933, protesting low wages and poor work conditions in the local berry industry, Hicks Camp residents along with other workers in the region struck against their employers, mostly Japanese tenant farmers—who were ironically also targets of discrimination.[25]

Gast played a role in the strike and gained a bit of notoriety. Working for the Los Angeles Chamber of Commerce under Frank Clements, Gast issued a report on the situation in El Monte. Clements opposed unionization but also restrictions on Mexican immigration. Gast related these concerns to the public, noting that "our particular interest is . . . to maintain our Mexican labor supply." Though Gast acknowledged the low wages paid by Japanese tenant farmers, he believed that they had acted in good faith and offered a fair compromise to Hicks Camp residents.[26]

The experiences of nonwhites, as evidenced by Hicks Camp and the Berry Strike of 1933, contrasts sharply with that of white El Monte and San Fernando Valley subsistence homesteaders and puts into stark relief the very different realities facing white, Japanese, and Mexican farmers and laborers during the Depression and afterward.

The End Results

Upon its completion, the local El Monte community welcomed the hundred-unit homestead project with open arms: "We are glad that you, the 100 federal subsistence homesteaders, have come to dwell among us, and we want you to know it." City officials created a homestead float for the Pasadena Tournament of Roses Parade in 1936. Later, El Monte High School students established a demonstration garden within the project and recorded their successes. The city's embrace of the community exceeded the expectations of Gast and other DSH leaders.[27]

However, Gast stepped down soon after the project's completion. In 1935, the DSH was placed under the more experimental RA. Gast did not share the RA's approach and resigned in October of that year. "None of the exotic social and economic theory which has ruled in the development of subsistence homesteads in some parts of the country was considered in carrying out the Rurban Homes," he stated in his final report, confirming his differences with the new management.[28] The Farm Security Administration (which had had the photographer Dorothea Lange document the development of the project) inherited Rurban Homes one year later, and in 1942 the Federal Public Housing Authority assumed responsibility for the project, but the agency mostly organized the homes' sale to homesteaders.

In the intervening years, local development largely erased the influence of the Rurban Homes on the El Monte landscape. However, in the nearly three decades following the homes' completion, 25,000 small farm households would be established in the region. One can even see the seeds of the small farm movement in current urban agriculture.

While Hall had promoted the conversion of vacant lots in New York in the early twentieth century into "gardens for the poor," today Compton's ten-acre Richland Farms community provides residents with access to gardens for cultivation and even livestock.[29] "It's a garden paradise," Lloyd Wilkens told the

Los Angeles Times in 2011. Smaller versions of Richland Farms have emerged in cities across the nation; in 2014, there were 900 in New York City alone.[30]

Though less about rugged individualism and more about providing residents with access to fresh vegetables and fruit (particularly in minority communities whose members lack access to fresh produce), the urban farming movement—like its small farms predecessor—also emphasizes the importance of nature in the lives of urban residents. Additionally, if the small farms movement and subsistence homesteads fretted about masculinity, the new urban gardening movement features far more women's faces than those of men. "City farmers will tell you that the green-collar work on these small holdings is the province of a largely pink-collar labor force," the *New York Times* columnist Michael Tortorello observed in 2014.[31]

More collective in nature and including more people of color, participants in the urban farm movement differ in many ways from the "gentleman farmers" of the 1920s, but El Monte has also changed over time. Today, the San Gabriel Valley has emerged as one of the most diverse regions of the nation. In 2010, with funding from the California Strategic Growth Council and help from BASE landscape architecture, the city established the El Monte Urban Agriculture Initiative Program. Over approximately ten months, plans for community gardens, farmers markets, and the like were developed. South El Monte's Earthworks Urban Farm has also contributed to the urban agriculture initiative. Matching the diversity of the local population, the farm grows a variety of produce, including crops native to Mexico and Asia. With an overabundance of stores selling junk food, no real supermarket, and an obesity rate that hovers around 27 percent for children and 28 percent for adults, El Monte struggles with access to healthy food. Through its crop production, community outreach, and educational programs, Earthworks performs an important task locally.[32]

In the end, the subsistence homestead of the early 1930s might have been problematic in terms of gender, race, and class, but it did establish and perpetuate a tradition in El Monte. Today, residents have reengaged with that tradition on different terms and with different goals, and perhaps they can improve on the past.

Notes

1 Ada Perry, "Gardeners Given Useful Hints in Gast's New Book," *San Diego Union Tribune*, April 9, 1933.

2 Becky M. Nicolaides, *My Blue Heaven: Life and Politics in the Working-Class Suburbs of Los Angeles, 1920–1965* (Chicago: University of Chicago Press, 2002), 27–30.

3 Quoted in Robert Carriker, *Urban Farming in the West: A New Deal Experiment in Subsistence Homesteads* (Tucson: University of Arizona Press, 2010), 91.

4 Charles C. Cohan, "Small Acreage Homes Here Beckon to Thousands," *Los Angeles Times*, September 9, 1934.

5 Carriker, *Urban Farming in the West*, 87.

6 Dona Brown, *Back to the Land: The Enduring Dream of Self-Sufficiency in Modern America* (Madison: University of Wisconsin Press, 2011), 156. See also Carriker, *Urban Farming in the West*, 98–101.

7 Brown, *Back to the Land*, 155 and 165–166; Carriker, *Urban Farming in the West*, 87 and 100.

8 Nicolaides, *My Blue Heaven*, 48–50.

9 Carriker, *Urban Farming in the West*, 81–82.

10 Quoted in ibid., 82–83.

11 Harold M. Finley, "Well, We Got It Across! Small Farm Home Idea, Worked Out Here, Now Being Tackled by Uncle Sam on a Tremendous Scale," *Los Angeles Times*, April 8, 1934.

12 Carriker, *Urban Farming in the West*, 93–98.

13 Quoted in ibid., 97–98 and 102.

14 Ibid., 100.

15 'Rurban Homes' Plan Explained," *Los Angeles Times*, March 25, 1934.

16 Lee Shippey, "Rurban Homes Offer Chance for 'Pioneers' to Increase Their Income," *Los Angeles Times*, May 6, 1935.

17 Carriker, *Urban Farming in the West*, 101.

18 Ibid., 100–101.

19 Quoted in ibid., 106.

20 Brown, *Back to the Land*, 36–38, 47, and 157.

21 Brown, *Back to the Land*, 126–127.

22 Brown, *Back to the Land*, 126–127; See also, Laura R. Barraclough, *Making the San Fernando Valley: Rural Landscapes, Urban Development, and White Privilege*, (Athens: University of Georgia Press, 2011), 42–44, 46, and 51.

23 Brown, *Back to the Land*, 129–131.

24 Barraclough, *Making the San Fernando Valley*, 29 and 51.

25 Matt Garcia, *A World of Its Own: Race, Labor, and Citrus in the Making of Greater Los Angeles, 1900–1970* (Chapel Hill: University of North Carolina Press, 2001), 69–70 and 74–75; Charles Wollenberg, "Race and Class in Rural California: The El Monte Berry Strike of 1933," *California Historical Quarterly* 51, no. 2 (Summer 1972): 155–164; Daniel Morales, "El Monte's Hicks Camp: A Mexican Barrio," KCET, July 18, 2014, https://www.kcet.org/history-society/el-montes-hicks-camp-a-mexican-barrio.

26 Gilbert Gonzalez, "The Los Angeles County Strike of 1933," eScholarship.org, Center for Research on Latinos in a Global Society, July 1, 1996, accessed August 24, 2018, https://escholarship.org/uc/item/740364cq; Abraham Hoffman, "The El Monte Berry Picker's Strike, 1933," *Journal of the West* 12 no. 1 (1973): 71–84; Ronald W. Lopez, "The El Monte Berry Strike of 1933."*Aztal-Chicano Journal of the Social Sciences and Arts* no. 1 (1970): 101–114.

27 Carriker, *Urban Farming in the West*, 102.

28 Quoted in "Rural Home Head Quits," *Los Angeles Times*, October 31, 1935.

29 Brown, *Back to the Land*, 51. See also "Richland Farms: An Introduction," KCET, October 4, 2010, https://www.kcet.org/shows/departures/richland-farms-an-introduction.

30 Ann M. Simmons, "Farming in Compton's Core," *Los Angeles Times*,

February 20, 2011, http://articles.latimes.com/2011/feb/20/local/la-me-richland-farms-20110220. See also Michael Tortorello, "Mother Nature's Daughters," *New York Times*, August 27, 2014, https://www.nytimes.com/2014/08/28/garden/mother-natures-daughters.html?rref=collection%2Ftimestopic%2FUrban%20Agriculture&action=click&contentCollection=timestopics&region=stream&module=stream_unit&version=latest&contentPlacement=9&pgtype=collection.

31 Michael Tortorello, "Mother Nature's Daughters," *New York Times*, August 27, 2014, https://www.nytimes.com/2014/08/28/garden/mother-natures-daughters.html?rref=collection%2Ftimestopic%2FUrban%20Agriculture&action=click&contentCollection=timestopics&region=stream&module=stream_unit&version=latest&contentPlacement=9&pgtype=collection. See also Michael Tortorello, "Growing Everything but Gardeners," *New York Times*, October 31, 2012, https://www.nytimes.com/2012/11/01/garden/urban-gardens-grow-everything-except-gardeners.html.

32 "City of El Monte, Urban Agriculture Initiative Program: Urban Greening Plan," City of El Monte, August 2014, accessed May 15, 2018, https://issuu.com/baselandscape/docs/uaip_issuu; Connie K. Ho, "Quenching the Thirst in a Food Desert at Earthworks Farm," KCET, January 5, 2015. https://www.kcet.org/shows/departures/quenching-the-thirst-in-a-food-desert-at-earthworks-farm.

17

A Community Erased

Japanese Americans in El Monte and the Greater San Gabriel Valley

ANDRE KOBAYASHI DECKROW

A visit to El Monte, California, reveals many official signs and markers that hark back to the town's pioneer past. The local history museum is designed to look like a frontier town in the American West, complete with wagon wheels and mannequins outfitted in long skirts and bonnets. With its fertile location between the San Gabriel River and Rio Hondo, El Monte is often presented as a dream destination for westbound wagon trains, not to mention the earlier indigenous populations and the Spanish. Not surprisingly, as happened throughout the West Coast, the verdant farmland that made the San Gabriel Valley attractive to white settlers in the late 1800s would prove inviting to agricultural migrants—specifically, Japanese and Mexicans—a few decades later.

Being Japanese American in El Monte

Japanese immigrants began arriving in the San Gabriel Valley in the early 1900s. By 1913, enough Japanese had settled in the region to warrant the establishment of the Japanese Farmers' Association of the San Gabriel Valley.[1] That year, the association hosted a celebration in El Monte to welcome a visiting delegation of the Japanese Navy to Southern California. Just over twenty years later, a 1936 Japanese American Citizens League census found fifteen hundred Japanese Americans, also known as Nikkei, living in the San Gabriel Valley, about five hundred first-generation and a thousand second-generation.[2]

In El Monte specifically, the vast majority of Japanese lived outside of the main areas of town. They settled on large farms, where they grew produce and flowers to sell at local farm stands or the larger farmers markets in Southern California. Such business relations meant that the Japanese of El Monte interacted on a daily basis with not only local white residents on whom they relied as customers, but also other Japanese from throughout the region. These daily economic interactions at Los Angeles–area produce markets only further engrained a sense of ethnic solidarity across Southern California's Nikkei that local organizations, such as the Japanese Chamber of Commerce of Los Angeles and the Japanese America Society, worked tirelessly to cultivate.[3] Until World War II, Japanese Americans from the San Gabriel Valley routinely participated in Japanese-language speech contests and other community celebrations, many of which were held in Los Angeles's Little Tokyo.

The experience of Rikizo Nishida and his young family illustrates the complicated communal ties of many prewar Japanese immigrants. Nishida left his home near Hiroshima, Japan, for the United States in 1903. After working on a Hawaiian sugar plantation for three years, he moved to San Francisco and then Nebraska, finally reaching Southern California in 1911. After a year, Nishida returned to his hometown near Hiroshima, in all likelihood with the intention of finding a wife to bring back to the United States to start a family. While further Japanese migration had been prohibited under the terms of the 1907 gentleman's agreement between the U.S. and Japanese governments, immigrants already in the United States—the majority of whom were single males—could invite immediate family members to accompany them.

As a result, just a year later, in 1913, Rikizo and his new wife, Iwano, returned to the Los Angeles area—settling first in Covina, where they opened a restaurant. In 1916, Nishida quit the restaurant business and took up farming. Four years later, he invested $10,000 to open a ten-acre berry farm in El Monte. As a resident of El Monte, Nishida was active in the local Japanese community, holding numerous positions in Nikkei organizations: he was a member of the San Gabriel Valley Men's Association, treasurer of the local Japanese Language School, and governor of the San Gabriel Valley Berry Growers Co-op.

On August 23, 1929, Nishida and his family headed to Los Angeles harbor to join a large number of other Japanese Southern Californians to greet two visiting Japanese naval cruisers.[4] However, a day that made Little Tokyo "gay with flags and bunting of America and Japan" proved tragic for the Nishida family, when the car they were riding in struck another vehicle on Lower Azusa

Road.[5] Rikizo was killed when a piece of the nearby guardrail struck his head, and three other passengers were injured in the accident.

In the aftermath, the now-widowed Iwano could not support her family single-handedly. Instead, she sent her middle daughter, Mary Kikuye, to live with an uncle and aunt in Japan, though she would return a few years later to attend high school in El Monte. Later, she would meet her husband, himself a second-generation Japanese American, at one of Los Angeles's farmers markets, where he was working for his family's fruit company. In maintaining a sense of a Japanese national identity, to the point of wanting to welcome Japanese naval vessels to Southern California, while living in the United States and also routinely moving between both countries, the Nishida family's experience reveals the transnational identities that first- and some second-generation Japanese Americans embraced prior to World War II.

Farm Management and the Berry Strike of 1933

For Japanese residents of El Monte, their geographic separation from the center of town mirrored their socioeconomic and legal position in the city. Understandings of class in El Monte were essentially triangulated along ethnic lines between the city's white, Japanese, and Mexican residents. Although California's Alien Land Laws prevented first-generation Japanese immigrants from owning land, upwardly mobile Japanese, like Rikizo Nishida, managed to either lease land from white landowners or own land through their second-generation Japanese children, who were American citizens.[6] Over time, an increasing number of Japanese immigrants in the San Gabriel Valley who had been farm laborers became farm managers, especially when the Depression caused a drop in land prices and compelled many white landowners to lease their lands to Japanese growers. With more land, the Japanese began hiring an increasing number of Mexican laborers. For these Japanese, the rough transition from farmworker to farm manager would culminate in the El Monte Berry Strike of 1933.

The same macroeconomic factors that contributed to increased Japanese control of San Gabriel Valley farmland led to a drop in agricultural labor prices throughout Southern California and left many Mexican pickers, including those residing in Hicks Camp, facing desperate conditions. In June 1933 outside labor groups, led by the Cannery and Agricultural Workers' Industrial Union, organized El Monte's Mexican berry pickers to demand higher wages from Japanese growers. The labor dispute would quickly become articulated in ethnic terms. While most historical analyses of the 1933 Berry Strike concern the Mexican pickers' important contribution to California labor history, the strike was also a significant moment for El Monte's Japanese community. When the growers refused to give in to the laborers' demands and the strike proceeded, members of the Japanese community mobilized to support their own.

The city's Japanese leaders successfully petitioned the principal of El Monte High School to dismiss Japanese students for three days to help with the berry harvest.[7] Moreover, according to the historian Charles Wollenberg, labor leaders managed to expand the strike beyond the San Gabriel Valley: throughout Southern California, Mexican farmworkers picketed Japanese-run farms.[8] The conflict would not end until six weeks later, when officials from the state Bureau of Labor Relations, along with the white-led El Monte Chamber of Commerce, grew concerned that the labor strife would begin to affect the bottom lines of non-Japanese growers. Not only did white property owners have a vested interest in ensuring that their farms, leased to Japanese, remained profitable, but community leaders feared that labor unrest might also spread to white-run farms in the area. Ultimately, the Bureau of Labor Relations issued a compromise ultimatum.

A happy *Los Angeles Times* article on berry farm conditions a year after the strike proclaimed that "while Japanese, Mexicans, and Filipinos work and live in harmony and gain subsistence in the fields, berry patches covering 200 acres in the Arcadia district are serving delicious ingredients for strawberry shortcakes and Youngberry pies to an appreciative audience." Otokichi Sakamoto, a grower dubbed the "Berry King of the San Gabriel Valley" and leader of the Japanese Farmers' Association of the San Gabriel Valley, explained: "No thoughts of strikes are in the minds of these people. . . . Pickers, who sometimes work from 6 A.M. to 6 P.M. . . . now earn twenty-two cents per hour. . . . Before the recent strike, they were receiving seventeen cents."[9]

The wage increase, however, fell short of the twenty-five cents per hour that pickers and labor leaders had originally demanded. Analyzing the final result of the Berry Strike, Wollenberg concludes that "the Japanese may have 'won' the El Monte strike, but . . . the strike demonstrated the ultimate power of white institutions over Japanese interests in rural California."[10] As much as the Japanese aimed to achieve social mobility in the first few decades of the twentieth century, they still retained little control over the economic and legal structures that governed Japanese American life in El Monte.

Segregated Schools

Nowhere was this inequality more apparent than in the city's segregated public school system. Aimed at separating poor, and often transient, Mexican students from established white schools, the practice of operating separate schools for racial minorities was a common practice, especially in agricultural areas, throughout much of Southern California.[11] Although the city's secondary schools were integrated, El Monte's primary schools (through the fifth grade) were not. And despite whatever progress the Japanese community had made in the previous half-century, it was here that the myth of Japanese equality with the town's white residents would be shattered: in El Monte, young Japanese and Mexicans attended the Lexington Grammar School, while white students attended separate, better equipped primary schools. While El Monte's leaders had come to the assistance of Japanese farmers in settling the Berry Strike of 1933, the same leaders forced Japanese children to attend the same schools as the children of families on the other side of the picket line.

In his interview with the Denshō Project, an online Japanese American oral history archive, Bacon Sakatani, a second-generation Japanese American who lived in El Monte for a time as a child, describes attending the Lexington School. He notes that of the school's forty or so students, 20 percent were Japanese and 80 percent were Mexican. Many of the Mexican students were very poor. Sakatani comments, "I have a photo that shows them barefooted and some of them were not even bringing lunches to school."[12] Moreover, though the premise for segregating primary school students was to prepare them for the rigors of higher grades, Sakatani remembers that the majority of Mexican students did not end up attending secondary school, while the Japanese students, who almost all attended secondary school, generally did not need such remedial support. In fact, Sakatani faults the segregated schools for what he believed to be his limited vocabulary once he began attending integrated schools in nearby La Puente. Although El Monte schools were some of the few segregated primary schools in the San Gabriel Valley, he states, "As I recall there were no protests. People just accepted those kind of schools."

El Monte's Japanese community may have grudgingly accepted segregated schools at the community level, but at the individual level, there was notable resistance. As a young child growing up in El Monte in the 1930s, Ike Hatchimonji's experience differed from that of most of his fellow second-generation Japanese. For starters, his father, Kumezo Hatchimonji, was one of the few first-generation Japanese in El Monte to have been educated in the United States. Having studied English with American missionaries in northeastern Japan, Kumezo came to the United States after taking a job on a merchant ship. He graduated from New York's Columbia University in 1927 and shortly thereafter moved to Southern California. In Los Angeles, he married Nobue Komoro, the daughter of a Japanese Christian minister, and the couple had twins, nicknamed Mike and Ike, in 1928. Then Kumezo moved the family to Phoenix, Arizona, where he established the Valley Seed Company, selling fruit and vegetable seeds commercially to Japanese and other small-scale farmers. The family moved again, this time to the San Gabriel Valley in 1934, where Kumezo continued to sell seeds commercially. A couple of years later, he opened a retail store for the Valley Seed Company at 402 East Valley Boulevard in

FIG. 20 Kumezo Hatchimonji in front of his general store. (Courtesy of Mike Hatchimonji.)

El Monte, and the Hatchimonji family lived in a small rented house behind the store. They were one of the few Japanese families who lived in town as opposed to on farms outside of the city.

Seeing the rundown conditions at the Lexington Grammar School, Kumezo Hatchimonji received permission from the principal of the Mountain View Grammar School, in the adjacent but integrated Mountain View School District, for his sons to attend that school instead. Every day, Ike and Mike walked half a mile each way to the boundaries of the Mountain View School District, where they would catch a bus to and from school. Ironically, Ike remembers that his home in El Monte actually abutted the grounds of an all-white elementary school that he was legally barred from attending. Moreover, he notes that he and his brother were allowed to attend an integrated primary school only because their father, an educated and fluent speaker of English, had personally spoken with the principal. In all likelihood, even if they had hoped for their children to attend integrated schools, many other first-generation Japanese would not have been comfortable making such requests of school officials. As both Sakatani and Ike Hatchimonji recall, in their childhood it was not just the primary schools that were segregated in El Monte. Japanese and Mexicans could sit only in certain sections of movie theaters and use public swimming pools only on certain days of the week. Despite this segregation, Ike does not remember experiencing any direct prejudice. Most of Hatchimonji's young friends were white, and their attitudes toward him did not seem to change even with the beginning of World War II. If anything, he sees his childhood in El Monte as a time of innocence, especially in comparison to the experience he and other Japanese would face just a few years later.

Forced Relocation and Internment

The indignity of attending segregated public school paled in comparison to the injustice that was forced relocation and internment during World War II. In the months preceding the bombing of Pearl Harbor, the Japanese in the San Gabriel Valley could not have imagined they would soon lose their homes and livelihoods. In fact, with the specter of war looming, many Japanese Americans were active in the local community's preparations for national defense. Less than six months before they would be sent there as detainees, local Japanese participated in the Japan Day celebrations at the 1941 Los Angeles County Fair at the Pomona Fairgrounds. Even during Japan Day, reports indicate that the fair's "national defense theme predominated."[13] Just two months later, in November 1941, the *Los Angeles Times* chronicled a local "Food for Defense Week Campaign" in El Monte, during which the area's farmers were expected to disclose their farms' production to local officials. Given the plethora of first-generation Japanese farmers in the area, "At each [high] school, Japanese interpreters were present to help Japanese—mostly farmers of truck crops—fill out their patriotic reports."[14] In all likelihood, the following year's agricultural production fell far short of the Food for Defense drive's estimates, as the area's Japanese residents would be relocated prior to the 1942 harvest.

On February 19, 1942, President Franklin Roosevelt signed Executive Order 9066, which set in motion the relocation of Japanese Americans from throughout the West Coast to internment camps in the interior of the country. For El Monte's Japanese, the time immediately following Pearl Harbor was one of great uncertainty. Hatchimonji recalls attending school the day after the attacks and things proceeding more or less as normal, though he credits his parents for shielding him and his siblings from the worst news. When the orders to evacuate the San Gabriel Valley came in late April, he remembers being called, along with his brother, to the principal's office, where the principal told them that he regretted that they had to go. With just a couple of weeks' notice and little knowledge of where their final destination would be, Japanese in the San Gabriel Valley prepared for their relocation, selling whatever belongings they could.

For the Hatchimonji family, the timing of their removal was especially harsh. Since farmers bought seeds on credit and paid after their harvests, a May evacuation meant that while most seeds had already been planted, the Japanese farmers could not reap what they had sown. As a result, Kumezo Hatchimonji's seed business suffered heavy losses, and he struggled to pay his bills. In addition to selling whatever belongings they could, Ike remembers that his family had to give away their German shepherd, as they were not allowed to take their pets with them.[15] In early May, the family, along with other El Monte Japanese, arrived at an assembly point in West Covina for the bus trip to their new temporary home at the Pomona Assembly Center on the Los Angeles County Fairgrounds.

By early April, the San Gabriel Valley was home to one of the largest assembly centers on the West Coast: Santa Anita Park, in Arcadia. The relocation of Japanese Americans proceeded over a period of six weeks, starting from the coasts before moving inland. By the time that Japanese in the San Gabriel Valley were ordered to evacuate in May, the makeshift barracks at the racetrack, including those in converted horse stables and under the grandstand, were already overcrowded.[16] Instead, residents were sent to the Fairplex. There, a series of hastily constructed barracks surrounded by high barbed-wire fences had been built from scratch, since few of the fairgrounds' existing facilities were suitable for human accommodation. Like Santa Anita, the Pomona Detention Center eventually became so overcrowded that horse stables were used to house detainees. Upon arriving at Pomona, El Monte's Japanese faced harsh conditions even compared to those in other detention centers. Outbreaks of food poisoning and athlete's foot were common, and older residents struggled with the summer heat.

Residents also struggled to achieve a semblance of normalcy in the camps. Ike Hatchimonji remembers celebrating his grammar school graduation in camp, as he had missed his own at the Mountain View Grammar School by just a few weeks. In addition, he fondly recalls the kindness of people from the American Friends Service Committee, a Quaker organization whose members brought books and supplies to the camp and made life somewhat easier for the Japanese Americans imprisoned there. However, Hatchimonji also notes that it was not until he arrived at Pomona and met other Japanese from throughout Southern California that he was instilled with a sense of Japanese identity and an understanding of the precariousness of his rights.

In August 1942, the vast majority of detainees in the Pomona Detention Center were relocated to their more permanent home: the Heart Mountain Relocation Center, in a barren area of northwestern Wyoming.[17] After leaving Pomona, many would never return to the San Gabriel Valley or even Southern California. When Japanese internment came to an end in early 1945, many internees resettled away from the West Coast, in cities like Chicago and Salt Lake City. Having lost their leased lands in the relocation, even those who returned to the San Gabriel Valley typically entered industries other than agriculture. In 1988, the U.S. Congress acknowledged the injustice of Japanese American internment when it passed the Civil Liberties Act. The act provided a small but symbolic sum of $20,000 in reparations for Japanese Americans who had been interned.

Memorializing Japanese American History

While El Monte and the San Gabriel Valley are still home to a small community of Japanese Americans, the demographics and economy of the region have undoubtedly changed since World War II. El Monte is now largely Latino, and the San Gabriel Valley is home to one of the largest Chinese populations on the West Coast. Few, if any, farms remain, and the towns of the valley are now bedroom communities whose economies are closely tied to Los Angeles. Today, there is almost no evidence of the Japanese American community that played such an important role in the region's development in the early twentieth century.

However, in this regard, El Monte and the San Gabriel Valley are not alone. Throughout the Western Hemisphere, communities have grappled with how best to commemorate Nikkei populations that either no longer exist or are diminishing. In Latin America, where towns that were once entirely Japanese are becoming increasingly heterogeneous, Nikkei commonly build Japanese-style gardens in public parks. For these immigrants, the marking of public space in a traditionally Japanese style serves as a lasting symbol of their city's history in the face of an uncertain future. Elsewhere on the West Coast, one of the largest and best-known public memorials to prewar Japanese Americans can be found on Bainbridge Island, Washington, just west of Seattle. Part of a local public history project, the Bainbridge Island Japanese American Memorial commemorates the lives and forced removal of the town's 276 Japanese American residents in March 1942.[18] The 276-foot-long walkway at the heart of the memorial features a story wall with numerous friezes depicting prewar Japanese American life. As it leads toward the water, the memorial allows visitors to retrace the final steps on the island of these Japanese Americans.

On a smaller scale, cities in Southern California have recently either dedicated or have planned Nikkei memorials. In April 2012, on the seventieth anniversary of the removal of the area's Japanese Americans, community leaders in Venice, led by the Venice Japanese American Memorial Marker Committee, culminated a decade-long effort to dedicate a monument to the Nikkei community at the major intersection that served as the city's assembly point.[19] And in February 2014, as part of the city's public trails project, Santa Ana in Orange County commissioned a public sculpture to commemorate its history as a Japanese American farming community.[20]

As the numbers of Japanese Americans who grew up in the San Gabriel Valley and of the area's residents with memories of Japanese American friends and classmates both continue to decrease, so too does the impetus for remembering El Monte's Japanese American history. Yet, now as much as ever, it is important to recognize not only the important contributions that the Nikkei made to the region but also the ease with which a vibrant immigrant community was effectively erased from public memory.

Notes

1 "Japanese Farmers Entertain Cadets: Are Hosts at Banquet Given at El Monte," *Los Angeles Times*, May 13, 1917.

2 "Nipponese List Births: Citizens' League Takes Census," *Los Angeles Times*, January 12, 1936.

3 For a broader examination of the transnational ties of Japanese in California in the early twentieth century, see Eiichiro Azuma, *Between Two Empires: Race, History, and Transnationalism in Japanese America* (Oxford: Oxford University Press, 2005).

4 The visit of Japanese naval forces in Southern California symbolizes the broader U.S.-Japanese competition that Akira Iriye argues was manifested in "the sense of estrangement across the Pacific at the turn of the twentieth century . . . related to the parallel development of [the United States and Japan] as expansionists" (*Pacific Estrangement: Japanese and American Expansion, 1897–1911* [Chicago: Imprint Publications, 1994]).

5 "'Banzais' Greet Naval Visitors: Japanese Training Ships at Harbor Welcomed," *Los Angeles Times*, August 24, 1929. See also "Three Killed in Traffic; Two Others Face Death," *Los Angeles Times*, August 24, 1929.

6 Scott Kurashige explains the effects of the Alien Land Laws on the economic structures and intraethnic relations of Japanese produce farmers in *The Shifting Grounds of Race: Black and Japanese Americans in the Making of Multiethnic Los Angeles* (Princeton, NJ: Princeton University Press, 2008), 68–70.

7 "El Monte Berry Crop Threatened by Strike," *Los Angeles Times*, June 7, 1933.

8 Charles Wollenberg, "Race and Class in Rural California: The El Monte Berry Strike of 1933," *California Historical Quarterly* 51 (1972): 158.

9 Quoted in "No Strike Here: Arcadia Berry Pickers Too Busy to Make Trouble," *Los Angeles Times*, July 1, 1934.

10 Wollenberg, "Race and Class in Rural California," 163.

11 It was not until 1946 that the Ninth Circuit Court of Appeals ruled in *Mendez v. Westminster* that segregated schools for Latinos in California were unconstitutional.

12 Bacon Sakatani, interview by Tom Ikeda, Denshō Digital Archive, August 31, 2010, http://ddr.densho.org/interviews/ddr-densho-1000-298-5.

13 "Fair Attendance Totals 176,498 for Four Days," *Los Angeles Times*, September 17, 1941.

14 "Farmers Begin Signing Up in Food for Defense Drive," *Los Angeles Times*, November 4, 1914.

15 Believing that he would eventually return to the San Gabriel Valley and reestablish his business, Kumezo Hatchimonji placed a considerable number of seeds in storage. While he would never return to El Monte, he was eventually able to get the seeds delivered to him at the Heart Mountain Relocation Camp in northwestern Wyoming. With the seeds, he helped found a successful victory garden program on the camp premises. Ike Hatchimonji, interview by Martha Nakagawa, Denshō Digital Archive, November 30, 2011, http://ddr.densho.org/interviews/ddr-densho-1000-381-13/.

16 At its peak, Santa Anita would hold over 18,000 Japanese Americans. Today, only a small plaque in front of the grandstand commemorates the racetrack's infamous history. See Konrad Linke, "Santa Anita (detention facility)," Denshō Encyclopedia, accessed July 29, 2019, https://encyclopedia.densho.org/Santa_Anita_(detention_facility)/.

17 Japanese Americans from Southern California were completely unprepared for their first winter at Heart Mountain, where temperatures sometimes reached −30 degrees Fahrenheit. See Mieko Matsumoto, "Heart Mountain," Denshō Encyclopedia, accessed July 29, 2019, http://encyclopedia.densho.org/Heart%20Mountain/.

18 Bainbridge Island Japanese American Community, "Bainbridge Island Japanese American Memorial—Introduction," accessed August 15, 2018, http://www.bijac.org/index.php?p=MEMORIALIntroduction.

19 Venice, "Japanese American Memorial Monument," accessed August 15, 2018, http://www.venicejamm.org/. See also "Japanese American Memorial Marker," KCET, July 31, 2012, https://www.kcet.org/shows/departures/japanese-american-memorial-marker.

20 Art Pedroza, "City to Fund Public Art Honoring the Japanese-American Farming Community," New Santa Ana, February 4, 2014, http://newsantaana.com/2014/02/04/city-to-fund-public-art-honoring-the-japanese-american-farming-community/.

18

Whittier Narrows Park

A Story of Water, Power, and Displacement

DAVID REID

A stroll through Whittier Narrows Park is a walk through many worlds. The scent of *carne asada* wafts on the breeze as a jogger moves by in full stride. The sound of buzzing model airplanes drawing figure eights above the trees is punctuated by shots from the shooting range. On weekdays local school groups visit the nature center and hike the trails, while on weekends the park is filled with rowdy soccer games and families flocking from distant corners of Southern California for reunions. The sound of rhythm and blues from stereos blends with birdsong as fishermen cast their lines into the lake.

At 1,492 acres, Whittier Narrows is one of Los Angeles County's largest parks. Not only is it part of the daily landscape for locals, it is also a landmark in the memories of many generations. It is a site of layered histories in a struggle between the natural and built environment, California water politics, and the uprooted communities that once called this region home.

How did a working-class neighborhood in drought-parched Southern California become the home for this park? The answer lies in the story of Whittier Narrows Dam, constructed in 1957 as part of a flood-control scheme central to the development of modern Los Angeles. The dam's construction and the controversy it roused is a microcosm of the West's sordid history of water—the story of how astonishing amounts of money and hubris transformed the landscape, usually at the expense of the marginalized and in favor of the powerful, and created a glittering society whose sheen of prosperity rests on the razor's edge of its dwindling water supply. Yet in an ironic twist, the story of Whittier Narrows is one instance when the voices of the marginalized won out over those of the powerful, and when the development of water infrastructure, so often ecologically destructive, prevented a historic natural area from disappearing.

For as long as humans have inhabited the San Gabriel Valley, Whittier Narrows has been important for its water. The narrows form a gap in the mountains that make up the southern edge of the valley, through which the Rio Hondo and San Gabriel River flow. The geology of the hills is mirrored underground, where an intrusion of bedrock forces groundwater up to the surface. For thousands of years, the abundance of water from the two rivers and the rich vegetation and tree cover of the hills created a bustling habitat for wildlife and a productive hunting ground for the Kizh Indians, also known as the Tongva—whose territory once stretched from Pomona to Catalina Island and the Sierra Madre. Later, the water also enticed Spaniards to Whittier Narrows. They built the Mission San Gabriel Arcángel in 1771, and the mission's name came to be adopted by the Kizh-Gabrieleño Indians, who were enslaved to help construct it. The Spaniards and Indians living on the mission effected enormous transformations on the land, constructing *zanjas* (ditches) to channel the rivers' water onto agricultural fields for irrigation. By the time the mission system was secularized in 1833, the San Gabriel Mission held an enormous amount of productive agricultural land.

The richness of the land drew more newcomers in the nineteenth century. While rights to mission lands had been awarded by decree to the Kizh-Gabrieleño inhabitants, in fact most fell into the hands of Mexican ranchers and land grantees as newly independent Mexico sought to populate its northern expanses. Yet even as the Mexican usurpers made claims on the San Gabriel Valley, the Mexican-American War turned the region into U.S. territory and started a new wave of land takeovers, led by Anglo settlers. El Monte remained an attractive site for agriculture throughout the nineteenth century and into the twentieth, when it became home to a growing population and a wide expanse of walnut, citrus, and other truck farms and—by the 1940s—to factories producing munitions for the war effort.

Memories of Whittier Narrows from the time before the dam paint a bucolic picture of agriculture, simplicity, and above all water. "In our well the water was delicious," remembers Manuel Martínez, whose family migrated from Michoacán to a rustic house in an unincorporated area along the river in 1939.[1] Life was not easy: the family built its own house out of boxcar wood, used an outhouse, and had to heat water for bathing on an outside fire. But Martínez recalls it fondly: the ducks and pheasants that inhabited the reeds along the river's edge, learning to swim with his sister, Ofelia, from a little island behind their house, and digging a well with his father—and hitting water only six feet underground. "It makes you into a better person, going through this," he says. Night brought the sound of frogs croaking and singing, giving the area its name of Canta Ranas.

"You could grow anything in El Monte," recalls Robert Irwin, who was born in Whittier in 1935.[2] Working on his Irish immigrant grandfather's walnut farm, Irwin's memories of youth swirl with the rhythms of agricultural life and the flow of water. Each year the Rio Hondo and San Gabriel River would flood, leaving a layer of rich topsoil on farmers' fields. Irwin helped his grandfather and did chores on neighbors' farms to earn extra money, and in his spare time, he would fish for trout in the streams: "It was a completely, totally different world."[3]

While the number of farms increased through the twentieth century, there was still plenty of plant and animal life along the rivers. Chief Ernie Salas of the Kizh-Gabrieleño Indians remembers his father teaching him how to hunt at El Rancho de Don Daniel, a riverside property whose owner allowed locals to use the riverside and that had once been Kizh land. They would shoot rabbit, quail, and wild doves, but never hawks. Then Salas's father would clean and cook the animals, and they would eat them right there. "Nobody does that anymore," Salas says.[4] This was also where he learned to swim as a young boy—by being thrown into the river! (It is to be hoped that nobody does that anymore, either.)

The abundance of water attracted another kind of interest as well. Around the time of Salas's swimming lesson, Whittier Narrows fell under the gaze of Los Angeles City officials, hydro engineers, and business interests, who determined that the Los Angeles Basin's rivers and groundwater could—and should—be dammed, channeled, diverted, or otherwise controlled. Flood prevention was the main objective. Annual rainfall in Los Angeles is low, but it tends to come in sudden torrents that overwhelm the dry soil's ability to absorb them and create flash floods. Urban sprawl exacerbates the problem, by paving over the ground and further reducing its ability to absorb water. Moreover, it places buildings, infrastructure, and people in the way, raising the stakes and consequences of floods. Destructive floods in the 1910s, 1920s, and 1930s heightened the apparent need for flood control in the Los Angeles Basin. This was also a time when the collective wisdom was that rivers—and the environment at large—were there to be altered. It was an era when "conserving" water literally meant building dams, and "wasting" water meant allowing rivers, lakes, and aquifers to burble away untouched in their natural state.

Indeed, in this era water all across the West became the object of a unique form of hydro-engineering hubris, a sort of Manifest Destiny of water. Marc Reisner, in his classic book *Cadillac Desert*, called these "the go-go years"—decades in which no project was too big or too small for the U.S. Bureau of Reclamation (which was tasked with managing irrigation projects) and the U.S. Army Corps of Engineers (which was in charge of flood control and navigation, although in reality the two agencies frequently competed for the same types of project).[5] Visionaries since John Wesley Powell had viewed water and irrigation as the key to settling the U.S. West, but the magic ingredient finally arrived during the Depression, when President Franklin Delano Roosevelt's New Deal poured previously unimaginable amounts of money into Western water development.

Projects like Hoover Dam are part of the American pantheon of technological success stories. Millions have been struck in awe by the dam and others, like Glen Canyon and Grand Coulee, whose mass and engineering magnificence seem to be outsize monuments to the American will.[6] But as Reisner shows, there is a dark side to these developments.[7] Their direct environmental effects are harmful enough, and they are compounded by what the dams enable: the settlement of millions of people in what are essentially desert areas—swimming pools, fountains, citrus groves, and lush golf greens notwithstanding. If you build it, they will come, in other words; and if you build it in a desert, they will come to be dependent on extremely scanty sources of water. Today, for example, some forty million people depend on the Colorado River alone for their water. The consequences of this dependence are becoming more and more apparent, as California faces increasingly severe droughts.

To make things worse, many irrigation projects benefited entrenched interests instead of the everyday people whose livelihoods they were initially meant to protect. Cheap irrigation water from financially dubious projects turned into an enormous taxpayer subsidy to large landowners and some of the nation's richest oil and insurance companies, who snatched up cheap land as a tax dodge and sometimes benefited from federal farm subsidies as well.[8]

The construction of the Whittier Narrows Dam lies in this context of runaway water infrastructure. Yet in some ways, it is an exception to the rule. As Sarah S. Elkind tells in *How Local Politics Shape Federal Policy*, the story of the dam is about one time when determined local voices managed to shape the course of federal water policy.[9]

A dam at Whittier Narrows was first proposed by the City of Long Beach in 1920, as a means of securing a city water supply independent from Los Angeles. When that need was rendered moot by the construction of what became the Hoover Dam, the proposed dam at Whittier Narrows became part of broader plans by the Los Angeles County Flood Control District (LACFCD), an agency tasked with managing a total-basin scheme for river diversion, harbor protection, and flood control.

Yet plans for the Whittier Narrows Dam languished until 1936 when, as part of the New Deal, Congress passed the Flood Control Act and turned oversight of flood control on all rivers to the Corps of Engineers. The Corps included the Whittier Narrows Dam in a 1938 plan to redevelop the San Gabriel River, which gained higher priority following a devastating flood in March of that year. The flood was the worst in Los Angeles history, claiming forty-nine lives and causing some $40 million in damage.[10] The Army Corps responded with "surgical precision," as Jared Orsi puts it, implementing a massive, basin-wide scheme of infrastructure and works to prevent the tragedy from recurring.[11] The present-day dam at Whittier Narrows is an artifact of that plan: it is a flood control dam, which in the event of heavy rainfall upstream can be closed, preventing a flood downstream and allowing the floodwaters to percolate back into the underground aquifer or be released at a safe volume.

The problem was that the site of the Corps's proposed dam at Whittier Narrows was home to thousands of people, several school districts, a number of farms, railroad tracks, oil wells, and an Audubon Society bird sanctuary. Concerned people in El Monte formed the El Monte Citizens Flood Control Committee to oppose the dam.[12] The committee hired former LACFCD hydrologists to scrutinize the Corps's plans and propose alternatives, and they also counted on the support of Jerry Voorhis, the Democrat who represented El Monte in the U.S. House of Representatives and received hundreds of letters opposing the dam.

The committee fought the Corps of Engineers through the 1940s. Instead of a dam, the committee insisted, the Corps should focus on deepening and fortifying the river channel downstream of Whittier Narrows; rather than attempting to impound floodwaters as a dam would do, these works would contain them within the riverbed and prevent flooding. Attempting to get the two sides to compromise, Voorhis suggested that the dam be built in a different place, a mile downstream of the Corps's proposed site, so as to affect fewer people. The Corps rejected both proposals out of hand.

The Corps was legally bound to undertake work only at the behest of local interests: only civic groups, not the Corps itself, could initiate the construction of a flood control dam. Yet the Corps subverted this rule to gain support for a dam at Whittier Narrows. Rather than surveying all stakeholders to determine whether the consensus was in favor of a dam or not, the Corps was extremely selective, endorsing only the views of those who supported a dam and dismissing the strong opposition from El Monte. At times the Corps went further, by cultivating—to use Elkind's word—support for the dam among business interests in Long Beach and other downstream areas. Instead of abiding by rules designed to make water infrastructure reflect the public will, in other words, the Corps weaponized those rules to dismiss opposition to a dam it was determined to build.[13] In 1946, for example, Congress ordered the Corps to hold public hearings on the proposed dam at Whittier Narrows, after Voorhis blocked appropriations for the dam as a last-ditch effort to halt its construction. The

FIG. 21 Crew of men paving the main channel, near Whittier Narrows, 1965. (Courtesy of *Los Angeles Herald Examiner* Photo Collection and Los Angeles Public Library.)

Corps delayed the public hearing for months to bolster support from the Long Beach Chamber of Commerce and other communities that it felt would support the dam.[14] Then, rather than use the hearings to gather public feedback and provide information on possible alternatives, the Corps used them as a venue to reject opposition to the dam as backward and alternative proposals as inferior.

It took until 1948 for the deadlock to end. Congressman Richard Nixon, who had replaced Voorhis in the fall of 1946, was able to broker a compromise: the Corps agreed to move the dam site a mile downstream (as Voorhis had suggested) and modify the plans to protect local landmarks and business interests—including oil wells, railroad tracks, and the Audubon Society bird sanctuary—thus making the plans more palatable to El Monte locals. Construction began in 1950 and was completed in 1957.

For El Monte, the outcome was bittersweet. The new dam, while much less disruptive than the original, still displaced more than 2,000 people and 560 homes to make room for the dam's works and spreading grounds (areas where floodwater can be stored to allow it to percolate back into the ground).[15] As Irwin remembers, "The state came in and built Legg Lake. They ripped everything down."[16] The construction altered the flow of groundwater, and Irwin's grandfather had to sell his once-thriving walnut orchard (a few surviving walnut trees can still be seen behind a chain-link fence in a vacant lot off Durfee Avenue). Before the dam, groundwater was so abundant that his grandfather was able to irrigate ten acres of walnut trees with a single windmill. In contrast, he says, "you could dig until your balls fell off now and not get any water!" The dam's construction disproportionately affected the poor. Many of the displaced were low-income Mexican Americans and immigrants whose semiofficial leases with local landowners gave them few legal rights. As Martínez recalls, "All they told [people] was that everybody had to get out." They were never compensated, and he comments, "We probably could have sued for that."[17]

Moreover, the prolonged fight over the dam left a bitter aftertaste for locals in El Monte, despite their apparent success in stopping the original plan. As Elkind writes, the process by which the Whittier Narrows Dam was created "was not antidemocratic in the pure sense."[18] A majority of people in the region supported it, and the dam has worked as it was supposed to (so far—see below). But the process left much to be desired. The Corps's deliberate efforts to thwart public dialogue left some in El Monte convinced that their opinions and indeed livelihoods were not valued by their government and left a lasting suspicion of federal or state proposals for public works or local programs supposedly in the public interest. As a result, the Whittier Narrows Dam controversy stands in people's memories as both an example of El Monte's political exclusion and an example of local people's ability to make their voices heard in spite of it.

As time goes by, though, the outcome of the Whittier Narrows Dam controversy seems more and more like a victory for El Monte and South El Monte. Perhaps ironically, opposition to the dam had been about protecting local industry, not the environment. Yet today it is the natural features of Whittier Narrows that are most cherished. Indeed, the acrimony and displacement the dam wrought have faded in memory (except, of course, for those who were displaced by it). Whittier Narrows today is a community gem.

"It was a wonderland for children," recalls Dana Law, who moved to El Monte as a boy in the early 1960s and spent many days of his youth fishing, wandering, and getting lost in and around Whittier Narrows.[19] The dam and its spreading grounds have ensured the survival of some 400 acres of forest, lakes, trails, lawns, and soccer fields—a rare natural site in the city and an important place for recreation, gathering, and having fun. The construction of the freeways that surround the park have helped maintain its hidden, semiwild allure. As Nick Juravich, who helped to record the oral histories cited in this chapter, tells me, happy memories from Legg Lake came up virtually every time someone from El Monte was asked about the past.

The infrastructure has also preserved a living link to the Whittier Narrows area's history and to the natural world. As Ernie Salas says, when you enter the forest, "you can hear nature, hear the birds, hear everything. It's like you're in a secluded area in the city itself." His son, Andy, adds that Whittier Narrows offers the first taste of the natural world to many locals: "a lot of the kids we take into there have never been into a place that's kind of wild." For many who live in El Monte and South El Monte, says Andy, "We can't go to the mountains, we've never been to Yosemite—[the park] was our Yosemite."[20] The existence of Whittier Narrows is an ironic quirk in the history of development in the Western United States: the same water infrastructure that caused so much ecological destruction by enabling settlement also helped preserve the hydrologic landscape at Whittier Narrows.

In 2006, the fight over the Whittier Narrows Dam was revived in the controversial plans for the San Gabriel River Discovery Center, which would replace the existing Whittier Narrows Nature Center. The plans call for the $30 million, 14,000-square-foot center, including a 116-space parking lot, to be constructed atop ten acres of what is currently parkland occupied by hundred-year-old trees and bird habitat. Opponents claim that the planned center is too big, too expensive, too destructive of natural habitat, and too much the brainchild of outside interests, not local people.[21] As Andy Salas says, "This big eraser called 'progress' is going to come in and take away the last native lands."[22]

Those plans—and much more—have been called further into question since the Army Corps of Engineers determined in 2017 that the Whittier Narrows Dam is at extreme risk of failure.[23] Heavy rain could cause the dam's floodgates to open prematurely or erode the dam by underground seepage or overtopping (when water flows over the top of a dam). Needless to say, that would pose an extreme risk to the estimated one million people who live in the San Gabriel River's floodplain. A contingency and repair plan is being developed, and the Corps has made it one of its highest-priority safety projects.

Once again, Whittier Narrows raises bigger questions about people and water in the West. Now that we've created this world through water, how do we sustain it? For whom? To what ends? Whose voices will be heard in the process? While the problems may be familiar, the answers remain uncertain.

Notes

1 Manuel Martínez and Ofelia Silva, oral history interview, January 15, 2015, South El Monte Arts Posse (SEMAP), East of East: Mapping Community Narratives in El Monte and South El Monte, http://www.semapeastofeast.com.

2 Robert Irwin, oral history interview, January 10, 2015, South El Monte Arts Posse (SEMAP), East of East: Mapping Community Narratives in El Monte and South El Monte, http://www.semapeastofeast.com.

3 Ibid.

4 Members of the Kizh-Gabrieleño Band of Mission Indians, oral history interview, January 10, 2015, South El Monte Arts Posse (SEMAP), East of East: Mapping Community Narratives in El Monte and South El Monte, http://www.semapeastofeast.com.

5 Marc Reisner, *Cadillac Desert: The American West and Its Disappearing Water* (New York: Penguin Books, 1993), 158.
6 David Nye, *American Technological Sublime* (Cambridge, MA: MIT Press, 1994).
7 Reisner, *Cadillac Desert.*
8 For more on the history of water in the West, see, among others, Philip L. Fradkin, *A River No More: The Colorado River and the West* (Berkeley: University of California Press, 1996); Norris Hundley Jr., *Water and the West: The Colorado River Compact and the Politics of Water in the American West* (Berkeley: University of California Press, 2009); Donald Worster, *Rivers of Empire: Water, Aridity, and the Growth of the American West* (New York: Oxford University Press, 1992).
9 My narrative of the dam's construction and controversy closely follows Elkind's account. See Sarah S. Elkind, *How Local Politics Shape Federal Policy: Business, Power and Environment in Twentieth-Century Los Angeles* (Chapel Hill: University of North Carolina Press, 2011).
10 Jared Orsi, *Hazardous Metropolis: Flooding and Urban Ecology in Los Angeles* (Berkeley: University of California Press, 2004), 110.
11 Ibid., 111.
12 Elkind, *How Local Politics Shape Federal Policy*, 96.
13 Ibid., 101.
14 Ibid., 106.
15 Ibid., 110.
16 Irwin, oral history interview, SEMAP.
17 Martínez and Silva, oral history interview, SEMAP.
18 Elkind, *How Local Politics Shape Federal Policy*, 86.
19 Dana Law, oral history interview, January 12, 2015, South El Monte Arts Posse (SEMAP), East of East: Mapping Community Narratives in El Monte and South El Monte, http://www.semapeastofeast.com.
20 Members of the Kizh-Gabrieleño Band of Mission Indians, oral history interview, SEMAP.
21 Laura Vena, "Shaping the Landscape at Whittier Narrows Nature Center," KCET, January 26, 2015, https://www.kcet.org/shows/departures/shaping-the-landscape-at-whittier-narrows-nature-center.
22 Members of the Kizh-Gabrieleño Band of Mission Indians, oral history interview, SEMAP.
23 Louis Sahagun, "U.S. Army Corps of Engineers Says Whittier Narrows Dam Is Unsafe and Could Trigger Catastrophic Flooding," *Los Angeles Times*, September 14, 2017, http://www.latimes.com/local/california/la-me-whittier-narrows-dam-20170914-story.html.

19

Transportational El Monte

From the Red Car to the Freeway

RYAN REFT

"I remember being in Los Angeles, reading about farms, it was very exciting," Marty Martinez, a longtime resident of El Monte and South El Monte, reminisced. "Hay, chickens, eggs, horses, cows, you read about all that, [but] it feels like a dream world." One day Martinez found himself on a school field trip to a farm in the San Gabriel Valley (SGV), eventually arriving at Durfee Ranch in El Monte. A few years later, in the late 1930s, his family moved from Southeast Los Angeles to El Monte, where Martinez discovered that his new home was exactly where he had journeyed with his classmates. "I recognized it right away, I've been here before. It was fantastic really, a real farm with a red roof."[1]

Martinez would eventually serve on the South El Monte planning commission during the 1980s and 1990s, and that work and his memories reflect the changes that unfolded over the next two decades that simultaneously reshaped the land, its demography, and politics. From the vantage point of El Monte, he and his fellow residents witnessed the SGV's metamorphosis from an agricultural Shangri-la, populated largely by whites with small but significant Latino and Asian communities, to the prototypical multicultural, urbanized suburb that has come to epitomize the SGV.

Though several forces contributed to the evolution of El Monte and South El Monte, the region's transportation networks played a critical role. Greater El Monte spent the first half of the twentieth century stitched into an expanding metropolitan Los Angeles by the world's largest interurban streetcar system. It experienced the century's second half threaded into a burgeoning Greater Los Angeles by highway construction. Both car and train facilitated exponential demographic growth and change, indicative of much of the SGV. The simultaneous demise of the interurban streetcar lines and the emergence of Southern California's freeway system led to what some have described as a fleeting "autotopia."[2] It failed to reduce traffic and victimized East Los Angeles inhabitants, but it did lay the groundwork for the SGV's evolution.

Agricultural labor had drawn the region's first Latino residents, but highway construction drove and facilitated the migration of mostly Latino residents of East Los Angeles while simultaneously erasing El Monte's agrarian past. Greater El Monte emerged as a clear but nuanced expression of what one Los Angeles writer summarized as the nation's long struggle between "the pastoral versus the technological," but it also exemplified America's suburban diversity in the twenty-first century.[3]

Riding the Big Red Car

In the early decades of the twentieth century, agriculture and the Pacific Electric railway (P.E., or popularly referred to as Red Car) served as anchors for a sizable Mexican and Mexican American community in El Monte. Even if wages remained low, the berry fields, walnut and citrus orchards, and other offerings required labor and provided employment. Fully extended in 1911, the P.E. provided mobility to working- and middle-class Latinos, African Americans, Asians, and whites, enabling them to traverse Southern California for work and leisure.[4]

The residential population of the region increased by 100 percent from 1920 to 1930, before the freeway reached the SGV. Of the forty-two municipalities incorporated into the region by the mid-1930s, thirty-nine could thank the P.E. for their growth.[5] During this period, El Monte more than doubled in size. Despite the valley's sizable growth, the gravity of downtown Los Angeles persisted, and El Monte remained bound in its orbit. The introduction of freeways to the SGV sparked a demographic boom that would remake El Monte, turning it from a rural enclave of just over 3,000 people in 1930 into an urbanized suburban city of over 100,000 people in 2010—while also freeing the region from downtown Los Angeles's gravitational pull.

For residents, the interurban streetcar system provided critical passage. Its over eleven hundred miles of track laid the foundation for what the historian Eric Avila calls "decentralized urbanization."[6] Ruth Gonzalez moved with her

FIG. 22 "Pacific Electric Railway Co., Los Angeles," 1910. (Courtesy of Library of Congress, Prints and Photographs Division.)

family from Compton to El Monte in the early 1940s. Her father and his brothers had purchased farmland from Japanese residents who had been forced into internment camps during World War II. She took the Red Car to her job in Los Angeles at Washington Avenue and Central Street, and on summer days, she and her girlfriends would slip bathing suits on under their clothes and ride it down to Long Beach.[7]

The causes of the P.E.'s demise remain a source of debate.[8] Some residents point to political corruption and conspiracy, but the reality is simpler. The P.E. struggled for decades with declining rates of ridership and return on its investment. The rail companies failed to invest in capital improvements and privileged freight over patronage. Add the economic interests of the oil, asphalt, and automobile industries and the political goals of municipal Los Angeles—General Motors representatives labeled Red Cars "mongrel vehicles," while

Los Angeles officials sometimes referred to them as "wheeled slums"—and one understands the perfect storm that sank streetcar fortunes.[9]

Consumers also bear some collective responsibility. By 1915, California led the nation in car ownership, with the number of private cars in the state increasing from 55,217 in 1915 to 110,000 in 1918 and 441,000 in 1924.[10] Industry officials and politicians criticized the interurban railway, but public dissatisfaction with it and the promise of automobiles also functioned to undermine its standing.[11]

In 1961, the P.E. made its final trip; the yellow cars of its counterpart, the Los Angeles Railway which served the downtown business district, halted operations in 1963. By the mid-1960s, California accounted for one-ninth of the nation's registered automotive vehicles, and collectively the state's drivers traversed 82 million miles annually.[12] In the end, as David Brodsly succinctly put it, "It required no conspiracy to destroy the electric railways; it would however, have required a conspiracy to save them."[13]

Highway to the SGV

The introduction of freeways—most notably the San Bernardino (I-10), the Pomona (CA-60), and the SGV (I-605)—recast the valley, and suburbanization and redevelopment transformed the region. The rural landscape and pace were realigned to suburban and sometimes industrial rhythms.

Los Angeles County added seven million people in the period 1940–1970. Having been denied access to other suburban regions and in some cases utilizing Department of Veterans Affairs (VA) loans made possible by the GI Bill, Asian and Mexican Americans looked to the SGV for home-owning opportunities. Beginning in the 1950s and accelerating in the 1960s and 1970s, Greater El Monte, like much of the SGV, emerged as a multicultural Valhalla for minority home owners.[14] "Proliferating subdivisions attracted World War II veterans looking to buy homes . . . and drew Mexican Americans from East Los Angeles, and Japanese Americans from the West Side and East Side, and Chinese Americans from Chinatown," the historian Wendy Cheng writes.[15] Today, the economic abundance derived from the countless interactions between Asian and Latino residents in Los Angeles generally, and the SGV specifically, distinguishes the region from other metropolitan areas. The end result, Mike Davis writes, is "the dim-sum-*con-salsa* suburbs" of the SGV.[16]

Yet though freeways created opportunity, they also snatched it away. For much of Los Angeles's Mexican American population, especially residents of Boyle Heights and East Los Angeles, highways have plagued their existence. The East Los Angeles Interchange and the seven freeways that meet there demolished communities and accelerated the regional culture's embrace of racial politics.[17] Freeways and industrial zones occupy over half of the area of Boyle Heights. "A resident walking from Cesar Chavez Avenue in Boyle Heights to Los Angeles County General Hospital, less than half a mile away," Gilbert Estrada points out, "would have to cross forty one lanes of highway."[18] East Los Angeles residents fled upon the very highways that had driven them out, settling along the asphalt spine in the formerly blue-collar suburbs that had made middle-class home owners of white Angelenos decades before them.

El Monte and the I-10

As early as 1939, El Monte residents resisted the idea of a freeway in their midst. While the outbreak of World War II delayed negotiations and construction, the passage of the 1947 Collier-Burns Act enabled the state to renew its efforts. The law increased the gasoline taxes that had been passed in 1923 and 1938 and earmarked revenue for freeway construction in urban and rural areas. With this new financial support, California once again struck out to create a network of highways knitting the state together, but El Monte attempted to subvert the state's plans.[19]

In 1948, El Monte Mayor Fred King rebuffed the California Highway Commission telling its members that the city preferred "a subway" and that a freeway threatened to slice the "city in half," which would diminish property values.[20] Three years later, the debate between El Monte's political leaders and the California Division of Highways flared again. Several business leaders suggested that the state's preferred route would "flow through the city's business district," increasing congestion and inconveniencing residents. Instead, city officials lobbied for one of two alternative routes, one to the north and the other to the south, but the state rejected both.[21] Five years later at a public event celebrating the town's centennial, Mayor R. C. Miller struck a similar chord, telling the audience that the state had asked him to "sign an agreement which will ruin" El Monte, and added that three city council members had won large electoral majorities due to their vocal opposition to the freeway.[22]

Outside of El Monte, however, views differed. Officials from Pomona and West Covina and the Alhambra Chamber of Commerce indicated their desire that the state proceed.[23] The *Los Angeles Times* questioned El Monte's motivation and asserted that the city's intransigence undermined the "welfare of thousands upon thousands of users of the public highway system."[24] Eventually, to secure the city's approval, the state acceded to "concessions here and there," but in general it won the battle.[25]

The San Bernardino Freeway (I-10) not only reshaped the physical landscape of El Monte but also the city's connection to metropolitan Los Angeles. Vernon Wickstorm—who was born in East Los Angeles in 1935 and later moved to El Monte, where his parents ran a store until 1943—remembered the San

Bernardino Freeway in its infancy. "I had just got my license," Wickstorm recalled. "I would get on and drive all the way to Los Angeles and hardly see any cars." Later, as the I-10 was extended further, "more and more cars" appeared on the freeway. Much as municipal officials feared, the freeway did split the city along a north-south divide, Wickstorm noted, commenting that "it is the way it is, we just live with it."[26]

Still, even in its earliest incarnation, the I-10's construction hinted at the demographic changes to come. Benita Bishop, author of the self-published *Lost Girl from El Monte*, grew up in the city as a direct result of the I-10. Though her mother hailed from Ciudad Juarez, her father—Lee Morgan, who was white—worked as a civil engineer and settled the family in the city after helping design and build the freeway. Her mixed racial heritage exemplified the town's impending future: "I grew up in El Monte being half white and [half] brown, half happy, half sad, half in trouble half the time and half searching but always curious."[27] If Bishop embodied the changes brought to El Monte by I-10, she also marked the midpoint of this process. The Pomona California State Freeway (CA-60), which followed, ultimately accelerated and deepened Greater El Monte's transformation.

South El Monte and CA-60

CA-60 had a much greater impact on South El Monte than on El Monte. Incorporated in 1958, South El Monte raised few objections to the freeway's construction, reflecting the city council's general probusiness orientation. Dana Law—whose father, James Law, played an active role in South El Monte's political culture—remembered playing on the highway before it opened: "Imagine [your parents saying]: 'you kids go out and play in the Freeway' which we did before it opened."[28] Other residents recalled the collision of the fading agrarian past and the automotive future, as horses would sometimes wander onto finished or nearly finished sections of the freeway.

By 1964, the state had secured agreements with over thirteen municipalities, including South El Monte, to build the Pomona Freeway. With much of the freeway's path still underdeveloped, the state proceeded easily with the acquisition of land.[29]

Some residents say that they heard very little about it until construction began.[30] Years earlier, Ruth Gonzalez had met her husband, Jonathan. They married, had children, and settled in East Los Angeles. They were living at Ditman Avenue and Fifth Street in 1962, when they were forced to move due to freeway construction. Hearing about opportunities in the SGV, they quickly purchased a new home in South El Monte.

Real estate agents never mentioned the impending freeway to the new home owners. "When [construction] started . . . everyone was like 'What?!,'" Ruth

Gonzalez recalled. Though the Gonzalezes might have reconsidered their purchase had they known about the Pomona Freeway, Ruth also admitted that they were so glad to have a new home it might not have made a difference—a testament to the discriminatory real estate market that defined Los Angeles County at the time. The couple also pointed out that many of their neighbors had migrated to South El Monte because of freeway construction in East Los Angeles, only to encounter it again after their move.[31]

Still, it would take several years for the Pomona Freeway to fully impact South El Monte. Even in the late 1960s, parts of the town maintained a rural lifestyle. Born in Boyle Heights and raised in East Los Angeles, James Rojas frequently visited his aunt's four-room home in South El Monte during the 1960s. She had moved there from East Los Angeles. Spending summer weekends in South El Monte, he marveled at the fauna, communing with chickens, horses, frogs, and ducks. "As a kid looking for intimacy with the built environment," he told an interviewer, "animals are [a] really powerful way to do that . . . I felt very privileged."[32]

Eventually, however, the Pomona Freeway altered daily life in numerous ways. Those residents living in close proximity to the freeway endured sound and air pollution, and it also recalibrated the rhythms of everyday life. "Before the freeway everything was real quiet, tranquil, nice . . . but after the freeway everything started changing," according to Jonathan Gonzalez. People felt more hurried, life began to move faster, and industry expanded. Gonzalez served as a member of the South El Monte City Council in the 1980s, a position from which he helped secure the construction of sound barriers for residents adjacent to CA-60.[33]

Opinions regarding the Pomona Freeway vary. Younger residents like Rojas, whose family had settled in Alhambra after moving from Boyle Heights, welcomed it. "When I was a kid I thought it was the best thing, I thought it was modern and quick," Rojas noted. "[It] wasn't until I went to M.I.T. when [*sic*] I learned all the freeways were so negative. I always thought they were cool."[34] Martinez credits the freeway with improving his small printing business by making travel to downtown Los Angeles more efficient and quicker. James Law, another entrepreneur, enjoyed an increase in his demolition business that was facilitated in part by the new highway.[35] Whatever their differences of opinion, most residents agreed that Greater El Monte's agricultural landscape quickly vanished, and population booms soon followed.

The pro-business city council and Mayor Joseph Vargas took advantage of the Pomona-Tyler Street interchange to move City Hall to its current location while adding a new civic center and library. The Pomona Freeway helped bring this redevelopment into reality, as state officials touted the economic benefits of CA-60. By 1968, the city's daytime population had increased to 30,000, as workers commuted to their jobs from other SGV municipalities. South El

Monte had grown nearly fourfold from its incorporation in 1958 and had 12,000 residents and 1,100 businesses, many of them industrial.[36]

The Highway to Political Representation

The industrially zoned land along the Pomona Freeway emerged as one of three corridors in Greater Los Angeles where once white blue-collar and suburban housing tracts soon turned Latino. However, the SGV's Latino population had long existed, even if its political power remained muted. In many valley communities, residents of Mexican descent had been settled for decades and had established tight-knit neighborhoods. The historian Matt Garcia described these settlements as *colonias*, segregated pockets of Mexican and Mexican American communities dotting the landscape in the Imperial, San Fernando, and San Gabriel Valleys. In El Monte, Hicks Camp and Medina Court (also known as Hayes Camp) best exemplify such developments.[37]

Though these could be hardscrabble encampments, they provided footholds in local municipalities that influenced demographic development. Freeways forced Eastside Latinos out but eventually provided housing and work opportunities for new arrivals. By the 1970s, the growth of the Latino population was undeniable: in 1979, 80 percent of South El Monte's population identified themselves as Latino. Moreover, in terms of community building, *colonias* "emerged as sites of collective identity formation and political activism that merged Mexican and American cultural practices," writes Jerry Gonzalez.[38]

In many SGV cities, *colonias* were victimized by highway and suburban subdivision construction and swept away by asphalt, automobiles, and contractors. El Monte's Hicks Camp did persist into the 1970s, but development razed it. "*Colonia* residents quickly saw their communities move from the rural periphery into the middle of a dizzying, sprawling metropolis," Gonzalez asserts.[39]

Having Mexican American representatives like Mayor Vargas in municipal government did not guarantee equity for working-class Mexican Americans across the SGV, as the prerogatives of urban renewal often trumped ethnic loyalties.[40] In addition, demographic dominance did not guarantee representation. Though El Monte's population was over 75 percent Latino in 1990, only one city council member was of Latino descent. In contrast, by the early 1980s, the majority of South El Monte's council members were of Latino origin. Despite such electoral disparities, by 1990, political operatives speaking to the *Los Angeles Times* were using I-10 and CA-60 corridor as a framing device for the voting power of the growing Greater Eastside: "the communities spread out along the Pomona and San Bernardino freeways now represent 'the greatest bloc of potential Latino voting strength in the Southwestern U.S.'"[41] At the turn of the twenty-first century, Mike Davis went further, describing it as "the most important

Latino political constituency in the nation."[42] By 2000, El Monte and South El Monte had become part of "a more affluent Chicano suburban belt" that contained the majority of the 400,000 Latinos earning at least $35,000 annually.[43]

Cultural Representation, Whittier Boulevard, and Whittier Narrows

Cultural expression of these demographic changes emerged in the late 1960s.[44] As highway construction reshaped the two cities, amid the flowering of the Chicano movement in the 1960 and 1970s, youthful Latino residents took to Whittier Boulevard, as a way to assert their burgeoning presence.

Stretching from East Los Angeles through Montebello, Pico Rivera, and Whittier, the eleven-mile expanse of Whittier Boulevard served as cultural lodestar for lowriders of the 1960s and 1970s. Lowriders functioned as "visual texts of working class life," and Whittier Boulevard served as the page upon which these narratives were written.[45]

In truth, Whittier Boulevard helped set the SGV on its demographic future path well before freeway construction and lowriders. City planners enacted policies that drove the Latino Eastside diaspora into the valley. Los Angeles's expansion of Whittier Boulevard in the 1930s ultimately deprived Eastsiders of valuable park and recreational spaces and established a pattern for road and freeway construction that would persist for decades afterward. "Sixth Street Bridge and Whittier Boulevard did not create the barrio, but they did establish the kind of path dependencies that are most difficult to overcome," the historian Matthew Roth argues, "the kind that are poured into concrete."[46]

As Avila and others have argued, the very automotive culture that victimized Latino communities provided an outlet for cultural expression. Chicano culture told its story of freeways "through wit, sarcasm, and satire, and other imaginative forms of cultural appropriation," writes Avila.[47] Lowriding operated as just one part of this larger collective statement.

Few aspects of U.S. culture, particularly California culture, could be seen as quintessentially American than the pervasive use of the automobile. The economic and physical mobility of cars and their identification with an American middle-class ideal made them perfect vehicles for identity, while enabling black and brown Angelenos (members of the two communities most affected by urban renewal and highway construction) to "transgress the boundaries of racially segregated neighborhoods" in and around Los Angeles, writes the cultural historian Denise Sandoval.[48]

Beyond the act of cruising, through the 1979 film *Boulevard Nights* and Thee Midniters' 1965 song "Whittier Boulevard," lowriders made claims to popular culture.[49]

Gang problems of the late 1960s and early 1970s led to police crackdowns on cruising, though lowrider aficionados were quick to point out that unruly types were the exception rather than the rule. "People think we're out to make trouble, but we're not," one twenty-two-year-old Whittier Boulevard biker told the *Los Angeles Times* in 1979. "It's the *cholos* that cause the problems." The character of Raymond in *Boulevard Nights* put it similarly: "It all changed when the *cholos* came around."[50]

Though its popularity ebbed and flowed over the years, lowriding boomed again around 2015. Eli Garcia, a thirty-seven-year-old La Puente resident, reminisced about his youth watching lowriders cruise the boulevard, describing it as a family-friendly atmosphere and promoting its resurgence: "It's like a way of life for us."[51]

In some ways history repeated itself, as lowriding's renewed popularity gained the attention of municipal authorities and the East Los Angeles Chamber of Commerce in 2017. Both expressed concerns about thousands of lowriders on the boulevard disrupting bus service, increasing congestion, and negatively affecting businesses along the strip.[52]

Whatever lowriding's fate along Whittier, one SGV location persists as a regular gathering place for these car enthusiasts: Whittier Narrows Park. Once home to smaller *colonias* and created by a 1954 flood control project, the park came into being contemporaneously with the I-10 and CA-60. Today it remains bound by the San Gabriel Freeway and I-10, while the Pomona bisects its 1,400-acre northern lobe. Mirroring the experiences of El Monte and South El Monte, Whittier Narrows emerged from a much larger, more pristine, agricultural region—or, as Rudolfo D. Torres and Victor M. Valle write, it functioned as a sacrificial zone for regional development.[53]

Yet it encapsulates the complexities and nuances of freeway construction in the SGV. The park draws lowrider enthusiasts, nature lovers, and picnicking Latino families. Martinez remembers all of East Los Angeles descending on the Narrows and having "a ball, corn tacos and music, you name it." Rojas's family used the Narrows as a destination point: his entire "East LA and Whittier family would come out" and picnic, he remembers, with "food, guitar and singing, all that Mexican stuff." White residents enjoyed the park as well. For example, Dana Law frequented Legg Lake regularly.[54]

By the early twenty-first century, Latinos accounted for nearly 65 percent of the park's patrons. "Strummed guitars" and "beer mellowed voices" flow between the smell of "scorched corn tortillas and carne asada," while bat-wielding birthday crazed children beat piñatas till they explode with confectionary treasures. At the same time, "Chicano club members and girls in tank tops gather around tricked out low riders some with hoods lifted, others bounding or tilting in the parking lots," observe Torres and Valle.[55]

Paradoxically, though freeway construction denuded the landscape of public space and shrunk what was once a sprawling agricultural region, it also made Whittier Narrows priceless. The intersection of freeways ferries visitors to its paths, trails, and lake. Though the highways have altered life in the SGV, as the longtime Whittier Narrows Nature Center docent Ed Barajas reflected in a 2015 interview, the Narrows has become a place apart: "If you go into that area between [the Rio Hondo and San Gabriel River] you can hear nature, you can hear the birds, you hear rabbits, you can hear everything."[56]

Whittier Narrows provides the youth of the Greater Eastside an access to wilderness that is often absent in metropolitan Los Angeles. Many kids have never experienced any sort of wilderness, and after they see and experience Whittier Narrows, "they go back to their schools and" tell kids all about it, noted Barajas.[57]

The Narrows serve as a grander, twenty-first-century version of Durfee Ranch and embodies the same dream world that enthralled Martinez. Admittedly, driving through the Narrows on the Pomona Freeway and its "crazy quilt of public spaces, factories, and sewage treatment plants" might render it "indecipherable" from the passenger side of an automobile, but it nonetheless remains emblematic of the SGV's transformation.[58]

The freeways destroyed it; the freeways created it; the freeways and the people most victimized by it sustain it. A similar narrative holds true for Greater East Los Angeles and has been inscribed in the homes and communities of El Monte and South El Monte. Undoubtedly, the story lacks clean lines, stock villains, clear heroes, and a succinct and unobtrusive resolution. Indeed, freeways are the messy but intriguing story of the SGV and Greater El Monte in the twenty-first century.

Notes

1 Marty Martinez, interview by Maryam Hosseinzadeh, February 22, 2015.

2 Reyner Banham, "Ecology IV: Autopia" in *Los Angeles: The Architecture of Four Ecologies* (Los Angeles: University of California Press, 2009), 195–204. See also, Joan Didion, "Bureaucrats" in *The White Album* (New York: Farrar, Straus and Giroux, 1979), 79–86.

3 David Brodsly, *L.A. Freeway: An Appreciative Essay* (Berkeley: University of California Press, 1981), 4–5.

4 Eric Avila, *Popular Culture in the Age of White Flight: Fear and Fantasy in Suburban Los Angeles* (Los Angeles: University of California Press, 2004), 188.

5 Brodsly, *L.A. Freeway*, 68 and 91–92.

6 Avila, *Popular Culture in the Age of White Flight*, 186–188.

7 Ruth and Jonathan Gonzalez, interview by Maryam Hosseinzadeh, February 22, 2015.

8 Robert Gottlieb, *Reinventing Los Angeles: Nature and Community in the Global City* (Cambridge, MA: MIT Press, 2007), 181–182.

9 Avila, *Popular Culture in the Age of White Flight*, 180; See also David Brodsly, *L.A. Freeway*, 92–93.
10 Brodsly, *L.A. Freeway*, 82.
11 Avila, *Popular Culture in the Age of White Flight*, 190.
12 "California Highways –1964," *California Highways and Public Works*, ed. Lester S. Koritz, 43 no. 11–12 (November–December 1964): 7.
13 Brodsly, *L.A. Freeway*, 96.
14 Gilbert Estrada, "If You Build It, They Will Move: The Los Angeles Freeway System and the Displacement of East Los Angeles, 1944–1972," *Southern California Quarterly* 87, no. 3 (Fall 2005): 295.
15 Wendy Cheng, *The Changs Next Door to the Díazes: Remapping Race in Suburban California* (Minneapolis: University of Minnesota Press, 2013), 27.
16 Mike Davis, *Magical Urbanism: Latinos Reinvent the U.S. City* (New York: Verso, 2000), 46.
17 The seven freeways are the Santa Ana I-5 Freeway (1944), the Hollywood U.S.101 Freeway (1948), the San Bernardino I-10 Freeway (1953), the Golden State I-5 Freeway (1955), the Santa Monica I-10 Freeway (connected in 1961), the Long Beach I-710 Freeway (1961), and the Pomona 60 Freeway (1965). See G. Estrada, "If You Build It, They Will Move," 290; Avila, *Popular Culture in the Age of White Flight*, 186.
18 G. Estrada, "If You Build It, They Will Move," 306.
19 Chester G. Hanson, "El Monte Freeway Showdown Near," *Los Angeles Times*, August 5, 1951; "El Monte Dispute on Freeway Aired," *Los Angeles Times*, August 15, 1952; Daniel J. B. Mitchell, "Earl Warren's Fight for California's Freeways: Setting a Path for the Nation," *Southern California Quarterly* 88, no. 2 (Summer 2006): 205 and 207.
20 "Freeway Idea Being Fought by El Monte," *Los Angeles Times*, December 17, 1948.
21 Hanson, "El Monte Freeway Showdown Near."
22 Ibid.; "El Monte Dispute on Freeway Aired."
23 Hanson, "El Monte Freeway Showdown Near"; "El Monte Dispute on Freeway Aired."
24 Hanson, "El Monte Freeway Showdown Near."
25 "Pact Signing Ends Dispute on El Monte Freeway Route," *Los Angeles Times*, August 24, 1953.
26 Vernon Wickstorm, oral history interview, January 12, 2015, South El Monte Arts Posse (SEMAP), East of East: Mapping Community Narratives in El Monte and South El Monte, http://www.semapeastofeast.com.
27 Quoted in Vickie Vértiz, "Lost Girl: Tales about Loving and Leaving 1970s El Monte," KCET, July 8, 2015, https://www.kcet.org/shows/departures/lost-girl-tales-about-loving-and-leaving-1970s-el-monte.
28 Dana Law, oral history interview, January 12, 2015, South El Monte Arts Posse (SEMAP), East of East: Mapping Community Narratives in El Monte and South El Monte, http://www.semapeastofeast.com.
29 Robert S. Diamond, "State Moves Ahead on Pomona Freeway," *Los Angeles Times*, October 25, 1964.
30 Martinez, interview; Gonzalez and Gonzalez, interview.
31 Gonzalez and Gonzalez, interview.
32 James Rojas, oral history interview, January 9, 2014, South El Monte Arts Posse (SEMAP), East of East: Mapping Community Narratives in El Monte and South

El Monte, http: www.semapeastofeast.com. See also George R. Voight, *South El Monte: The History of a City* (South El Monte, CA: Municipal Services Bureau, 1983); Law, interview, SEMAP.

33 Gonzalez and Gonzalez, interview.

34 Rojas, oral history interview, SEMAP.

35 Martinez, interview; Law, oral history interview, SEMAP.

36 "Mayor Asks Change in Site for City Hall," *Los Angeles Times*, May 17, 1964; "South El Monte to Dedicate Civic Center," *Los Angeles Times*, December 9, 1966; Robert S. Diamond, "$93 Million Freeway Moving East," *Los Angeles Times*, December 9, 1965; "'City of Achievement': South El Monte Thriving and All-American," *San Gabriel Valley Tribune*, June 16, 1968.

37 Matt Garcia, *A World of Its Own: Race, Labor, and Citrus in the Making of Greater Los Angeles, 1900–1970* (Chapel Hill: University of North Carolina Press, 2001), 19, 109, and 119. See also Laura R. Barraclough, *Making the San Fernando Valley: Rural Landscapes, Urban Development, and White Privilege* (Athens: University of Georgia Press, 2011), 54; Mike Davis, *Magical Urbanism*, 43.

38 Jerry Gonzalez, "'A Place in the Sun': Mexican Americans, Race and the Suburbanization of Los Angeles, 1940–1980" (PhD diss., University of Southern California, 2009).

39 Ibid.

40 Ibid 5–6, 151, and 156.

41 Edmund Newton, "San Gabriel Valley Becomes the New Power Base of Latino Voters," *Los Angeles Times*, January 21, 1990, accessed August 12, 2016, https://www.latimes.com/archives/la-xpm-1990-01-21-me-1023-story.html.

42 Mike Davis, *Magical Urbanism*, 48.

43 E. Newton, "San Gabriel Valley Becomes the New Power Base of Latino Voters"; Davis, *Magical Urbanism*, 46–48.

44 Law, oral history interview, SEMAP; Wickstorm, oral history interview, SEMAP.

45 Denise M. Sandoval, "The Politics of Low and Slow/Bajito y Suavecito," in *Black and Brown in Los Angeles: Beyond Conflict and Collision*, ed. Josh Kun and Laura Pulido, (Los Angeles: University of California Press, 2014), 182; See also Denise M. Sandoval, "Cruising through Low Rider Culture: Chicana/o Identity in the Marketing of Low Rider Magazine," in *Velvet Barrios: Popular Culture and Chicana/o Sexualities*, ed. Alicia Gaspar de Alba (New York: Palgrave Macmillan, 2003), 184.

46 Matthew Roth, "Whittier Boulevard, Sixth Street Bridge, and the Origins of Transportation Exploitation," *Journal of Urban History* 30, no. 5 (July 2004): 731.

47 Eric Avila, *The Folklore of the Freeway: Race and Revolt in the Modernist City* (Minneapolis: University of Minnesota Press, 2014), 52.

48 Sandoval, "The Politics of Low and Slow," 185.

49 Gonzalez, "'A Place in the Sun,'"197–199; *Boulevard Nights*. Michael Pressman. Los Angeles: Warner Brothers, 1979.

50 Jay Horowitz, "Whittier Cruising: A Tradition Gone Sour," *Los Angeles Times*, August 8, 1979; see also, Gonzalez, "'A Place in the Sun,'" 204.

51 Brittny Mejia, "Officials Looking to Curb Cruising on Whittier Boulevard Once More," *Los Angeles Times*, July 24, 2017, http://www.latimes.com/local/california/la-me-ln-cruising-whittier-boulevard-20170721-story.html#.

52 Ibid.

53 Torres and Valle, *Latino Metropolis*, 146 and 158.

54 Martinez, interview; Rojas, oral history interview, SEMAP; Law, oral history interview, SEMAP.

55 Torres and Valle, *Latino Metropolis*, 158.

56 Members of the Kizh-Gabrieleño Band of Mission Indians, oral history interview, January 10, 2015, South El Monte Arts Posse (SEMAP), East of East: Mapping Community Narratives in El Monte and South El Monte, http://www.semap eastofeast.com.

57 Ibid.

58 Torres and Valle, *Latino Metropolis*, 146.

20

The Starlite Swap Meet

JENNIFER RENTERIA

The space occupied by Starlite Swap Meet, an ephemeral gathering place that facilitates sales and bartering in what otherwise would be a vacant lot in the industrial suburb of South El Monte, can best be described as a void in the urban landscape, only becoming a place upon the arrival of the people who occupy it on weekends. Not only does the space become occupied, but it also comes to house what can be considered a true shopping center, whose "retailer" variation and livelihood are perhaps nearly comparable to that of the brick-and-mortar shopping establishments of the Americana in nearby Glendale and the Grove in Los Angeles—though of course it is in a class of its own. Like the latter entities, though, the swap meet is also privately owned. Vendors pay to occupy parts of the space, and customers are charged a 75 cent fee to enter it.

Despite being occupied only two days of the week, the space has managed to sustain a strong following, attracting many to its temporary "streets" and lively "public" sphere. It has continually retained such a large following that opposition—of which there has been much, particularly from health and safety officials with legitimate and justifiable concerns—has been relatively easily quelled by the space's owners and the many vendors and customers linked to its existence.

The following account is primarily based on a lifetime of observations: my family has sold items at the swap meet for more than twenty years. My family's bicycle business, purchased from another dedicated bicycle vendor, began as a hobby and eventually became the base of my family's income, as my parents'

FIG. 23 Jennifer Renteria, "Starlite Sign," April 2009. (Courtesy of Jennifer Renteria.)

work situations changed. The entire family, as well as the day laborers, teens, and occasional uncle we have employed over the years, have worked the stand at the swap meet, engaging in its demands alongside the other approximately 200 vendors.

The Swap Meet

Opened in the 1950s, the Starlite Swap Meet once operated as a drive-in theater that housed up to 860 vehicles.[1] The otherwise empty lot simultaneously began operating as a daytime outdoor swap meet shortly after the theater's opening. Over time, the swap meet proved to be more successful than the space's cinematic use. Despite the eventual demise of the theater in the mid-1990s, the swap meet continues to thrive in the shadow of the Art Moderne–like marquee that once marked the theater's main entrance and now welcomes swap meet visitors. Aside from the marquee, the only notable infrastructure is the fence that denotes the space's boundaries in relation to its light manufacturing and residential neighbors, and two relatively modest buildings located at the center of the swap meet, where a cafeteria, administrative office, and restrooms are located. Sold at the swap meet are toiletries, herbal medicines, pet clothing, and seemingly everything in between.

The swap meet's demographic and cultural components are largely defined by its community, the majority of whose members are Latino, immigrant, and low-income. However, South El Monte, neighbored by other San Gabriel

PRIMARY SWAP MEET ENTITIES

Bottle Collectors	individuals who sort out swap meet trash piles and cans in search of bottles that are then taken to recycling centers in exchange for monetary gain
Cart Vendors	individuals who sell goods out of shopping carts; typically, these vendors do not have permits
Day Laborers	individuals who work for daily wages, especially as an unskilled laborer; in the case of the swap meet, day laborers seek work as sales and stand maintenance assistance
Swap Meet Customers	visitors who pay a small fee to enter the swap meet to use its services
Extended Vendors	swap meet vendors who have paid to set up a swap meet stand for vending a particular item but also sell otheitems out of their stands, such as food or beverages, which they deliver around the swap meet; typically, other swap meet vendors are their customers
Sidewalk Vendors	individuals who vend along the swap meet's nearby or adjacent sidewalks and fences, taking advantage of the influx of people visiting the swap meet
Swap Meet Staff	individuals employed by swap meet management, including administrative staff, cafeteria staff, maintenance staff, security guards, ticket booth staff, and trash collectors
Swap Meet Vendors	individuals who pay a fee to vend at the swap meet within an allocated space; they are either regular vendors who pay a monthly fee or temporary vendors who only pay on the days a space becomes available to them; spaces are available to temporary vendors only when regular vendors do not arrive by the 8 AM cutoff time, at which point spaces are distributed to interested vendors on a first-come, first-served basis; regular vendors are required to have permits and report sales to the IRS
Transient Vendors	swap meet customers who bring items to the swap meet to sell; typically, swap meet vendors are their customers; these vendors may walk around the swap meet taking orders for food, for example, and later return with items stored in their vehicles; as well, these vendors may carry items, such as beverages, and sell them as they walk around the swap meet premises

FIG. 24 Jennifer Renteria, "Primary Swap Meet Entities," April 2009. (Courtesy of Jennifer Renteria.)

Valley[2] cities, is also significantly influenced by the many Asian or Asian American residents who characterize much of the valley.[3] Thus, the swap meet's landscape has been altered by the region's varied cultural influences and can be seen as one walks through the swap meet and learns of the interactions among vendors and between vendors and customers. It would be negligent, though, to say that the influences are obvious, except the language barriers that exist between the groups—broken English often being the only language that ties the communities together. The entrepreneurial spirit certainly thrives throughout the entire swap meet; however, unlike their Latino counterparts, Asian vendors appear to actually subscribe to the principle of remaining inside the spaces for which they have paid. Latino participants take a more anarchistic approach, more fluidly taking on varying roles as primary swap meet entities.

On any given weekend day—rain or shine—vendors begin arriving at dawn, driving their packed vehicles through the swap meet's west entrance. As the urban theorist James Rojas might say, vendors enact, or begin enacting, the environment with their presence, their arrival marking the birth of a new swap meet day.[4] By midmorning, vehicles are unloaded and stands set up in time to welcome early customers. Vehicles, particularly those containing the components of a larger stand, are often modified and outfitted with shelves, metal crossbars, and netting to better store merchandise. The stands themselves are props, or "movable items, easily manipulated by the user who provides instant modification."[5] They serve to connect the user to the space in the enacted environment created by the vendors who occupy the property's void.

Stands sometimes occupy more than one space, each space totaling approximately 400 square feet and costing about $25–$50 a day to lease. The structures are, for the most part, modest in size and design, but occasionally they reach heights equivalent to that of a two-story building and may sinuously weave around the many trucks, equal extensions of these entrepreneurial enterprises, that are parked between the stands. Several hours are often spent building the structures, which are typically composed of metal poles, tarps, and the joints and cables that hold them together. Working a stand can be rigorous and requires a certain kind of physical stamina that can endure seasonal weather changes and heavy lifting.

Remaining relatively intact for only a few hours of the swap meet's 10–12-hour days, the stands usually begin to see their end at about 2:00 in the afternoon. The ritual of erecting and dismantling the stand is largely determined by natural time, in that the swap meet is solely lit by sunlight, yet a stand sometimes remains despite evening's darkness: some vendors are stubborn enough to work according to abstract time to make an extra buck.

The swap meet, although legal, has often been a source of concern to local officials, who have regularly identified health and safety violations. As a result,

SWAP MEET WEEKEND DAY TIME LAPSE*

TIME	VISIBLE ACTIVITY	ENTITIES PRESENT	DENSITY
0600	swap meet staff arrive and open ticket booth at main vendor entrance; regular swap meet vendors arrive, drive vehicles through main entrance; swap meet vendors seeking to obtain a one day permit begin lining up near entrance	• swap meet staff • swap meet vendors	
0700	swap meet vendors continue to arrive; stands are assembled; customers begin to arrive; sales begin to take place	• swap meet staff • swap meet vendors • customers • transient vendors	
0800	main vendor entrance shut down; available spaces are distributed to temporary vendors; temporary vendors allowed entrance; stands continue to be assembled	• swap meet staff • swap meet vendors • customers • transient vendors	
0900	stand set-up; sales	• swap meet staff • swap meet vendors • customers • transient vendors • sidewalk vendors	
1000	customers arrive and depart; sales	• swap meet staff • swap meet vendors • customers • transient vendors • sidewalk vendors	
1100	customers arrive and depart; sales	• swap meet staff • swap meet vendors • customers • transient vendors • sidewalk vendors	
1200	customers arrive and depart; sales	• swap meet staff • swap meet vendors • customers • transient vendors • sidewalk vendors	
1300	customers arrive and depart; sales	• swap meet staff • swap meet vendors • customers • transient vendors • sidewalk vendors	
1400	customers arrive and depart; sales; stand breakdown begins	• swap meet staff • swap meet vendors • customers • transient vendors • sidewalk vendors	
1500	customers arrive and depart; sales; breakdown continues; cart vendors begin to arrive; bottle collectors arrive	• swap meet staff • swap meet vendors • customers • bottle collectors • cart vendors	
1600	swap meet closed to customers; last few sales made by swap meet vendors; trash collectors begin to appear	• swap meet staff • swap meet vendors • customers • bottle collectors • cart vendors • trash collectors	
1700	last few vendors exit swap meet; trash collectors continue to work	• swap meet staff • swap meet vendors • trash collectors	
1800	swap meet shuts down	• swap meet staff • trash collectors	

* Based on observations made in April and November 2009.

FIG. 25 Jennifer Renteria, "Swap Meet Weekend Day Time Lapse," April 2009. (Courtesy of Jennifer Renteria.)

property owners have often felt pressured to close the swap meet—or at least pressured enough to alarm vendors about the possibility of closure if they continue to violate regulations. The swap meet manager will periodically—approximately every six months or so—try to clean up vendors' violations, which may be anything from placing items outside of a demarcated vending

THE LIFE CYCLE OF A SWAP MEET STAND

FIG. 26 Jennifer Renteria, "Life Cycle of a Swap Meet Stand," April 2009. (Courtesy of Jennifer Renteria.)

space to selling food out of one's truck. For the most part, vendors will comply but eventually go back to their old habits.

The entire sequence—from officials showing up to the eventual vending of uninspected foods—happens so regularly that it almost seems like an inherent part of the swap meet's workings. Of course, the concerns officials bring to light are often legitimate and ones that can and should, perhaps, be addressed more efficiently. Some architectural and planning solutions, such as simply repainting lines to create more generous egress and ingress passageways for safety vehicles or providing spaces where people could prepare food in compliance with health code regulations, could resolve the ongoing and regular concerns.

Conclusion

The solid sense of community that exists despite the seeming ephemeral nature of the whole operation is impressive. Despite its thriving weekends, by Sunday evening and straight into the end of the week (after the trash and bottle collectors have stocked their supplies), this loud, eclectic place, where raw capitalism settles the score, becomes a desolate, concrete landscape where runaway plastic bags, caught on fences, rustle in the wind. Always becoming, it follows a constant cycle of rowdy occupation and silent emptiness. Once again, it is what it was last week, and come the following weekend, the swap meet will appear and disappear another time.

This consistency within a seemingly transient existence—as marked by the immediateness of the transactions, the exchanges, the relationships, the potential for growth, the ability to mobilize and move ahead into new spaces, relatively easily reshaping one's business as one goes—is perhaps part of the reason why spaces like the swap meet thrive as they do and have long appealed to folks like my family and the many others who shape them. To be able to go from drive-in theater to swap meet to vibrant community all in one space and in such a little time is both exciting and inspiring to witness and live.

These observations are sprinkled with bits of theory, evidence of my background in urban design, and are also based on my increasing appreciation for the happenstance innovation that comes into play as a part of the swap meet's and similar institutions' habitation of potentially lost urban spaces, their vast emptiness seeming to be their greatest asset.

Notes

A previous version of this chapter was published as Jennifer Renteria, "The Ephemeral Anatomy of the Starlite Swap Meet," American Planning Association, January 2010, https://www.planning.org/ (article link discontinued).

1 Cinema Treasures, "Starlite Drive-In," accessed July 14, 2009, http://cinematreasures.org/theater/10747/.

2 The San Gabriel Valley is a Southern California region located east of downtown Los Angeles. Included in its 200 square miles are thirty-one cities and five unincorporated communities, one of which is Monterey Park—the first American suburb to boast an Asian majority. Other notable cities include Pasadena and San Marino, both of which house widely recognized institutions such as the Norton Simon Museum and the Huntington Gardens.

3 "Visit San Gabriel Valley," accessed June 30, 2009, http://www.visitsangabrielvalley.com (article link discontinued); City of South El Monte, home page, accessed June 30, 2019, http://www.ci.south-el-monte.ca.us/.

4 James Rojas, "The Enacted Environment: Examining the Streets and Yards of East Los Angeles," in *Everyday America: Cultural Landscape Studies after J. B. Jackson*, ed. Chris Wilson and Paul Groth (Berkeley: University of California Press, 2003), 275–292.

5 James Rojas, "The Enacted Environment: The Creation of 'Place' by Mexicans and Mexican Americans in East Los Angeles" (Masters diss., Massachusetts Institute of Technology, 1991), 23.

Part IV

Popular Culture

FIG. 27 Fernando Mendez Corona, "El Monte History." (Courtesy of South El Monte Arts Posse and Fernando Mendez Corona.)

The so-called cultural turn in the humanities and social sciences provided academics with a new set of objects and methods. Building on the effort of social historians to include the voices of the working class, minorities, and women into larger historical narratives, academics began turning to culture to discern meaning. These essays on the historic and contemporary popular culture of El Monte and South El Monte further our understanding of the relationship between them and Los Angeles City, as well as the ways that working-class communities adapt mainstream cultures to create their own sense of place. The construction of Gay's Lion Farm in the 1930s was possible only because Los Angeles residents imagined El Monte as an exotic and nature-filled periphery. Distance from the city, however, proved to be an advantage for Art Laboe, his fellow musicians, and their fans as they created the first multiracial dance hall in Los Angeles. Decades later, Chicanos enlivened the punk movement in the San Gabriel Valley (a story that has been largely overlooked in the literature on punk), finding in large backyards and industrial areas the ideal settings for their underground parties and radical politics. Queer women created a safe space at the LGBTQ bar Sugar Shack, while Spanish-speaking migrant women have rented out vacant and underused properties in strip malls, building a *rasquache* barrio feminism to practice their distinctive approach to Zumba.

21

El Monte's Wild Past

A History of Gay's Lion Farm

MICHAEL S. WELLER

Gay's Lion Farm, once a defining symbol of El Monte, has left relatively few traces in today's city. El Monte High School may be the home of the Lions, boasting a statue of a lion that was once part of the farm, but a perfectly bland McDonald's stands on Valley Boulevard where the entrance to the farm once saw fancy cars and tour buses disgorging their passengers to visit the tourist attraction. About three hundred yards west, an overpass of Interstate-10 looms like a conqueror over a memorial to the fallen farm on the southeast corner of Valley and Peck Road. The memorial is easy to miss for drivers hurrying through the intersection. It's also unlikely to be visited by pedestrians, since the space is next to a busy intersection and below a freeway with no convenient parking nearby. Across the intersection, near a bus shelter on the northeast corner, is another ignored commemoration. The glass plating on this marker is scraped so badly that it renders the text almost entirely illegible.

Yet Jack Barton, longtime El Monte High School principal and the author of "A Brief History of El Monte," said the Lion Farm had "been likened to the Disneyland of the 1920's and 30's,"[1] and a brochure of the era boasted that the farm was comparable to the pyramids of ancient Egypt.[2] This latter claim is undoubtedly the hyperbole of the showman. Still, the farm had visitors as distinguished as Albert Einstein and Eleanor Roosevelt, and many of El Monte's "leading lights" were patrons and friends of the farm in the 1930s.[3] It is surprising,

FIG. 28 Gay's Lion Farm, circa 1936. (Courtesy of California Historical Society Collection at the University of Southern California Digital Library.)

then, that such a prominent feature of the city should have left so few markers of its existence.

Born in 1886, Charles Gay was a French performer who met his wife, the English-born Muriel, when he was performing in a circus in London. The Gays moved to California with Charles's circus in 1914 or 1915[4] and began raising lions near Westlake (now MacArthur) Park in 1919.[5] They relocated their operation to El Monte in 1924 and opened it to the public on July 1 of the following year.[6] The Gays established the farm to train lions that they could rent out to Hollywood studios for use in movies. Apart from Jackie and Leo, the lions who roar to introduce MGM films, Numa was probably the farm's most famous performing lion, appearing in several films in the 1920s—most notably Charlie Chaplin's *The Circus*.[7]

As a tourist attraction, we can situate the Lion Farm within the rise of amusement parks such as Coney Island, which discarded the traditional separation between "genteel and proletarian leisure."[8] Moreover, resort owners redefined the crowd, moving away from the "unpredictability of the throng" to a more sedate image of "family clusters focused on children and child-like fantasies," according to the social historian Gary Cross.[9] Los Angeles featured its own seaside amusement parks in Venice, Ocean Park, and Santa Monica.[10] However, the Lion Farm was more closely related to the other "animal-focused amusements" of the day than to these West Coast Coney Islands. These animal-themed spaces included another lion farm, Goebel's (later known as Jungleland), just across the county line in Thousand Oaks;[11] the Barnes Circus Zoo and the Monkey Farm near Culver City; the Alligator Farm in Lincoln Heights; and, on the western end of the San Gabriel Valley, Cawston Ostrich Ranch in South Pasadena.[12]

Among the Lion Farm's million visitors were Secretary of War Henry L. Stimson; Nina Douglas-Hamilton, Duchess of Hamilton; Kermit Roosevelt, son of President Theodore Roosevelt and cousin of First Lady Eleanor Roosevelt; the polar explorer Lincoln Ellsworth;[13] and a young Marilyn Monroe.[14] The farm also became a destination for student-athletes playing in the Rose Bowl. (Unsurprisingly, they kept their distance from the lions.)[15]

El Monte High School adopted "Lions" as the school nickname in 1925, and the Gays even provided a lion to serve as mascot for important football games.[16] The farm also hosted civic events, notably the Lions Club annual banquet—where barbecued lion was on the menu. The 1941 banquet drew 890 Lions Club members from across Los Angeles County.[17] A 1929 Bastille Day celebration by the "French Colony of Los Angeles" included an event at the farm in which a baby lion was to be baptized with the name "Marshall Foch," after the World War I French military leader.[18]

Working with lions was dangerous, of course, and the farm was not immune to tragedy. In September 1928, the trainer John Rounan suffered fatal injuries when three lions (including a lion named, incredibly enough, Nigger) escaped as they were being moved from one cage to another. Two of the lions were shot in the ensuing ruckus.[19] In another accident, the trainer Herman Zeigler was killed after he stumbled during a show and was attacked by a lion.[20]

Despite its role as a tourist attraction and its proximity to the glamour and glitz of Hollywood, the Lion Farm's place in El Monte history is framed by a problematic discourse on race. Scholars such as Eric Avila have discussed the role of amusement parks as spaces of whiteness, away from the frightening "darkness" of the multicultural inner city.[21] In this context of white flight and suburbanization, Avila analyzes Disneyland, for example, as a sanitized version of America, a "counterculture of visual order, spatial regimentation, and social homogeneity."[22] Other scholars have noted that circuses pitted representations of civilization against those of primitiveness. For example, Yoram S. Carmali explains how lion-taming spectacles depict the triumph of "culture" (the lion tamer) over "nature" (the lions, which are "caged in, captured, and dominated").[23] Furthermore, scholars such as Stuart Hall have discussed how this culture-nature opposition is often racialized: "culture" or "civilization" equals Western or white, while "nature" or "savagery" equals nonwhite or non-Western.[24]

In some ways, the Lion Farm became a stand-in for a tropical "other," in stark contrast to a region whose climate is Mediterranean and semiarid. In fact, the geography of El Monte and its environs in the early twentieth century was significantly different from that of today. These changes in the landscape are crucial in understanding how the Lion Farm came to be a racialized space. Before they were encased in flood-control channels, the floodplains of the San Gabriel River and Rio Hondo were heavy with vegetation. In addition to the "island" of El Monte between the two rivers,[25] the vegetation was especially thick at Whittier Narrows, and Hollywood discovered this fertile area as a space for location shooting.[26] Whittier Narrows had a rather inauspicious debut as a location: in 1915, it stood in for the American South in D. W. Griffith's infamous pro-Confederacy film *The Birth of a Nation*.[27] Almost twenty years later, it would serve as the "Africa" of Edgar Rice Burroughs in the film versions of the *Tarzan* novels that starred Johnny Weismuller and Maureen O'Sullivan. The films were very popular, and the Lion Farm capitalized on the publicity surrounding them to promote its own version of an exotic setting. As Daniel Medina writes, the Narrows and the Lion Farm fit into the narrative of a "semitropical California" that local promoters attempted to sell to tourists.[28]

This recasting of the Whittier Narrows as Africa and the Lion Farm's attempt to create an African jungle between the San Gabriel River and the Rio Hondo are both critical to understanding the farm's role in the discourse on race and whiteness. Though it existed well before the era of white flight, the Lion Farm prefigures Disneyland's appearance as a racialized space, using lions as symbols of the primitive. People of color had lived and worked in El Monte before its establishment as what the *Los Angeles Times* called the "first white settlement in Southern California,"[29] but in the 1920s and 1930s El Monte remained a predominantly white city with segregated schools. Anglos dominated the city's political and economic leadership.[30] In this context, the Lion Farm can be seen as an image of Africa and of the primitive to be tamed—in this case, by white men.

A remarkable photo of the 1934 El Monte Lions Club banquet in Jorane King Barton's *Images of America* supports this idea: twenty or so pillars of society pose with guns around a table covered with what is supposed to be jungle foliage.[31] The men pictured include the school superintendent, Frank Wright, for whom the modern middle school is named; Lester Burdick, El Monte's first police chief;[32] Sam Leffler, the husband of Nellie Leffler, who would become El Monte's mayor in 1938;[33] and Harold Pearson, a horticulturalist who had once been a gardener for the queen of Sweden.[34] Incidentally, Roy Addleman, whose funeral home on Valley Boulevard would host Charles Gay's service in 1950, is also in the picture.[35]

The accident that led to the death of the trainer John Rounan also provided a photo that supports the reading of the Lion Farm as a white version of a tamed Africa. Rounan's colleague—Joe Hoffman, a Lion Farm guide—stands with a gun beside one of the two lions killed in the incident (recall that one of the lions was named Nigger). The article does not specify which lion is pictured, but it does mention that Hoffman posed for photographs immediately after the shooting![36]

World War II brought about the demise of the farm, as a wartime meat shortage made it prohibitively expensive for the Gays to feed their lions. Hoping to continue the operation after the war ended, the Gays offered 150 of their approximately 200 lions for sale and also loaned lions to privately owned zoos.[37] In a *Los Angeles Times* article, Charles Gay stated that he planned to keep about fifty lions as breeding stock so that he could reopen after the war.[38] However, his health faltered, and when the war ended, he was not well enough to relaunch the farm. In 1949, the Gays put the property up for sale, and they retired to Balboa Island.[39] Charles Gay died of a heart ailment in 1950, while Muriel Gay passed away in 1966.[40]

In 1950, the lion statue that sits in front of the El Monte High School auditorium arrived on campus. It had been in storage after the closing of the farm and then spent two years at the Lower Azusa Road "cauliflower patch" of J. Emmett Cushing, president of the school's alumni association.[41] As the San Gabriel River and Rio Hondo were encased in concrete in the 1950s, El Monte's population was growing, from 8,101 in the 1950 census[42] to 13,163 in 1960.[43] The growth of the city was mirrored by the interstate highway project, which brought I-10 to the San Gabriel Valley. The land where the lions once roamed is now gone; the section of the freeway that paved over much of what was once the Lion Farm was completed in 1955–1957.[44]

Perhaps, given its problematic nature, it is just as well that the Lion Farm has faded from view. The animal-focused amusement parks of yesteryear have all vanished as well and have no chance of returning, given the profound changes in both legal regulations and people's attitudes about the relationship between humans and animals. Moreover, in the twenty-first century El Monte, though still fraught with inequality, is significantly more diverse and urban than its prewar incarnation. It is impossible to imagine today's chief of police and the superintendent of schools posing as big-game hunters, as Burdick and Wright did in 1934. Perhaps, after all, it is good that the most significant remaining trace of the farm is the statue at El Monte High School, which is connected more with school pride than civic pride, and that the city's efforts to honor the former park are shrouded in both physical and metaphorical obscurity.

Notes

1 Jack Barton, "A Brief History of El Monte," April 1988, https://web.archive.org/web/20100801231324/http://home.earthlink.net/~jackbarton/ElMonteHistory.htm.

2 Gay's Lion Farm, "Gay's Lion Farm," n.d., advertising brochure in Rick Thomas Collection.

3 Cecilia Rasmussen, "L.A. Scene: The City Then and Now," *Los Angeles Times*, April 6, 1992.

4 A 1927 newspaper article states that Charles Gay came to California "shortly after the war " ("Running a Lion Farm," *Woodbridge Leader*, July 1, 1927). However, Anthony Balducci writes that Gay arrived in California in 1914 (*The Funny Parts: A History of Film Comedy Routines and Gags* [Jefferson, NC: McFarland, 2012], 60–62). The Internet Movie Database lists Gay as a performer in a number of short films produced in the United States in 1915, which would support Balducci's date. "Charles Gay," IMDB, accessed September 22, 2014, https://www.imdb.com/name/nm0349797/?ref_=ttfc_fc_cl_t7.

5 John Church, *Pasadena Cowboy: Growing Up in Southern California and Montana, 1925 to 1947* (Novato, CA: Conover-Patterson, 1996), 38.

6 Jorane King Barton, *El Monte: Images of America* (Charleston, SC: Arcadia, 2006), 79.

7 Balducci, *The Funny Parts*, 60–62; Rasmussen, "L.A. Scene."

8 Gary Cross, "Crowds and Leisure: Thinking Comparatively across the 20th Century," *Journal of Social History* 39, no. 3 (2006): 631.

9 Ibid., 637.

10 City of Santa Monica Office of Pier Management, "Pier History," accessed August 15, 2018, https://www.smgov.net/Departments/OPM/content.aspx?id=30821.

11 Myron Levin, "Jungleland Founder Leaves Town but Takes Her Memories with Her," *Los Angeles Times*, November 13, 1986.

12 Herbert E. Floercky, "Amusement Map of Los Angeles County," 1929, Los Angeles Public Library Map Collection, https://tessa.lapl.org/cdm/ref/collection/maps/id/71.

13 "Door Shut for Always, Lion Farm Owners Say," *Los Angeles Times*, October 28, 1949.

14 Caitlin Flanagan, "Inventing Marilyn," *Atlantic*, February 20, 2013.

15 Jeff Prugh, "For the Players, the Rose Bowl Is Party Time," *Los Angeles Times*, December 26, 1975.

16 Maritza Velasquez, "As El Monte Celebrates Centennial, Locals Recall Wild History with Gay's Lion Farm," *San Gabriel Valley Tribune*, March 24, 2012.

17 "Lion Feast Attracts 890," *Los Angeles Times*, August 28, 1941.

18 French Here Celebrate Bastille Day," *Los Angeles Times*, July 14, 1929.

19 Balducci, *The Funny Parts*, 62; "Maddened Lions Battled: Two Slain and Another Captured at Gay Farm as Beast Mauls Manager Seriously," *Los Angeles Times*, September 27, 1928.

20 John Smith Clarke, *Circus Parade* (New York: C. Scribner's Sons, 1936), 111.

21 Eric Avila, "Popular Culture in the Age of White Flight: Film Noir, Disneyland, and the Cold War (Sub)Urban Imaginary," *Journal of Urban History* 31, no. 3 (2004): 3–22.

22 Ibid., 13.
23 Yoram S. Carmeli, "Lion on Display: Culture, Nature, and Totality in a Circus Performance," Poetics Today 24, no. 1 (2003): 65–90.
24 Stuart Hall, "The West and the Rest: Discourse and Power," in *Formations of Power*, eds. Stuart Hall and Bram Gieben (Cambridge, UK: Polity Press, 1992), 275–318.
25 Enrique Diaz, *The San Gabriel Valley: A 21st Century Portrait* (San Antonio, TX (Historical Publishing Network, 2005), 42.
26 Daniel Medina, "Tarzan on the Rio Hondo! When Hollywood Invaded the Whittier Narrows," KCET, May 1, 2014, https://www.kcet.org/shows/departures/tarzan-on-the-rio-hondo-when-hollywood-invaded-the-whittier-narrows.
27 Ibid.
28 Ibid.
29 K. H. Young, "Location Boon to Community," *Los Angeles Times*, March 6, 1927.
30 Census, United States Census (1930), accessed September 21, 2014, http://www.census.gov/prod/www/decennial.html; E. Diaz, *The San Gabriel Valley*, 44.
31 Jorane Barton, *El Monte*, 81.
32 Craig Quintana, "El Monte Seeks Landmark Status for Its Pioneer Jail," *Los Angeles Times*, September 4, 1988.
33 "Former Woman Mayor Suing, Husband Consents to Move," *Los Angeles Times*, November 26, 1940; Isobel Millier, "Madam Mayor," *Los Angeles Times*, July 3, 1942.
34 Peggi Ridgway and Jan Works, *Sending Flowers to America: Stories of the Los Angeles Flower Market and the People Who Built an American Floral Industry* (Los Angeles: American Florists' Exchange), 56.
35 Untitled second obituary, *Los Angeles Times*, February 24, 1950.
36 "Maddened Lions Battled."
37 "Famed Gay's Lion Farm at El Monte to Close," *Los Angeles Times*, December 25, 1942.
38 "Gay's Lion Farm Closes, Victim of War Rationing," *Los Angeles Times*, December 28, 1942.
39 Deepa Bharath, "Balboa Island Home Celebrates 100 Years," *Orange County Register*, December 15, 2013; "Door Shut for Always, Lion Farm Owners Say," *Los Angeles Times*, October 28, 1949.
40 Untitled second obituary; "Mrs. Muriel Gay, of Lion Farm, Dies," *Los Angeles Times*, August 29, 1966.
41 "Lion Farm Statue Moved to School Site," *Los Angeles Times*, May 27, 1950.
42 Census, United States Census (1950), accessed September 6, 2014, http://www.census.gov/prod/www/decennial.html.
43 Census, United States Census (1960), accessed September 6, 2014, http://www.census.gov/prod/www/decennial.html.
44 "Final Bids to Be Let on San Bernardino Freeway," *Los Angeles Times*, January 16, 1955; Paul O. Harding, "A Concrete Ribbon Unwinds," *Los Angeles Times*, January 3, 1955; Ray Hebert, "Vast Network of Freeways Rapidly Linking L.A. Area: Big Strides Achieved in Last Year," *Los Angeles Times*, February 11, 1957.

22

Memories of El Monte

Art Laboe's Charmed Life on the Air

JUDE P. WEBRE

The oldies station is one of the most tried-and-true formats on the FM radio dial, seemingly ubiquitous yet often absorbed subconsciously. Whether heard in the produce aisle at the local supermarket, planting an earworm that lasts for days, or while driving on the interstate through an unfamiliar city, "great hits" of the 1950s, 1960s, 1970s, and so on can reliably be found—or find you.

Depending on the depth of a station's playlist, a warm, nostalgic doo-wop track by the Penguins (featuring Cleve Duncan) might float past. Over the same stately chords as the Penguins' best-known hit, "Earth Angel," Duncan sings of lost love and happier times:

> I'm all alone.
> Feeling so blue.
> Thinking about you
> And the love we once knew.
> And each time I do,
> It brings back those memories
> of El Monte.

In the fleeting two minutes and forty-six seconds of a 45 rpm vinyl record, what seems like sentimental oldies fare turns out on closer inspection to be a fascinating artifact, a reminder of the intercultural promise that early rock and roll held for the youth of Southern California.

Curiously enough this song, "Memories of El Monte," was penned by Frank Zappa, later a major figure in 1970s progressive rock with his band the Mothers of Invention, and arguably one of the most innovative composers in American avant-garde music. The doo-wop track for the Penguins was one of the first songs that Zappa wrote and reflects his adolescence, steeped in the fertile rhythm and blues scene of Greater Los Angeles. When Zappa wrote the song in 1962 with his friend (and future Mothers singer) Ray Collins, he had been listening to *Memories of El Monte*, a 1960 compilation of singles from the mid-1950s heyday of doo-wop put out by Original Sound Records, an independent label owned by the local radio celebrity and concert promoter Art Laboe. In fact, Zappa brought the song to Laboe, who agreed to pay to record it and release it as a single on his label. Laboe used his connections to help recruit the lead vocalist of the Penguins, Cleve Duncan, backed by the tenor Walter Saulsberry and the Viceroys (another local doo-wop group), with Zappa joining on the xylophone.[1]

Ever the shrewd, understated impresario, Laboe asked Zappa to include in the lyrics mentions of classic doo-wop songs that happened to be tracks on the Original Sound compilation. As a result, the second verse, spoken by Duncan, is a poignant call and response that recalls dances past:

> If only they'd have those dances again,
> I'd know where to find you, and all my old friends.
> The Shields would sing . . . "*You cheated. You lied . . .*"
> And the Heartbeats . . . "*You're a thousand miles away . . .*"
> And the Medallions with "The Letter" and . . . "*Sweet words of his mortality . . .*"
> Marvin and Johnny with . . . "*Cherry Pie . . .*"
> And then, Tony Allen with . . . "*Night owl . . .*"
> And I, Cleve Duncan, along with the Penguins, will sing,
> "*Earth angel, Earth Angel, Will you be mine?*"
> At El Monte.[2]

The resulting single is, on one level, a curious postmodern pastiche of the doo-wop genre, not out of place with the affectionate parodies of American popular music that Zappa later wrote. But on another level, with Laboe's stewardship as well as its evocation of El Monte, the song taps into a hidden reservoir in the cultural history of Southern California, in particular its Chicano/a/x community.

Beginning with the dances he threw at El Monte's Legion Stadium in 1955, through five decades as a beloved oldies DJ connecting with his audience on a nightly basis, Laboe remains an iconic voice for Californians who do not fit the more glamorous conception that many Americans hold of Los Angeles. As the essayist Susan Straight has lyrically suggested, these are the people "cruising, boxing groceries, welding mufflers, changing tires, sewing prom dresses, picking oranges, teaching kids," and calling Laboe every night to dedicate songs to their loved ones.[3]

By his own telling, Laboe grew up with the radio. He was born Art Egnoian to immigrant parents of Armenian descent in Salt Lake City on August 7, 1925, a mere three years after the radio pioneer Gugielmo Marconi began wireless broadcasts of entertainment programming. From an early age, Laboe remembers being "completely enthralled by the box that talked." His fascination became a hobby and then a profession when he moved to Los Angeles in 1934 to live with his sister, after his parents divorced. As a teenager, Laboe became involved in ham radio circles and even started a station out of his bedroom in 1938.

As Laboe related the story in an interview with the historian Josh Kun, it was during his service in the Navy Reserve during World War II that he received his first break in commercial broadcasting. While stationed on Treasure Island in San Francisco Bay in 1943, Art Egnoian showed up one day at KSAN, a local station, to ask for airtime. Despite his inexperience, he was able to secure a one-hour time slot (11:00 P.M. to midnight) due to a shortage of licensed DJs during the war. Fortuitously, young Art had acquired the relevant broadcast license during a brief stint at Stanford University to study radio engineering. The station manager at KSAN suggested that Egnoian change his name, so he borrowed the last name of a secretary working there—Laboe.[4]

During his first program at KSAN, Laboe stumbled upon the technique that has become his signature broadcasting style: the personal dedication. In 1943, there were few records played on the radio, which then focused on news, information, and live theatrical and musical performances. When there was airtime to fill, a station would play records, mostly of big bands and pop vocalists—a task that fell to Laboe in his time slot. He quickly discovered that a prime segment of his audience were young women who called in to dedicate songs to their brothers, boyfriends, and husbands serving in the military.

For Laboe, then as now, the personal dedication was a tangible way for the DJ, alone with the microphone in studio, to connect with the invisible audience hearing his broadcast. But it also has helped him gain the loyalty and personal investment of listeners. When a listener calls to dedicate a song to a loved one, Laboe serves as an intermediary between his listeners, connecting two points across space, while offering recognition with his voice of a personal experience or emotion. Throughout his career, the dedication has been fundamental to Laboe's approach. Bridging the distance of military service has been extended to other kinds of absence—that of loved ones in prison, those traveling for migrant labor, or even just the solitary worker on a graveyard shift.[5]

Laboe's focus on taking requests also helped him—again fortuitously—anticipate the groundswell of rock and roll within postwar teen culture in the mid-1950s. After the war, Laboe had a difficult time finding work, when more experienced DJs returned from the service. He bounced around stations east of Los Angeles in Palm Springs and the Pomona Valley before trying out a mobile DJ booth for KPOP in Los Angeles. His most popular location, which he occupied from 1951 to 1959, was in the parking lot of Scrivener's Drive-In at the corner of Sunset and Cahuenga boulevards in Hollywood.

Only a few blocks from Hollywood High, Scrivener's became the epicenter of Los Angeles's effervescent teen culture that combined automobiles, mass culture, and discretionary income to set a new standard of freedom through consumption for young people nationwide. Laboe began doing a late show at Scrivener's that lasted until 4:00 A.M., broadcasting to teens cruising at night throughout the region. He eventually added an after-school broadcast (what he called "record hops"), taking song recommendations from the kids he interviewed. When the national craze surrounding the first rock and roll hits of Elvis Presley, Jerry Lee Lewis, and Little Richard reached Los Angeles in late 1955, Laboe became the first DJ to play these artists' singles on the West Coast, largely based on tips from his teen informants at Scrivener's. While continuing to play the doo-wop and rhythm and blues records that had been the staple of his broadcasts up to then, Laboe achieved wider local celebrity because of rock and roll, as his show became the highest-rated on Los Angeles radio and served as a promotional destination for the new brand of pop stars.[6]

The runaway popularity of the Scrivener's broadcasts created traffic jams around the drive-in, convincing Laboe that he should organize "dances and shows" for his radio audience. This led him to El Monte Legion Stadium, a nondescript, rundown, boxy auditorium that had been built as a wrestling venue for the 1932 Olympic Games and later served as the site of boxing, professional wrestling, and roller derby events. Legion Stadium had also recently hosted raucous rhythm and blues shows featuring saxophone "honkers" like Big Jay McNeely, whose "Pachuco Hop" was a big hit with the zoot-suit crowd on the Eastside. Laboe's friend and fellow DJ, Dick "Huggy Boy" Hugg, emceed those shows and shared his huge popularity among Latino audiences with Laboe in suggesting the venue for rock and roll dances. Starting in 1955, Laboe hosted an event every other weekend at Legion Stadium, drawing enthusiastic teenagers from all over the region to the 3,000-person venue. The events alternated between dancing to records and live performances by local artists, such as the rockabilly duo Don and Dewey, as well as rising stars like Jackie Wilson,

FIG. 29 Vincent Ramos, "El Monte Legion Stadium Nocturne." El Monte Station. (Courtesy of Los Angeles County Metropolitan Transportation Authority.)

Sam Cooke, and Ritchie Valens—the Latino heartthrob who tragically died in a plane crash in 1959.[7]

Laboe cemented a bond with his audience by going into the crowd to meet people. He would talk with groups of teens and ask them about themselves and their favorite songs, just as he had done at Scrivener's. Laboe also visited with people waiting on line outside to get into the venue. Shows at Legion Stadium typically cost \$3.00, but when a big name such as Jerry Lee Lewis or Jackie Wilson appeared, the cover went up to \$3.50, leaving some concertgoers short of the extra fifty cents. As Laboe related in a recent oral history interview, "I remember filling both my coat pockets with half dollars—there were a lot of half dollars around then—and I went outside where everybody was waiting in line and went up and down the line and I could see who was trying to dig up some money—people were real honest about it—and I was handing out these half dollars to some of these kids." When the promoter chastised him for leaving the stage and giving away money before the show, Laboe replied that this was how he wanted to do it, allowing everyone the chance to get into the show.[8]

During the six years when Laboe put on shows in El Monte, he provided the space for a spontaneous community of youth that cut across ethnic, racial, and class lines. While the shows drew affluent fans from the Westside who had made up the Scrivener's crowd, the core audience for the events was drawn from the local Mexican American enclaves in East Los Angeles, the San Gabriel Valley, and El Monte, as well as black and white working-class neighborhoods south and east of there. As the historian Matt Garcia has described, radios and automobiles helped facilitate an informal network of young rock and roll fans across Los Angeles, who, united by Laboe's personality and love of the music, converged at Legion Stadium for an intercultural exchange remarkably free of the racial tensions within social spaces that had characterized their parents' generation.[9]

Laboe remembers that the events were meant to be "fun, fun, fun," and the atmosphere encouraged nonconformist fashion (due to lack of a dress code), self-expression, and a general goodwill that seems almost utopian in retrospect.[10] Memories of El Monte Legion Stadium—in only the recent past when Zappa wrote the song—have left a strong impression to this day on Laboe, the performers, and the young people who went there. It remains a question for further research whether the harmonious atmosphere that Laboe and others remember reflects a nostalgic veneer or a genuine collective spirit that tolerated and perhaps encouraged interethnic mixing, dancing, and dating in an era when crossing such boundaries was often deeply fraught. The social mixing across racial and ethnic lines seems to have been enough of a threat to cause local authorities eventually to shut down the Legion Stadium shows over the objections of DJs and performers.

As with many such conjunctions in American popular music, this moment of promise proved to be fleeting, as the emerging record industry in Los Angeles absorbed, elaborated, and transformed the energy of early rock and roll into a more predictable and manageable product. The El Monte shows inspired a wave of local bands who enjoyed success as live performers in dance halls across the Eastside, but these groups were increasingly overshadowed in the 1960s and 1970s by the popularity of national acts on the radio. One group that emerged from the late 1950s scene to achieve national success, keeping alive its multiethnic spirit, was War, whose 1975 hit "Low Rider" captures one of the colorful sights of a night out in El Monte. By the time Legion Stadium was torn down in 1974 to make way for a post office, the concerts there had truly passed into memory, even as the music of that time persisted on the radio with the emergence of oldies stations.[11]

Laboe's brand of nostalgia has never been rueful, however, and his career over the past several decades reflects the optimism and resilience that characterized his personality from the beginning. Laboe arguably invented oldies as a format, coining the term on a fifteen-volume series of compilations on Original Sound titled *Oldies but Goodies*. According to Laboe, he came up with the concept at Scrivener's Drive-In to refer to tracks only three or four years old that his audience would still request. The key point, in his words, is that "it's old but it's gotta be good," which still serves as a guiding principle on his radio shows today. Laboe has also maintained long-standing almost familial relationships with several performers who appeared at El Monte, including the Penguins and Rosie Hamlin of Rosie and the Originals, whose music Laboe continues to play on his show and present at oldies concerts in the Los Angeles area. Likewise, Laboe helped Hugg reestablish his DJ career, offering him an oldies radio slot in the early 1980s after Hugg had fallen on hard times.[12]

Through the many transformations of radio, from AM to FM and then cable and into the era of Clear Channel, Laboe has always leveraged his popularity to retain full autonomy in the presentation of his show. Now in his nineties, Laboe continues to appear for thirty-one hours over six nights a week on stations throughout California and Arizona, as well as worldwide on the internet. In an era when many oldies stations are automated, sticking to a limited, market-tested playlist without DJs, Laboe draws on his own deep knowledge of popular music and the musical affections of his listeners to intersperse perennial hits with singles that might be more obscure to his younger audience. He remains popular across a wide range of age groups, however, and proudly takes dedications from ten-year-olds as well as *abuelas*. As Laboe slyly notes, he puts people on the air "from womb to tomb."[13]

It is this intergenerational appeal, built on his affable stewardship of the El Monte "dances and shows," that has made Laboe an honorary voice of the Mexican American community in Southern California, his radio program providing a sound track for Chicano/a/x identity. Gil Cedillo, a member of the Los Angeles City Council, vividly recalls cruising through Boyle Heights in the early 1970s with Antonio Villaraigosa in the future mayor's canary yellow 1964 Chevy listening to Laboe, whom he likened to "everyone's favorite uncle in the neighborhood."[14] The comedian Paul Rodriguez told the *Los Angeles Times* that Laboe "is more Chicano than some Chicanos, and everyone from the toughest *vato* to the wimpiest guy would say the same."[15] Laboe's reputation remains strong even among younger Mexican Americans today, such as a twenty-one-year-old student who told Straight: "Art Laboe! Man, I grew up in Baldwin Park and the whole neighborhood listens to him! The women love him."[16]

Laboe typically shrugs off such compliments, however, and one has the sense that he is a strong believer in the universal appeal of oldies: everyone chipped in over the years to make great music and have a good time. In the shark tank that commercial radio and the record industry can often be, Laboe's serene, unassuming approach throughout his career is remarkable. But his longevity makes complete sense in that he seems to have a wise understanding of the meaning that the music has for his listeners—in their memories and relationships—and he gladly makes himself the conduit for that meaning. If Art Laboe has led a charmed life on the radio, he has shared it with countless listeners.

Notes

1 Barry Miles, *Zappa: A Biography* (New York: Grove, 2004), 72–73. See also Barney Hoskyns, *Waiting for the Sun: Strange Days, Weird Scenes, and the Sound of Los Angeles* (New York: St. Martin's, 1996), 110.
2 The Penguins, *Memories of El Monte*, Original Sound Records 27, 45 rpm.
3 Susan Straight, "Listening to Art Laboe," *Boom: A Journal of California* 1, no. 1 (2011): 5.
4 Josh Kun, "Art Laboe in Conversation with Josh Kun at Original Sound Studios," Dublab, July 11, 2013, http://dublab.com/art-laboe-in-conversation-with-josh-kun-at-original-sound-studios-07-11-13/.
5 Straight, "Listening to Art Laboe," 3.
6 Art Laboe, oral history interview, November 22, 2013, South El Monte Arts Posse (SEMAP), East of East: Mapping Community Narratives in El Monte and South El Monte, http://www.semapeastofeast.com. See also Hoskyns, *Waiting for the Sun*, 37–41.
7 Hoskyns, *Waiting for the Sun*, 33–34.
8 Laboe, oral history interview, SEMAP.
9 Matt Garcia, "Memories of El Monte: Intercultural Dancehalls in Post-WWII Greater Los Angeles," in *Generations of Youth*, ed. Joe Austin and Michael Nevin Willard (New York: New York University Press, 1998), 157–172.
10 Kun, "Art Laboe."
11 Garcia, "Memories of El Monte," 167. See also Hoskyns, *Waiting for the Sun*, 237–239.
12 Kun, "Art Laboe."
13 Ibid.
14 Esmerelda Bermudez, "At 84, Art Laboe's an Oldie but Still a Goodie," *Los Angeles Times*, November 12, 2009.
15 Ibid.
16 Straight, "Listening to Art Laboe," 3.

23

El Monte's Wildweed

Biraciality and the Punk Ethos of the Gun Club's Jeffrey Lee Pierce

TROY ANDREAS ARAIZA KOKINIS

During the 1970s, El Monte was still being transformed from a semi-agrarian walnut grove town to a concrete-washed suburb so typical of the San Gabriel Valley by the 2000s. The suburban sprawl thirty minutes east of Hollywood does not typically get mentioned in the story of first-wave Los Angeles punk, yet it served as the backdrop for the upbringing of one of the scene's most musically talented and conceptually innovative front men, Jeffrey Lee Pierce (JLP), guitarist and vocalist of Los Angeles's the Gun Club. Just a San Gabriel Valley punk kid drawing from references as far-reaching as lowrider funk legends War, the blues artist Howling Wolf, Jamaican reggae, and the Viet Cong, JLP's oeuvre offers a unique sound track for thinking about race and space in Southern California. This chapter analyzes JLP's cultural production and punk ethos as products of his biracial upbringing in post–Chicano movement El Monte, California.

Scholarly work, documentary narratives, and popular common sense often represent punk rock as a white youth subculture and misidentify the genre's history, which is inseparable from the creative energies and contributions of racialized populations. Dick Hebdige's monumental book, *Subculture: The*

Meaning of Style, views the U.K. punk aesthetic as a "white translation" of black urban youth culture, citing the West Indian rude boy influence on the development of the genre across the Atlantic.[1] In Los Angeles, this experience has generally been associated with a predominantly white Hollywood scene. For example, Penelope Spheeris's *The Decline of Western Civilization* and Marc Spitz's *We Got the Neutron Bomb: The Untold Story of L.A. Punk*—both cited as classic documentations of punk in Los Angeles—focus almost exclusively on Hollywood and thus omit references to the thriving punk rock scene of the Eastside, the racialized working class suburbs east of downtown's LA River.[2]

More recently cultural studies scholars and DIY record labels have set out to resurrect a historical memory of what is referred to as the East Los Angeles Renaissance: a 1980 local punk scene whose backbone consisted of Fatima Records, a DIY label run by the Plugz's front man Tito Larriva, and East Los Angeles's first punk venue, the Vex. The East Los Angeles Renaissance's creative circuits did not follow linear paths—Fatima went bankrupt after releasing only three records and operating for only nine months, and the Vex eventually closed after a riot broke out during a Black Flag show (a group of white Huntington Beach punks threw chairs out of the windows, broke copy machines and art equipment, and vandalized paintings by local artists).[3] This incident shows the difficulty in merging the punk worlds of the Chicano Eastside with white Hollywood (and Orange County, by extension). It also demonstrates the way that Southern Californian racialization manifested in the punk scenes of the area, highlighting broader societal conflicts in the worst moments while enacting popular forms of multiracial solidarity through collaboration in the best of times.

I contend, however, that race and geography in the first-wave Los Angeles punk scene can be explored as much more than the white-brown antipode, Hollywood-Eastside binary. In fact, many suburban-born white, Mexican American, and biracial punks from the San Gabriel Valley and Inland Empire moved West and left an indelible imprint on the Hollywood punk scene. Their presence shattered this geographic and racial divide. Some viewed punk as a common ethos and identity to transgress the borders established by the racialized division of space in Los Angeles's urban sprawl. JLP, lead singer and guitarist of Los Angeles's the Gun Club, saw punk as a way to disidentify with hegemonic whiteness. JLP grew up in El Monte with his Mexican mother and Anglo American father. His childhood experiences led him to strongly identify with Mexicanness, likely due to being surrounded by fellow racialized youths in the San Gabriel Valley (SGV).

Even though he passed as white and found acceptance in white spaces, JLP unashamedly channeled his Mexican self-identification through his creative expression. Rather than feel trapped by what Gloria Anzaldúa has referred to as the *choque*, or culture clash, JLP drew inspiration and influence from his

Mexican identity and other nonwhite cultures, for which he had an affinity.[4] His creative production represents a post–Chicano movement cultural form that was attuned to the social and political realities of Los Angeles in the era of both Governor and President Ronald Reagan. JLP epitomizes the zeitgeist of Southern California in the early 1980s by embracing the biracial Chicano experience while not front-loading it in his lyrical and aesthetic content. Yet he proudly referred to his Mexicanness frequently in interviews and public interactions. JLP performed a post–Chicano movement identity that broke from previously defined forms of authenticity. His genius lay in his ability to escape from the traps of rigid forms of identification.

Born in Montebello, California, in 1958, JLP attended El Monte's Valle Lindo Middle School and Mountain View High School before moving with his family to Pacoima, in the San Fernando Valley. He began playing the guitar at age ten and served as the president of Blondie's U.S. fan club during his late teens. He met Brian Tristan (aka Kid Congo Powers), a La Puente native and Basset High School alumnus, in 1978 at a Pere Ubu show in Hollywood, when JLP recruited Kid Congo to play in a band. Kid Congo recalls: "On this particular night I was like 'Who is this guy anyways?' He was wearing a white vinyl trench coat with white girl's cowboy boots and a polka dot shirt."[5] Although Kid Congo did not play an instrument and refused to sing, JLP offered to teach him how to play guitar. The two collaborated on a few tracks that were eventually released on the Gun Club's classic debut LP, *Fire of Love* (1981). Although Kid Congo left the band to join the Cramps before the LP's release, he maintained a close relationship with JLP and eventually returned to the Gun Club to release *The Las Vegas Story* (1984) and *Mother Juno* (1987).

The two maintained an especially close relationship that was strongly influenced by their shared experience as Chicanos in the San Gabriel Valley. Kid Congo recalls:

> We bonded a lot on common areas, things like El Monte Legion Stadium or the Tumblewood theater. You know, things we grew up with and memories we had of there. We would say things like, "We have this guitar riff that sounds like it is coming out of a garage in La Puente, or the San Gabriel Valley." You know this kind of soul-y, psychedelic thing, like War or something like that. We would often reference that. We would often talk about how we felt very Mexican but we didn't speak Spanish. Like how you could feel the culture within you and what a strange thing that was.
>
> Our music, we definitely reference the SGV and Chicano culture a lot, and it does not always come out in an obvious way. It was some kind of otherness that we had always felt. And we would talk about our high school experiences and how that shaped us. How funny that we were these weird people in this

> community—that we felt very apart from it, like how we always knew we were going to leave. But we always found a lot of love for the area, and worth. The older we got, we would go backwards into that music. We would talk about how we felt like beatniks, like rock 'n' roll kids, and weirdos. And, you know, I was gay. I always felt like we had to leave from there, and we could never be ourselves there, for whatever reason. You know, I was young so—I don't know. But the more I think about it, the more I see a more open culture. Does this make any sense? I see a more open culture than I thought there? These limits were probably my own.[6]

As a white-passing biracial Chicano, JLP identified more closely with the Mexican identity transmitted via his mother than with the whiteness transmitted via his Korean War veteran father. He reflected: "All my life, people have been pushing me around. Mr. & Mrs. DRILL SERGEANT and their 50's Korean War ways, I will immediately go the other way. Authority, I do not respect. Unless it's the respectful authority of a street educated human being . . . War! Is in the streets! For the Blacks, the Mexicans, and the Japanese! We can understand each other."[7] His self-identification was manifested in a near obsession with race and an affinity for nonwhite peoples and cultures. Upon meeting fellow punks with racially ambiguous features, he commonly inquired about their racial identity and swiftly established himself as half-Mexican, jokingly identifying himself as a "half-breed."[8] Although the Gun Club is remembered for its blues punk sound, it initially drew more influence and inspiration from soul and reggae.[9] JLP resided for many years in the predominantly black South Los Angeles city of Inglewood, during the height of the Crips and Bloods feud. He ventured to Jamaica with Kid Congo to follow his love for reggae and dub. He also spent a significant amount of time in Vietnam and Japan. He recognized a shared historical experience among racialized peoples globally—a sort of late twentieth-century postmodern reiteration of *tercermundismo*.[10]

JLP's affinity for his Mexican identity can be identified in his choice to release the band's first EP on Tito Larriva's Fatima Records. He recalls: "I enjoyed the comfort of an all Mexican label, since I was raised by a Mexican mother in El Monte and had spent my entire life in her family environment. I was even briefly in a gang at Valle Lindo Junior High School. I understood Spanish and spoke a little. Tito's label consisted of The Plugz, The Brat, and The Gun Club." However, Fatima went bankrupt and was not able to fund the project. The band kept the Larriva recording but eventually released it with the predominantly white Slash Records.[11] This was at a time when clear racial distinctions were being made in the Los Angeles punk rock scene. According to Will Herron, front man of Los Illegals, nearly all bands with Chicano members were being labeled as "East Los Angeles" bands—the Plugz were referred to as "Los Plugz" and Los Illegals as "Lost Illegals," nicknames showing the

Westsiders' habit of othering Chicano bands from the same city.[12] Yet JLP's El Monte Mexican upbringing led him to risk potential pigeonholing by the Westside audience. Were it not for the shortage of resources, the first Gun Club recordings would have been released on Fatima, possibly changing the band's entire trajectory.

The band's affiliation with Slash Records gained them entry into the Westside scene. Whereas East Los Angeles bands faced exclusion for their blatant nods to Mexicanness and Chicanismo (they were seen as too ethnic), JLP and Kid Congo gained more acceptance in the Hollywood scene because the Mexican American influences in their music were subtle and did not leave the recognizable imprints that white audiences by then were able to identify. Kid Congo describes his perspective on otherness and punk rock culture in Los Angeles:

> The idea in punk was really no labels. So for me, I was a very tenacious kid—so I was like, well, no labels. That was what I immediately could see. Also that being a minority was very punk, I thought. You still had a feeling of not belonging. You know, it is like, America is white culture and Anglo culture. No matter how I do not even speak Spanish; I was raised as anyone would be in LA. But you still felt like an outsider. So punk was actually the perfect place for us—quite a bridge, you know. It was somewhere I did not feel the need to be Chicano, and it didn't matter that I was not white. It was actually a good thing, you know, sexually. A good thing to feel this otherness and to say, "Okay, this is a community of misfits or people who want to buck this system." You know, that was the requirement. Labels were taboo, but bucking the system was required. So playing into Chicano culture—it was like, I have this built-in otherness and built-in bucking the system. So this is somewhere I can shine and belong, to others.[13]

While Kid Congo viewed the Hollywood punk scene as a site of refuge for weirdos and outsiders of all types, including racialized people and gender queers, JLP remained uncomfortable with whiteness throughout his life. In his autobiography, *Go Tell the Mountain*, he declares:

> I still find Anglo-Americans strange and foreign. I have a penchant for black-haired girls and deliver a fearsome street rap. It's all part of my Mexican upbringing. . . . Later in my life, that comfort was always still there. Among Latinos or Asians, I always felt quite at home. I even experienced some militancy when my family moved to the San Fernando Valley, being unable to get along with the wealthy Anglo kids. I was always reading Eldridge Cleaver or Huey Newton, supporting the Viet Cong, who were then my idols. Needless to say, I didn't have many friends.[14]

After releasing *The Las Vegas Story* (1984), JLP and Kid Congo ventured together to Yucatan, Mexico, to discover their roots. They drunkenly snorkeled, roamed the jungle, and climbed pyramids for a week before returning to tour for the album. While neither traced any lineage to Mayan ancestry, the pilgrimage seemed essential for connecting them to what they both understood as a deeper—perhaps spiritual—Mexican identity. The Mexico trip was one of many examples of what the scholar Leonard Nevarez has called "rootless cosmopolitanism," a stateless moral freedom.[15] Admittedly, JLP liked being a foreigner and an unknown—something he often talked about in the interviews he gave while traveling in places like Greece, Japan, and England in the latter part of his musical career. He spent the last ten years of his life living between Japan and London, and making occasional trips to Vietnam. He was open about not wanting to return to Los Angeles and proudly drew influences from all around the world. JLP's obsession with difference can be interpreted as a result of his feelings as an outsider in Anglo America, an obsession that led him to produce poignant lyrics and explosive music that in turn led to the making of what might be some of the most remarkable punk albums ever to come out of Southern California.

There is only one clear reference to El Monte in JLP's lyrics. In the song "Hey Juana" from the solo album *Wildweed* (1985), JLP seems to be conversing with a fictitious Mexican lover from back home in El Monte. He frequently inquires about what everyday life is like. He gossips about various punk celebrity friends, such as Nick Cave and Romi Mori, and refers to various foreign places where he had lived. In the last five lines he moves between Spanish and English:

> *Konnichiwa,* Juana! Let's go home!
> Ah, hey Juana, baby?
> What are you gonna do today?
> Ah, Juana, *mi novia*
> *Qué pasa esta noche*?

While biracial people are commonly pathologized as stuck between two conflicting realities, JLP's lyrics in this song situate his racial identity and geographic origins within his global influences and experiences. Yet as wild as the wildweed may grow, this song reminds listeners that it can never break from its roots.

Conclusion

Whereas The Vex sought to bridge the East and West sides of Greater Los Angeles by providing a shared space, JLP and Kid Congo punctured these divisions in their musical and creative trajectory. As the Vex concluded its first chapter with a riot, JLP's feeling of estrangement from the hegemonic whiteness in punk propelled him to pursue innovative sounds inspired by the Black Power movement, the Vietcong, and the de facto segregated suburb where he grew up. In a strange way, the Gun Club's otherness speaks to the way white supremacist logic permeated the epoch's most progressive, deviant, and subversive subcultural scenes. It shows that even in circles whose members had open minds, biraciality confounds those hegemonic racial scripts that seek to make sense of entire racial categories by homogenizing entire populations, and thus it cannot be neatly situated in the antipodal corners predefined by the culture industry and the state.

In the end, the Gun Club never played the role of prodigal son. Although the group's core members JLP and Kid Congo both grew up in the San Gabriel Valley, the Gun Club never played a show in the community. As fate would have it, the band developed a larger fan base on the East Coast and in Europe than it had in Los Angeles. In 1993, the Gun Club released its seventh and final full-length LP, *Lucky Jim.* On March 31, 1996, JLP died of a brain hemorrhage at the age of thirty-seven. He was in the process of making more music with the Gun Club and his lifelong friend Kid Congo Powers. He wanted to live.

Notes

1 Dick Hebdige, *Subculture: The Meaning of Style* (London: Routledge, 1979).

2 Penelope Spheeris, *The Decline of Western Civilization* (New York: Home Media Entertainment, 1981); Marc Spitz, *We Got the Neutron Bomb: The Untold Story of L.A. Punk* (New York: Three Rivers Press, 2001).

3 On March 22, 1980, Will Herron (formerly a member of ASCO and a front man for Los Illegals) and Sister Karen Boccalero (a radical Chicana nun involved with the Catholic Youth Organization) opened the Vex on the third floor of Self-Help Graphics, at the corner of Brooklyn Avenue and Gage Street. See Josh Kun, "Vex Populi: At an Unprepossessing Eastside Punk Rock Landmark, Utopia Was in the Air, until the Day It Wasn't," *Los Angeles Magazine*, March 2003.

4 Gloria Anzaldúa wrote, "Like all people, we perceive the version of reality that our culture communicates. Like others having or living in more than one culture, we get multiple, often opposing messages. The coming together of two self-consistent but habitually incomparable frames of reference causes un choque, a cultural collision," *Borderlands/La Frontera: The New Mestiza* (San Francisco: Aunt Lute Books, 1987), 78.

5 Kid Congo Powers, "An Oral History of the Gun Club," *Razorcake* (December 2005–January 2006), http://razorcake.org/oral-history-gun-club-ryan-leach.

6 Kid Congo Powers, oral history interview, February 13, 2014, South El Monte Arts Posse (SEMAP), East of East: Mapping Community Narratives in El Monte and South El Monte, http://www.semapeastofeast.com.

7 Quoted in Leonard Nevarez, "In Exile: The Rootless Cosmopolitanism of Jeffrey Lee Pierce and the Gun Club," *Musical Urbanism*, June 23, 2015, http://pages

.vassar.edu/musicalurbanism/2015/06/23/in-exile-the-rootless-cosmopolitanism-of-jeffrey-lee-pierce-and-the-gun-club/.

8 Kurt Voss, dir., *Ghost on the Highway: A Portrait of Jeffrey Lee Pierce and the Gun Club* (Los Angeles: Power Factory Films, 2006).

9 Powers, "An Oral History of the Gun Club." JLP's mother collected soul and rhythm and blues vinyl records that he listened to and loved as a child.

10 *Tercermundismo* was a political ideology that embraced nonaligned socialism, anti-imperialism, and Third World solidarity. It gained popularity in Latin America throughout the 1950s and continues to be a mobilizing political force in certain countries today.

11 Jeffrey Lee Pierce, *Go Tell the Mountain* (Los Angeles: 2.13.61 Publications, 1998), 28.

12 Will Herron, interview by author, East Los Angeles, CA, January 16, 2014.

13 Powers, oral history interview, SEMAP.

14 Pierce, *Go Tell the Mountain*, 27–28.

15 Nevarez, "In Exile."

24

Punk and the Seamstress

APOLONIO MORALES

I started going punk in eighth grade at Kranz Junior High School back in 1990. At first I didn't know what to make of the music. I was still wearing those polo shirts with a tiger on the breast that were popular with the *cholos*, combing my hair back, and listening to Metallica—go figure. The feedback and noise that filled my ears was something new yet subversive. It seemed timeless and relevant. It was definitely not the hair band sound that prevailed on the airwaves or the gangsta rap that was starting to get popular at the time. Danny, my cousin George's friend, brought us all together. Danny was a tall lanky kid with a sense of humor; incredible charm; and, most importantly, parents who let him throw gigs in his backyard.

Before I knew it, I was part of a group of youth whose older brothers and sisters passed on new wave, skate, and punk rock to their younger siblings. We listened to Subhumans, the Misfits, the Exploited, Bad Religion, Minor Threat, Black Flag, and the Dead Kennedys on beat-up rerecorded cassettes. Bad Religion's melodic choruses and lyrics caught my attention. *Against the Grain* had been released in November 1990, and it had become punk rock's underground triumph. I listened to that tape on my fake Walkman through blown-out headphones over and over again:

> Here labeled as a lunatic, sequestered and content,
> There ignored and defeated by the government,
> There's an oriented public whose magnetic force does pull,

But away from the potential of the individual, against the grain.[1]

The words rang clear amid the distorted guitars—though I have to admit I barely understood the lyrics and found myself pulling out the dictionary more than a few times to decipher their meaning. I had finally found a way to interpret what my experience had been as someone who felt like an outsider to the saved-by-the-bell make-believe world on television. My friends and I rented the only copy of *The Decline of Western Civilization* at the local Blockbuster. I watched the movie with my friend Alex at the mobile home park down on Elliott Avenue. We watched X and Black Flag talking about life, death, and politics. Then we watched FEAR go on a homophobic and sexist rant. When Darby Crash told a story about a "wetback," Alex's dad overheard the word and walked across the room and screamed at the TV, "Wetback? Fuck you!" We agreed. Punk wasn't perfect; it had its issues, too. With punk you find what fits with you. I felt like I was part of something that had meaning behind it. It wasn't just mohawks and tattoos—there was rebellion behind it. The other most influential band for me at the time was the peace anarchist band Crass. I remember listening to *The Feeding of the 5000*. That album blew my mind and shattered every perception I was brought up with from class to religion:

Banned from the Roxy. . . . O.K.
I never much liked playing there anyway.
They said they only wanted well-behaved boys;
do they think guitars and microphones are just fucking toys?
Fuck 'em, I've chosen to make my stand
against what I feel is wrong with this land.
They just sit there on their overfed arses,
feeding off the sweat of less fortunate classes.
They keep their fucking power 'cause their finger's on the button;
they've got control and won't let it be forgotten.[2]

Punk music gave meaning to the things that were out of our control in our lives. It provided a serious sociopolitical analysis of our reality. Deep within both of these interpretations was the inevitable violence that existed in El Monte. No one knew how to talk things out except through aggression. It felt like there was a reason for it, like a last stand against invisible forces penetrating every aspect of our lives. There were reasons for our poverty. I suddenly found that there was something of value to be discovered within every band and every song, and it also helped explain why the cycle of oppression repeated itself in our lives.

In high school, I took refuge from the monotony by spending my time struggling to get into college prep courses and listening to punk. The backyard gigs were exciting, with punks in all shapes and sizes, with mohawks, and wearing leather jackets or Doc Martens with somewhat of a cholo twist. The smell of clove cigarettes and cheap beer still lingers in my mind. We watched bands like Non-Tolerance, Anti-Social, Schleprock, YAPO, the Death Mickies, X-O Toxins, and Beeker's Army. I was inspired and thought, "I can play this stuff, too." It wasn't long before my friends Hector Casillas, Johnny Montejano, Manny Andrade, and I started our own band. Johnny and I both bought the Mr. Entertainment guitar-amp specials from the Montebello Mall. The first guitar I ever owned was a no-name GTX, and I had a Peavey amplifier with built-in distortion. My first guitar burned to a crisp through a freak accident in my friend Hector's brother-in-law's truck. He was fixing some crossed wires on the GTX and decided to change the distributor cap on his engine at the same time. The wires on the distributor cap were crossed, and the truck blew up while he was driving on the freeway. He survived, but my guitar wasn't so lucky.

Manny left the band, so I convinced my mom to buy me a bass guitar. We became the Unwanted and later the Indigents. We kept changing names because every time I read *Maximum Rock 'n' Roll*, I'd see that someone with our name had put out an EP. We didn't have what you would call quality instruments. The wail of distortion and feedback became a wall of sound to the rattle of secondhand drums and barely audible bass. We made a whole lot of noise before we got any better, but the experience taught me that I could play music without formal education.

It seemed like everyone was starting a band at the time. I discovered KSPC 88.7 FM by accident. I tuned in religiously through a makeshift antenna made out of coaxial cable connected to my little boom box, and I started picking up a show called Rebel Girl Radio. It was the first time I heard Bikini Kill talking about revolution and feminism. The Riot Grrrl movement seemed to resonate with me, because I always felt close to my mother's struggle. For me, the airwaves were now filled with local bands and their demos, and they were playing punk rock just like us here in El Monte.

I wrote what my friends called "political" songs, taking inspiration from the *Los Angeles Times* and my English classes. Playing punk filled me with a rush I couldn't quite explain. The backyard gigs were a place where I felt a sense of community. For three bucks, you could see a couple of bands and get one of those red cups for the keg. The warm summer nights usually ended with fights breaking out and dirt flying around from all the slam dancing. When someone fell, we picked them up. At one of those gigs, the cops came in and got everyone out onto the street in the cul-de-sac with their guns drawn. They frisked us and claimed we were shooting guns into the air. It was Fourth of July, and the skyrockets next door were still popping. When we asked why we were being frisked, they put their guns near our ear and said, "Do you know what we get if we shoot you? Two weeks paid vacation." Black Flag's "Revenge" came into my head at that moment: "It's not my imagination, I got a gun on my back." I had never felt so powerless and humiliated.

We played a handful of gigs here and there, and as luck would have it, when I couldn't balance school with the band anymore, my friends went on to form No Offense and Tangwich without me. For folks not from that area, they were two bands that would go on to play for many years.

I didn't know it at the time, but I was developing a class consciousness—to be clear, a consciousness of my mother and family as working class. I felt like an observer watching the sacred lamb work six or seven days out of the week to keep us from homelessness and starvation. My mom spent seventeen years of her life making her boss rich. I was lucky enough to go to school to get an education. As an eighth grader, I came to understand that in this world it was very easy to be exploited, and it was a long history of exploitation.

Our history of enduring exploitation started with my grandfather, Fidel De La Torre, who was a bracero back in the 1960s. He traveled up and down California working the fields in various capacities. It was hard seasonal work, and he would come and go from Villa Guerrero, Jalisco, in Mexico and back. My grandfather didn't earn much as a bracero. He couldn't unionize and couldn't complain, or he would find himself with a revoked work permit. His hands were those of a guitarist and campesino—rough, weathered, and with the ability to bring joy though he was prone to violence against his own family.

When the bracero program ended, my mother, Ofelia, decided to follow in his footsteps—though he was not quite a role model—and find opportunity where workers were paid in dollars. She had had a premonition in a dream in which she found herself walking from Tijuana to Los Angeles and later recalled it was actually San Ysidro. My mother convinced herself that she was going to go to the United States for a year and make enough money to study in Guadalajara and become a nurse. The idea was to get an education and escape poverty. She came to the United States as an undocumented immigrant in the early 1970s and ended up in El Monte with its decaying suburban home exterior, which seemed like a haven at the time.

Not long thereafter, she met my father, who didn't stick around long enough to meet me. My sister came afterward, and her father didn't stay very long either. As the years passed, my mother's dream of becoming a nurse slowly disappeared. Instead, she became a hard worker with dreams and aspirations for her children. My mom worked at Modan Sportswear as a seamstress for as long as I could remember. She chose that factory because the other major sewing factory, Sirena, had work for only nine months out of the year at the time. The factory was first located on Durfee Avenue and then off Chico Street in South El Monte.

On the weekends and some weeknights, my mother took us to the factory. We'd wake up early in the morning. She'd buy my sister, Mayra, and me each a doughnut and a glass of milk for breakfast. The stacks of fabric on the side of the giant factory were where we made our little beds and tried to sleep as the roar of the machines and radio KLOVE blasted through the sound system. We entertained ourselves by pushing each other around on wooden carts, making doll clothing, and waiting around endlessly until my mother was finished. At the end of the day and on our way back to our roach-infested apartment my mom would tell us, "*Mi' jo, mi' ja*, don't ever work with your hands. Finish your education and don't end up breaking your back like I do for a living." I remember hearing her say this as I looked at a Band-Aid on her index finger covering a puncture from a needle made by the machine.

My mother's boss came in one day snapping his fingers at my mother, and he said he needed the work to be completed faster. My mom looked around the floor as he asked her, "Why aren't you responding to me?" She turned to him and said, "I'm looking for the dog you're snapping your fingers to. I'm not a dog. Don't snap your fingers at me." Rebellious at heart, she knew how to keep her dignity even when circumstances were stacked against her. She had given years of her loyalty to the company and knew every machine backward and forward. Her boss stormed off and slammed the door to his office.

At home we had always taken for granted that my mother was undocumented. She had been deported in 1975, and we had a detailed plan laid out in case it happened again. My sister and I would go live with my aunt Fidencia should that day come. This was a constant fear in my life. This fear would be exacerbated during the Pete Wilson era of the early 1990s, as the Republican governor's Proposition 187 reminded us that we did not belong in California. Sixty percent of registered voters agreed. My sister and I were citizens, but that hardly seemed to matter at the time.

I was watching two parallel realities play out. On the one hand, you had those terrible commercials of immigrants jumping over fences and allegedly destroying the great state of California. On the other hand was my mother's daily toil in the sewing factory. It was the first time I felt like I wasn't an American. I remember I couldn't stand for the flag salute after Proposition 187 was passed. My math teacher asked me why, and I simply told her, "We're not wanted here. Why would I pledge allegiance to a country that doesn't want me here?" She shook her head and said, "Well, you have to stand anyway." I disagreed, and for the rest of the year, a Jehovah's Witness kid and I sat it out in shared protest every morning.

Thanks to a handful of teachers who believed in me and the Harvey Mudd College Upward Bound program, I made it to college. When I got the thick package from the University of California, Berkeley, I told my mom as soon as she got home, and her response was a tired, "That's nice, *mi' jo*. The rice should be done in a little while." She had no clue what that meant.

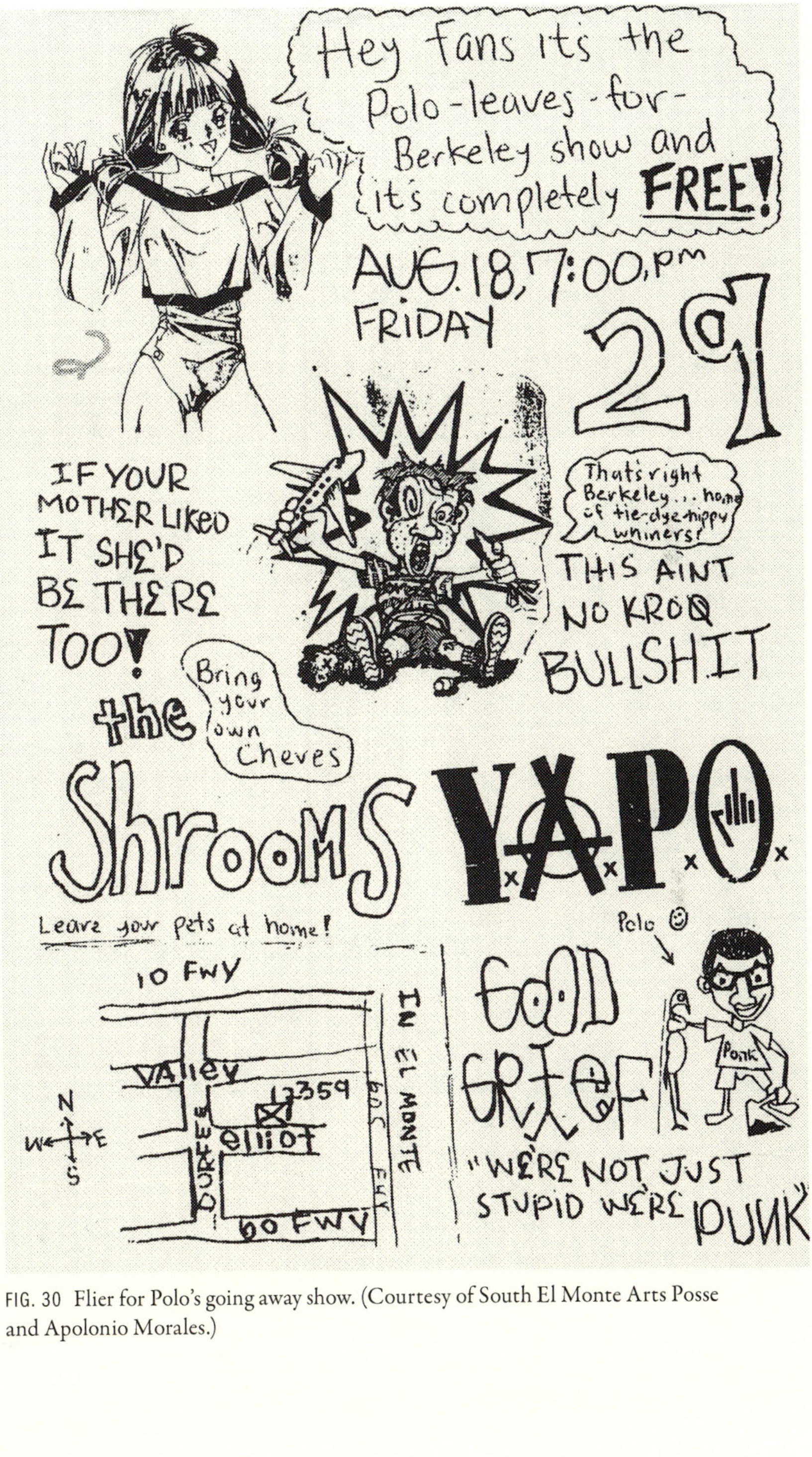

FIG. 30 Flier for Polo's going away show. (Courtesy of South El Monte Arts Posse and Apolonio Morales.)

As graduation drew near, I convinced my mom to let me have a gig at our place for a big send-off with all of my friends. We shared an empty lot with two other families down on Elliott Avenue, and that was the perfect place to have a hundred people come out to a free show. We made fliers and passed them around in different cities and record stores. Before I knew it, there were hundreds of people to see No Offense, the Shrooms, and a couple of other bands I can't even remember. As the gig went into the night, the cops came, a helicopter shone its light on us, and all hell broke loose. Fortunately, there was no violence at this gig, and folks went home with a lasting memory of some guy named Polo going off to college.

A year into college, I got a call from my sister, who told me that Mom had had a stroke. At forty-two, all of the hard work and stress had finally caught up to her. I went to Oakland and got on the Greyhound midnight express. I finally made it to Los Angeles County–University of Southern California Medical Center, where my mom was still waiting in the emergency room for a bed upstairs. I walked up to her and saw her broken for the first time in my life. Half paralyzed, she looked at me, and we both started to cry. I sat next to her and told her it was going to get better and that I was going to quit school and take care of her. She was barely able to speak, but she told me: "*Mi' jo*, you're crazy. You're going back to college to take the opportunity I never had." Those words stuck in my head, and all of a sudden I remembered the Proposition 187 commercials and the anti-immigrant hatred that consumed every level of society and decided that something needed to change. I took my mother's advice and finished school.

After college, I taught for a few years and eventually landed a job as a labor organizer. This is where I learned that workers had power and where I saw immigrants fighting back for basic rights and a decent wage. I went off to do community organizing, and over the years I have managed to take the issue of immigration reform head on.

Over the course of many years, my mother became a citizen. Though her health problems persist, she overcame her paralysis and began living a normal life again. Yet the situation for immigrants remains pretty much the same. I think about all the things that brought me where I am today and how my mother's immigrant experience and punk played a big part in that. My outlook, perception, and skepticism have sharpened over the years. Still, I've convinced myself that we can unite, organize, and fight. I realize now that it takes courage to change our society, and now and again the Subhumans still echo in my mind:

> A world of strength and clarity, the alternative reality,
> But creating a new lifestyle could never come to much.
> Everyone had the ideas but no one had the guts.[3]

With its impact on and longevity in El Monte, punk continues to be a source for creativity and is deeply rooted in the immigrant experience of youth seeking an alternative to a very dismal reality. I learned a lot through my mother's sacrifices. This was my experience, yet it is echoed in the generation that followed. The music and the scene were neither here nor there. It was distinct and unique. Punk was a style of music that some of us embraced and began to create on our own in our frustration and anger. It was a chance to make something out of nothing and break every stereotype in the process, despite all the things that were going against us. That same rebellious spirit still lives within me and finds peace of mind in challenging the status quo. Even as uncertain as the future may be, it keeps me hopeful and inspired.

Notes

1 Bad Religion, "Against the Grain." *Against the Grain*, Hollywood, CA: Epitaph Records, 1990.

2 Crass, "Banned from the Roxy." *The Feeding of the 5000*, London: Crass Records, 1979.

3 Subhumans, "Worlds Apart." *Worlds Apart*, Melksham, UK: Bluurg, 1985.

25

A Gay Bar, Some *Familia*, and Latina Butch-Femme

Rounding Out the Eastside Circle at El Monte's Sugar Shack

STACY I. MACÍAS

What if El Monte served as a central geographic node in the reimagining of lesbian and gay social history in the last quarter of the twentieth century? Whose stories would we privilege if El Monte was positioned as a relevant point of departure for exploring gay and lesbian bar cultures? How much would this working-class, suburban city with its majority Latina/o/x population—situated in the eastern part of Los Angeles (LA) County and east of the Latino urban juggernaut that is East LA—matter to a consideration of gay and lesbian modes of social existence? For Sandee Estrada and other self-identified gay Latinas hailing from local environs, the Sugar Shack in El Monte was the last stop for the last call in a Sunday night ritual of bar hopping and community building.[1] Sandee, a self-identified gay Chicana from Hacienda Heights, nostalgically recalls what she and her *comadres* named the Eastside Circle: a ring-shaped route of travel along the Latina lesbian bar corridor starting from home off the 605 Freeway and heading to the furthest east spot (Redz, in Boyle Heights), then moving east and north to the Plush Pony in El Sereno, and finally making a path homeward to the Shack in El Monte (and on occasion Infinities in South El Monte), before calling it a night.[2] The Eastside Circle not only constitutes a significant local Latina lesbian orbit of the 1990s for the likes of Sandee, but it also represents an understudied, disregarded, and peripheralized history of communities of lesbian, gay, bisexual, transgender, and queer (LGBTQ) working-class people of color whose queer—or outsider—status place them in search of affinities beyond the glitter and flash of "Gay L.A."[3]

Existing on the literal and metaphorical outskirts from what Audre Lorde calls the "mythical norm,"[4] subterranean social sites and cultural outlets like the Sugar Shack emerge in the conditions created by differences in geography, race/ethnicity, sexuality, class, and gender. Historically, LGBTQ communities form such publics and stage such practices not only as a result of sexual non-normativity, but also in response to class, race, and gender disenfranchisement and commonly through the active construction of place. "The Gay Bar" as the premier locale that metonymically functions to hail what Jose Muñoz calls "queer worldmaking" is ground zero for processes of identity affirmation, chosen family making, queer pleasure taking, and "minoritarian belonging."[5] In the sphere of gay bar life, amid the rhythms from a jukebox, the drink specials of the house, and the din of local denizens exists the sometimes glorious, sometimes fractious, but always singular story of the place itself. This is the story of such a place, El Monte's Sugar Shack, in homage to what Debi Tinker, a South El Monte native and regular at the Shack described as "one of those great lil' dive bars that was rich in character and rich with characters."[6]

The Shack before the Sugar: Historically Reimagining 4101 North Arden Drive

While Rosalinda "Rose" Rivas opened the Sugar Shack under this beloved moniker in 1987, the small shack-like space at 4101 North Arden Drive in El Monte has a longer history that, according to city records, dates back to the mid-twentieth century.[7] In September 1957, city documents indicate that the first official owner, Chas A. Bersani, submitted an application for a certificate of occupancy at 4103 North Arden Drive[8] and proceeded to name it the House of Heartburn. The stated business purpose was a "café," presumably a place where food and nonalcoholic drinks would be sold. It is plausible to discern, however, that a place called House of Heartburn in El Monte in the late 1950s was less like a restaurant and more akin to a bar providing cooling beverages as a balm to those whose hearts had been broken or set ablaze by romantic love. In the period 1960–1963, 4101 North Arden Drive underwent approximately four changes in ownership, in turn becoming Utters Café, Rugie Café, and

TJ Sugler before being named the Whistle Stop by November 1963.[9] Charles E. and Norma Price were then the owners of record, and they indicated for the first time that the purpose of the business was "a *beer tavern* and café."[10]

As other chapters in this volume attest, El Monte was often narrowly invoked to symbolize the vestiges of a raucous, unlawful, and degenerate white past. This narrative in part also paved the way for the city's auspicious status as a hip destination for LA County's youth of color and liberal white populations, who unabashedly wanted to enjoy the popular music of the time. The Sugar Shack also provided a haven for African American women who were often rejected and mistreated in LA gay and lesbian bars like the Canyon Club, as Faderman and Timmons describe in their interviews of African American lesbians.[11] It is also important to note that the authors' reference to the Sugar Shack does not include its attendant city. Therefore, another bar named the Sugar Shack likely existed in another timeframe elsewhere in LA County. This might explain the unaligned history between Faderman and Timmon's mention of the Sugar Shack in the 1950s and the fact that the Sugar Shack in El Monte did not acquire its name until the late 1980s. Alternatively, this might also raise productive questions about the relationship among individual storytelling, community memory, and the historical record.

While we can surmise that the Prices might have chosen the apropos name Whistle Stop due to the fact that 4101 North Arden Drive is situated just south of a railroad track and on the corner of Railroad Drive, it might also be valuable to reimagine fictive pasts in which places sharing the moniker Whistle Stop or Sugar Shack come into being across time, space, and form through affective modes of queer belonging and felt knowledges that exceed simple rationales.

The Whistle Stop kept its name despite at least six changes in ownership from late 1963 through 1978. Not until July 14, 1978, when Edgar E. Ufers and Howard L. Booth petitioned to take over the ownership did the place become renamed "Eddie's," an establishment for the "sale of beer and food."[12] Unlike the Whistle Stop before it, Eddie's experienced just two changes in ownership before Bert Rivas (sister to Rose Rivas, the owner of record) and her wife, Olivia, began managing the space and laid claim to the contemporaneously renowned name of Sugar Shack. Beginning with its tenure as Eddie's, 4101 North Arden Drive publicly earned its reputation as a gay and lesbian bar attracting working-class communities of color to sip cheap beer, play pool, sing to the jukebox, and greet habitués with hugs and kisses.

From Eddie's to the Shack: Forming Old School and New School *Familias*

In the late 1970s, Shelley Ponce recalls ending up at Sugar Shack (then called Eddie's), a little corner bar in El Monte without any signage and a back entrance into what resembled a garage with a busted pool table, L-shape bar, and homey feel. Shelley, a straight-identified Latina who grew up in East LA and attended Garfield High School, was deep into the disco music scene, citing black musicians like the queer icon Sylvester and the classically trained Jesse Green as among her favorites.[13] When I asked specifically how she ended up at the Shack (as she and other patrons affectionately referred to it), especially because she was accustomed to larger gay club venues like Ginos or Circus in Hollywood, she said she was not sure. Like Sandee, Shelley remembers touring the gay Latina bar circuit of greater East LA, where the Plush Pony became the first local lesbian bar that she made her way into on account of her now compadre and then coworker at Zody's (a Southern California-based discount retail chain). Neither Shelley nor her companion identified then or now as gay, but they had both heard about a friendly gay watering hole near a railroad that shook from its core like the train was cutting directly through it. For Shelley, her foray into gay public space was instigated by several factors, including her love of disco music and dancing, her interest in fashion and clothing design, and the fact that her younger sisters would come out as lesbian and bisexual, respectively. Fresh out of high school, Shelley was the first sibling to venture into the nightlife scene of the late 1970s, and although she was not yet twenty-one, she charmed her way into bars like the Shack that were seemingly more lenient about screening for drinking age and requiring legal identification than they are now. Eventually, the Shack caught the attention of her youngest sister, whom Shelley described as "butch," and in due course Shelley was followed by her sisters into the scene.[14] Shelley's experiences at the Shack mirror those of the other patrons, who cobbled together a sense of *familia* in the tiny dive bar whose presence was larger than its physical stature.

Like Shelley, Sandee Estrada, Rose Peinado, and Debi Tinker relay memories of the Shack through a shared frame of family networks—both biological and built. These familial bonds were staged through a Latina/o kinship system informed by Chicano cultural values and expressed through Chicana/o cultural vernacular. For example, Sandee recounted that most people were welcomed with the warmth reserved elsewhere for family members, while Debi recalled being greeted with the Mexican endearment *mi' ja*. Despite social identity differences, bar patrons conveyed a deep appreciation for a space that felt familiar, unpretentious, and intimate and that stood apart from other gay bars of the region. In fact, the Shack catalyzed several of these women into forming lifelong connections beyond the space of the bar. The friendly, familial environment that they all praised could be attributed to the partnered couple Bert and Olivia, who managed the bar and maintained the tightknit-community feel that it had had when it was Eddie's. With its coming of age in the late 1970s as the only openly gay bar in El Monte, the institution transmitted an anthropomorphic sensibility. Most of the women I interviewed repeatedly and fondly invoked the trope of family to emphasize the bar's role not only as a structure and place that held meaning, but also as a family member able to hold you up compassionately to withstand the vicissitudes of lesbian and gay existence and to sober you up with old school *borracho* (music to sing to while drunk) melodies belted out of the jukebox. For LGBTQ communities, formulating *familias* from scratch, as the Xicana lesbian author Cherríe Moraga proclaims, is a vital part of community survival and self-care, especially in a dominant culture that deems queer of color sexualities as aberrant formations or outright betrayals.[15]

While making *familia* from scratch was a commonplace practice among the bar patrons, there is a persistent role that biological family relations play in queer of color public space making. Unlike white populations, in which sexuality and narratives of coming out are often cordoned off and imagined apart from biological family relations, the Shack's LGBTQ community members incorporated queer and straight family members into their social and cultural practices. Scholars who theorize queer kinship structures shed light on these conventions, which also upend traditional conceptualizations of working-class people of color as more likely to subscribe to homo- and trans-phobic attitudes than their white counterparts.[16] For Shelley and her two younger gay sisters, the Shack was a special place to hang out with family and friends alike. Some of Sandee's most endearing memories of the Shack are of the special occasions that brought out her family members—including her mother, a straight, beguiling high femme who attracted the ardor of regulars. Sandee (who met her wife, Rose, through her own older gay sister) told how she and Rose held an impromptu postwedding rehearsal dinner get-together at the Shack. Realizing the night was still young after the formal rehearsal dinner concluded at Salvatore's in Montebello, Sandee phoned the bar to ask if they could put the beer on ice and keep the doors open. The owners gladly obliged, and soon almost the entire wedding guest list was partying the night away, dancing to Kirk Franklin's New Age gospel tunes—which lent a church-like atmosphere to the infectious jubilation.

Rose and Debi also linked biological family members to their significant memories of the Shack. Rose's elder gay sister, Nena, a person with a developmental disability, was a dear friend of the owners. They would look after Nena and alert Rose if Nena ever found herself in a quandary. Rose reported that Nena was so fond of the bar and its owners that she said her dying wish would be to have her ashes scattered all over the El Monte bars, including the Shack. Debi also had a family connection to the Shack: At one point, her aunt worked behind the bar, pouring beer into red plastic cups and opening tabs for locals. And with Dee Dee, Debi's gay sister who was separated by just ten months and who passed away a few years ago, Debi shared an affinity for the Shack and the family connections that the space fostered.

Knowing the owners by name and being a regular certainly affected whether and how one could integrate oneself into the family-like atmosphere at the Shack. Bert and Olivia were flexible and shrewd owners equally attuned to the desires of their patrons and the imperatives of their business venture. For Shack regulars, Sundays were leisure days of post-softball mingling and beer imbibing, whether to lament the game played hard but lost at Sunny Slope Park in nearby Monterey Park or to watch a Sunday football game live on the television set unloaded from a regular's truck. Rounding out the Eastside Circle at the Shack was a weekend ritual that involved catching up with friends, collecting quarters for the jukebox, or simply spending time at what another interviewee, Marty Castillo, called the "lesbian 'Cheers.'"[17] For its regulars, it was a treasured spot where calling ahead to ask the owners to stock the fridge, stay open after hours, or host a potluck was like calling on a *tia* or homegirl to lend a hand. This model of social exchange among given and made *familias* was also deeply entrenched in the signs and sounds of Chicana lesbian aesthetics and cultural practices, which were primary and explicit forms of self- and community expression.[18]

The Couplet That Endures: Latina Butch-Femme Culture at the Shack

In his essay chronicling 1990s queer of color life in LA's working-class bars and barrios, Joel Barraquiel Tan paints a picture of his initial foray into the Sugar Shack: "The first time someone called me a Homothug, I took it as an insult. Turned out I was being hit on. It was summer 1994, during Oldies Tuesday and dollar beer at the Sugar Shack in El Monte, a tiny bar that attracted aging Chicana lesbians, older *vatas* that looked and acted like men with their heavily made-up *hainas* in tow. The Shack was old school, nothing but '50s Elvis records with a smattering of Bloodstone, Smokey Robinson, Shirelles, and other golden-oldie selections in the jukebox."[19] Like Barraquiel Tan's vivid impressions, Shack regulars stressed the presence of both Chicana butch and butch-femme cultural signs. For masculine-presenting lesbian women, the gangsta or cholo style of cotton tanks, dark denim jeans, and crisp white athletic shoes predominated. When femme women showed up to the Shack either as part of the requisite butch-femme duo or decoupled with a crew of their own, they were described as garnering attention for their fragrant allure and eye-catching outfits. These quintessential Chicana/o aesthetics, paired with the "old school" Chicano sounds streaming from the jukebox, marked the Shack as an expressly Latina/o racialized, suburban, working-class dive bar dealing in the currency of butch-femme.

Unmistakable in its class appeal, the Shack was an explicitly Mexican American, nonwhite bar that mainly served the east of East LA gay and lesbian set whose members faithfully practiced a degree of butch-femme. Scholars who study lesbian publics and gay women's bar culture reveal the significance of social practices like butch-femme that are channeled into embodied, erotic, and quotidian forms. In her monograph about the centrality of butch-femme culture in gay and lesbian bars through the 1970s, Marie Cartier notes: "In women of color communities, butch-femme has been, and is still, often the way gay women's/lesbian sexuality has been enacted. It was when women of color left their communities and dated outside, in white communities . . . that butch-femme was shameful role-playing."[20] Thus, during the late 1970s and through the 1980s, when Eddie's and the Shack were drawing a decidedly butch-femme Chicana/o clientele, mainstream and lesbian feminists were advocating that women abide by gender-neutral codes of behavior and aesthetics. The belief held by these mostly white and middle-class women was that butch-femme reproduced the oppressive heterosexual dynamics between men and women, with butches assuming the patriarchal gender position of men and rendering femmes inferior—a sentiment echoed in the passage above from Barraquiel Tan. However, using a heterosexual normative framework through which to interpret lesbian of color culture is deeply flawed. Lesbian cultural practices like butch-femme often emerge in resistance to dominant norms, norms that are not always accessible to nonheterosexual women of color to inhabit or embody by virtue of their racialized gender identity and lesbian sexuality. Furthermore, as Madeline Davis and Elizabeth Kennedy submit in their now canonical ethnographic study of lesbians in mid-twentieth century Buffalo, New York, butch-femme is an everyday strategy of survival that working-class and women of color lesbians specifically rely on to resist their violent encounters with a homophobic, racist, and classist society.[21]

If, as Cartier asserts, gay women's bars in the period 1940–1975 "served as cultural community centers or institutional foundations for gay women and were organized primarily by butch-femme individuals," then what do we make of butch-femme bars and their owners after 1975, the period during which butch-femme fell out of favor?[22] Sometime in the early 1990s, the Latina butch-femme owners, Bert and Olivia, became the beloved married couple behind the bar. I spoke to Greg Rivera, a straight Latino and the owner of Pinky's, a custom autobody and paint shop that currently sits in the space behind the now-closed Sugar Shack. Greg recalled an earlier time when he hung out at the business behind the Shack that his friend Ronnie then owned and when Greg worked elsewhere as a chauffeur. He was scheduled to pick up customers for a special occasion and was surprised when one of the owners of the Shack, a butch woman dressed in a sharp black tuxedo, approached the limousine door. She had ordered the car service on her wedding day, and Greg proceeded to pick up her fiancée, "the feminine owner dressed in a long, creamy white gown," and ferry them to a Long Beach location for their ceremony and celebration.[23]

It was clear that Greg, an El Monte local, was familiar with the lexicon of butch-femme as well as with the Shack regulars, who welcomed him inside the bar to grab a soda or who brought him hot dogs and nachos, the few items sold when the bar's kitchen was working.

According to Greg and the various butch-femme couples with whom I spoke, Olivia and Bert seemed to bestow on their patrons—most of whom were working-class Chicana/Latina gays—a sense of validation, pride, and visibility. Representative of both the community it served and El Monte business owners of a different ilk, Bert and Olivia's butch-femme coupling was a testament to the venerable and vulnerable racialized sexual politics that Chicanas/Latinas possessed. Chicana/Latina lesbians are already always socially marked because of their deviant sexuality, racialized gender, and working-class status. Due to this nexus of nonnormative differences, Chicana/Latina lesbians especially abide by the codes of butch-femme culture, in which the affective flair and expressive beauty of butch-femme becomes a way to assert agency over their sexual and gender identities and creatively mold their culture.[24] Cartier's larger argument, in which she reveals how butch-femme culture holds power on a par with a sacred experience of religion, is a much better (albeit unorthodox) framework with which to apprehend the reliance on butch-femme dynamics among gay Chicana/Latinas at the Shack. Like Davis and Kennedy before her, Cartier depathologizes butch-femme public performances in the space of the gay bar. Cartier may critically err by generalizing that as of the 1990s, butch-femme was "no longer the primary organizing principle for gay women," which is also her rationale for concluding her book's research on gay women's bars with that decade.[25] Contrary to this statement stand the spaces that lesbian of color communities created and sustained throughout the 1990s and well into the 2000s. Latina butch-femme pairings like Bert and Olivia and the Shack's regulars epitomize a devotion to butch-femme that cannot be mislaid temporally or written off as misogynist, backward, or derivative. In essence, Latina butch-femme adherence demonstrates that working-class, gay women or lesbians of color organize their social and erotic lives in this system daily and devoutly rather than as a fad or phase.

Last Call: The Politics of Disappeared Lesbian and Gay Bar Histories

On April 4, 1992, a fire broke out at the Sugar Shack. The source of the fire was undetermined, according to the City of El Monte Fire Department report.[26] This report, along with a recommendation for repairs to return the bar to operating code, an estimated cost of repair worksheet (the total cost was $500), and a follow-up report on repairs, constitutes the majority of available, material, and historical public information on the Sugar Shack; the remainder comes from individual recollections. Without the city's public records, the Sugar Shack and a few other selected manifestations of 4101 North Arden Drive might well have existed only in the hearts and minds of its devoted patrons, some of whom have now passed away or lost the prized ability to remember with ease. Such is the story of places like the Sugar Shack, which tug at our collective consciousness and urge us to write, record, save, and legitimize the value of non-hegemonic queer sites of social history.

The memories, *familias*, and cultural practices forged through times spent at the Shack remain bittersweet reminders of a less complicated time for queer community members of the San Gabriel Valley who made the rounds and connected in the flesh. Exhausted after nearly twenty years of keeping the Shack afloat, Bert and Olivia sold the bar and its contents in 2006. Debi and Sandee still mourn the beloved gay bar, noting that few public places remain in which people can maintain community and check in on each other outside of Facebook, which effectively has replaced the gay bar as a hub of social interaction.

The original Eastside Circle (consisting of Redz, the Plush Pony, the Sugar Shack, and sometimes Infinities in South El Monte) represents the circumference of gay bar life in the 1980s—2010s for many LGBTQ Latina/os of Greater East LA and the San Gabriel Valley. For other people, lesser known spots like the Island in Highland Park, Amber Light in San Gabriel, Industry Bar in Hacienda Heights, and the Tender Trap in South El Monte widen the circle of queer Latina/o cultural and social history, and thus extend the dimensions of the Eastside Circle, too. Beyond the frame of the fantastical (like the bar fire) or the fateful (like its closure), the history of the Sugar Shack rests most affectionately and securely not in mere recovery but in reimagining the genealogy of places off the main gay map. Such places might be suppressed in historical memory, but they continue to exist at least ephemerally in the personal and collective archives of resistant communities everywhere. The story of the Sugar Shack brings into sharp relief the fact that Latina/o cultural and social history archives are living, and they have to be fully explored and honored in all their mundane details and unique grandeur.

Notes

I thank and honor the women I met while researching the Sugar Shack, including Deb Andrade, Marty Castillo, Sandee Estrada, Rose Peinado, Shelley Ponce, Debi Tinker, and Nancy Vasquez. Without hesitation, each of them made time in their busy lives to talk or meet with me so that I could help bring this story to life. I especially acknowledge Shelley Ponce, the first respondent who quickly and graciously connected me to every other narrator; Debi Tinker, who organized a group of Shack regulars to gather with me over dinner; and Sandee Estrada, who shared the name of the circuitous gay women's bar route for East LA and San Gabriel Valley inhabitants, the Eastside Circle.

1 I use the term "gay" to describe the bar and its attendees' sexuality because it is the primary term of reference that they use. I also use "lesbian" and "queer" to refer more broadly to the sexual cultures of working-class women of color bar spaces that I contend in this chapter frame the history of the Sugar Shack and the beginning of a lesbian, gay, bisexual, transgender, and queer (LGBTQ) history of El Monte.

2 Sandee Estrada, interview by author, August 23, 2018.

3 See Lillian Faderman and Stuart Timmons, *Gay L.A.: A History of Sexual Outlaws, Power Politics, and Lipstick Lesbians* (New York: Basic Books, 2006).

4 Audre Lorde, *Sister Outsider: Essays and Speeches* (Berkeley, CA: Crossing Press, 2007), 116.

5 José Esteban Muñoz, *Disidentifications: Queers of Color and the Performance of Politics* (Minneapolis: University of Minnesota Press, 1999).

6 Debi Tinker, text message to author, August 23, 2018.

7 The El Monte City Clerk's Office provided archival records that are regularly made accessible via public requests. I especially acknowledge Jonathan Hawes, El Monte's city clerk, for his diligent and timely efforts to respond to my requests.

8 This address appears in the earliest application for a certificate of occupancy. However, it appears that by 1962, 4103 had become an obsolete address and been absorbed by 4101 North Arden Drive, perhaps due to a street excavation project completed by the owners in 1958. As of December 2017, Google Maps reverts to 4101 for an address search for 4103.

9 I use the word "approximately" because some of the handwriting on the applications for a certificate of occupancy and the certificates that I perused was difficult to decipher, given the age of the documents and the method of record keeping.

10 Application for Certificate of Occupancy, 4101 North Arden Drive, November 13, 1963, submitted by Charles E. and Norma Price, El Monte City Clerk's Office (emphasis added).

11 Faderman and Timmons, *Gay L.A.*, 102.

12 Application for Certificate of Occupancy, 4101 North Arden Drive.

13 Shelley Ponce, discussion with the author, August 7, 2018.

14 Shelley Ponce, text exchange with the author, July 30, 2018.

15 Cherríe Moraga, *Heroes and Saints & Other Plays* (Albuquerque, NM: West End Press, 1994), 35.

16 See, for example, Marlon M. Bailey, *Butch Queens up in Pumps: Gender, Performance, and Ballroom Culture in Detroit* (Ann Arbor: University of Michigan Press, 2013); Gayatri Gopinath, *Impossible Desires: Queer Diasporas and South Asian Public Cultures* (Durham, NC: Duke University Press, 2005); Richard T. Rodríguez, *Next of Kin: The Family in Chicano/a Cultural Politics* (Durham, NC: Duke University Press, 2009).

17 This is a reference to the popular NBC sitcom *Cheers*, which featured the trials and tribulations of a set of regulars who gathered daily at the eponymously named bar in Boston. The sitcom aired in the period 1982–1993.

18 For an extended analysis of the meaning of kin in queer Latina/o communities with a focus on gay Latino formations, see Richard Rodríguez's groundbreaking *Next of Kin*.

19 Joel Barraquiel Tan, "Homothugdragsterism" in *Total Chaos: The Art and Aesthetics of Hip-Hop*, ed. Jeff Chang (New York: BasicCivitas, 2006), 211.

20 Marie Cartier, *Baby, You Are My Religion: Women, Gay Bars, and Theology before Stonewall*. (Durham, UK: Acumen, 2013), 14–15.

21 Madeline Davis and Elizabeth Kennedy, *Boots of Leather, Slippers of Gold: The History of a Lesbian Community* (New York: Routledge, 1991).

22 Cartier, *Baby, You're My Religion*, 3.

23 Greg Rivera, discussion with author, July 31, 2018.

24 See Stacy I. Macías, "Latina and Chicana Butch/Femme in Literature and Culture," In *Oxford Research Encyclopedia of Literature* (Oxford University Press, 2015).

25 Cartier, *Baby, You're My Religion*, 218.

26 City of El Monte Fire Department, Fire Report to Building Department, April 16, 1992.

26

All the Zumba Ladies

Reclaiming Bodies and Space through Serious Booty Shaking

CARRIBEAN FRAGOZA

If a summer drought were to defrost an undiscovered chunk of ice buried deep in the San Gabriel Mountains and reveal a stunned Spanish explorer, à la the movie *Encino Man*, and if he were to stumble down past Arcadia and Temple City into El Monte and peer into one of many Zumba studios, drawn by its hypnotic rhythms and neon-colored facade, his wildest colonial fantasy would have come true: he would have finally reached the mythical island of California, ruled by Amazon warrior women. Inside the studio he would see a small clan of women, shaking and shimmying, kicking and punching, hooting and howling in a sweaty trance-like state to blasting, high bass music. This ritual dance must be in preparation for war. Their leader, Queen Calafia, must surely be near, probably getting her nails done up the street at the Valley Mall.[1]

Throughout the city, neon-colored flags drape over windows and flutter out on sidewalks like bastions of a newly declared nation: Zumba. And like other nations, Zumba demands sovereignty and claims territory. Over the past several years, its territory has notably expanded into small storefronts all over Greater Los Angeles. In El Monte, it has claimed many units that had either remained unoccupied for years or had gone through a series of flimsy, short-lived businesses. Zumba has also carved out niches for itself in community centers, churches, parks, and pretty much any public or semipublic space.

Zumba is a worldwide brand-name fitness trend that consists of Latin-inspired music and exercise choreography. Founded in Miami in 2002 by Alberto "Beto" Perez, Zumba is easily identifiable by its line of brightly colored exercise apparel that includes clothing, shoes, sweatbands, and other accessories and its videos. The music and moves are drawn from *cumbia*, salsa, merengue, bachata, and reggaeton and are fused with more typical cardiovascular exercise programs such as aerobics.

While most know Zumba as a wildly popular international fitness trend, poor and working-class women in El Monte have hybridized Zumba, evolving it from exercise to performance and then a way of life. Women who practice Zumba develop and embody a kind of barrio feminist aesthetic that helps them reclaim their bodies and public space.

Zumba's popularity among girls and señoras of all ages is exciting and intriguing for a number of reasons. First, an unprecedented number of ladies have become regular exercisers and committed booty shakers. Second, the Zumba aesthetic fully embraces its place at the bottom of the fitness and fashion food chain. Part of its charm is its *paisa-* and *pocho-*ness that comfortably and inelegantly mashes together *banda*, hip hop, and reggaeton; wraps neon spandex over everything; and runs the whole hot mess through a copier to make copies of copies of copies of itself. Third, Zumba creates safe public spaces for women while allowing them to build real networks of support and friendship that extend beyond the studio.

Bodies Reclaiming Space

At a Zumba studio, one song never gets old:

> When I walk in the spot (yeah), this is what I see (ok).
> Everybody stops and they staring at me.
> I got passion in my pants and I ain't afraid to show it, show it, show it, show it.
> I'm sexy and I know it.[2]

Women of all ages, shapes, and sizes find their own sexiness in their bodies and then carry it right out of the studio and onto the street. In El Monte and South El Monte, Zumba studios can be found every couple of blocks along Garvey Avenue, one of the major commercial streets. For decades Garvey has been plagued by its two main sources of commerce, seedy car sales lots and prostitution, making this street a particularly unwalkable space for women. The misuse or lack of use of public space in working-class suburbs such as El Monte renders the space less hospitable and more oppressive for all bodies, but particularly female ones. Urban settings and vibrant public spaces in other communities are often more conducive to public female interaction. Women hanging out on corners to chat or shouting down the street is nothing to be surprised about.

However, the Zumba phenomenon, coupled with the aftermath of the 2008 economic recession, made it momentarily possible for women of El Monte to lease unused storefronts for studios and Zumba-inspired retail space. By pooling their resources and charging instructors and participants modest fees, leaseholders (mostly women) injected energy into the struggling local economy and rekindled sparks of life in El Monte's moribund commercial strip.

On Garvey Avenue, women become hyperaware of their bodies and how they are carried. In patriarchal communities such as El Monte, female bodies become publicly accessible as soon as they enter public view.[3] No matter how they are dressed or what they are doing, they are subject to public scrutiny, desire, and judgment. According to these patriarchal rules, a sensual or embodied body (that is, one that does not hide itself) announces itself as accessible, for pay or otherwise. In short, exhibiting any signs of embodied sensuality or sexuality puts the female body at risk of anything from insult to outright physical violence.

Zumba studios on Garvey Avenue and other main streets in El Monte provide rare places of safety for women. Once inside, a body can be whatever it pleases. This space is protected. Zumba ladies are quick to protect and defend themselves and each other loudly and aggressively. Oftentimes this sphere extends outside the door, encompassing even public sidewalks. Clusters of women stand outside, talking, laughing, cussing, confiding, eating, and sometimes dancing (and even smoking after Zumba—don't tell anyone). Zumba ladies claim the sidewalks they stand on. By extension, a true Zumba lady claims all ground she walks on, both in her home and on the street. It is her right to be where she is and who she is.

Standing outside the studio smoking cigarettes, they will not lower their eyes when someone passes by. They cast daring glares from behind burning cigarettes, glowing in clusters with each drag like a constellation of stars. Of course, if you are nice to them, they will invite you to Zumba class and sweetly advise you not to smoke.

The Zumba Aesthetic

Zumba is not the kind of place where people dress in slick gym wear that shows off chiseled bodies (or sometimes deliberately conceals the doughier ones). Shredded and rewoven T-shirts and neon spandex blend into a sort of *banda-cumbia Flashdance* on acid. Spandex and colors are good. Glitter is great. Full makeup is good, too, although not required. Some ladies practice in studded stretch jeans and tank tops.

Austere in my yoga-inspired exercise gear (black and gray), I wouldn't have imagined that lip gloss and cute socks could have any real physiological impact on a workout. But as it turns out, it does. When I see the determination in the dozens of lovely blue-shadowed eyes shimmering like their owners' sequined tank tops and sweat dribbling down faces like strings of gems, I know that these ladies are the real thing. They are cutely clad warriors.

"Style is very important. Even though we don't judge each other, we care about how we look," says Daniel "Danny" Hernandez, a local Zumba instructor and El Monte native. He notes that his Zumba students become very invested in their workout gear, sometimes purchasing pricey Zumba brand clothes but most often personalizing their own to flaunt their style. "They wear it to work, they wear it to the store, they wear it to pick up their kids from school. They show it off," says Hernandez.[4]

A very well-manicured middle-aged woman, known simply as La BonBon, struts into the studio with a freshly altered T-shirt. Everyone immediately notices it, admiring the unique twist-tied pattern on the back. She promises to teach them how she did it. Zumba fashion and aesthetic, though strongly protected by the corporate brand, is also characterized by its DIY quality. To be specific, it is more of a DIT (do-it-together) approach because ladies like La BonBon help each other with their outfits and in the process build friendships. Style becomes part of the glue that binds these women into a subculture of their own.

We can think of Zumba attire as being part of an aesthetic tradition known as *rasquachismo*. In Tomás Ybarra-Frausto's 1989 essay "Rasquachismo: A Chicano Sensibility," a touchstone in Chicano arts discourse, *rasquachismo* is "a working class aesthetic based upon lived reality." He continues: "To be rasquache is to be unfettered and unrestrained, to favor the elaborate over the simple, the flamboyant over the severe. Bright colors are preferred to somber, high intensity to low, the shimmering and sparkling to the muted and subdued." He might well have been describing Zumba well before its invention. Most importantly, *rasquachismo* is an aesthetic with a particular attitude that is "rooted in resourcefulness and adaptability, yet mindful of stance and style."[5]

While stance and style are expressed in fashion, they may be more significantly expressed in the body. The ladies invert conventional tastes not only in style but also in body image as they become more comfortable and confident in their own bodies.

Reclaiming Female Bodies

By most standards, particularly patriarchal ones, working-class Latina mothers' performing sexuality can hardly be considered tasteful. Yet in El Monte, the performance of sexuality gives Zumba its special zest: "Ese cuerpecito, mami, que dios te dio / No es para que se lo coman los gusanos, es para que lo gozemos los humanos."[6] Nothing gets the ladies going like forceful *reggaeton* pelvic thrusts, sexy waist writhing, and vigorous shoulder shimmying. There is no time for self-consciousness about jiggling breasts or shaking asses. In all literalness, the objective is to use what you've got. Skinny ladies seem at a loss. If you have an ass, no matter what it looks like, please, please let it jiggle. Hard bodies are not expected or necessarily desired here.

In terms of ass shaking, feminist conversations about Nicki Minaj's *Anaconda* music video put into question its play on the public gaze and ownership of black women's sexual bodies. To a less obvious extent, Zumba puts brown bodies back into the ownership of brown women. But unlike Minaj's booty quiver, Zumba ceases to be a performance for and contestation of the public gaze, despite its taking place in a public space. The gaze takes place in the mirror, and it's personal. It's an observation of the personal physical body that belongs to oneself. And because at the heart of the whole thing there is joy, the gaze is also a celebration. Booty, thighs, arms, tummies of all shapes and sizes—you take joy in shaking whatever you've got.

This is not to be confused with vanity. Hernandez signals to a wall of mirrors at the front of the room. "It takes courage to stand in front of a mirror and watch yourself dance for an hour," he says.[7]

The performance also takes part in the collective gaze shared with the other ladies in class. In Veronica Marquez's Zumba classes up the street, dances can spin off into impromptu call-and-response choreographies or spontaneous dance battles. At peak moments, ladies allow themselves to get carried away in the pleasure of dance, often improvising their own moves while the others cheer them on. "The girls come to have fun. Also, they become very supportive of each other," says Marquez.[8]

In short, Zumba can be considered a barrio feminist practice because it helps build bonds among women who may not otherwise be able to establish friendships. "Many of these women are housewives and have kids. A lot of women are dedicated to just their families. But they come here and they can relate to each other. They become friends," says Hernandez.[9] Indeed, participants become more than classmates by carpooling their children to school or giving each other rides to doctor's appointments and grocery stores. Eventually they become weekend party pals, rolling in packs to baptisms and *quinceañera* parties. On Mondays, they come back to class jovially comparing *panzas* and *lonjas* through their zebra-print stretchies. After class, the women take a breath of fresh air, feeling good about their bodies that are glistening with sweat.

Zumba as a Nonpedagogical Tool

Frankly, Zumba doesn't do much to help women understand their bodies or how healthy weight loss works—but to be fair, not many trendy exercise programs do. Unlike the severity of training programs such as CrossFit, Zumba is clearly about having a good time. After all, the official Zumba motto is "Ditch the workout. Join the party." "An instructor is not a trainer. We are here to guide a class," states Hernandez. "The class is not the instructor. It belongs to the students."[10]

Over time, Hernandez has learned that the first and most important thing that Zumba participants can do to get fit is to let go of their fears and insecurities. "I just want you to enjoy yourself. The weight loss will follow," he tells them. According to him, "Most women in this community have never exercised before. They don't want to work out because it's so unfamiliar to them."[11]

One of these women was Judith Olalde, who had virtually no interest in Zumba or exercising when she attended her first class. To be more exact, she was tricked by her sister into coming. But after the first class, she was hooked.

She notes her own transformation over the last two years. When she started Zumba, she was an exhausted mother of three with no energy or interest in exercise. She had gained weight over the years and did little to take care of her appearance. She laughs, remembering her early Zumba outfits: oversized sweatpants over plastic body wraps. Now she is one of the Zumba class queen bees, sporting tights, spunky zebra-print tops and electric-color socks that match her headband and shoes.

What keeps Olalde coming to class five days a week is not its attention to proper form or the science of body sculpting. Like so many ladies, she's become devoted to the study of what happens when exercise becomes a pleasurable part of your daily life. They are students of what it feels like to be energized from head to toe by a song you really like. They learn that while they build bonds with other women, there is also something empowering about being committed to something that just makes you feel good.

Olalde's laughter during class is probably the only thing louder than the music or the fashion. If the defrosted Spanish explorer were to stick around the studio long enough, her jokes would make him blush. He would also see young mothers seeking brief respite from the never-ending demands of their kids and grandmothers who in middle age have rediscovered the pleasure of dancing to sweet *cumbias* they once danced to in their hometown as young women. He would see babies lulled to sleep by noise in their strollers and prepubescent girls learning to dance *bachata*. He would see that Olalde, La BonBon, and all the other Zumba ladies are not preparing themselves in the art of war but in the more rare and sophisticated art of joy.

Notes

A version of this chapter was previously published on KCET as "All the Zumba Ladies: Reclaiming Bodies and Space through Serious Booty-Shaking," September 9, 2014, https://www.kcet.org/history-society/all-the-zumba-ladies-reclaiming-bodies-and-space-through-serious-booty-shaking.

1 Garcia Rodríguez de Montalvo's novel *Las sergas de Esplandián* (The adventures of Esplandián), published in the early sixteenth century, introduced Queen Calafia to Spanish audiences, particularly would-be explorers.
2 LMFAO, "Sexy and I Know It," *Sorry for Party Rocking*, Santa Monica, CA: Interscope, 2011, CD.
3 Laura Mulvey introduced the concept of the "male gaze" in 1975 ("Visual Pleasure and Narrative Cinema," *Screen* 16, no. 3 [1975]), 6–18.
4 Daniel Hernandez, interview by author, August 12, 2014.
5 Tomás Ybarra-Frausto, "Rasquachismo: A Chicano Sensibility," in *Chicano Art: Resistance and Affirmation, 1965–1985*, ed. Richard Griswold del Castillo, Teresa McKenna, and Yvonne Yarbro-Bejarano (Los Angeles: Wight Art Gallery, University of California, Los Angeles, 1991): 155–162.
6 Los Hijos del Pueblo, "El Botecito," *El Botecito*, Mexico City: Musart, 2009, CD.
7 Hernandez, interview.
8 Veronica Marquez, interview by author, August 17, 2014.
9 Hernandez, interview.
10 Ibid.
11 Ibid.

Part V

Literary Cartographies

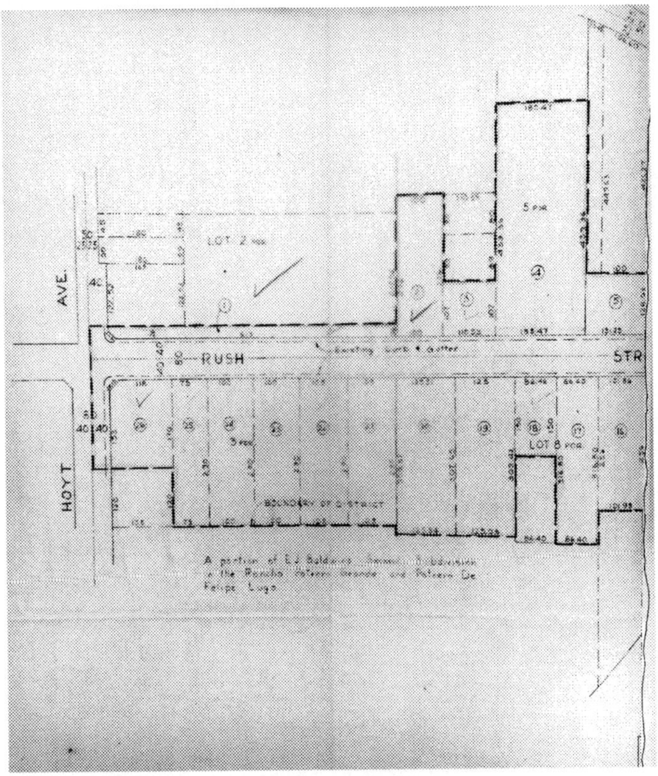

FIG. 31 Unsigned and undated blueprint for Rush Street. (Courtesy of South El Monte Arts Posse and South El Monte City.)

For a place that has done so little to support creative practices and so much to control narratives about itself, a surprising number of writers have emerged from El Monte and South El Monte. Perhaps that is at least in part because South El Monte and El Monte writers have insisted on telling stories that are as much about place as they are about personal experiences.

While there is currently no formal literary scene in El Monte or South El Monte, numerous notable authors have emerged from the area, and the imagination of each has been fed by Greater El Monte's historic, natural, and built landscape. Writers from Greater El Monte and surrounding areas show how literature and language are not very different from cartography. They are as much about marking and representing space as they are about storytelling. And like most cities, what are El Monte and South El Monte if not collections of stories? Collectively, stories give shape to intensely detailed maps and flesh out otherwise uncharted and unaccounted geographies.

The authors in this part of the book—Michael Jaime-Becerra, Alex Espinoza, Toni Margarita Plummer, Carribean Fragoza, and Salvador Plascencia—provide on-the-ground perspectives, illustrating the many ways in which the city and self merge, and private and public space overlap. In the process, they make Golfland Arcade, the railroad tracks, and ordinary streets like Rush, literary landmarks. Their writings guide us through personal landscapes, giving readers entry into El Monte and South El Monte's geography of densely layered family, community, and historical narratives. The essays in this section demarcate the contours of neighborhoods with memories, emotional markers, and passageways that are tied to a landscape of contradictory personalities—sometimes idyllic, sometimes cruel, yet all precious in their mundane detail.

27

1181 Durfee Avenue

1983 to 1986

MICHAEL JAIME-BECERRA

Between the fourth and sixth grades, you are seized by three deep and compulsive obsessions:

> Marvel comic books (all things Daredevil and X-Men and Spiderman).
> BMX bicycles (yours: a secondhand Mongoose, unwieldy and spray-painted black after you stripped the frame down to its bare chrome-moly tubing).
> And video games.

Your parents find all three activities doubtful. Comic books are allowed since they get you reading something else besides *MAD* magazine and therefore seem remotely educational. And when you're on your bicycle, you're out of the house, out of your parents' way, and doing something sort of athletic, even if the extent of this athletic activity is you and your friends racing up and down Parkway Avenue, seeing whose tires can leave the longest skid, and assembling ramps from plywood scraps. (One day, your friends will shove a few extra bricks under one of these ramps, raising it higher than they're willing to attempt, and you won't notice. Moments later you'll fly higher and farther than ever, sailing beautifully, historically, over lengths of sidewalk, and then you'll crash into the low brick wall dividing the Delgado and Murillo properties, knocking the wind out of your lungs and fracturing a rib that will bend forever outward.)

Your parents are most resistant to video games because they have no redemptive value. A waste of quarters. A waste of time. You are not allowed an Atari. No Intellivision or ColecoVision either. The closest thing you have is a nameless knockoff, presented one Christmas by your estranged grandfather. (His presence in your life is shadowy and distant; he does not know about video games being unwelcome.) This beige console lets you play three blocky, black-and-white variations of *Pong*. Since you already know the good stuff, it entertains you for less than an hour.

There are other arcades: Chuck E. Cheese on the north side of town; Showboat in Puente Hills; and somewhere off the 605 Freeway, Golf 'n' Stuff Fun Center, which you've never visited yet exists in your elementary-school imagination with a golden, mythological glow. And you have also played interesting, solitary video games in other places: *Track & Field* at the Santa Fe Farms liquor store; *Jungle Hunt* inside Crawford's Market; *Tempest*—a confusing waste of quarters—at the Food Barn on Ramona Boulevard. But it is the Golfland arcade that has collected your favorites all in one place:

Spy Hunter.
Star Wars.
Zaxxon.
Pole Position.
Gyruss.
Punch-Out!!

Golfland becomes the center of your universe. It is adjacent to the 60 Freeway's Peck Road off-ramp, so whenever you go anywhere with your parents, you're welcomed home by its four miniature golf courses with their bright green and yellow dragons, their expressions silly and slightly crazed.

At this point, you're too young to notice girls, though you already sense that unless you're on a date, or needing to entertain younger cousins, you won't ever really give a shit about mini golf. Instead you will commit the location of the video games inside the arcade to memory. Wall after wall of them, the space dimly lit by the flashing screens of the machines, the air somehow smoky in your recollection. To be at Golfland is to do something outside of your parents' approval. This is your first taste of rebellion. The thrill feels seedy and vaguely self-destructive, the nascent equivalent of being in a casino, a nudie bar, and a street fight all at once. Each week, you are drawn there with the sort of magnetic, gravitational pull experienced by wayward meteors and doomed astronauts returning to Earth.

On Friday evenings, usually after dinner, your father takes out his money clip and hands you your allowance. For helping with the lawn, dragging out the trash cans, and picking up the dogs' shit all week, you receive five dollars. He enjoys telling you not to spend it all in one place.

On Saturday mornings, your mother turns the bathroom into a hair salon, her clients a few holdovers from her former life as a beautician. The ladies arrive early and are there until the middle of the day, the house filling with the acrid smell of permanent-wave solution, the steady noise from the salon-style hair dryer that sits on the kitchen table and fits over their heads like a golden space helmet.

Your father works every weekend. (While he'll claim that Saturday money at time-and-a- half, double-time on Sundays, is too good to pass up, later on you'll have to understand that he simply preferred his life at the supermarket, a life where he was free to order everyone around as he pleased.) He leaves before dawn, and he doesn't return until your mother's ladies have gone.

This is why you're free to roam around on Saturday mornings. Golfland opens at ten, and if you're not out of the house by nine-thirty, you feel hopelessly behind schedule. You tell your mother that you'll be back, choosing a moment where she's too preoccupied with a curling iron or applying hair dye to ask where you're going. You retrieve your bicycle from the shed where the lawnmower is stored. You wind the length of duct-taped chain around the seat post and secure it with the fat Master lock. You leave through the side gate, stomping your feet at the dogs to keep them inside.

These morning rides are crisp, the air cold against your forearms, your hands starting to ache. (You don't have the black, knit gloves that you'll eventually copy off the riders in *BMX Action*; and you can't ride with both hands in your pockets instead of on the handlebars.) You pedal west on Parkway, the lock knocking against the frame as you pedal, the sun at your back, low and bright. You continue until the street ends.

There you veer onto the bike path, the San Gabriel River to your left. In the summer, the river reduces to a series of stagnant puddles. In wintertime, collected rain rushes past sandy islands, overturned shopping carts, and clusters of leafy bamboo. The water cascades over concrete retainers meant to slow it, and it eddies around bunches of wild carp. Sometimes you spot a crane, a shard of white against the green, before it opens its wings and leaps effortlessly into flight. Aside from the occasional team of ten-speeders, who blur past in a whiz of neatly clicking gears and coordinated blue Lycra, you are alone.

When you reach the 60 Freeway, you are minutes away from Golfland, and this excitement is uncontainable. The trail dips downward and you pedal your hardest, gaining double speed. When you're under the Freeway, the unceasing roar of cars overhead, you shout as loud as you can.

The sound of four quarters falling out of a change machine is a delight, and the jackpot sound of twenty falling after you've inserted a five-dollar bill is rapturous. If Golfland's change machines produced tiny snacks instead of quarters, you'd be salivating. Even though you've gotten there early, other kids are already crowded around the games you've waited all week to play. In the fourth-grade, there is no statement more bad-ass than the placing of a quarter at the edge of a video-game screen. The tap of the coin against the glass declares that you're playing next. It also implies that you will play the game better than whoever is at the joystick, and your looming presence over their shoulder will insist that they get it over with already.

You are not bad-ass, so you walk around until your opportunities come. When they do, you love the digitized versions of Bach and Henry Mancini used as theme music, the robotic voices asking that you prepare to qualify, the different chimes and chirps that signal incremental accomplishments. A bracing thud as your spacecraft is equipped with double cannons. A high whine when you shift into high gear. The hyperspace trill bringing you one warp closer to Earth. You love the idea of your lasers winging Darth Vader's Tie Fighter and sending him spinning into space as you advance on the Death Star. You love the challenge of destroying your enemies before they can destroy you.

Of all the games, *Punch-Out!!* is the one you love most. It lets you be a boxer, your green character looking something like a graph-paper diagram of Bruce Banner half-transformed into the Hulk. After you drop in a quarter, the game asks you to enter your initials, to declare an identity before your first match. Sometimes you get brave and put "M♥V." Most often you are "MIK," ignoring that the "E" won't fit.

Your fourth-grade sensibility finds the opponent characters intriguing. Glass Joe is goofy and Piston Hurricane seems tough and Bald Bull, who reminds you of Marvin Hagler, repeatedly reveals your lack of hand-eye coordination with his devastating uppercut. You infrequently make it to a fourth fight. Each time you manage one, Kid Quick lives up to his name and dispatches you with a relentless flurry of punches that you are helpless to counter. When you go down, his pixilated taunting prompts another quarter into the machine.

It will take you a while to realize the secret of your opponents' eyes flashing yellow right before they try to punch you. When you are knocked down, the game will encourage you to get up, and in an effort to regain strength, you will tap the left and right buttons as fast as you can. You've seen other kids do it, but you don't know if it actually works.

There will be the occasional game when it all comes easy, when you lock in on the pattern of each opponent and their special move doesn't faze you. You will avoid their jabs and hooks and body blows and strike back with purpose, your strength gaining. When it peaks, the right-hook punch enabled, the game will tell you to put your opponent away and you will.

(Many years later, you will begin dating a girl that loves vintage clothing and art-deco furniture. Holding hands, you'll notice that she has a permanent callous that she calls her "Nintendo Thumb." There will be a subsequent afternoon when her brother dusts off their old system, and with *Mike Tyson's Punch-Out!!* in the console, the girl will proceed to easily defeat the game's opponents, the muscle memory in her hands still sharp, her reflexes instinctive and automatic. On her first try, she will take down Glass Joe and then Von Kaiser, Piston Honda and then Don Flamenco, King Hippo and Great Tiger and Bald Bull. It will be one of the most pure and beautiful displays of skill that you'll ever witness. Ultimately she'll lose to Mr. Sandman, an opponent that you hadn't actually seen before. You'll want her to keep going, only she'll be bored by the game and will set the controller aside as if it were an empty glass or an old magazine. The memory of her turn will nevertheless remain and it will become one of the many reasons you ask her to marry you.)

You are not a great video-game player. You are not even good. Only sometimes, when a magical game occurs, will your name make it to the high-score list. This is the opportunity Golfland offers you. A chance to be recognized. To make your mark. No matter if that mark is just three letters in the middle of a list of fifty other scores, if the recognition is essentially the final command in a computer program. It does not matter that your name will disappear when the machine is unplugged. This moment, this illusion of being accomplished at something, is the exact moment that you had hoped for. When it happens, you will wait for the screens to cycle through so that you can see your name again.

When your pockets are finally empty, you will check the game to see the high-score screen one last time. You will then head down the long hallway that leads to the exit. The cacophony of all the games going at once will echo off the orange tiles, and it will make you miss the arcade before you've even left it. Outside, you will unlock your bicycle and regard the vast, hot stretch of asphalt that is Golfland's parking lot, blinking at the midday sun as if you've emerged from a cave. Your trip, like many of life's narcotic pleasures, has been intense and is over quickly, but it will seem like a big part of the day has gone by without you. By now you'll be expected back at home. You'll take your time getting there.

28

Train versus Pedestrian on Valley Boulevard

ALEX ESPINOZA

We lived in the shadows of factories and processing plants. I remember the tall smokestacks off of Seventh Street, lit up like massive Roman candles at night. I remember the smell of chemicals and solvents mixing with the scent of vinegar from the Vlasic Pickle Factory, fresh bread from the Golden Foods Bakery, or strawberries and cherries from Hansen's bottling plant. I grew up with the sound of semis barreling down Nelson Avenue and Orange Boulevard, steel plates banging and grinding against one another, and the low, droning hum of train wheels gliding over the metal tracks running parallel to Valley Boulevard—that long stretch of thoroughfare running west into South El Monte, Rosemead, and East Los Angeles and east into South San Jose Hills, Walnut, and Diamond Bar.

As a young boy, I would ride my bike through a wide empty field that lay just north of Valley Boulevard and the railroad tracks, a lot sandwiched between a junkyard and yet another factory. Bits of paper bags and torn strips of newsprint would get caught in the thorny stems of wild bushes that grew in the grime-coated soil, and I'd pedal through the thin trails that wound through the field, smashing the countless stink beetles that skimmed across my path. A rusted chain-link fence separated the perimeter of the field from the railroad tracks. I'd hear the whistle first, the sharp howl that pierced through the endless roar of rush-hour traffic on Valley.

That whistle, so mournful, so aching. I heard it at night as I slept with the windows open on summer evenings in our house in La Puente. I used to imagine those trains traveling through mountains and tunnels, across forests and deserts, venturing well past our ramshackle homes and dilapidated strip malls (their cheap stucco exteriors flaking and bubbling off like reptiles molting their skin), past the steel and metal towers of the factories and processing plants, far away to places someone like me would never see.

Every month, I had a doctor's appointment at the Orthopedic Hospital in downtown Los Angeles. My mother didn't speak English, but she knew how to read numbers and could navigate the byzantine RTD bus system, which we'd use to get there. Early mornings once a month, we'd walk down Orange toward Valley, step over the steel ruts of the tracks, and wait for the Number 484. This would carry us down Valley, under the 605 Freeway, to the South El Monte bus terminal, then to the 10 West, past Cal State Los Angeles, and into downtown. I remember miles of walking down crowded streets, standing in front of the courthouse, watching lawyers in suits toting leather briefcases with shiny brass buckles. I remember traveling back home, arriving exhausted, the suspicious glances and menacing nods of those doctors lingering in my mind no matter how hard I tried to forget them.

My father drank heavily throughout my childhood and into my high-school years. Of the bars along Valley Boulevard, there was one in particular, El Chaparral, that was his favorite. He was there the night that he died. He'd been celebrating his retirement from the carpet mill. He planned on leaving my mother and returning to Michoacán, to live out his last days on the parcel of land that had been in our family for decades. It was late in the evening. I'd come home from pulling a shift at the Puente Hills Mall, where I worked at a store that sold greeting cards and "over the hill" gag gifts. My mother and sister were at my sister-in-law's baby shower in Whittier; she was nine months pregnant with my niece, and they would spend the evening eating cake and unwrapping gifts. The house was empty, and I had ordered Domino's pizza and was watching music videos well past midnight when I saw the headlights of my sister's car pull into the driveway. An hour later, as I was about to crawl into bed, the taste of pepperoni and cheese and garlic still on my tongue, there came a knock on the front door.

A police officer was on the stoop. With him was a boy I recognized from my high school named Rudy. He was popular and good-looking; all the girls liked him because he was Latino but had blond hair and cool, green eyes. I ran with a completely different crowd. I was sure he had no clue who I even was. Rudy wore a polo shirt with the word "Explorer" stitched in gold thread across the right front pocket. My mother had woken up by now and was standing in the living room with us. My sister, a deep sleeper, was out, I was sure—her head buried beneath the blankets. I don't remember what the officer said exactly, but by the time they had stepped out of the house, walked down the driveway, and hopped back into the squad car, I knew that my father's body had been found, the side of his skull cracked and bleeding, a few feet from the railroad tracks along Valley Boulevard. I knew that he'd been rushed to Queen of the Valley Hospital in West Covina, where he had been pronounced dead. I had to translate all of this for my mother.

One witness said he was at El Chaparral when he watched my father stumble across Valley Boulevard. Once on the other side, this witness reported, my father encountered a man. A few minutes later, there came the sirens, a helicopter circling in the night air above. Then my father's body was being strapped to a gurney and placed inside the ambulance.

"That man," the witness said to us, "I think he robbed your father. Took his money, smashed his head in with a rock, and left."

It made sense, we thought. There were all sorts of shady characters who hung out around that place at night. And his wallet was never found. That was the story we told people, the myth we created around my father's demise—that he'd been robbed and beaten coming home one evening. We never asked for an official police investigation. We mourned, laid my father to rest, and moved forward.

It seems that wherever I live, railroad tracks are always within close proximity. I never plan this. It just happens. Even now, in the Central Valley, miles away from the spot where my father died, my home is less than half a mile from two rail lines that snake through the city of Fresno. Random train whistles punctuate my days and drift into my bedroom on chilled currents of night air. I hear them when I'm out running errands or at my desk writing. In this way, I often think, my father is with me. It was that sound, pulling and tugging at me all those years, that made me decide to order his autopsy report. The envelope arrived on a hot July afternoon, but I didn't open it right away. It sat on my dining room table for a few weeks before I mustered up the courage to peel back the adhesive and review what was inside.

The truth is that he wasn't beaten and robbed that night. The evidence suggests that my father decided to end his life by lying down on those railroad tracks. But he must have come to his senses at the last minute. Maybe the air sobered him up, because he heard the approaching train and tried getting up and out of the way, but it was too late. It sideswiped him on the side of the head. By the time his body was found, he was unresponsive, void of any vital signs.

Since I discovered the truth about my father's death, the lie we grew up telling—about a strange man, an encounter beside a pair of rusty railroad tracks, his missing wallet—has, in many ways, become a myth, something my siblings tell their children. And now that I know the truth, I don't correct them, and I don't know why. Perhaps it's easier for us to reconcile so much of the shame we harbored about my father while he was alive, when we would watch him stumbling home drunk from the bars. Perhaps it's easier for us to confront the regret of not having done more to help him deal with his addiction while he was with us.

"If only we had more time with Dad," my brother told me over the phone one time. "But he was killed."

"Yeah," I said. "Whoever did it is still out there, too."

And at night, when I hear the whistle of the train, just before I'm about to drop off to sleep, I think how easy it is to hold on to a beautiful lie rather than an ugly truth.

Yes, I tell myself. It's easier this way.

Notes

A version of this chapter was previously published on KCET as "Train Versus Pedestrian on Valley Boulevard," June 10, 2015, https://www.kcet.org/history-society/train-versus-pedestrian-on-valley-boulevard.

29

Epiphany Catholic Church

TONI MARGARITA PLUMMER

After my home, Epiphany was the place that loomed largest in my South El Monte life. It was where I attended elementary school. It was the church where we went to Mass every Sunday, and where I received my first Holy Communion and first reconciliation in a tiny room with shaggy carpet on the walls. It was where I went to confirmation classes for two years during my freshman and sophomore years in high school, before being confirmed and choosing an obscure saint's name because I needed to be different from all the Agnes's and Bernadette's. (You never heard of Saint Lutgardis?) It was where I first started lusting after boys and where I would meet my first sexual partner. It was where I was baptized as an infant and where I first saw a dead body at a funeral. It encompassed all of life and is the backdrop for countless memories—special and mundane, joyful and sad.

In fact, Epiphany is one of the reasons I call South El Monte my hometown. When they met, my parents were both working in downtown Los Angeles. They found a stucco bungalow in South El Monte, very reasonably priced at $44,000 and built the same year my mother was born. My mother liked that there was a Catholic school nearby, for the children they would have. They bought it, and just like that, Epiphany became my destiny.

When I attended the school, there were grades 1–8. Recesses were spent playing four square or hopscotch. In junior high, Chinese jump rope was my preferred pastime: ankles, calves, knees, thighs, underbutts, waists! Two of us would hold the long loop of rubber bands around our bodies while the third girl took her turn jumping from one side to the next, inside, outside, onto both strands, then off. On "scratchies" you had to be especially careful not to let a strand slip out from under you. For "skinnies" we'd use just one leg, and for "fatties" we'd spread our legs apart. If it was raining, we'd stay seated at our desks and play Seven Up or watch a Disney movie or "Davey and Goliath" on the TV mounted in the upper corner of the classroom.

Every year we were required to sell World's Finest chocolate bars to help raise money for the school. Hopefully a pitying relative would buy a case or half a case from you, so you didn't have to peddle them one by one. I'd end up eating my fair share, dutifully stuffing a dollar bill into the envelope kept in the refrigerator. I loved the ones with almonds; later there was a crispy kind. My sisters and I would dress in our uniforms and go door to door. Our mom would drop us off at the Alpha Beta supermarket on Durfee Avenue, and we'd stand outside pitching shoppers. The kid in my class who always sold the most was the one whose family worked at the swap meet. If you sold a lot, you'd get prizes. The big one was a trip to Disneyland on a weekday; you could be in Fantasyland while the rest of your sorry classmates were stuck in school, having to wait until you returned before any new material could be covered.

The library was a solitary stucco building past the field, inhabited, it seemed, by the scariest of the nuns. We would do science tutorials on the computers. There were also huge headphones that squeezed your head, and you'd listen to a story about Rikki-Tikki-Tavi and answer questions about it. The nuns wore brown habits and wimples. You could see their bangs, but that was it for visible hair. Sister Paul Marie was principal, and there were a handful of other Bernardine nun teachers. They all lived in a convent behind the school, and you tried to avoid bouncing your basketball over their wall. Once I ran into them while at Disneyland with my family; it was rather disconcerting to see them in plainclothes. They were raving about the new President Lincoln attraction.

There were lay teachers too: Mr. Cannon played guitar for us, including his original "I'm a Mean Teacher." Mrs. White was the first black person I had any real amount of contact with, and I delighted in mimicking her southern accent with phrases I learned from her, such as, "You are slow as molasses." Ms. DeFrancesco adored pigs, and her desk was bedecked with all kinds of them. And the sisters Ms. Llewellyn and Mrs. Spencer commuted all the way from Apple Valley. Before PE class, the boys having been sent out of the classroom, we girls would change into our shorts and navy shirts emblazoned with the golden eagle. Then we'd walk out to the asphalt and Mr. Korogianos would lead us in warm-ups, making circles with ours arms and touching our toes. There was no gym.

The building that had been intended to be a gym instead opened as Epiphany Church in 1956, and as students we attended weekday Mass there. The teachers seated us boy-girl-boy-girl, with empty seats between us. I would hope and fear that I'd be put next to a boy I liked and get to hold his hand during the "our father." If I was by the outer aisle, I'd imagine I was holding hands with whatever saint was pictured in the stained-glass window across from me.

On Sunday mornings, our mother would take us to Mass. The congregation at large was always bisected naturally by language. There were masses, groups, and events for the English speakers and different ones for the Spanish speakers. Of course, Mexican culture permeated everything. We celebrated Las Posadas at Christmas time, and there were menudo breakfasts in the cafeteria. Every June was the annual parish fiesta, where you could win goldfish by throwing ping-pong balls into a bowl or doing the cakewalk. Rides included a big yellow slide you rode down on a rough, brown sack; the bumper cars; the funhouse; and the legendary "Zipper." Vendors would sell *buñelos* and *elotes*. A small stage would host bands and groups of children in costume performing traditional Mexican dances.

I will always think of Epiphany as having a golden age. This was when midnight masses actually started at midnight. When regular masses—in English, too—were well attended. Really, this was when the beloved Father Joe and Father Cumberland were in charge. White men from Long Beach and Alaska, respectively, they had learned Spanish and spoke it so well and were so personable that they were adored by both the English- and Spanish-speaking parishioners.

Father Joe had a conversational sermon style. He would take the microphone down the aisle like we were at a comedy club, and he'd ask the kids questions—withdrawing, coming back up, ebbing like the tide. I can't remember anything he said, but I can recall how he said it: the tone of his voice, his rhythm, and cadence. My grandmother loved his blue eyes. Father Joe introduced the Systematic Integral New Evangelization program, or SINE, to Epiphany. People would attend a retreat, and then they'd go into what were called small communities—groups of around twelve people that would assemble at someone's house. They'd pray and discuss some facet of church teaching. These people were the core of the church, the ones who ushered and served Communion at Mass and who could be counted on to volunteer. The regulars. My mother was in a small community, and we'd frequently have people over to the house. My sisters and I would play in our rooms with the other members' kids while the adults sat at the dining-room table and had their mysterious conversations.

When Father Joe got transferred to another church after sixteen years, it was a big deal. Because he loved camping, part of his farewell was transforming the field to a campground where we set up tents and stayed overnight. At his farewell Mass, I read a poem I had written for the occasion. It was my first reading in public of something I had written.

Father Cumberland was popular, too, and the priest I felt the closest connection with. Tall and red-haired, he stood out in a crowd. I remember that in grade school he'd come by the classes to talk to us. He had a more understated sense of humor and was great with kids and teenagers. I have a picture of me with him standing outside the church, my forehead shiny from the oil they had anointed me with at confirmation. For my *quinceañera*, I didn't want a big party like some of my friends had. I got a green, tea-length dress with lace around the top; had my hair done up in ringlets; and put on nylons and high heels, and Father Cumberland said the Mass. He was invited to a family party back at our house afterward, where I changed into shorts and a sleeveless flannel shirt and played musical chairs with my cousins. He would eventually leave Epiphany, too, to go to a nearby church. When I told him I was going to major in philosophy in college, he expressed concern, saying that philosophy majors often fell away from the church. I found this pretty funny, as I was going to Notre Dame University.

Father Cumberland and my mother kept in touch over the years; she's on his mailing list for letters about his trips home to Alaska. Six years ago, he presided over my sister's marriage in San Dimas. As for the subsequent pastors and priests at Epiphany, let's just say they weren't the type you or your grandmother would have a crush on. And some spoke English with such a heavy accent that it was difficult for English speakers to understand them. The church got a makeover, too. The tabernacle was moved from its place under the crucifix, behind the altar, to the side; the priest thought he shouldn't have his back to it. The crucifix, a very large cross with a striking sculpture of Christ, was moved to the side, too, and replaced with stained-glass windows and molding. On the outside of the church, where there had been the three kings on their camels and the words "Sharers in the promise in Christ Jesus through the preaching of the Bible," now there were simply three crowns. It's an odd feeling to have the church you know so well rearranged on you. You find that you are nostalgic for the wooden lecterns—you think these newfangled glass ones expose the lectors too much. (The beautiful statue of Our Lady of Guadalupe has maintained her place, though; on her feast day she gets showered with flowers, and some brave soul climbs up a ladder to place a crown on her head.) With so many changes, and so many changes in leadership over the years, some people went to other churches. My family continued attending.

After I graduated from Epiphany in 1993, I went to Cantwell Sacred Heart of Mary High School in Montebello. I didn't drive, and none of my Cantwell friends lived that close to me. I mostly hung out with the kids I knew from Epiphany. That was my social life. And when I'd come back from college, for Christmases and summers, I'd meet up with the same crowd. It shifted over the years—new friends were made, and others fell out. But there was always a group. We went to Mass and had our own small community. There was a youth group for a while. Once we had a "lock in" in the cafeteria—this consisted of us, boys and girls, being physically locked in the cafeteria overnight. (There was a chaperone, I'm sure.) We prayed, holding hands with our eyes closed. We witnessed more than one teenage pregnancy. I never got close to that fate, but the group did provide me with more male friendships than I'd ever had or would have again. It wasn't unusual for me to be the only girl in the group, and I enjoyed being thought of as one of the guys. Together we frequented the McDonald's by Golfland, played pool at the Golden Cue and other pool halls, drank, loitered, cruised, went dancing in Hollywood and Los Angeles, bowled, saw movies, threw house parties, and smoked cigars in Santa Monica. We were all over the place. But if we had any home turf, it was Epiphany.

I live across the country now, and when I visit South El Monte, I usually concentrate on seeing my family. If I go to Epiphany, I know I'm likely to see at least a few people I know. Most of my old crowd doesn't attend anymore, but it's still the closest thing I have to a center for the city.

Epiphany for me will always be the people that it brought together and that it continues to gather in its church and school, its hallways and parking lots, its cafeteria and "covered area" (where the students eat lunch).

It is Brenda Gutierrez, my classmate at Epiphany and in high school, and cheerful and loyal friend. During high school our mothers would carpool. One day I made the mistake of telling her that we had "free dress"—a day when you didn't have to wear a uniform to school—when that was not the case. She did not hold it against me. Brenda became Ms. Gutierrez, a first-grade teacher at Epiphany.

It is Dolores Gomez, a pianist and vocalist, whose beautiful voice for me will remain the clearest, most basic expression of church music. I still remember her pulling me out of a class and asking me to sing "Mary Had a Little Lamb": she was auditioning us. I sang in her choir on and off, sometimes getting solos; after college I followed her to a church in Montebello.

It is Pat Tudor, a tall elderly woman with thick glasses who won millions of dollars from a lottery ticket she bought at a liquor store on Durfee. She fixed up her house, shared the money with her family, and contributed to Epiphany each year, paying for the food for retreats and snacks for meetings.

It is Alma Casillas, who with her husband cleaned the church and rectory. Her son, my version of Jordan Catalano, was in my small community, and once I heard his band Good Grief play in their backyard. I still have the band's bumper sticker stuck inside a Hello Kitty case.

My last time at Epiphany, I saw a young woman who I used to spend a lot of time with. We don't really speak anymore. She has a daughter whom I've never met. During Communion, she walked by my pew on her way back to hers, and I stood up and gave her a hug. This wild girl I'd known, who I'd gone out with all over Los Angeles and Orange County, drinking, dancing, and meeting guys with—she smiled, and there was this new silence and somberness to her. A new maturity. She walked on, and I sat back down in the wooden pew, one I'd sat in many, many times before as a child, a teenager, a young adult. I listened to the ending of the Mass teary eyed, struck by the loss of that relationship but also by the simple passing of that time of my life.

People drive by Epiphany every day. They have to stop at that blinking red light with the crosswalk. They hear the bell chiming, and some cross themselves as they drive by and some don't. It is intensely important for some, not worth a second thought for others. For me, it was the first place in which I was part of a larger community that extended beyond my family. It's my youth and integrally linked to my memories of South El Monte.

30

Rush Street

CARRIBEAN FRAGOZA

Rush Street is a main artery in South El Monte that runs from one end of the city to the other, and it has come to mean different things to different people. Rush Street can be the street that you took to the Starlite Swap Meet on Rosemead Boulevard every weekend with your parents, usually against your will. Rush can be the street you took with your father to get to the soccer fields at Whittier Narrows, also against your will. Or perhaps it is the street that you took on your own time when you got older, to get to either the San Gabriel River on the eastern end, or the Rio Hondo on the western end—cemented or raw, both riverbanks good for smoking crudely rolled joints.

Rush itself, however, is hardly a destination or scenic route (much like the rest of the city, which only marks its name on maps via traffic reports as the place where freeway congestion knots itself the tightest—a place to avoid). Its own name recommends how it should be navigated: as quickly as possible. Yet this street has marked itself upon me, silently engrained its name in phantom scars. It started as an unlikely destination, and one day, unexpectedly, it became a landmark.

The truth is, I sought out Rush Street for one simple reason: to be alone.

Twenty-five years old, I was a graduate student working a part-time job, and I found myself nestled again in the tight quarters of my parents' home. For over thirty years, they had rented a single-story two-bedroom bungalow where my two siblings and I grew up. At various times, we've sprawled into unlikely corners for sleep and privacy. I wrote wherever I found vacant space, during the day in a bedroom using a bed as a desk or late in the evening at the kitchen table, keeping a single light on so as to not disturb the sleep of living-room dwellers. In the middle of the night, I read in the small walk-in closet, again like when I was an adolescent. And sometimes, on a day like Sunday, I just had to get out completely.

I found that bike riding was a good way to let off steam. It allowed me to contemplate the city I had grown up in and explore parts of the neighborhood that I'd never been to and would not have accessed by car or foot. I became fascinated with Rush Street's desolate landscape the same way that many people grow to love the desert. Sundays were the best days, when the city rested, off guard in its dominical lull.

I'd ride through the tight residential streets until the short, chain-link-gated homes were abruptly replaced by Rush's rows of cinderblock warehouses and welding and car repair shops. Unmarked clusters of buildings in various shades of gray and dirty beige witnessed my passing in silence. And behind dog-guarded gates, I caught glimpses of constellations of more buildings, everything heavily garlanded with barbed wire. All of this sprawled out before me, below a great burning blue sky.

On these shadeless summer days, the asphalt roads and dirty concrete sidewalks scorch the life out of everything. All is covered in dirt and soot and grime. But late in the afternoon, the sky blushes out the earth's heat, and the asphalt seems to darken in relief. A lonely bar opens its front door for the first time all day and from its darkness lets out the strain of an accordion's song.

On this particular Sunday, like all Sundays, I was relieved, too. As usual, I occupied an entire lane where during the week flatbed trucks compete for sharp turns, and big rigs perform daunting traffic feats. Today, it was mine. I was not dressed to shield myself from penetrating gazes or to protect myself from the elements of the street and weather, as I usually would have been. Instead I wore flimsy shorts, a tank top, and sandals. It was an absurd outfit, but I didn't care. I enjoyed feeling the sharp breeze filter through the thin fabric of my clothes. My exposed toes thrilled in their proximity to the gritty asphalt as the pedals descended to only inches from the ground.

Although I can no longer remember the details of the car except its unexpected presence as a large predatory body that came up fast in my peripheral vision, suddenly I could hear and feel its dangerous nearness. Instead of changing lanes, it seemed to pull closer. Quickly I pulled toward the curb, directing my wheel to the sloping plane of a driveway.

By then, I'd already learned that when your wheel doesn't hit the lip of the driveway precisely straight on, it slides uncontrollably, and you drop to the ground. However, on this day I learned that if you're biking fast enough, you drop and keep going until you run out of momentum—or in my case, until your course is broken. I hit the concrete and continued to slide across the sidewalk, slamming wheels first against the metal wall of a welder's shop. The wheel hit the wall; the bike seat hit my sitting bones; and my entire thigh dragged against the concrete, collecting in its exposed raw flesh all of the trajectory's dirt, gravel, and rocks.

I lay stunned under my twisted bike. The car that had nearly pushed me off the road was long gone, as if it had never existed. But in the distance, I saw another bike rider approaching me. He was a middle-aged man, darkly tanned under a baseball cap pulled low against the sun. He wore a grease-stained, navy blue uniform. But as he neared me, he lowered his gaze to the asphalt and did not alter his pace. He continued to pedal, as if I were a phantom that had failed to appear. He acknowledged my presence by blatantly ignoring me. I did not hurry to stand up. I lay there on this industrial landscape, feeling like the only living being and made more alive now by my pulsating wounds.

I limped home, the whole endless way. My bike wobbled on its now crooked wheel, and its loosened seat hung at an awkward angle. My sitting bones blared with pain. Blood dribbled down my leg. On my journey I recall encountering only one other car. The passenger, a woman, watched me and then turned her gaze away to avoid eye contact. I hobbled down my own street, where all of my neighbors had retreated with the fading sun into their homes.

When I arrived home, I found the house empty. My mother and siblings had gone to church, and my father . . . who knew. I wasn't sure whether to feel relieved or desperate—it was more solitude than I'd bargained for.

I sunk into the bathtub, still dressed, dirty feet muddying the white porcelain walls of the tub. I let the water run lukewarm as I inspected my dirt-encrusted wound. I call the grime embedded into the meat of my leg and the fleshy part of the palm of my hand "dirt" simply to signify filth. I wish it had been dirt, which is earth or soil, but true dirt is hard to come by in places like Rush Street. Instead there are grease, dust, metallic flakes, rust, and jagged pebbles—never worn smooth by water or wind but broken down like many little teeth knocked out of the busy mouth that is the street. Today, on Sunday, the debris had rested, waited in its week's worth of breaking and grinding, for other bodies, out of synch with its industrial flow, to come crashing down. I let the water gurgle around me and cover my wounds. As I tried to pick out the larger pieces, I felt overwhelmed not only by the stinging pain but also by a kind of defeat I did not have words for or understand. I rubbed the bright coral skin in the water and watched plumes of blood dance and dissolve as I abandoned myself to tears. Truly, one of the greatest rewards of being alone is being able to cry with no shame.

I lay on the couch and fell asleep waiting. My mother woke me up, horrified, wanting to know exactly what had happened. She stared at my leg, panicked, not knowing what to do. But she knew who might. She called Doña Mari, a sweet elderly woman who lived down the street with all five of her grown children and all of their children in a small wood-frame house. Doña Mari is one in a series of grandmothers my mother turns to for advice—say, when she cannot remember an ingredient in a particular dish her mother used to make, or when she needs an herb for a child's stomachache.

Or today, when my thigh is ballooning and the scraped area is too deep and wide for alcohol or Band-Aids. We watched the wound and looked at each other helplessly as we waited for our neighborhood grandmother. Doña Mari arrived a few minutes later, accompanied by half a dozen of her grandchildren ranging in age from three to ten. They were a lively pack of cousins ready to explore all nooks of a new environment. But nothing attracts a crowd, even a very young one, like gore. The children solemnly joined their grandmother around the couch to witness the mess. I had my shorts rolled up halfway up my scuffed butt cheek. The blood in the scrape had congealed into a deep red-pink gelatin studded with grains of dirt and gravel. A biking accident. It happens to children, and it happens to adults—twenty-something women who ordinarily should be nursing the cuts and bruises of children of their own. The visitors stared at everything—my butt cheek, my leg and knees, the palms of my hands held up to the ceiling like a martyr in agony. But there was no martyrdom and no cause. No real reason. I was riding, I explained; I fell. That's all there was to it. The wound and the woman, I was aberration all around: a spectacle to be witnessed and somehow learned from, though the lesson was too obscure.

Doña Mari stood over me, inspecting my body and thinking very hard. She peered through her bifocals to get a closer look at each limb. The living room was heavy with a rare silence. Finally, Doña Mari's face lit up with a solution. She had just the thing in her magical bag full of time-tested remedies. As she rustled through white plastic grocery bag, I felt relieved that I could rely on a special non-FDA-approved herb or exotic pomade concocted by ancestors and inherited over many generations. I'd recently watched a show on PBS about all of the stunning medicinal properties of near-extinct animals in remedies made by native medicine people in straw huts all over the world. As long as it wasn't made out of axolotl or sea turtle, I thought. I'd have to ask Doña Mari. I just hoped my inquiry would not offend her.

Neosporin, she stated with great authority, as she pulled out the tiny plastic tube with the orange label. This will do it. Neosporin. I doubted there was enough Neosporin in that tube to even begin covering the large area, and I graciously thanked her anyway. At least there was no axolotl in Neosporin. I advised the children to be careful riding their bikes as they filed out of the house—all of their playful effervescence had long ago fizzed out.

"Should we go to the emergency room?" my mother offered.

Instead, I decided to allow the routine of my daily life to deflate my leg back to normality. It didn't work. Instead it made me a freak show at the front desk of the YMCA, where I worked greeting people and scanning their membership cards as I attempted to conceal my undressed wound. I concentrated on summoning the axolotl's regenerative powers. Unfortunately, too grotesque for public view, I was soon sent home.

Later that day, I decided it was time to call the woman I'd been house- and cat-sitting for in the several weeks prior to my accident. She lived high on a steep hill in Highland Park, in one of those old renovated homes that members of the creative middle class had just started taking over. She was a professor of mine. She had asked me to watch her kitty for a week while she was away on a trip to New York. Cat-sitting mainly consisted of leaving the grumpy old cat alone except when it was time to give it its medications—tablets ground into small balls of fine soft cheeses that I pried into its mouth and syringes full of clear fluids to be injected under its skin. In exchange, I could help myself to all of the gourmet hummus and tea I wanted, and I could sleep in my professor's bedroom with a spectacular view of the Los Angeles Basin.

In the first few nights, I had marveled at her bookshelves and her office, where she wrote books and plays and prepared lesson plans for her art-school students who were quick to love and respect her left-leaning ways. I thought how wonderful it would be to have a place of your own with all of your stuff and no one to bug you or hassle you about what you're wearing or how late you come home after hanging out with those good-for-nothing who-knows-whos. But after a day or two, I had grown lonely in that adorable hilltop house. Books that usually brought me great solace and refuge in my suffocating life kept me no company. This loneliness surprised and irritated me. So I descended from that hill and had returned to my crowded family home in the San Gabriel Valley, where I sought respite from my cramped quarters with persistent desperation. I had returned to the hilltop house only to perform my cat-sitting duties. Regularly, I had escaped on random bike rides through my dirty little hometown. Each time, wherever I went, my only true destination was solitude. Especially on Rush. Over the course of my life, I have found solitude in unexpected iterations and in various concentric circles, each different in characteristics—sometimes soothing and sometimes unbearable.

After my fall, as I contemplated my wounds, I realized that I would not be able to (1) drive my rusty stick-shift car, (2) climb up the steep hill to the professor's house, or (3) stomach sticking another needle through that ancient cat's skin when really it should have been left alone to die on its own terms under the porch or by the persimmon tree in the garden. I explained my dilemma on the phone to the unsympathetic professor, who refused to speak to me for the following year.

After a few days, scabs finally began to form over my wounds. I was relieved by my healing (perhaps the axolotl spirit had been at work after all), but I could not shake the thoughts about all the crap trapped under that scabrous layer. Finally I went to the emergency room, where a doctor—after a brief inspection—knew exactly what to do. He pulled out a wire brush from one of his sterile bins, something nearly identical to the tool my father used to scrub the charred grime off the barbecue grill. "We can use anesthesia or not, what do you prefer?" he asked. The scabs had grown thick and in some parts bulbous. My gnarled skin vaguely reminded me of the broken-up gritty asphalt that I had grated my leg on. "Anesthesia," I answered. He proceeded to stick long syringes into numerous parts of my wounds. He applied additional pressure to break through the areas where the crust had hardened more thickly. The pain was always greatest when the needle came close to a bone. Was there such a thing as anesthesia for the anesthesia, I wondered. (Later, on an unrelated series of visits to my dentist, I learned that yes, there is such a thing.) He scraped everything off with great vigor. Clearly, he was a very thorough doctor. My thigh, knees, and one of my palms were scraped clean and then packaged in those plasticky pads used to absorb blood in packaged meat at the supermarket. He explained that they would allow me to heal while preventing scabbing and scarring.

I hid my other crusty palm from his view—I was willing to live with a disfigured hand—yet he caught sight of it and demanded it from me. Again he prompted: "Anesthesia or no anesthesia?" Fuck it, I thought. "No anesthesia," I said. And he scraped.

The pain of the bike accident and all of its aftermath is impossible for me to really describe. Yet the telling of its story strangely assuages the fire-ants-in-my-pants need that had driven me into odd corners of my parents' house, across town, and back again onto Rush Street. Greater than a need to be alone was my need to create a space that simply belonged to me. Grinding into Rush Street's dirt and grime in a bike accident was a way to do it. Embedded into my body, Rush Street belongs to me even more now. Or rather, we belong more to each other. And yes, there is solace in that.

31

Durfee Avenue

SALVADOR PLASCENCIA

Pried from the park benches and trash cans, the soaring rocket that once flew across El Monte's city seal vanished. The ship's nose scuffed the atmosphere—a friction stitched as a broken line on police officers' and firefighters' sleeves. The trajectory was not interplanetary but a mobius path. A sagging sash announced the destination and civic motto: "Where Future Meets Past." On the other side of the seal, a covered wagon waited for the spacecraft.

Clods of the imaginary pastoral plowed under all evidence of the supersonic. The official stationery is now stamped with a pair of oxen pulling a wagon along a forking river, the San Gabriel Mountains blurry in the background, with two cumulus gauzes hanging in an unpierced sky.

But I write to you from that once bent and looping chronology. From the out of tense of my remembering and an avenue tottering in time. A sheen still streaks across the municipal airspace, but just under my feet—below the buried jugs of burned motor oil and shards from shuttered ceramic factories—also lie the dented casing and fins of a once hopeful futurity.

The avenue, named after a walnut tycoon who lost his fortune to a tree fungus, surrenders its clots of traffic and name to a winding thoroughfare. At its northern end, neighborhood lanes and courts chop Durfee Avenue into sleepy cul-de-sacs. For shady stretches, gangling oaks and the sickly progeny of orchards dangle over lawn chairs and barbecues. The rows and rows of almond and walnut trees that once canopied the land have been pruned, felled, and burned into housing tracts.

The Santa Anas are, of course, eternal. They blow through the Gabrelino villages, shake the husked nuts from their branches, and nudge TV antennas from their frequency.

In our elementary school, also named after a tree nut tycoon, we sit in a circle, drooling fluoride into waxy paper cups. Floating in the baby blue fluid, flecks of cavities bob to the surface. A turbine pushes the Santa Anas past canisters of Freon and into our classroom. The rot of our enamel has been averted, and the treated room protects us from the swelter of the day.

Despite the taming of the winds and the formulated gargle, ancient noises haunt the school's plumbing. A fourth grader hung himself in the boy's restroom, using a double knot to dislodge his Adam's apple from his throat. When the toilets flush and faucet knobs turn, ghostly moans sluice through the building.

Just a few blocks away, some decades after my elementary school days, my grandmother rests in a cot at the Subacute Center, the medical name for an understaffed facility with gummy floors. Her exact whereabouts are protected by a series of unlatched iron gates, turning corridors, and decoy doors leading to the gurneys of haggard and immodestly robed strangers.

An *anciana*—not just an old lady with blotched skin and a single tooth but one of those ancient beings you see on hillsides carrying loads of twigs on their backs, around from the days when the earth was still scabbing into continents—sits across from my grandmother.

"Are you all going to stay here until she dies?" the suction from her face says.

In the spring and summer breaks when my parents sent me away to the rancho, one of these ancients tapped on the bus, scraped at the glass, and held up bags of boiled roots splattered in hot sauce. The bus route wound from Guadalajara through a canyon carved by the soapsuds of a murky river and stopped at lookouts to unload passengers who carried bulging bags of city goods into the switchbacks. Without diesel engines, the canyon trapped its people in a snare of up and down.

It was during these stopovers that they battered the windows and shouted the melancholy price of their *camotillos*. Only once did I slide open the window and hand them my money. But as the bus lurched away and they held up their pocked quinces and spears of sugar cane, I spit the cud of starch back into the bag. I have felt the scorn of these people ever since.

My grandmother—like them, perhaps a descendant from this gulch where a simple livelihood requires infinite motion—is also an immortal. Even after her liver bursts into a cryptic Rorschach and the nurses, suddenly displaying an urgent proficiency, enter to unhook the snarls of tubing, the electricity of her pacemaker still throbs.

And at this moment, even if it is a faraway hour, her signal continues to pulse.

Spatial glitches overcorrect for the misalignments in time. Sidewalks run in jagged staggers and then unceremoniously dematerialize. The avenue spreads itself in a formation of self-refutation: it sinks and then swiftly rises, the spongy asphalt hardens, a disordered lot of weeds and couch carcasses adjoins a rigidly labeled system of storage sheds. Fissures open up in the ZIP codes—portals where you enter through one door and exit a block away.

El Gallito, a repressed Nicaraguan restaurant masquerading as Mexican, serves banana leaf tamales and a corn mush called Indio Viejo only on weekends. Valley Boulevard intersects Durfee Avenue, leading to the perdition that is the City of Industry—a band of strip clubs and massage parlors terminating in a bellyache of bargain buffets and claim jumper portions. The irony of the city is the shameful languidness of those walking across its parking lots. El Gallito is mistaken—some say slanderously—for El Gallo Giro, a cloned taqueria desiccating taste buds across seven Southern California locations. And farther away, en route to Rio Hondo College, a giant golden rooster perches on top of a seafood restaurant.

At one of these rooster places, I watch pickups loaded with stacks of cardboard and scrap metal amble by. I slurp at tiny tubs of salsa and think about my grandmother in her hospital bed, the machine-laundered sheets tucked around her, the cylinders of fluorescent light emitting their antiseptic glow. She complained that the doctors were lousy. But the doctors were not doctors, just a herd of nursing students wearing ironed-on patches. In the babble of pain, she asked to be sent home to the rancho. And then, as if teleported back to health and into her sooted kitchen, she said, "Your grandfather goes away for years and then walks in like he was just upstairs."

Now when I drink an O'Doul's with my grandfather, I see my grandmother walking to the arroyo, a basket of laundry balanced on her head as my aunts and uncles scatter. Each item of clothing to be soaped, rubbed against a stone, rinsed, and then hung over thorny huisaches to dry. The froth of the detergent drifts downstream. My aunts play under the tented bushes and forage for herbs. Fifteen hundred miles to the north, my grandfather leans over a sink in the bowels of the *Queen Mary* ship rinsing dishes, telling jokes to busboys, and after work shooting pool with his pruney hands. The ad campaigns are not wrong—drinking forges a bond, but some days O'Doul's is just a diuretic requiring too much pretending.

In Spanish, though maybe it's just my literalist misunderstanding of the word, a sudden confusion can overtake your internal compass and fix the needle in place. If you become *norteado*, the pointer will not budge no matter which way you turn. So I can only say that I head north and end up at one of those bars where I have to wear a Cruz Azul jersey to avoid being mistaken for a white person. There, I bump into my grandfather in all his eras: a man in a yellowed Stetson and Wrangler pants drinking near beer, hunched over, and chatting with the bartender—mumbling the names of players and formations that have not been cited for generations; the sinewy laborer in cement- and paint-specked pants holding a Corona bottle; at the billiards table, the glister of brilliantine and the white of a crisply starched shirt circles to find the best geometry. All of these are embodiments of my grandfather, all lonely for their village life but toiling and loitering away in the promise and daze of El Norte.

They glance at my jersey and make a joke that can be used no matter what the season or tally of losses, and after any number of convoluted trades and loans. A transhistorical club constant: Man, that Cruz Azul goalie sure is old and ugly.

I nurse a beer until the match ends, but then a blackout saps the wattage from the lamps and television set. A change of ownership pushes out the bartender and regulars. The familial fraternity is transformed into a karaoke joint with a menu of sugared drink specials. And regardless of what shirt I wear, my beer is poured with an indifferent courtesy.

As a child, I sat in the back seat of my father's car as we drove by the bar and down the adjoining driveway. There, my father picked up bags stuffed with scraps of fabric and loaded them into the trunk. Back at our apartment, my mother sewed them into shirt pockets and sleeves.

For some reason the Chevy, our first family vehicle, was called a pony car. And my father, a lean and slight man, was often mistaken for a jockey. His coworkers—men who also had to crawl through the vents of industrial ovens and smelled of cereal and sweat—mockingly called him Shoemaker, the name of an El Monte High dropout who won a dozen Triple Crown races. (Many years later as we ate dinner at the Derby, my father looked skeptically at a plate of steak tartare and then at a framed picture on the wall. "I look nothing like that person," he said.)

In my reasoning, this double diminutive—sitting in a pony car driven by a jockey—reminded me of my own smallness, and I shrunk down into the seat where I could not be seen. One shame might have led to another in a chain reaction of private humiliations.

After my father dropped me and the bags of cloth off, and my mother was in the living room pressing on the sewing-machine's pedal—the sound fixing her safely in place—I would open my mother's drawer and slip her bra over my shoulders, hold the cups in my palms, and then, in a panic, shove it away again. And one time, as my baby sister napped on my parents' bed, I went into the restroom and stretched one of my dirty shoelaces and held it like a garrote against my neck.

I do not know the logic of these actions. If they foreshadow some buried desire or demise, if it was just a curiosity of texture and that uneasy thrill of feeling something that shouldn't be wrapped around me, or if the significance is obvious and plain but imperceptible to me. The meaning may be only that my mind often idles over these moments looking for meaning.

Now, driving down the boulevard and the crisscross of roads, trying to verify the location of buildings and the fidelity of my memory, I stop in front of the apartment where we lived back then. I expect to find the building razed and converted into a driveway of townhomes. But they collapsed only the carport, hung air-conditioning units, and patched the windows with plywood. Those details aside, 2331½ Burkett Rd—in a town that took a wrecking ball to Legion Stadium and plasters over hundred-year-old clapboards—has perfectly preserved, down to the hue of the stucco, the duplex where I tried on my mother's bra.

In the discourse of El Monte, a common rhetorical move (one I have used many times and have watched others also turn to) is to invoke the crime writer James Ellroy's bleak description of the city—a smoggy void with evil-looking pachucos hosing down cars on the lawns—and then counter it with resident tenderness to disprove Ellroy's characterization of our hometown. We use stories of what we assume to be variations on universal rites: the initial discovery of the Hostess Bakery thrift shop on Ramona, the first kiss behind a barrier we would come to learn is called a backstop, the psychobilly shows in friends' patios. Anecdotes of immigrant frugality: newsprint trimmed into toilet paper squares, soles discreetly taped and glued back into shoe form, sad TV sets rescued from curbsides. The yield of the resourcefulness: two-hour airplane flights replaced with days on a rattling Tres Estrellas bus, down payments stowed in Folgers cans, a fleet of used pickup trucks for a rising lawn-care empire. The contrite retelling of moral blunders illustrating a new self-awareness and Americanness: the Jehovah's Witnesses (though they were more likely to have been Mormon missionaries) your grandmother shooed away while holding up her rosary, the holes in the yard used to bleed oil changes into, the Peruvian *morenito* we cornered at recess to touch the yarn on his head.

As I sit in the car, a tourist to my own childhood, a haze of soot and exhaust tints the evening, and on a patch of dirt a dusty car pins a dry tuft of grass to the ground. Ellroy's El Monte enters my thoughts, and I'm traitor to my own town. If a rocket sails above—the symbol of the city's brighter future—the particulates in the air obscure its flight.

But this day will return. It will cycle back and meet its past. Even in reading this far you have triggered the day yet again—and maybe in that hatch mark of time the El Monte skies are clear, painted in the mythical azure of the city seal, and the shuttle returns to gently hover above.

Epilogue

Suburban Cosmopolitanism in the San Gabriel Valley

WENDY CHENG

FIG. 32 Ernesto Chaves, Carribean Fragoza completing "ay corazon." (Courtesy of South El Monte Arts Posse and Ernesto Chaves.)

In July 2012, the artist Carribean Fragoza wove braided white plastic bags into the green tarp and chain-link fence flanking a vacant lot near an entrance to the 60 Freeway in California's San Gabriel Valley (SGV). The SGV begins about ten miles east of downtown Los Angeles and continues east all the way to Pomona. It is bordered by the massive San Gabriel Mountains in the north and the northeastern edges of Orange County in the south. Approximately two million residents of Los Angeles County make their homes there. When Fragoza was done, the plastic bags spelled out in cursive "ay corazon" (translated roughly, "oh my heart"). Fragoza's installation was part of a multisite public art project called Activate Vacant, implemented by the arts collective South El Monte Arts Posse (SEMAP) in the working-class municipality of South El Monte, the majority of whose population is Latino/a/x and Asian.[1]

According to Fragoza, who is also a codirector of SEMAP, "The 'ay corazon' audience is all the commuters that leave their homes and families every morning and return to them every evening. 'Ay corazon' is meant to evoke the loved one and whatever emotion the two words arouse in them." It could be an exasperated "regaño or scolding" or "evoke the name of someone's long lost love. . . . Ay corazon . . . might be whispered to oneself in delicious memory or yearning anticipation. . . . In effect, ay corazon [*sic*] is an emotional holograph for the community."[2] A native of South El Monte, Fragoza reappropriated used plastic bags from her mother's kitchen cupboard to make the message.[3] At once high art and suburban, political, sentimental, and *rasquache* in its aesthetics and intentions, Fragoza's contribution to the Activate Vacant project exemplified the "east of east" spirit of SEMAP, and of the area more broadly.

The "east" that SEMAP uses to identify itself as "east" of is East Los Angeles (LA), long the symbolic and political core of Chicano/a/x LA. Just as the poet, essayist, and playwright Cherríe Moraga wrote of being adjacent to, but apart from, the Chicano movement "spilling out of barrio high schools and onto police-barricaded streets" in East LA "just ten minutes from my tree-lined working-class neighborhood in San Gabriel"[4] (several miles northwest of South El Monte), SEMAP locates itself as adjacent to, but distinct from, the urban core sensibilities of East LA. "East of east" is "everything that exists outside the reach of the city of Los Angeles," says Fragoza.[5]

The two "easts" in SEMAP's self-description resonate figuratively with Asian and Asian American histories in both East LA and the San Gabriel Valley. In the early to mid-twentieth century, East LA became home to a diverse array of working- and middle-class whites and people of color, many of them from immigrant backgrounds.[6] Similarly, the valley's population in the early twenty-first century was Latino/a/x, Asian American, heavily immigrant, and working and middle class. And the valley currently constitutes the largest majority Latino/a/x and Asian American region in the country.[7]

FIG. 33 Phung Huynh, "In the Meadow." El Monte Station. (Courtesy of Los Angeles County Metropolitan Transportation Authority.)

Since the 1990s, the San Gabriel Valley has become best known for being the first "suburban Chinatown" and "ethnoburb."[8] The landscapes of many SGV cities have certainly been transformed by ethnic Chinese investment and settlement from both sides of the Pacific.[9] However, these familiar facts can serve to obscure the reality that the SGV is a large and vibrantly multiethnic and multiracial area with a complex and layered past.[10] In the western cities of the valley, over half of the population is Asian and almost one-third is Latino/a/x, making the area over 90 percent Asian and Latino/a/x. In contrast, many of the eastern municipalities developed out of racially hierarchical agricultural and industrial economies and have rich Mexican and multiracial working-class histories. Traveling eastward along the southern portion of the valley, one finds majority Latino/a/x municipalities such as South El Monte, El Monte, and La Puente, with Asians—including larger numbers of Vietnamese and other Southeast Asians—constituting the second largest group.[11] Continuing east, the Asian population again increases in SGV cities like Rowland Heights and Hacienda Heights.[12]

In the past few decades, heated struggles over urban development, civic landscapes, and identity in the western portion of the valley have challenged the status quo and made it clear that the region's identity and who gets to have a say in that is up for grabs.[13] In this long moment of rapid demographic change, voices from different strata of the social order have risen up and refuse to be forgotten, whether they are those of whites, Mexican Americans, or Asian Americans who came to the area in pursuit of homeownership after World War II; descendants of Mexican Californio families; or Gabrielinos whose roots go back hundreds of years. Other voices have emerged to assert their presence and histories in the region, too, in dual processes of invention and recovery. In particular, away from city halls and formal politics, distinctive identities tied to place have begun to emerge.[14] Cultural producers such as SEMAP have begun to express their own visions of the area. In the emerging literary, cultural, and artistic practice of the region, multiracial, nonwhite, and suburban forms of cosmopolitanism—what we might think of as an "east of east" cosmopolitanism—are emerging that may alter the racial and class dimensions of what it means to be American.

Cosmopolitanism (the idea of being a citizen of the entire world) is an old ideal.[15] In seeking to apply cosmopolitanism anew to the world we live in today, the philosopher and cultural theorist Kwame Anthony Appiah emphasizes two threads: first, the idea that we have obligations to others "that stretch beyond those to whom we are related by the ties of kith and kind, or even . . . shared citizenship"; and second, an interest in and respect for difference: "People are different . . . and there is much to learn from our differences. . . . Because there are so many human possibilities worth exploring, we neither expect nor desire that every person or every society should converge on a single model of life."[16] Appiah writes that cosmopolitans are found among both the "best off" and the "worst off" in society, noting that in fact, "ignorance about the ways of others is largely a privilege of the powerful."[17]

Typically, U.S. suburbs are not associated with cosmopolitanism. Developed and perpetuated with exclusionary principles, they have served as spatial expressions of inequality and class and racial homogeneity since the mid-twentieth century, being typically middle-class and wealthy, white, flush with resources, and perceived as lacking in culture. Central city ghettoes, barrios, and Chinatowns, in contrast, have constituted inverse mirrors of suburbs: poor; brown, yellow, and black; starved of resources; and stereotyped as culturally excessive.

Most scholarship on race, class, and culture has focused on these readily apparent contrasts in urban centers. However, demographic transformation in the United States as well as the "browning" of U.S. suburbs demand more attention to majority-nonwhite, multiracial, suburban metropolitan areas.[18] As the historian Scott Kurashige has pointed out, in "a new polyethnic majority," racial integration depends less on the "spatial distribution" of people of color in relation to whites and more on the relationships among multiple ethnic and racial communities.[19]

In the SGV, many cultural producers, scholars, and activists are articulating a suburban, cosmopolitan ethos that will be increasingly relevant to broader swaths of the United States and has the potential to challenge long-held associations of whiteness, middle-class status, and suburban as normative ideals. In the past twenty years, literary and cultural productions emerging from the SGV have included a number of works of literary fiction and short stories, a mystery novel about Asian American parachute kids, several comedic rap songs, and a streetwear brand.[20] In 2014, a play about Toypurina, the Gabrielino woman who led a failed revolt against the Spanish at the San Gabriel Mission, was mounted at the Mission Playhouse, and more recently the feature film *Varsity Punks* was set in El Monte.[21] And this is not even to mention the vibrant, ever-evolving, and internationally known food culture that has spawned a Chinese-language-only blog and twitter feed that has tens of thousands more followers than LA's beloved, Pulitzer Prize–winning food critic, the late Jonathan Gold (who lived in the SGV).[22] These developments are notable because they signify the coming of age of a multiracial, majority-nonwhite, place-specific culture on its own terms. The SGV is a region apart from central LA, and large portions of the valley have been able to retain their class heterogeneity and multiracial, majority-nonwhite populations for multiple generations, without suffering the degree of gentrification and displacement to which central city neighborhoods are constantly vulnerable.

The cities of El Monte and South El Monte have emerged as key nodes in the burgeoning SGV arts and culture scene. Like the members of SEMAP, the writer Michael Jaime-Becerra—who grew up in El Monte and still lives there—balances multiple sensibilities at once. His outlook is deeply local and connected to a specific place, but he also has an expansive openness to the complexities of the SGV in the world. His world is El Monte, but it isn't only El Monte. In his two books set in and around the city—*Every Night Is Ladies' Night* and *This Time Tomorrow*—Jaime-Becerra renders the mundane landscapes of the SGV with tremendous love, name-checking places and streets without commentary throughout his narratives, as though to assert to readers that they should know these places (for example, "Georgie decides to go down Valley Boulevard instead of taking Garvey into El Monte").[23] While his characters are primarily working-class Mexican immigrants and Mexican Americans—truck drivers, mechanics, forklift operators, and fast-food workers—they are always also something else, such as Goth teens, former prisoners, brothers, sisters, uncles, lovers, and dreamers.

While earlier generations of Chicano/a/x writers were writing with justifiable urgency about "field labor, immigration, [and] our parents' struggles to feed the family,"[24] growing up in El Monte as the son of a union meat cutter and an elementary school clerk, Jaime-Becerra realized that he could "hang with low riders and skateboarders, groove to Juan Gabriel and Siouxsie and the Banshees."[25] Like so many Latino/a/xs and Asian Americans in the SGV, he was also able to carve out an ethnic identity distanced from dominant ideas about race: "Everybody around me, they were either Mexican or Mexican American or Vietnamese," he has said. "I didn't really identify in terms of race in LA."[26]

There is freedom in the ambiguity that comes with loosened cultural boundaries, when old stereotypes are no longer used to keep people in place, and when people are comfortable crossing cultural lines to find their place in a community—the place where they feel they belong, not where they are told that they do. This is the "east of east" ideal, in which working- and lower-middle-class people of color are able to simply be (and be seen by the wider community) in their full and complex personhood.[27] This is what Jaime-Becerra describes as his coming-of-age experience and is apparent in the world he creates for his readers.

This is true in the work of the El Monte writer Salvador Plascencia, too, although in entirely different ways. Plascencia set his 2005 novel, *The People of Paper*, in his hometown. His "meta-fiction" was intended "partly as a parody of traditional immigration narratives"—or, as one reviewer put it, is "part memoir, part lies."[28] This is how Plascencia introduces the locale: "The town was called El Monte, after the hills it did not have."[29] A page later, he elaborates: "El Monte was one thousand four hundred forty-eight miles north of Las Tortugas and an even fifteen hundred miles from the city of Guadalajara, and while there were no cockfights or wrestling arenas, the curanderos' botanica shops, the menudo stands, and the bell towers of the Catholic churches had also pushed north, settling among the flower and sprinkler systems."[30]

The transnational migrants have settled among the suburban "flower and sprinkler systems," but they made the landscape their own. Throughout the book—which also playfully busts genre conventions with scribbled-out words, blocked text, blank pages, and graffiti—an assortment of vivid characters (including migrant lettuce pickers and gang members) battle against the godlike Saturn, who is gradually revealed to be the author, Salvador Plascencia. Saturn/Plascencia loses control of his characters and the narrative because he is languishing over a breakup with his girlfriend, who has left him for a white guy. Plascencia's El Monte is both grounded and surreal, his portrayal of its denizens heartfelt and absurd. "In a way," Plascencia has said, both he and Jaime-Becerra "are trying to talk about an El Monte that's not the news copter, watching a cop kick a gangster in the head"[31]—that is, a place grounded in its true range of subjectivities, experiences, and imaginative possibilities, not constrained by externally imposed stereotypes and power hierarchies.

> Let me tell you about a place out east
> Just fifteen minutes from the LA streets
> Hollywood doesn't even know we exist
> Like it's a mystical land, filled with immigrants
> —Fung Brothers, "626"[32]

In 2013, a small, local, streetwear company based in Monterey Park that called its brand SGV produced a T-shirt with a design that blended the elements of the flags of the People's Republic of China, Mexico, and the United States. The company's website said: "The SGV is a region of America where a lot of Chinese and Mexicans have learned to live together, most of the time in harmony. Welcome to Chimexica."[33] Here was a simple, pop culture expression of cosmopolitanism: to coexist with mutual respect for difference, without denial or exclusion. Other SGV designs featured repurposed logos for Sriracha, a well-known hot sauce that was created in Rosemead by a Chinese-Vietnamese immigrant and Tres Flores, a hair cream popular with working-class Chicano/a/x youth, as well as the woven sandals popular with older Asian immigrant men. Another T-shirt featured curse words in Chinese, Vietnamese, Spanish, and Tagalog. As Paul Chan—the designer as well as the company's founder, and a child of immigrants from Hong Kong, who moved to Alhambra as a young child in the 1980s—put it: "I . . . learned quickly that in the SGV you play your position and don't over step your boundaries. I've always had a huge appreciation for that. The way those unwritten rules work. . . . It was part of survival to know about all the different cultures so I don't end up disrespecting people and getting my ass kicked."[34]

In his essays in *Postcolonial Melancholia*, the historian Paul Gilroy wondered how everyday cosmopolitanism "from below," such as what Chan describes, could be magnified and given greater purpose.[35] At its best, this is an explicitly antiracist cosmopolitanism that does not gloss over differences between cultures or violent histories to create a false universalism, but instead reckons with formative histories and still-present realities of racism and colonialism.[36] This is a cosmopolitanism that does not look to states or nations for the realization of its hopes but "glories in the ordinary virtues and ironies—listening, looking, discretion, friendship—that can be cultivated when mundane encounters with difference become rewarding."[37] It is a "radical openness,"[38] a "planetary consciousness"[39] made even more real and important by its awareness of the harms done by racism and inequality. Ideally, it does not stop at awareness but rejects xenophobia and violence and "culminates in a new way of being at home in the world through an active hostility toward national solidarity, national culture, and their privileging over other, more open affiliations."[40]

In the love poem "It's Not New York," Moraga, a child of the SGV, wrote:

> This is joy.
> It has the name and look of her,
> her black eyes, my childhood eyes staring back at me
> and nothing in our mutual LA sub-urban pasts prepared us
> for this moment.[41]

The familiar and familial are made new in this moment of connection.[42] Moraga's poem affirms the importance of affinity and chosen commonality, yet there's something in those "mutual LA sub-urban pasts" that already connects the two lovers—a way of thinking, a framework of experience that moves away from those overdetermined centers, that moves "east of east" to a moment of utopian promise.

Indeed, the "it" Moraga refers to is not New York City. It is not Queens or the Bronx or Manhattan, the paradigmatic models of American urbanism, but it is as diverse as those boroughs, and it is spread over a much larger physical area—one that encompasses El Monte and South El Monte, the SGV, and Greater LA and all its peripheries. In broader networks of trade, work, kinship, culture, and migration, it is linked with Mexico, China, Vietnam, Thailand, and many other places. It is centrifugal and centripetal, a crossroads and a destination, a central part of the great drama of a multiethnic, metropolitan, urban-suburban life that continues to transform cities across the United States in the twenty-first century. The SGV is not only where many of these forces converge but where many of them began—whether labor radicalism, civil rights, or punk rock. And the rest of its stories have yet to be told.

Notes

A version of this chapter was previously published as "East of East: The Global Cosmopolitans of Suburban LA," *Boom: A Journal of California* 5, no. 1 (Spring 2015): 20–28.

1 As of 2010, South El Monte's population of 20,116 was 85 percent Latino/a/x (of which 78 percent was Mexican), 11 percent Asian (of which 55 percent was Chinese and 40 percent was Vietnamese), and 4 percent non-Hispanic white. U.S. Census Bureau, 2010 Census Summary File 1, https://factfinder.census.gov/faces/nav/jsf/pages/index.xhtml, accessed July 29, 2019.

2 Carribean Fragoza, "ay corazon," South El Monte Arts Posse, July 14, 2012, http://semartsposse.wordpress.com/2012/07/14/ay-corazon/.

3 Ibid.

4 Cherríe Moraga, *The Last Generation: Prose and Poetry* (Boston: South End Press, 1993), 146.

5 Carribean Fragoza and Romeo Guzmán, interview by author, October 12, 2014.

6 See George J. Sánchez, "'What's Good for Boyle Heights Is Good for the Jews': Creating Multiracialism on the Eastside during the 1950s," *American Quarterly* 56, no. 3 (2004): 633–662.

7 The population was approximately 45 percent Latino/a/x and 28 percent Asian as of 2010. See Kevin Smith, "Economic Snapshot: San Gabriel Valley Working to Regain Jobs," *San Gabriel Valley Tribune*, April 24, 2012.

8 Timothy Fong, *The First Suburban Chinatown: The Remaking of Monterey Park, California* (Philadelphia: Temple University Press, 1994); Wei Li, *Ethnoburb: The New Ethnic Community in Urban America* (Honolulu: University of Hawai'i Press, 2009).

9 See Min Zhou, Yen-Fen Tseng, and Rebecca Kim, "Rethinking Residential Assimilation: The Case of a Chinese Ethnoburb in the San Gabriel Valley, California," *Amerasia Journal* 34, no. 3 (January 2008): 53–83.

10 This past dates back hundreds of years to indigenous Gabrielino/Tongva settlement in the area and continues through Spanish colonization, the Mexican period, and U.S. conquest—each of which had its own racialized regimes of land dispossession and labor exploitation. After World War II, whites and then an increasing number of Mexican Americans and Asian Americans came to the western portion of the valley from central and East LA in pursuit of homeownership opportunities. This part of the valley is home to Monterey Park, which is directly adjacent to East LA and became famous in the 1980s and 1990s as the "first suburban Chinatown." See Wendy Cheng, "A Brief History (and Geography) of the San Gabriel Valley," KCET, August 4, 2014; http://www.kcet.org/socal/departures/columns/east-of-east/a-brief-history-and-geography-of-the-san-gabriel-valley.html.

11 Specifically, El Monte is 69 percent Latino/a/x (of which 88 percent is Mexican) and 25 percent Asian (of which 54 percent is Chinese and 30 percent Vietnamese). See U.S. Census Bureau, 2010 Census Summary File 1.

12 Rowland Heights is approximately 60 percent Asian and 27 percent Latino/a/x, while Hacienda Heights is 39 percent Asian and 46 percent Latino/a/x (ibid).

13 Examples of such struggles include slow growth and English-only initiatives, the favoring of "mainstream" businesses as opposed to ethnic Chinese businesses in development, and more recently a fight to prevent alterations to the city of San Gabriel's mission-based logo and city motto. See Leland Saito, *Race and Politics: Asian Americans, Latinos, and Whites in a Los Angeles Suburb* (Urbana: University of Illinois Press, 1998); Wendy Cheng, *The Changs Next Door to the Diazes: Remapping Race in Suburban California* (Minneapolis: University of Minnesota Press, 2013); Adolfo Flores, "Gabrielinos Balk at San Gabriel's Plan to Change City's Motto," *Pasadena Star-News*, September 8, 2010.

14 In my research on the western SGV in the late 2000s, I found that many Asian American and Latino/a/x residents of the area felt this deeply in their everyday lives. They regularly expressed feelings of comfort and familiarity across nonwhite racial and ethnic groups, and they often contrasted these feelings of commonality with dominant social norms associated with whiteness. See Cheng, *The Changs Next Door to the Diazes*.

15 Kwame Anthony Appiah, *Cosmopolitanism: Ethics in a World of Strangers* (New York: W. W. Norton, 2006).

16 Ibid., xv.

17 Ibid., xvii–xix.

18 See William H. Frey, "Melting Pot Cities and Suburbs: Racial and Ethnic Change in Metro America in the 2000s," Brookings Institution, May 2011, https://www.brookings.edu/wp-content/uploads/2016/06/0504_census_ethnicity_frey.pdf.

19 Scott Kurashige, "The Many Facets of Brown: Integration in a Multiracial Society," *Journal of American History* 91, no. 1 (2004): 56–68.

20 The literature includes Alex Espinoza, *Still Water Saints* (New York: Random House, 2007); Michael Jaime-Becerra, *Every Night Is Ladies' Night* (New York: Rayo, 2004) and *This Time Tomorrow* (New York: Thomas Dunne Books, 2010); Salvador Plascencia, *The People of Paper* (Orlando, FL: Harcourt, 2006); Denise Hamilton, *The Jasmine Trade* (New York: Scribner, 2001). Also see Daniela Gerson, "SGV for Life?," *Alhambra Source*, November 30, 2011, https://www.alhambrasource.org/story/sgv-for-life; Fung Brothers, home page, accessed October 15, 2014, http://fungbrothers.com.

21 San Gabriel Mission Playhouse, *Toypurina: A Story of Love, Determination and Loss*. Accessed June 22, 2019. http://www.toypurina.org; "Varsity Punks," website, accessed October 15, 2014, http://varsitypunks.com/.

22 "San Gabriel's Evolving Food Scene," KCRW, June 1, 2014, http://blogs.kcrw.com/goodfood/2014/06/san-gabriel-valleys-evolving-food-scene.

23 Jaime-Becerra, *Every Night Is Ladies Night*, 122. See also Jaime-Becerra, *This Time Tomorrow*.

24 Vickie Vertiz, "El Monte Forever: A Brief History of Michael Jaime-Becerra," December 16, 2014, http://tropicsofmeta.wordpress.com/2013/12/16/el-monte-forever-a-brief-history-of-michael-jaime-becerra/.

25 Reed Johnson, "Writers Salvador Plascencia and Michael Jaime-Becerra Share a City and Common Inspiration: El Monte," *Los Angeles Times*, April 25, 2010, http://articles.latimes.com/2010/apr/25/entertainment/la-ca-el-monte-20100425.

26 Quoted in ibid.

27 On complex personhood, see Avery Gordon, *Ghostly Matters: Haunting and the Sociological Imagination* (Minneapolis: University of Minnesota Press, 1997).

28 Johnson, "Writers Salvador Plascencia and Michael Jaime-Becerra Share a City and Common Inspiration."

29 Plascencia, *The People of Paper*, 33.

30 Ibid., 34.

31 Quoted in Johnson, "Writers Salvador Plascencia and Michael Jaime-Becerra Share a City and Common Inspiration."

32 Fung Brothers, "626," Music video, February 19, 2012, http://youtu.be/3n3HQ9ugeog.

33 SGV brand website, http://www.sgvforlife.com; accessed July 2012 (site discontinued).

34 Quoted in Gerson, "SGV for Life?"

35 Paul Gilroy, *Postcolonial Melancholia* (New York: Columbia University Press, 2005), 67.

36 Ibid. Also see Michelle A. McKinley, "Conviviality, Cosmopolitan Citizenship, and Hospitality," *Harvard Unbound* 5: no. 1 (March 2009): 55–87.

37 Gilroy, *Postcolonial Melancholia*, 67.

38 Ibid., xv.
39 Ibid., 75.
40 Ibid., 68.
41 Moraga, *The Last Generation*, 105.
42 On queer suburban imaginaries, see Karen Tongson, *Relocations: Queer Suburban Imaginaries* (New York: New York University Press, 2011).

Acknowledgments

This book is the product of years of labor, transdisciplinary collaborations, institutional support and grants, and, most importantly, a deep love and commitment to two working-class cities in the San Gabriel Valley. Its arrival was made possible by a community of scholars, artists, writers, community members, organizations, and family.

Our public history project "East of East: Mapping Community Narratives in El Monte and South El Monte" emerged as a collaboration between La Casa de El Hijo del Ahuizote in Mexico City and the South El Monte Arts Posse (SEMAP). Our dear friends Diego Flores Magón and Froylán Enciso took weeks away from their homes and work to launch "East of East" and help us imagine how to build an archive. Together we worked, lived, cooked, and organized a series of events. Sara Quezada has been a constant source of inspiration, and together we held a conference at South El Monte High School in 2013. We are beyond fortunate to have had Jennifer Renteria on this journey with us from the beginning.

Since our first series of events, we have collaborated with a number of institutions and organizations. Working with David Diaz, formerly of Day One, and Marco Vera of Mexicali Rose, we explored the history of 1960s El Monte and South El Monte and used the archive and the past to physically alter the landscape. Fernando Corona and Alonso Delgadillo's mural is waiting for you on Central Avenue, just across from New Temple Park.

Working with Columbia University's History Department and Michael S. Weller of Mountain View High School, we brought historians, high school educators, and community members together to begin building a curriculum based on the "East of East" archive.

La Historia's effort to preserve the history of the barrios is a constant source of pride. Together we conducted oral histories, scanned photographs, and hosted a community discussion about the barrios. While Doña Olga Gutiérez is no longer with us, we know she would have been proud to see this book come to fruition.

Bridgetown in La Puente hosted a punk-flier digitizing event, which helped us collect dozens of the fliers from Greater El Monte and the San Gabriel Valley.

Columbia's Center for Oral History and the University of California, Los Angeles (UCLA) loaned us audio recorders to conduct oral histories on numerous occasions. We thank Mary Marshall Clark and Virginia Espino for their early support and their exemplary work as oral historians.

Rio Hondo Community College, the Jeff Seymour Family Center, the Cities of South El Monte and El Monte, and the El Monte Library on Tyler Avenue housed our events. We thank them for allowing us to use their space. The City of South El Monte provided us with access to city documents, which resulted in the finding of invaluable and forgotten archival material like a 16mm film reel. This book is that much better for it.

All our contributors took time to conduct primary and secondary research. Many of them also conducted oral histories, scanned documents for our archive, and presented their research in El Monte and South El Monte. Their efforts to build an archive and history of South El Monte and El Monte were aided by a number of individuals. Laura Gutierrez, Janett Barragan Miranda, Efrain Oquendo, Kevan Antonio Aguilar, Apolonio Morales, and Christopher Luke Trevilla conducted oral histories or scanned documents.

Throughout this process we conducted dozens of interviews and scanned hundreds of photographs, fliers, newspaper clippings, and city documents. We are forever grateful to everyone who shared their stories and personal archives with us. This book is as much theirs as it is ours.

KCET helped us amplify our work, and we are grateful for our collaboration. A big thanks goes to Alvaro Parra, Rubi Fregoso, Justin Cram, Juan Devis, and the rest of the KCET team.

Everyone who has written for and read Tropics of Meta (ToM) has helped build a community of scholars dedicated to writing for a popular audience. This book is a product of that labor and beautifully captures the ToM ethos: historiography for the masses.

SEMAP is an arts organization, and artists played an important role in shaping our approach to the archive and scholarship. J.T. Roane and Huewayne Watson's artists' residency with SEMAP in the summer of 2012 provided a blueprint for La Casa's time in South El Monte and El Monte. Álvaro Márquez and Daniel González made original art. Lester Lawenko, Ernesto Chavez, Michael Beserra, Jason Gutierrez, and Christopher Anthony Velasco photographed El Monte and South El Monte, and some of their photographs are in this book. A big thanks goes to Henry Pacheco for documenting some of our events.

Various institutions and curators invited Carribean Fragoza to make art about El Monte and South El Monte, enabling us to further explore the intersections of fiction, history, and place. We thank Vincent Ramos, Robert Miller, Jen Hofer and Woodbury University's Nan Rae Gallery, the Los Angeles County Museum of Art's Charles White Gallery, the UCLA Hammer Museum, and the SUR:biennial at Rio Hondo College.

We received funding from the Los Angeles City Department of Cultural Affairs, National Performance Network, the History in Action program at Columbia University's History Department, and the American Library Association to work on "East of East." The History Department and the College of Social Science at California State University (CSU), Fresno, provided funds to offset expenses associated with the production of this book. We thank them all.

Matt Garcia's scholarship and very early public history work is a source of inspiration. We thank him for his support and are honored that this book is part of the Latinidad series. Our acquisitions editor, Nicole Solano, and the anonymous reviewers provided valuable feedback.

We are grateful for all the historians, poets, and novelists who have written about El Monte, South El Monte, and the San Gabriel Valley. It is our hope that like their work, this book will pave the way for future scholars and artists.

This book is also dedicated to Roberto "Bobby" Salcedo, a tireless champion of our communities who sparked new generations of advocates in South El Monte and El Monte. We will always honor his memory in our work.

We like to think that we are building community one party at a time, and thus we thank everyone who has provided music to dance to. Alejandro Rosas (aka DJ Horchata) is a true homie and threw a backyard party for the launch of our chapbook *Burn the Wagon*. We also thank Bastidas and the Hashishans for their music and playing at our events, Space Primo for DJing on numerous occasions, and the Zumba ladies for always dancing and always being fierce. We look forward to more parties, in the back or front yard. Thanks to Progress Brewery for the refreshments and support.

SEMAP received a lot of love inside and outside of El Monte and South El Monte, and we are especially thankful to everyone who has attended our events, invited us to speak, or provided other forms of support. We thank Sesshu Foster, Dolores Bravo, Rubén Martínez, Devra Weber, Elias Serna, Vickie Vertiz, Kenji Liu, Aimee Suzara, Maryam Hosseinzadeh, Janet Sarbanes, Ben Ehrenreich, Pilar Tompkins Rivas, Adrian Rivas, Saul Sarabia, Israel Pastrana, Josh Kun, Hector Tobar, Laura Vena, Phung Huynh, Angela Anderson Guerrero, Gloria Arellanes, Art Laboe, Joanna Morones, Frank Molina, and the crew at *Boom* (particularly Jason Sexton).

We would also like to thank the community of scholars in the history departments at Georgia State University and at CSU Fresno, a community that includes many friends and allies who are committed to groundbreaking work in digital humanities and public history and who have supported this project with enthusiasm. Our homies from Columbia—such as Betsy Blackmar, Ansley Erickson, Nara Milanich, Pablo Piccato, Mae Ngai, Alex Gil, Eric Frith, Daniel Morales, and Nick Juravich—have been a constant source of much appreciated encouragement, too.

East of East has also been a family affair. Carribean and Romeo welcomed their daughter Aura a few days before SEMAP's first event, a photo exhibit on Tyler Avenue titled "How's the Water?" Years later, their second daughter, Camila, arrived as Daniel González delivered the cover art for this completed book. The Guzmán and Fragoza families are part of SEMAP and have provided support in numerous ways: Ceci Fragoza cared for Aura while we jumped over fences, took over vacant lots, and organized public events; Pati Guzmán cooked on several occasions and is always excited to talk culture and politics; and Ray Guzmán has yet to miss a SEMAP event. Saira Mazhar and Joel Suarez have been generous and indefatigable interlocutors through all the years of this project's evolution. Francisca Guzmán has supported us in a number of ways, including lending us and our collaborators her house. We also thank Aimee Guzmán for her design and ideas; Melissa, Dante, and Jamie for their enthusiasm; and Nicolás and Jaime for instilling in us a desire to explore, always from below.

Selected Bibliography

Adams, James Truslow. *The Epic of America*. Boston: Little, Brown, 1931.

Alamillo, José. *Making Lemonade out of Lemons: Mexican American Labor and Leisure in a California Town, 1880–1960*. Urbana: University of Illinois Press, 2006.

Allende, Isabel. *Zorro*. London: Harper Collins, 2005.

Anzaldúa, Gloria. *Borderlands/La Frontera: The New Mestiza*. San Francisco: Aunt Lute Books, 1987.

Appiah, Kwame Anthony. *Cosmopolitanism: Ethics in a World of Strangers*. New York: W. W. Norton, 2006.

Aron, Stephen. "Convergence, California, and the Newest Western History." *California History* 86, (2009): 4–13 and 79–81.

Avila, Eric. *The Folklore of the Freeway: Race and Revolt in the Modernist City*. Minneapolis: University of Minnesota Press, 2014.

———. *Popular Culture in the Age of White Flight: Fear and Fantasy in Suburban Los Angeles*. Los Angeles: University of California Press, 2004.

———. "Popular Culture in the Age of White Flight: Film Noir, Disneyland, and the Cold War (Sub)Urban Imaginary." *Journal of Urban History* 31, no. 3 (2004): 3–22.

Azuma, Eiichiro. *Between Two Empires: Race, History, and Transnationalism in Japanese America*. Oxford: Oxford University Press, 2005.

Bailey, Marlon M. *Butch Queens Up in Pumps: Gender, Performance, and Ballroom Culture in Detroit*. Ann Arbor: University of Michigan Press, 2013.

Balducci, Anthony. *The Funny Parts: A History of Film Comedy Routines and Gags*. Jefferson, NC: McFarland, 2012.

Bancroft, Hubert Howe. *The Works of Hubert Howe Bancroft*. Vol. 25, *History of Nevada, Colorado, and Wyoming, 1540–1888*. San Francisco: History Company, 1890.

Banham, Reyner. "Ecology IV: Autopia" in *Los Angeles: The Architecture of Four Ecologies*. Los Angeles: University of California Press: 2009, 195–204.

Barraclough, Laura R. *Making the San Fernando Valley: Rural Landscapes, Urban Development, and White Privilege*. Athens: University of Georgia Press, 2011.

Barrows, Henry D. "Pio Pico: A Biographical and Character Sketch of the Last Mexican Governor of Alta California." *Annual Publication of the Historical Society of Southern California, Los Angeles* 3, no. 2 (1894): 55.

Barton, Jorane King. *El Monte: Images of America*. Charleston, SC: Arcadia, 2006.
Beebe, Rose Marie, and Robert M. Senkewicz, eds. *Lands of Promise and Despair: Chronicles of Early California 1535–1846*. Norman: University of Oklahoma Press, 2015.
Bell, Horace. *On the Old West Coast: Being the Further Reminiscences of a Ranger-Major Horace Bell*. New York: Grosset and Dunlap, 1930.
———. *Reminiscences of a Ranger: Early Times in Southern California*. Norman: University of Oklahoma Press, 1999.
Bernal, Dolores Delgado. "Chicana School Resistance and Grassroots Leadership: Providing an Alternative History of the 1968 East Los Angeles Blowouts." PhD diss., University of California, Los Angeles, 1997.
Blackwell, Maylei. *¡Chicana Power! Contested Histories of Feminism in the Chicano Movement*. Austin: University of Texas Press, 2011.
Boulevard Nights. Michael Pressman. Los Angeles: Warner Brothers, 1979.
Brodsly, David. *L.A. Freeway: An Appreciative Essay*. Berkeley: University of California Press, 1981.
Brooks, Charlotte. *Alien Neighbors, Foreign Friends: Asian Americans, Housing and the Transformation of Urban California*. Chicago: University of Chicago Press, 2009.
Brown, Dona. *Back to the Land: The Enduring Dream of Self-Sufficiency in Modern America*. Madison: University of Wisconsin Press, 2011.
Carmeli, Yoram S. "Lion on Display: Culture, Nature, and Totality in a Circus Performance." *Poetics Today* 24, no. 1 (2003): 65–90.
Carriker, Robert. *Urban Farming in the West: A New Deal Experiment in Subsistence Homesteads*. Tucson: University of Arizona Press, 2010.
Cartier, Marie. *Baby, You Are My Religion: Women, Gay Bars, and Theology before Stonewall*. Durham, UK: Acumen, 2013.
Castillo-Muñoz, Verónica. *The Other California: Land, Identity, and Politics on the Mexican Borderlands*. Berkeley: University of California Press, 2016.
Chavez, Ernesto. *"¡Mi Raza Primero!" (My People First!): Nationalism, Identity, and Insurgency in the Chicano Movement in Los Angeles, 1966–1978*. Berkeley: University of California Press, 2002.
Cheng, Wendy. *The Changs Next Door to the Diazes: Remapping Race in Suburban California*. Minneapolis: University of Minnesota Press, 2013.
———. "The Changs Next Door to the Diazes: Suburban Racial Formation in Los Angeles's San Gabriel Valley." *Journal of Urban History* 39 (November 2012): 15–35.
Church, John. *Pasadena Cowboy: Growing Up in Southern California and Montana, 1925 to 1947*. Novato, CA: Conover-Patterson, 1996.
Clarke, John Smith. *Circus Parade*. New York: C. Scribner's Sons, 1936.
Cohen, Deborah. *Braceros: Migrant Citizens and Transnational Subjects in the Postwar United States and Mexico*. Chapel Hill: University of North Carolina Press, 2011.
Cohn, Raymond L. *Mass Migration under Sail: European Immigration to the Antebellum United States*. New York: Cambridge University Press, 2009.
Cole, Martin. "Pío Pico Mansion: Fact, Fiction, and Supposition," in *Pío Pico Miscellany*. Ed. Martin Cole. Whittier, CA: Governor Pico Mansion Society, 1978, 15–38.
Connolly, N.D.B. *A World More Concrete: Real Estate and the Remaking of Jim Crow South Florida*. Chicago: University of Chicago Press, 2014.
Correa, Jennifer G. "The Targeting of the East Los Angeles Brown Berets by a Racial

Patriarchal Capitalist State: Merging Intersectionality and Social Movement Research." *Critical Sociology* 37, no. 1 (2010): 83–10.

Critchlow, Keith, and Walter Parkes, dirs. *The California Reich*. Los Angeles: Intercontinental Releasing Corporation, 1975.

Cross, Gary. "Crowds and Leisure: Thinking Comparatively across the 20th Century." *Journal of Social History* 39, no. 3 (2006): 631–650.

Culver, Lawrence. "America's Playground: Recreation and Race," in *A Companion to Los Angeles*. Eds. Lawrence Deverell and Greg Hise. (Hoboken, NJ: Blackwell Publishing, 2010).

Curtis, Erin, Jessica Hough, and Guisela Latorre. *¡Murales Rebeldes! L.A. Chicana/Chicano Murals under Siege*. Santa Monica, CA: Angel City Press, 2017.

Davis, Madeline, and Elizabeth Kennedy. *Boots of Leather, Slippers of Gold: The History of a Lesbian Community*. New York: Routledge, 1991.

Davis, Mike. *City of Quartz: Excavating the Future in Los Angeles*. New York: Verso, 1990.

———. *Magical Urbanism: Latinos Reinvent the U.S. City*. New York: Verso, 2000.

Deverell, William. *Whitewashed Adobe: The Rise of Los Angeles and the Remaking of Its Mexican Past*. Los Angeles: University of California Press, 2004.

Diaz, Enrique. *The San Gabriel Valley: A 21st Century Portrait*. San Antonio, TX: Historical Publishing Network, 2005.

Diaz, Vicente M. *Repositioning the Missionary: Rewriting the Histories of Colonialism, Native Catholicism, and Indigeneity in Guam*. Honolulu: University of Hawai'i Press, 2010.

Didion, Joan. "Bureaucrats," in *The White Album*. New York: Farrar, Straus and Giroux, 1979, 79–86.

Donato, Rubén, and Jarrod S. Hanson. "Legally White, Socially 'Mexican': The Politics of De Jure and De Facto School Segregation in the American Southwest." *Harvard Educational Review* 82, no. 2 (Summer 2012): 202–225.

Duara, Prasenjit. *Rescuing History from the Nation: Questioning Narratives of Modern China*. Chicago: University of Chicago Press, 1995.

Elkind, Sarah S. *How Local Politics Shape Federal Policy: Business, Power, and Environment in Twentieth-Century Los Angeles*. Chapel Hill: University of North Carolina Press, 2011.

Ellroy, James. *My Dark Places: An L.A. Crime Memoir*. New York: Alfred A. Knopf, 1996.

Engh, Michael E. *Frontier Faiths: Church, Temple, and Synagogue in Los Angeles, 1846–1888*. Albuquerque: University of New Mexico Press, 1992.

Espinosa, Lisbeth. "The Changing Aesthetics of Murals in Los Angeles." Master's thesis, California State University, Los Angeles, 2011.

Espinoza, Alex. *Still Water Saints*. New York: Random House, 2007.

Espinoza, Dionne. "'Revolutionary Sisters': Women's Solidarity and Collective Identification among Chicana Brown Berets in East Los Angeles, 1967–1970." *Aztlán* 26, no. 1 (2001): 17–58.

Espinoza, Dionne, Maria Eugenia Cotera, and Maylei Blackwell, eds. *Chicana Movidas: New Narratives of Activism and Feminism in the Movement*. Austin: University of Texas Press, 2018.

Estrada, Gilbert. "If You Build It, They Will Move: The Los Angeles Freeway System and the Displacement of East Los Angeles, 1944–1972." *Southern California Quarterly* 87, no. 3 (Fall 2005): 287–315.

Faderman, Lillian, and Stuart Timmons. *Gay L.A.: A History of Sexual Outlaws, Power Politics, and Lipstick Lesbians*. New York: Basic Books, 2006.

Faragher, John Mack. *Eternity Street: Violence and Justice in Frontier Los Angeles*. New York: W. W. Norton, 2016.

Flores, Edward Orozco. *God's Gangs: Barrio Ministry, Masculinity, and Gang Recovery*. New York: New York University Press, 2013.

Foner, Nancy. "Then and Now or Then to Now: Immigration to New York in Contemporary and Historical Perspective." *Journal of American Ethnic History* 25, nos. 2–3 (Winter–Spring 2006): 33–47.

Fong, Timothy. *The First Suburban Chinatown: The Remaking of Monterey Park, California*. Philadelphia: Temple University Press, 1994.

Four Directions Institute. "Gabrielino." 2007. http://www.fourdir.com/gabrielino.htm.

Fradkin, Philip L. *A River No More: The Colorado River and the West*. Berkeley: University of California Press, 1996.

Freund, David. *Colored Property: State Policy and White Racial Politics in Suburban America*. Chicago: University of Chicago Press, 2007.

García, David G. *Strategies of Segregation: Race, Residence, and the Struggle for Educational Equality*. Oakland: University of California Press, 2018.

García, Mario T. "Americans All: The Mexican American Generation and the Politics of Wartime Los Angeles, 1941–45." *Social Science Quarterly* 65, no. 2 (1984): 278–289.

García, Mario T., and Sal Castro. *Blowout! Sal Castro and the Chicano Struggle for Educational Justice*. Chapel Hill: University of North Carolina Press, 2011.

Garcia, Matt. *A World of Its Own: Race, Labor, and Citrus in the Making of Greater Los Angeles, 1900–1970*. Chapel Hill: University of North Carolina Press, 2001.

———. "Memories of El Monte: Intercultural Dancehalls in Post-WWII Greater Los Angeles." In *Generations of Youth*, edited by Joe Austin and Michael Nevin Willard. New York: New York University Press, 1998, 157–172.

Garreau, Joel. *Edge City: Life on the New Frontier*. New York: Anchor Books, 1991.

Gates, Paul. "The California Land Act of 1851." *Southern California Historical Quarterly* 50, no. 4 (December 1971): 395–430.

Gerber, David A. *American Immigration: A Very Short Introduction*. New York: Oxford University Press, 2011.

Gerstle, Gary. *American Crucible: Race and Nation in the Twentieth Century*. Princeton, NJ: Princeton University Press, 2001.

Gibbons, Andrea. *City of Segregation: One Hundred Years of Struggle for Housing in Los Angeles*. Brooklyn, NY: Verso, 2018.

Gilroy, Paul. *Postcolonial Melancholia*. New York: Columbia University Press, 2005.

Gomez, Alan Eladio. *The Revolutionary Imaginations of Greater Mexico: Chicana/o Radicalism, Solidarity Politics, and Latin American Social Movements*. Austin: University of Texas Press, 2016.

Gonzalez, Gilbert G. *Chicano Education in an Era of Segregation*. Denton: University of North Texas Press, 2013.

———. *Labor and Community: Mexican Citrus Worker Villages in a Southern California County, 1900–1950*. Urbana: University of Illinois Press, 1994.

González, Jerry. *In Search of the Mexican Beverly Hills: Latino Suburbanization in Postwar Los Angeles*. New Brunswick, NJ: Rutgers University Press, 2017.

Gonzalez, Jerry. "'A Place in the Sun': Mexican Americans, Race and the

Suburbanization of Los Angeles, 1940–1980." PhD diss., University of Southern California, 2009.

Goodman, Adam. *The Deportation Machine: The Undocumented History of Expulsion in America*. Princeton, NJ: Princeton University Press, forthcoming.

Gopinath, Gayatri. *Impossible Desires: Queer Diasporas and South Asian Public Cultures*. Durham, NC: Duke University Press, 2005.

Gordon, Avery. *Ghostly Matters: Haunting and the Sociological Imagination*. Minneapolis: University of Minnesota Press, 1997.

Gottlieb, Robert. *Reinventing Los Angeles: Nature and Community in the Global City*. Cambridge, MA: MIT Press, 2007.

Gray, Paul. *A Clamor for Equality: Emergence and Exile of Californio Activist Francisco P. Ramirez*. Lubbock: Texas Tech University Press, 2012.

Gutiérrez, Olga. "Analyzing Segregation in El Monte: The Lexington School," MA thesis, California State University, Los Angeles, 1981.

Gutiérrez, Ramón. "Contested Eden: An Introduction," *California History* 76, no. 2/3 (1997).

Guzmán, Romeo. "Rebel Archive: A History of La Casa de El Hijo Del Ahuizote," in *Regeneración: Three Generations of Revolutionary Ideology*, ed. Pilar Tompkins Rivas. Mexico City: Vincent Price Art Museum and La Case de El Hijo del Ahuizote, 2018.

Hackel, Steven. *Children of Coyote, Missionaries of Saint Francis: Indian-Spanish Relations in Colonial California, 1769–1850*. Chapel Hill: University of North Carolina Press, 2005.

———. "Sources of Rebellion: Indian Testimony and the Mission San Gabriel Uprising of 1785." *Ethnohistory* 50, no. 4 (Fall 2003): 643–669.

Hamilton, Denise. *The Jasmine Trade*. New York: Scribner, 2001.

Herrera, Juan. "Spatializing Chicano Power: Cartographic Memory and Community Practices of Care." *Social Justice* 42, nos. 2–3 (2015): 46–66.

———. "Unsettling the Geography of Oakland's War on Poverty: Mexican American Political Organizations and the Decoupling of Poverty and Blackness." *Du Bois Review* 9, no. 2 (2012): 375–393.

Hester, Torrie. *Deportation: The Origins of U.S. Policy*. Philadelphia: University of Pennsylvania Press, 2017.

Highsmith, Andrew. *Demolition Means Progress: Flint, Michigan and the Fate of the American Metropolis*. Chicago: University of Chicago Press, 2014.

A History of El Monte: The End of the Sante Fe Trail. Los Angeles: El Monte Lodge No 424 - I.O.O.F., 1923.

Hobsbawm, Eric. *Primitive Rebels: Studies in Archaic Forms of Social Movements in the 19th and 20th Centuries*. New York: Norton, 1959.

Hoffman, Abraham. "The El Monte Berry Picker's Strike, 1933." *Journal of the West* 12, no. 1 (1973): 71–84.

Hooper, Colleen. "Ballerinas on the Dole: Dance and the US Comprehensive Employment Training Act (CETA) 1974–1982." *Dance Research Journal* 49, no. 3 (2017): 70–90.

Hoskyns, Barney. *Waiting for the Sun: Strange Days, Weird Scenes, and the Sound of Los Angeles*. New York: St. Martin's, 1996.

Hughes, Langston. *Let America Be America Again: And Other Poems*. New York: Vintage, 2004.

Hundley, Norris, Jr. *Water and the West: The Colorado River Compact and the Politics of Water in the American West*. Berkeley: University of California Press, 2009.

Huynh, Francesca. "Frances Huynh." Narrating the Chinese Vietnamese Identity. Accessed June 28, 2019. http://chinesevietnamese.com/frances-huynh.

Hyra, Derek. "The Back-to-the-City Movement: Neighbourhood Redevelopment and Processes of Political and Cultural Displacement." *Urban Studies* 52 (2015): 1753–1773.

Iriye, Akira. *Pacific Estrangement: Japanese and American Expansion, 1897–1911*. Chicago: Imprint Publications, 1994.

Jackson, Kenneth T. *Crabgrass Frontier: The Suburbanization of the United States*. New York: Oxford University Press, 1985.

Jaime-Becerra, Michael. *Every Night Is Ladies' Night*. New York: Rayos, 2004.

———. *This Time Tomorrow*. New York: Thomas Dunne Books, 2010.

Joseph, Gilbert M., and Timothy J. Henderson, eds. *The Mexico Reader: History, Culture, Politics*. Durham, NC: Duke University Press, 2002.

Katznelson, Ira. *When Affirmative Action Was White: An Untold History of Racial Inequality in Twentieth-Century America*. New York: W. W. Norton, 2005.

Keely, Charles B. "Effects of the Immigration Act of 1965 on Selected Population Characteristics of Immigrants to the United States." *Demography* 8 (May 1971): 157–169.

Kelley, Robin D. G. *Race Rebels: Culture, Politics, and the Black Working Class*. New York: Free Press, 1994.

Kimmelman, Michael. "Karl May and the Origins of a German Obsession." *New York Times*, September 12, 2007. https://www.nytimes.com/2007/09/12/travel/12iht-12karl.7479952.html.

King, William F. "El Monte, An American Town in Southern California, 1851–1866." *Southern California Quarterly* 53, no. 4 (December 1971): 317–332.

Kruse, Kevin M., and Thomas J. Sugrue, eds. *The New Suburban History*. Chicago: University of Chicago Press, 2006.

Kurashige, Scott. "The Many Facets of Brown: Integration in a Multiracial Society." *Journal of American History* 91 (2004): 56–68.

———. *The Shifting Grounds of Race: Black and Japanese Americans in the Making of Multiethnic Los Angeles*. Princeton, NJ: Princeton University Press, 2008.

La Tour, Jesse. "A History of the Kizh (Orange County's Native Inhabitants)." Accessed June 22, 2019. http://jesselatour.blogspot.com/2012/07/a-history-of-tongva-tribe-orange.html.

Lamar, Howard R. *Texas Crossings: The Lone Star State and the American Far West, 1836–1986*. Austin: University of Texas Press, 1991.

Lewthwaite, Stephanie. *Race, Place, and Reform in Mexican Los Angeles: A Transnational Perspective, 1890–1940*. Tucson: University of Arizona Press, 2009.

Li, Wei. *Ethnoburb: The New Ethnic Community in Urban America*. Honolulu: University of Hawai'i Press, 2009.

Limerick, Patricia. *The Legacy of the Conquest: Unbroken Past of the American West*. New York: W. W. Norton, 1987.

Ling, Huping. *Voices of the Heart: Asian American Women on Immigration, Work, and Family*. Kirksville, MO: Truman State University Press, 2007.

Lopez, Ronald W. "The El Monte Berry Strike of 1933." *Aztlán: Chicano Journal of the Social Sciences and Arts* 1, no. 1 (1970): 101–114.

Lorde, Audre. *Sister Outsider: Essays and Speeches*. Berkeley, CA: Crossing Press, 2007.

Loza, Mireya. *Defiant Braceros: How Migrant Workers Fought for Racial, Sexual, and Political Freedom*. Chapel Hill: University of North Carolina Press, 2016.

Magón, Ricardo Flores. "Speech in El Monte, California, 1917." In Ricardo Flores Magón, *Dreams of Freedom: A Ricardo Flores Magón Reader*. Edited by Charles Bufe and Mitchell Cowen Verter, 280–281. Oakland, CA: AK Press, 2005, 280–282.

Massey, Douglas S., Jorge Durand, and Nolan J. Malone. *Beyond Smoke and Mirrors: Mexican Immigration in an Era of Economic Integration*. New York: Russell Sage Foundation, 2002.

McGirr, Lisa. *Suburban Warriors: The Origins of the New Right*. Princeton, NJ: Princeton University Press, 2001.

McKinley, Michelle A. "Conviviality, Cosmopolitan Citizenship, and Hospitality." *Harvard Unbound* 5, no. 1 (March 2009): 55–87.

McWilliams, Carey. *Southern California: An Island on the Land*. Salt Lake City, UT: Gibbs Smith Publishers, 1973.

Miles, Barry. *Zappa: A Biography*. New York: Grove, 2004.

Minian, Ana Raquel. *Undocumented Lives: The Untold Story of Mexican Migration*. Cambridge, MA: Harvard University Press, 2018.

Mitchell, Daniel J. B. "Earl Warren's Fight for California's Freeways: Setting a Path for the Nation." *Southern California Quarterly* 88, no. 2 (Summer 2006): 205–238.

Modell, John. *The Economics and Politics of Racial Accommodation: The Japanese of Los Angeles 1900–1942*. Urbana: University of Illinois Press, 1977.

Mohl, Raymond A. "Asian Immigration to Florida." *Florida Historical Quarterly* 74 (Winter 1996): 261–286.

Molina, Natalia. *Fit to Be Citizens? Public Health and Race in Los Angeles, 1879–1939*. Berkeley: University of California Press, 2006.

Möller, Maria, and Kathryn E. Wilson. "Images of Latino Philadelphia: An Essay in Photographs." *Pennsylvania Magazine of History and Biography* 128 (October 2004): 385–398.

Moraga, Cherríe. *The Last Generation: Prose and Poetry*. Boston: South End Press, 1993.

———. *Loving in the War Years: Lo que nunca pasó por sus labios*. Boston: South End Press, 1983.

Mulvey, Laura. "Visual Pleasure and Narrative Cinema." *Screen* 16, no. 3 (1975): 6–18.

Muñoz, José Esteban. *Disidentifications: Queers of Color and the Performance of Politics*. Minneapolis: University of Minnesota Press, 1999.

Nelson, Alondra. *Body and Soul: The Black Panther Party and the Fight against Medical Discrimination*. Minneapolis: University of Minnesota Press, 2011.

Nevarez, Leonard. "In Exile: The Rootless Cosmopolitanism of Jeffrey Lee Pierce and the Gun Club." *Musical Urbanism*, June 23, 2015.

Newmark, Harris. *Sixty Years in Southern California, 1853–1913, Containing the Reminiscences of Harris Newmark*. New York: Knickerbocker Press, 1916.

Ngai, Mae. *Impossible Subjects: Illegal Aliens and the Making of Modern America*. Princeton, NJ: Princeton University Press, 2004.

Nguyen, Viet Thanh. *The Sympathizer*. New York: Grove Press, 2015.

Nickerson, Michelle. "Beyond Smog, Sprawl, and Asphalt: Developments in the Not-So-New Suburban History." *Journal of Urban History* 41 (2015): 171–180.

Nicolaides, Becky M. *My Blue Heaven: Life and Politics in the Working-Class Suburbs of Los Angeles, 1920–1965*. Chicago: University of Chicago Press, 2002.

Nugent, Walter. *Crossings: The Great Transatlantic Migrations, 1870–1914*. Bloomington: Indiana University Press, 1992.

Nye, David. *American Technological Sublime*. Cambridge, MA: MIT Press, 1994.

Obler, Susan Sellman, ed. *Personal Stories from the El Monte Communities*. Whittier, CA: Rio Hondo College, 1978.

Orleck, Annelise, and Lisa Hazirjian. *The War on Poverty: A New Grassroots History*. Athens: University of Georgia Press, 2011.

Oropeza, Lorena. *¡Raza Si! ¡Guerra No! Chicano Protest and Patriotism during the Viet Nam War Era*. Berkeley: University of California Press, 2005.

O'Rourke, Kevin H., and Jeffrey G. Williamson. *Globalization and History: The Evolution of a Nineteenth-Century Atlantic Economy*. Cambridge, MA: MIT Press, 1999.

Orsi, Jared. *Hazardous Metropolis: Flooding and Urban Ecology in Los Angeles*. Berkeley: University of California Press, 2004.

Perlmann, Joel. *Italians Then, Mexicans Now: Immigrant Origins and Second-Generation Progress, 1890 to 2000*. New York: Russell Sage Foundation, 2005.

Plascencia, Salvador. *The People of Paper*. Orlando, FL: Harcourt, 2006.

Reisner, Marc. *Cadillac Desert: The American West and Its Disappearing Water*. New York: Penguin Books, 1993.

Ridgway, Peggi, and Jan Works. *Sending Flowers to America: Stories of the Los Angeles Flower Market and the People Who Built an American Floral Industry*. Los Angeles: American Florists' Exchange, 2008.

Rodríguez, Luis J. *Always Running: La Vida Loca: Gang Days in L.A.* New York: Touchstone, 1993.

Rodríguez, Richard T. *Next of Kin: The Family in Chicano/a Cultural Politics*. Durham, NC: Duke University Press, 2009.

Rojas, James. "The Enacted Environment: Examining the Streets and Yards of East Los Angeles." In *Everyday America: Cultural Landscape Studies after J. B. Jackson*, edited by Chris Wilson and Paul Groth, 275–292. Berkeley: University of California Press, 2003.

Rosas, Ana Elizabeth. *Abrazando el Espíritu: Bracero Families Confront the US-Mexico Border*. Berkeley: University of California Press, 2014.

Roth, Matthew. "Whittier Boulevard, Sixth Street Bridge, and the Origins of Transportation Exploitation." *Journal of Urban History* 30, no. 5 (2004): 729–748.

Rothstein, Richard. *The Color of Law: A Forgotten History of How Our Government Segregated America*. New York: Liveright, 2017.

Ruiz, Vicki. *From Out of the Shadows: Mexican Women in Twentieth-Century America*. New York: Oxford University Press, 1999.

Said, Edward. *Culture and Imperialism*. New York: Vintage, 1994.

Saito, Leland. *Race and Politics: Asian Americans, Latinos, and Whites in a Los Angeles Suburb*. Urbana: University of Illinois Press, 1998.

Salomon, Carlos Manuel. *Pio Pico: The Last Governor of Mexican California*. Norman: University of Oklahoma Press, 2010.

Sánchez, George J. "'What's Good for Boyle Heights Is Good for the Jews': Creating Multiracialism on the Eastside during the 1950s." *American Quarterly* 56, no. 3 (2004): 633–662.

Sanchez, Rosaura, and Beatrice Pita. "The Literature of the Californios." In *The Cambridge Companion to the Literature of Los Angeles*, edited by Kevin R. McNamara. Cambridge, MA: Cambridge University Press, 2010, 13–22.

Sandos, James A. "Between Crucifix and Lance: Indian-White Relations in California, 1769–1848." *California History* 76, nos. 2–3 (1997): 196–229.

Sandoval, Denise M. "Cruising through Low Rider Culture: Chicana/o Identity in the Marketing of Low Rider Magazine," in *Velvet Barrios: Popular Culture and Chicana/o Sexualities*, ed. Alicia Gaspar de Alba, New York: Palgrave Macmillan, 2003.

———. "The Politics of Low and Slow/Bajito y Suavecito." In *Black and Brown in Los Angeles: Beyond Conflict and Collision*, edited by Josh Kun and Laura Pulido, 182. Los Angeles: University of California Press, 2014.

Sandoval-Strausz, Andrew K. "Latino Landscapes: Postwar Cities and the Transnational Origins of a New Urban America." *Journal of American History* 101 (2014): 804–831.

Self, Robert. *American Babylon: Race and the Struggle for Postwar Oakland*. Princeton, NJ: Princeton University Press, 2003.

Shults, Jane Beemer. "The Ku Klux Klan in Downey in the 1920s." Master's thesis, California State University, Long Beach, 1991.

Sides, Josh. *L.A. City Limits: African American Los Angeles from the Great Depression to the Present*. Los Angeles: University of California Press, 2003.

Soja, Edward W. *Postmodern Geographies: The Reassertion of Space in Critical Social Theory*. London: Verso, 1989.

Starr, Kevin. *Americans and the California Dream, 1850–1915*. New York: Oxford University Press, 1973.

———. *California: A History*. New York: Modern Library, 2007.

Straight, Susan. "Listening to Art Laboe," *Boom*, Spring 2011.

Straus, Emily E. *Death of a Suburban Dream: Race and Schools in Compton, California*. Philadelphia: University of Pennsylvania Press, 2014.

Strum, Philippa. *Mendez v. Westminster: School Desegregation and Mexican-American Rights*. Lawrence: University Press of Kansas, 2010.

———. *Race for Profit: Black Housing and the Urban Crisis of the 1970s*. Chapel Hill: University of North Carolina Press, forthcoming.

Temple, Thomas Workman, II. "Toypurina the Witch and the Indian Uprising at San Gabriel." *Masterkey* 32, no. 5 (1958): 136–152.

Teutimes, Ernest P. Salas, Andrew Salas, Christina Swindall Martinez, and Gary Stickel. *Toypurina: The Joan of Arc of California*. San Gabriel, CA: Kizh Tribal Press, 2011.

Thangaraj, Stanley. *Desi Hoop Dreams: Pickup Basketball and the Making of Asian American Masculinity*. New York: New York University Press, 2015.

Tichenor, Daniel J. *Dividing Lines: The Politics of Immigration Control in America*. Princeton, NJ: Princeton University Press, 2002.

Tongson, Karen. *Relocations: Queer Suburban Imaginaries*. New York: New York University Press, 2011.

Trieu, Monica Mong. "Ethnic Chameleons and the Contexts of Identity: A Comparative Look at the Dynamics of Intra-National Ethnic Identity Construction for 1.5 and Second Generation Chinese-Vietnamese and Vietnamese Americans." PhD diss., University of California, Irvine, 2008.

Trouillot, Michel-Rolph. *Silencing the Past: Power and the Production of History*. Boston: Beacon Press, 1995.

Tseng, Yen-Fen. "Chinese Ethnic Economy: San Gabriel Valley, Los Angeles County." *Journal of Urban Affairs* 16, no. 2 (June 1994): 169–189.

United States Commission on Civil Rights. *Mexican American Education Study*. 6 vols. Washington: Government Printing Office, 1971.

Valle, Victor M., and Rodolfo D. Torres. *Latino Metropolis*. Minneapolis: University of Minnesota Press, 2000.

Vermúdez, Rosie C. "Alicia Escalante, the Chicana Welfare Rights Organization, and the Chicano Movement." In *The Chicano Movement: Perspectives from the Twenty-First Century*, edited by Mario T. Garcia, 95–116. New York: Routledge Press, 2014.

Vigil, James Diego. *Barrio Gangs: Street Life and Identity in Southern California*. Austin: University of Texas Press, 1988.

Voight, George R. *South El Monte: The History of a City*. South El Monte, CA: Municipal Services Bureau, 1983.

Voss, Kurt, dir. *Ghost on the Highway: A Portrait of Jeffrey Lee Pierce and the Gun Club*. Los Angeles: Power Factory Films, 2006.

Weibel-Orlando, Joan. *Indian Country L.A.* Urbana: University of Illinois Press, 1991.

Wiese, Andrew. *Places of Their Own: African American Suburbanization in the Twentieth Century*. Chicago: University of Chicago Press, 2004.

Wild, Mark. *Street Meeting: Multiethnic Neighborhoods in Early Twentieth-Century Los Angeles*. Berkeley: University of California Press, 2005.

Wilkins, Frederick. *The Legend Begins: The Texas Rangers 1823–1845*. Austin, TX: State House Press, 1996.

Wollenberg, Charles. "Race and Class in Rural California: The El Monte Berry Strike of 1933." *California Historical Quarterly* 51, no. 2 (1972): 155–164.

Worster, Donald. *Rivers of Empire: Water, Aridity, and the Growth of the American West*. New York: Oxford University Press, 1992.

Ybarra-Frausto, Tomás. "Rasquachismo: A Chicano Sensibility." In *Chicano Art: Resistance and Affirmation, 1965–1985*, edited by Richard Griswold del Castillo, Teresa McKenna, and Yvonne Yarbro-Bejarano, 155–162. Los Angeles: Wight Art Gallery, University of California, Los Angeles, 1991.

Young, Phoebe S. K. *California Vieja: Culture and Memory in a Modern American Place*. Berkeley: University of California Press, 2006.

Zhou, Min, Yen-Fen Tseng, and Rebecca Kim. "Rethinking Residential Assimilation: The Case of a Chinese Ethnoburb in the San Gabriel Valley, California." *Amerasia Journal* 34, no. 3 (January 2008): 53–83.

Notes on Contributors

YESENIA BARRAGAN is a historian of race, gender, slavery, and emancipation in nineteenth- and twentieth-century Latin America. She is currently an assistant professor of Modern Latin American History at Rutgers University.

MARK BRAY is a historian of human rights, terrorism, and politics in modern Europe. He is the author of *Antifa: The Anti-Fascist Handbook* and *Translating Anarchy: The Anarchism of Occupy Wall Street* and co-editor of *Anarchist Education and the Modern School: A Francisco Ferrer Reader.* He is a currently a lecturer at Rutgers University.

DAN CADY is an associate professor of history at California State University, Fresno.

WENDY CHENG is an associate professor of American studies at Scripps College. She is the author of *The Changs Next Door to the Díazes: Remapping Race in Suburban California* and coauthor of *A People's Guide to Los Angeles.*

ALEX SAYF CUMMINGS is an associate professor of history at Georgia State University and a senior editor of the blog *Tropics of Meta*. Her book, *Democracy of Sound: Music Piracy and the Remaking of American Copyright in the Twentieth Century,* was published in 2013.

ANDRE KOBAYASHI DECKROW is currently a visiting scholar at the Center for Japanese Studies at the University of Michigan. He received his Ph.D. in the History-East Asia program at Columbia University. His research examines Japanese state-directed agricultural migration to Brazil in the 1920s and 1930s and places this history within the broader contexts of Japanese imperial expansion and anti-Asian immigration regimes in the Western Hemisphere during the early twentieth century.

ALEX ESPINOZA was born in Tijuana, Mexico, and raised in La Puente. He is the author of two novels, *Still Water Saints* and *The Five Acts of Diego León*, and the nonfiction *Cruising: An Intimate History of a Radical Pastime*. He lives in Los Angeles and is the Tomás Rivera Endowed Chair of Creative Writing at the University of California, Riversaide.

MELQUIADES FERNANDEZ was born in the Dominican Republic and grew up in Brooklyn, New York. He received a bachelor's degree in history from Columbia University and has worked as a community organizer in California and Virginia. He is currently a student at the University of Michigan Law School.

CARRIBEAN FRAGOZA is a journalist, fiction writer, and artist from South El Monte. She is the founder and codirector of the South El Monte Arts Posse and coeditor at *Boom California*. Her short story collection is forthcoming with City Lights Publishers.

ADAM GOODMAN is an assistant professor of history and Latin American and Latino studies at the University of Illinois at Chicago. His articles, essays, and reviews have appeared in academic outlets like the *Journal of American Ethnic History* and popular publications like the *Nation* and the *Washington Post*.

ROMEO GUZMÁN is the codirector of the South El Monte Arts Posse and an assistant professor of U.S. and Public History at California State University, Fresno, where he is the founding director of the Valley Public History Initiative: Preserving Our Stories. He is the coeditor at *Boom California*.

JUAN HERRERA is assistant professor of geography at the University of California, Los Angeles. His book, *Care Is Political: Social Movement Activism and the Production of Space*, will be published by Duke University Press.

MICHAEL JAIME-BECERRA is an associate professor of creative writing at University of California, Riverside. He is also the author of *Every Night Is Ladies' Night* and *This Time Tomorrow*.

MARIA JOHN is an assistant professor of Native American history at the University of Massachusetts Boston. Her research interests include twentieth-century urban indigenous histories, comparative histories of settler colonialism, social and political histories of health and health care, histories of health activism, and the history of indigenous sovereignty.

NICK JURAVICH is an assistant professor of history and labor studies and the associate director of the Labor Resource Center at the University of Massachusetts Boston. His first book, *The Work of Education: Community-Based Educators in Schools, Freedom Struggles, and the Labor Movement*, will be published by the University of Illinois Press.

TROY ANDREAS ARAIZA KOKINIS received his PhD in Latin American history at the University of California, San Diego. He studies Latin American anarchism, dissident labor, and armed struggle within the Uruguayan New Left during the Dirty War–era (1967–1985).

DANIEL LYNCH is an instructor of history and social science at Marlborough School in Los Angeles and a historian with a PhD from the University of California, Los Angeles. His research focuses on the intersection of masculinity, race, and politics in nineteenth-century Southern California.

STACY I. MACÍAS was born and raised in South El Monte. She is currently an assistant professor in the Department of Women's, Gender, and Sexuality Studies at California State University, Long Beach. Her research and teaching focus on Chicana/x-Latina/x studies, women of color feminist theory and praxis, and queer of color cultural production.

DANIEL MEDINA was born and raised in the San Gabriel Valley. A graduate of Vassar College, he has worked as a staff writer and editor for KCET public media in Los Angeles.

APOLONIO MORALES was born in Los Angeles and raised in El Monte. He has dedicated his life to serving immigrants and workers as a former teacher and organizer and now political director. When not fighting for social justice, he spends time with his loving wife, while raising his two boys to appreciate the humanity that exists in others.

DANIEL MORALES, from Azusa, California, is an assistant professor of history at James Madison University. His forthcoming book, *The Making of Mexican America: The Dynamics of Transnational Migration, 1900–1940*, examines the creation of transnational migratory networks across Mexico and the United States in the twentieth century.

RACHEL GRACE NEWMAN received her PhD in international and global history at Columbia University. She is the author of *Los niños migrantes entre Michoacán y California: Pertenencia, educación y Estado-nación*.

SALVADOR PLASCENCIA is an assistant professor of creative writing at Harvey Mudd College. He is the author of *The People of Paper*.

TONI MARGARITA PLUMMER grew up in South El Monte and is the author of *The Bolero of Andi Rowe*, a story collection set in the San Gabriel Valley. A winner of the Miguel Mármol Prize and a Macondo Fellow, she has published widely.

RYAN REFT is a historian of the modern United States in the Manuscript Division at the Library of Congress.

DAVID REID has a PhD in Latin American history from Rutgers University. His forthcoming book (based on his dissertation), *Salt in the Wound: The Colorado River Salinity Crisis, the Cold War, and the Mexican State, 1961–1974*, is on the politics of water in Cold War–era Mexico. He teaches history at Poly Prep Country Day School in Brooklyn, New York.

JENNIFER RENTERIA is a designer, artist, and writer whose work and research focuses on the interpretation and representation of natural history in informal learning environments; urban informality and the built environment; and the relationship between landscape, humans, and nature. She serves as a visual communication and experience designer for the Smithsonian's National Museum of Natural History.

AURELIE ROY holds a PhD from Columbia University, where she worked on the legal representation of Native American affairs in the 1960s and 1970s based on interviews with Indian rights lawyers. She left academia to be a writer and an empowerment and wellness entrepreneur.

JUDE P. WEBRE received his PhD in U.S. history from Columbia University and has taught at Columbia, New York University–Gallatin, Yeshiva University, and the Brooklyn Institute for Social Research. His teaching and research engage the intersection of creative expression, especially poetry and music, and radical democratic movements. Besides his academic life, he has been a rock and jazz bassist for over two decades in Austin, Texas, and New York City.

MICHAEL S. WELLER teaches at Mountain View High School in El Monte. In addition to his interest in incorporating local history into the curriculum, he is interested in teacher leadership in educational change efforts, teacher education and induction, and the teaching of writing.

KAREN S. WILSON is a writer, lecturer, and historian with a PhD from the University of California, Los Angeles. Her current research focuses on social networks and their influences on cross-cultural relations in the American West in the nineteenth century. She curated the Autry National Center's 2013–2014 exhibition titled "Jews in the Los Angeles Mosaic" and edited a companion volume of the same name.

Index

Page numbers in italics refer to figures.

Available titles in the Latinidad: Transnational Cultures in the United States series

María Acosta Cruz, *Dream Nation: Puerto Rican Culture and the Fictions of Independence*
Rodolfo F. Acuña, *The Making of Chicana/o Studies: In the Trenches of Academe*
Mike Anastario, *Parcels: Memories of Salvadoran Migration*
Xóchitl Bada, *Mexican Hometown Associations in Chicagoacán: From Local to Transnational Civic Engagement*
Maritza E. Cárdenas, *Constituting Central American–Americans: Transnational Identities and the Politics of Dislocation*
Adriana Cruz-Manjarrez, *Zapotecs on the Move: Cultural, Social, and Political Processes in Transnational Perspective*
T. Jackie Cuevas, *Post-Borderlandia: Chicana Literature and Gender Variant Critique*
Marivel T. Danielson, *Homecoming Queers: Desire and Difference in Chicana Latina Cultural Production*
Allison E. Fagan, *From the Edge: Chicana/o Border Literature and the Politics of Print*
Jerry González, *In Search of the Mexican Beverly Hills: Latino Suburbanization in Postwar Los Angeles*
Rudy P. Guevarra Jr., *Becoming Mexipino: Multiethnic Identities and Communities in San Diego*
Colin Gunckel, *Mexico on Main Street: Transnational Film Culture in Los Angeles before World War II*
Romeo Guzmán, Carribean Fragoza, Alex Sayf Cummings, and Ryan Reft, eds., *East of East: The Making of Greater El Monte*
Marie-Theresa Hernández, *The Virgin of Guadalupe and the Conversos: Uncovering Hidden Influences from Spain to Mexico*
Anita Huizar-Hernández, *Forging Arizona: A History of the Peralta Land Grant and Racial Identity in the West*
Lisa Jarvinen, *The Rise of Spanish-Language Filmmaking: Out from Hollywood's Shadow, 1929–1939*
Regina M. Marchi, *Day of the Dead in the USA: The Migration and Transformation of a Cultural Phenomenon*
Desirée A. Martín, *Borderlands Saints: Secular Sanctity in Chicano/a and Mexican Culture*
Isabel Martinez, *Becoming Transnational Youth Workers: Independent Mexican Teenage Migrants and Pathways of Survival and Social Mobility*
Marci R. McMahon, *Domestic Negotiations: Gender, Nation, and Self-Fashioning in US Mexicana and Chicana Literature and Art*
A. Gabriel Meléndez, *Hidden Chicano Cinema: Film Dramas in the Borderlands*
Priscilla Peña Ovalle, *Dance and the Hollywood Latina: Race, Sex, and Stardom*

Amalia Pallares, *Family Activism: Immigrant Struggles and the Politics of Noncitizenship*

Luis F. B. Plascencia, *Disenchanting Citizenship: Mexican Migrants and the Boundaries of Belonging*

Cecilia M. Rivas, *Salvadoran Imaginaries: Mediated Identities and Cultures of Consumption*

Jayson Gonzales Sae-Saue, *Southwest Asia: The Transpacific Geographies of Chicana/o Literature*

Mario Jimenez Sifuentez, *Of Forest and Fields: Mexican Labor in the Pacific Northwest*

Maya Socolovsky, *Troubling Nationhood in U.S. Latina Literature: Explorations of Place and Belonging*

Susan Thananopavarn, *LatinAsian Cartographies*

Printed in the United States
By Bookmasters